Other A to Z Guides from The Scarecrow Press, Inc.

1. *The A to Z of Buddhism* by Charles S. Prebish, 2001.
2. *The A to Z of Catholicism* by William J. Collinge, 2001.
3. *The A to Z of Hinduism* by Bruce M. Sullivan, 2001.
4. *The A to Z of Islam* by Ludwig W. Adamec, 2002.
5. *The A to Z of Slavery & Abolition* by Martin A. Klein, 2002.
6. *Terrorism: Assassins to Zealots* by Sean Kendall Anderson and Stephen Sloan, 2003.
7. *The A to Z of the Korean War* by Paul M. Edwards, 2005.
8. *The A to Z of the Cold War* by Joseph Smith and Simon Davis, 2005.

HISTORICAL DICTIONARIES
OF WAR, REVOLUTION, AND CIVIL UNREST
Edited by Jon Woronoff

The A to Z
of the Cold War

Joseph Smith and Simon Davis

The Scarecrow Press, Inc.
Lanham, Maryland • Toronto • Oxford
2005

SCARECROW PRESS, INC.

Published in the United States of America
by Scarecrow Press, Inc.
A wholly owned subsidiary of
The Rowman & Littlefield Publishing Group, Inc.
4501 Forbes Boulevard, Suite 200, Lanham, Maryland 20706
www.scarecrowpress.com

PO Box 317
Oxford
OX2 9RU, UK

British Library Cataloguing in Publication Information Available

Library of Congress Control Number: 2004115075

ISBN 0-8108-5384-1

⊖™ The paper used in this publication meets the minimum requirements of
American National Standard for Information Sciences—Permanence of
Paper for Printed Library Materials, ANSI/NISO Z39.48-1992.
Manufactured in the United States of America.

Contents

Acronyms and Abbreviations

ABM	anti-ballistic missile
ACDA	Arms Control and Disarmament Agency
AID	Agency for International Development
ANZUS	Australia–New Zealand–United States Alliance
CEEC	Committee on European Economic Cooperation
CENTO	Central Treaty Organization
CFE	Conventional Forces in Europe Treaty
CFM	Council of Foreign Ministers
CIA	Central Intelligence Agency
COMECON	Council for Mutual Economic Assistance
COMINFORM	Communist Information Bureau
CORDS	Civilian Operations and Rural Development Supports
CSCE	Conference on Security and Cooperation in Europe
EC	European Community
ECA	Economic Cooperation Administration
ECSC	European Coal and Steel Community
EDC	European Defense Community
EEC	European Economic Community
ERP	European Recovery Program (Marshall Plan)
EU	European Union
EURATOM	European Atomic Energy Community
FNLA	National Front for the Liberation of Angola
FRG	Federal Republic of Germany (West Germany)
GATT	General Agreement on Tariffs and Trade
GDR	German Democratic Republic (East Germany)
HSWP	Hungarian Socialist Workers Party
HUAC	House Un-American Activities Committee
ICBM	intercontinental ballistic missile
IDCA	International Development Cooperation Agency
IMF	International Monetary Fund
INF	intermediate-range nuclear forces

IRBM	intermediate-range ballistic missile
KGB	Komitet Gosudarstvennoy Bezopasnosti or State Security Committee
MAD	mutually assured destruction
MBFR	mutual and balanced force reductions
MDAP	Mutual Defense Assistance Program
MEDO	Middle East Defense Organization
MI	military intelligence
MIRV	multiple independently targetable re-entry vehicle
MLF	Multi-Lateral Force
MPLA	Popular Movement for the Liberation of Angola
MRBM	medium range ballistic missiles
MRLA	Malayan Races Liberation Army
NACB	Non-Aligned Coordinating Bureau
NATO	North Atlantic Treaty Organization
NSA	National Security Agency
NSC	National Security Council
OAS	Organization of American States
OAU	Organization of African Unity
OEEC	Organization for European Economic Cooperation
OPEC	Organization of Petroleum Exporting Countries
OSS	Office of Strategic Services
PD	Presidential directive
PDPA	People's Democratic Party of Afghanistan
PLO	Palestine Liberation Organization
PRC	People's Republic of China
PUWP	Polish United Workers' Party
RDF	Rapid Deployment Force
ROC	Republic of China
SAC	Strategic Air Command
SALT	Strategic Arms Limitation Talks
SDI	Strategic Defense Initiative
SEATO	South-East Asia Treaty Organization
SHAPE	Supreme Headquarters Allied Powers Europe
SIGINT	Signals Intelligence
SLBM	submarine-launched ballistic missile
START	Strategic Arms Reduction Treaty
UAR	United Arab Republic
UN	United Nations
UNAEC	United Nations Atomic Energy Commission

UNCTAD	United Nations Conference on Trade and Development
UNITA	National Union for the Total Independence of Angola
UNRRA	United Nations Relief and Rehabilitation Administration
US	United States
WEU	Western European Union

Chronology

1939

September 1   Germany invades Poland; World War II begins

1941

June 22   Germany invades Soviet Union

December 7   Japan attacks Pearl Harbor and brings United States into the war

1943

November 28 – December 2   "Big Three" meet at Teheran Conference

1944

June 6   Allied invasion of Western Europe

June 26 – August 2   Soviet summer offensive in White Russia and Poland

August 23 – October 7   Dumbarton Oaks conference, Washington, D.C., to negotiate the draft of the United Nations Charter

October 9 – October 18   British Prime Minister Churchill visits Moscow and negotiates with Soviet Premier Stalin on respective percentages of great power influence in postwar Yugoslavia, Hungary, Romania, Bulgaria, and Greece

1945

January 1	Soviet Union unilaterally recognizes "Lublin Committee" as provisional government of Poland
February 2 – 12	Big Three meet at Yalta Conference
April 12	Death of Franklin D. Roosevelt, who is succeeded as U.S. President by Harry S. Truman
April 23	Truman castigates Soviet Foreign Minister Molotov during his courtesy visit to Washington D.C., for the Soviet Union's continuing manipulation of the Polish state
April 25 – June 26	San Francisco Conference meets to draw up constitution of the United Nations Organization
May 8	Surrender of Germany marks end of war in Europe
June 5	Four-power Allied Control Commission in Berlin assumes governmental power in Germany
July 16	Successful U.S. atomic bomb test at Alamogordo, New Mexico
July 17 – August 2	Big Three meet at Potsdam Conference; the Council of Foreign Ministers (CFM) is established to make peace treaties with defeated enemy nations
August 6	U.S. atomic bombing of Hiroshima, Japan
August 8	Soviet Union declares war on Japan
August 9	U.S. atomic bombing of Nagasaki, Japan
August 15	Japan surrenders to the Allies; World War II ends
August 18	Ho Chi Minh declares Vietnam independent from France
September 3	Soviet forces occupy Korea, north of the 38th parallel; U.S. forces occupy Korea south of this line
September 11 – October 2	CFM meets in London but fails to make progress on terms of peace treaty for Germany and its former satellites
October 5	French forces return to Indochina

November 27	U.S. General George C. Marshall sent to China as a mediator to avert imminent civil war between nationalists and communists
December 16	In Soviet-occupied northern Iran, separatist Azeris declare statehood under Red Army protection

1946

January 10	Inaugural UN session in London; Trygvie Lie chosen as secretary-general
January 18	Iran formally complains to the UN Security Council against Soviet activities in its northern provinces
February 9	Stalin makes speech in Moscow on incompatability of communist and capitalist systems
February 22	George Kennan, the U.S. chargé d'affaires, Moscow, sends his "long telegram" to Washington, D.C., urging "firm and vigilant containment" of inevitable Soviet expansionism
March 5	At Fulton, Missouri, Winston Churchill delivers his "Iron Curtain" speech
March 6	Ho Chi Minh rejects independence within French Union
March 24	After U.S. diplomatic pressure and Iranian concessions on northern autonomy and Soviet oil rights, the Soviet Union agrees to remove its troops from Iran
April 25 – July 12	CFM resumes in Paris; treaty terms agreed for the former German satellites
May 3	U.S. military governor in Germany, General Lucius Clay, suspends Soviet reparations from U.S. occupation zone
June 4	U.S. announces Baruch Plan for UN control of atomic energy and weapons
July 29 – October 15	Paris peace conference concludes Allied treaties with Bulgaria, Finland, Hungary, Italy, and Romania

August 7	Soviet note to Turkey demands naval transit and base rights in the Dardanelles
August 18	Truman sends note to Stalin expressing U.S. support for Turkish sovereign rights
September 6	U.S. Secretary of State Byrnes makes speech in Stuttgart, Germany, committing U.S. to economic reconstruction of Germany
November 4 – December 12	CFM convenes in New York to confirm amendments to the treaties agreed at the Paris peace conference
December 2	Creation of the Anglo-American "Bizone" in Germany is announced
December 19	Vietminh attacks French citizens and property in northern Vietnam; Indochina War starts

1947

January 8	General Marshall leaves China, having failed to avert civil war
February 10	Bulgarian, Finnish, Hungarian, Italian, and Romanian peace treaties signed in Paris
February 21	Britain informs U.S. it will end aid to Greece in six months
March 4	Britain and France sign Dunkirk Treaty
March 10 – April 24	CFM meets in Moscow to draft Allied peace treaties with Germany and Austria. No agreements are reached
March 12	In asking Congress for $400 million in aid for Greece and Turkey, President Truman announces the "Truman Doctrine"
June 5	At Harvard University, Secretary of State Marshall outlines the need for economic aid to Europe, which will eventually emerge as the European Recovery Program (ERP), or "Marshall Plan"
June 27 – July 2	British, French, and Soviet delegations meet in Paris to define terms of reference for the Marshall Plan. Soviet Foreign Minister

	Molotov walks out of discussions and compels Poland and Czechoslovakia not to participate in the plan
July 1	Under the pseudonym "X," George Kennan publishes the "Long Telegram" in *Foreign Affairs.* "Containment" is now acknowledged U.S. policy
July 12 – September 22	16 Western European states confer in Paris on a detailed European Recovery Program
July 26	Truman signs U.S. National Security Act into law; a single National Department Establishment (now Department of Defense), Central Intelligence Agency (CIA), and National Security Council (NSC) are set up
September 2	Rio Pact establishes U.S. defense relations with the South American nations
September 22	Establishment of the Communist Information Bureau (COMINFORM) through which the Soviet Union coordinates the activities of the Eastern European, French, and Italian communist parties
November 25 – December 16	CFM meets abortively in London on German and Austrian treaties. It dissolves with no date for reconvening
December 24	Greek communists declare countergovernment, precipitating concerted monarchist offensive against northern guerilla strongholds

1948

February 16	Kim Il Sung declares establishment of People's Democratic Republic of Korea (North Korea), in the northern former Soviet occupation zone
February 25	Communist coup in Czechoslovakia, followed by political purges of opposition parties
March 17	Britain, France, Belgium, Luxembourg, and the Netherlands sign the Brussels Treaty

March 20	The Soviet delegate to the Allied Control Commission in Berlin boycotts meetings in protest over separate Anglo-American-French discussions on the future government of the Western zones of Germany
April 2	U.S. Congress approves the European Recovery Program (ERP)/Marshall Plan
June 11	U.S. Senate approves the Vandenberg Resolution, authorizing the formation of alliances with anticommunist powers
June 16	Britain declares state of emergency in Malaya, which is beset by a communist insurrection
June 18	Britain, France, and the U.S. introduce a single reformed currency in their occupation zones of Germany and sectors of Berlin
June 24	Soviet Union initiates overland blockade of Western allied sectors of Berlin
June 26	Anglo-American airlift of supplies begins in Western allied sectors of Berlin
June 28	Yugoslavia expelled from the COMINFORM, which denounces Tito as a "deviationist"
July 6	U.S., Canada, and the Brussels Treaty signatories open security talks in Washington, D.C.
July 17	60 U.S. B-29 "atomic" bombers deployed to Britain as Berlin crisis continues
August 3	Whittaker Chambers testifies before House Un-American Activities Committee (HUAC) that he spied for the Soviet Union in the 1930s with Alger Hiss, a prominent U.S. former diplomat
August 15	Republic of Korea (South Korea) declared south of 38th parallel
September 1	German delegates from the British, French, and U.S. occupation zones meet in Bonn to formulate a "basic law" for a new German state
November 2	Harry Truman reelected as U.S. president
December 15	At the urging of Congressman Richard Nixon, HUAC indicts Alger Hiss for perjury

for denying past Soviet connections. In January 1950, Hiss is sentenced to five years in prison

1949

January 22	Chinese communists capture Beijing
January 25	Soviet Union sets up Council for Mutual Economic Assistance (COMECON), to help direct the Eastern European satellite economies
April 4	North Atlantic Treaty signed in Washington, D.C.
April 8	Britain, France, and the U.S. agree to terms for a federal German state to be formed out of their occupation zones
April 20 – 22	Chinese communists cross the Yangtse River and seize Nanking
May 8	German parliamentary council in Bonn approves "Basic Law" of the Federal Republic of Germany (FRG)
May 12	Berlin Blockade ends
May 25	Chinese communist forces take Shanghai
May 30	Socialist Unity Party government formed unilaterally by Soviet Union in its occupation zone of Germany
July 25	President Truman sends Mutual Defense Assistance Program (MDAP) for military aid to the North Atlantic Treaty signatories to the U.S. Congress
September 17	North Atlantic Treaty signatories meeting in the North Atlantic Council agree to form North Atlantic Treaty Organization (NATO)
September 21	British, French, and U.S. military governments in Germany transfer power to the FRG under Chancellor Konrad Adenauer
September 23	Truman announces U.S. detection of Soviet atomic bomb test on August 29
September 28	Congress approves MDAP

October 1	Mao Zedong declares the formation of People's Republic of China (PRC)
October 7	German Democratic Republic (GDR) proclaimed in the Soviet occupation zone of Germany
October 16	Greek civil war ends after Tito cuts support to Greek communists
December 8	Chiang Kai-Shek sets up Nationalist Chinese government on Taiwan
December 16	Mao arrives in Moscow for his first meeting with Stalin

1950

January 10	Soviet Union boycotts UN Security Council for retaining Republic of China (ROC) as a permanent member of Security Council
January 31	President Truman announces the U.S. will develop the hydrogen bomb
February 9	Senator Joseph McCarthy claims that the U.S. State Department knowingly employs 205 communists
February 10	British nuclear scientist Klaus Fuchs arrested for espionage
February 14	Mao and Stalin conclude formal alliance in Moscow
April 25	President Truman approves expanded U.S. defense programs recommended in NSC-68
May 9	French Foreign Minister Robert Schuman proposes formation of European Coal and Steel Community (ECSC)
June 25	Korean War begins
June 27	With the Soviet Union absent, the UN Security Council determines North Korea as aggressor, legitimizing the dispatch of UN forces to defend South Korea
September 15	UN landings at Inchon, Korea
September 29	UN forces in Korea cross the 38th parallel, ignoring PRC warnings not to do so

October 26	French Prime Minister René Pleven announces plan for a European Defense Community (EDC), which will contain FRG military units
November 20	UN forces reach Yalu River, Korea's border with the PRC
November 26	PRC troops attack UN forces in Korea, forcing them into full retreat

1951

April 2	U.S. General Dwight Eisenhower assumes post of Supreme Allied Commander Europe, making NATO operational
April 5	Ethel and Julius Rosenberg sentenced to death by U.S. Federal Court for nuclear espionage
April 11	Truman dismisses U.S. General Douglas MacArthur as UN commander in Korea, following the latter's public advocacy of an all-out offensive against the PRC
July 10	Korean War cease-fire talks begin at Kaesong
August 30	U.S.-Philippine mutual defense treaty signed
September 1	ANZUS defense treaty signed by U.S., Australia, and New Zealand
September 8	U.S.-Japan security treaty signed
September 14	Britain proposes a Middle East Defense Organization (MEDO), which Egypt rejects
October 22	Korean War armistice talks resume at Panmunjom

1952

February 20 – 25	NATO Conference in Lisbon agrees on terms for EDC and adopts conventional rearmament plans; Greece and Turkey admitted to the alliance
May 27	EDC treaty signed in Paris by France, the

	FRG, Italy, Belgium, Luxembourg, and the Netherlands
July 23	Egyptian monarchy overthrown in military coup under General Neguib, aided by Colonel Gamal Abdel Nasser
October 3	Britain explodes its first atomic bomb
November 1	U.S. tests experimental hydrogen bomb
November 4	Dwight Eisenhower elected U.S. president
November 10	Trygvie Lie resigns as UN secretary-general after sustained Soviet criticism of his alleged pro-U.S. bias, particularly in Korea
November 27	Public trials begin in Czechoslovakia in which Rudolf Slansky and 11 other leading communists are condemned to death

1953

March 5	Death of Stalin. Georgi Malenkov assumes Soviet premier's post, but on 14 March he concedes Communist Party secretaryship to Nikita Khrushchev
May 8	Eisenhower increases U.S. aid to France in Indochina after Vietminh forces invade Laos. By 1954, the U.S. will be covering 80 percent of French war costs
June 16 – 18	Strikes and demonstrations in East Berlin against onerous work norms. These spread across the GDR, necessitating Soviet military intervention to restore communist authority
July 2 – 5	In Hungary, the Stalinist leader Matyas Rakosi forced to concede premier's post to reformist Imre Nagy, although Rakosi retains Communist Party secretaryship
July 10	Soviet Union announces arrest of Lavrenti Beria, Stalin's former state security chief. He is executed in December
July 27	Korean War armistice announced
August 8	Soviet Union tests hydrogen bomb
August 19 – 22	Iranian military coup, orchestrated by the

CIA, overthrows Premier Mohammed Mossadegh and restores the Shah's political power

December 16   At the North Atlantic Council in Paris, U.S. Secretary of State John Foster Dulles threatens "agonizing reappraisal" of U.S. commitment to NATO, if FRG rearmament within the EDC is not expedited

1954

January 12   Dulles publicly outlines "New Look" U.S. defense strategy based on deterrence via the threat of nuclear massive retaliation against Soviet aggression

April 7   Eisenhower propounds "domino theory" to justify U.S. interest in the Indochina War

April 26   Geneva peace conference on Korea and Indochina opens

May 7   French defeat at Dien Bien Phu by Vietminh; France requests a cease-fire in Indochina

June 18 – 27   CIA-backed invasion and military coup overthrows government of Jacobo Arbenz Guzman in Guatemala

July 21   Indochina War ended at Geneva conference; provisional partition of Vietnam at 17th parallel, north of which the Vietminh consolidates the Democratic Republic of Vietnam (North Vietnam)
Nationwide elections are set for 1956, although neither the U.S. nor the southern Vietnamese government of Ngo Dinh Diem sign the Geneva Accords

August 30   French National Assembly rejects EDC treaty

September 8   South-East Asia Treaty Organization (SEATO) set up at the Manila conference

September 30   PRC begins shelling coastal islands of Quemoy and Matsu

October 23	Paris Agreements signed on FRG rearmament in NATO
December 2	U.S. Senate condemns Senator McCarthy for intemperate attacks on alleged communists in the U.S. Army

1955

February 8	Malenkov replaced as Soviet premier by Nikolai Bulganin
February 24	Baghdad Pact founded by Turkey and Iraq
April 18 – 24	Bandung Conference of 29 Asian and African nations
May 9	FRG enters NATO
May 11 – 14	Soviet Union and Eastern European satellites form Warsaw Pact
May 15	Britain, France, U.S., and Soviet Union sign the Austrian State Treaty with Austria in Vienna
May 26 – June 2	Khrushchev and Bulganin visit Yugoslavia and restore Soviet relations with Tito
June 11 – 25	India's Prime Minister Jawaharlal Nehru visits the Soviet Union, which accepts the principle of "nonalignment"
July 18 – 23	Geneva Summit between U.S. President Eisenhower, Soviet Prime Minister Bulganin, British Prime Minister Anthony Eden, and French Prime Minister Edgar Faure. Despite "the Spirit of Geneva," there are few tangible results
September 9 – 13	FRG Chancellor Konrad Adenauer visits Moscow, formally opening diplomatic relations with the Soviet Union
September 27	Egyptian arms transfer agreement with Czechoslovakia
November 17 – December 18	Khrushchev and Bulganin tour India, Burma, and Afghanistan, where they reach trade and aid agreements

December 9	FRG announces Hallstein Doctrine: it will not hereafter open relations with states recognizing the GDR

1956

February 14 – 26	20th Soviet Communist Party Congress, where Khrushchev's "secret speech" causes a sensation by criticizing Stalin for many alleged errors
June 28	Pro-reform demonstrations in Poznan, Poland, are violently suppressed
July 18	In Hungary, after Soviet intervention, the Stalinist Matyas Rakosi is replaced as Communist Party secretary by Ernö Gerö
July 26	Nasser nationalizes the Suez Canal after the U.S. and Britain terminate talks on economic aid
October 19 – 21	Khrushchev and other Soviet leaders visit Poland, and to avert further unrest there, accept the appointment of Wladysaw Gomulka as Communist Party secretary
October 23	Hungarian demonstrations begin and lead to the ouster of Gerö in favor of Janos Kadar as party secretary and the restoration of Imre Nagy as premier
October 29	Israel invades Egypt, having planned with Britain and France to furnish a pretext for their seizure of the Suez Canal and overthrow of Nasser
October 30	Nagy announces the end of one-party rule in Hungary
October 31	Britain and France bomb Egyptian air bases, following Nasser's refusal to withdraw his forces from the Suez Canal zone
November 1	Nagy announces Hungarian neutrality
November 4	Soviet invasion of Hungary
November 5	Anglo-French invasion of Egypt. The next day Britain is asked by the U.S. to accept a

	cease-fire. The operation is stalled and Anglo-French troops are removed by mid-December
December 2	Fidel Castro and a small revolutionary group secretly return to Cuba to begin an armed struggle against the dictator Fulgencio Batista

1957

January 5	"Eisenhower Doctrine" announced; U.S. pledges support to anti-Soviet/anti-Nasser regimes in the Middle East
January 29	Soviet Union agrees to aid construction of Egypt's Aswan Dam
March 6	Ghana becomes independent under Kwame Nkrumah
March 25	Treaty of Rome creates the European Economic Community (EEC)
May 15	Britain tests hydrogen bomb
October 2	Poland's "Rapacki Plan" proposes nuclear-free zone in Central Europe
October 4	Soviet Union launches Sputnik; a strategic panic ensues in the U.S.

1958

January 10	U.S. tests its first intercontinental ballistic missile (ICBM)
January 21	Adenauer vetoes Rapacki plan; U.S. follows suit on May 3
March 27	Khrushchev assumes post of Soviet premier, in addition to Communist Party leadership
July 15	U.S. marines invade Lebanon to support its pro-Western government
July 17	British paratroopers flown into Jordan to maintain King Hussein against pro-Nasser radical pressure
November 10	Khrushchev challenges the Western Allied

position in Berlin by threatening a full peace
treaty in six months with the GDR, dissolv-
ing Four-power occupation rights in the city

1959

January 1	Castro's forces enter Havana, the Cuban capital, ousting Batista
January 10	Soviet Union proposes all-German peace conference in return for which Khrushchev withdraws his ultimatum on Berlin
May 11 – June 20	Four-power discussions in Geneva fail to reach German settlement. Further talks in July and August also fail
July 31	Laos declares emergency after communist Pathet Lao attacks outlying army posts
September 15 –27	Khrushchev visits U.S., attends Camp David minisummit with Eisenhower
December 21	Britain, France, and the U.S. invite Khrushchev to full summit in Paris in 1960
December 30	Castro expropriates U.S.-owned plantation land in Cuba

1960

January 11	U.S. protests Cuba's continuing expropriation of American-owned economic assets
February 4	Cuban-Soviet trade agreement is signed
February 10 – March 5	Khrushchev tours Asia; he concludes significant aid and trade agreements with India and Indonesia
February 13	France explodes its first atomic bomb
May 1	Soviet Union downs U.S. U-2 spy plane and captures its pilot, Francis Gary Powers. Eisenhower's refusal to apologize to Khrushchev leads to the collapse of the Paris Summit on its first day, 16 May
June 30	Belgian Congo declared independent; the Congolese Force Publique mutinies July 5-8,

	leading to Belgian intervention. Congo Premier Patrice Lumumba appeals to the UN
July 11	Katanga secedes from the Congo
July 14	UN troops sent to the Congo
July 30	Malayan Emergency officially ended by Britain
September 2	Soviet Union promises aid to Lumumba
September 5	Lumumba dismissed by Congo President Joseph Kasavubu; civil war begins between the two factions
September 23 – October 30	Unruly UN sessions on the Congo crisis during which Khrushchev demands the resignation of UN Secretary General Dag Hammarskjöld
October 19	U.S. announces trade embargo against Cuba
November 8	John F. Kennedy elected U.S. president
December 20	In South Vietnam a National Liberation Front is set up against President Diem by the communists (Vietcong)

1961

January 3	U.S. severs diplomatic relations with Cuba
January 16	Lumumba handed over to Katangese troops, who murder him
January 18	Khrushchev introduces sweeping agricultural reforms, blaming state administrators for concealing the failures of his previous programs
March 13	President Kennedy proposes Alliance for Progress to furnish U.S. economic aid to Latin America
April 17 – 20	Cuban exiles trained by the CIA attempt disastrously to overthrow Castro in the Bay of Pigs invasion
May 3	Cease-fire in Laos
June 3 – 4	Kennedy and Khrushchev hold Vienna Summit, which ends in mutual recrimination over Berlin

August 3	Soviet Union threatens unilateral peace treaty with the GDR, which would render the British, French, and U.S. presence in Berlin technically illegal
August 12	To stop an exodus of GDR citizens via Berlin to the FRG, the Berlin Wall is erected, sealing off the Western sectors and dividing the city
September 1 – 6	Non-Aligned Movement meets in Belgrade, Yugoslavia
September 13 – 21	UN invasion of Katanga repulsed
October 17 – 31	Sino-Soviet disagreements emerge at 22nd Soviet Communist Party Congress over Khrushchev's attacks on unreconstructed Stalinism in Albania
November 14	On the advice of the Taylor-Rostow mission, U.S. President Kennedy increases the number of U.S. advisers in South Vietnam to 16,000

1962

May 12	U.S. and British Commonwealth troops sent to Thailand as fighting resumes in Laos
June 11	Laotian cease-fire, followed by neutrality agreement. U.S. and British Commonwealth forces in Thailand withdraw
October 14	U.S. detects Soviet intermediate range ballistic missile (IRBM) sites under construction in Cuba; Cuba Missile Crisis begins
October 20 – November 21	Sino-Indian War; PRC victories on northern Indian border
October 28	Khrushchev agrees to withdraw Soviet IRBMs from Cuba
December 28	UN forces renew fighting Katanga separatists after Congo negotiations collapse

1963

January 14	Charles De Gaulle vetoes British entry into the EEC
January 15	Katanga secession ended in the Congo
January 22	De Gaulle signs cooperation treaty with Adenauer
June 20	"Hot-Line" set up between Washington, D.C. and Moscow
June 26	Kennedy visits West Berlin, addresses huge audience and declares "Ich bin ein Berliner" ("I am a Berliner")
August 5	Britain, the U.S., and Soviet Union sign Partial Nuclear Test Ban Treaty in Moscow
November 1	President Diem of South Vietnam is overthrown in a military coup, with U.S. complicity. He is murdered the next day
November 22	President Kennedy assassinated in Dallas; Lyndon Johnson becomes U.S. president

1964

February 4	PRC denounces Soviet Union as scheming with the U.S. for world domination
August 2	North Vietnamese torpedo craft attack U.S.S. *Maddox* in the Gulf of Tonkin
August 7	Congress passes the Tonkin Gulf Resolution, permitting Johnson to "prevent further aggression" by North Vietnam. Retaliatory U.S. air strikes follow, but the resolution will also serve to permit a build up of advisers, and later, U.S. combat troops in South Vietnam
October 14	After a disastrous harvest and further proposed military retrenchment, the Soviet Politburo forces Khrushchev to retire. He is replaced as Communist Party secretary by Leonid Brezhnev, and as premier by Alexei Kosygin
October 16	PRC tests its first atomic bomb

November 3   Lyndon Johnson reelected U.S. president
December 30   UN peacekeeping mission in the Congo
                   ended

1965

February 5 – 10   Soviet Premier Kosygin visits North Vietnam
                   and agrees to arms supplies for operations
                   against South Vietnam
February 7   Systematic U.S. bombing of North Vietnam
                   begins after Vietcong attack on U.S.A.F. base
                   at Pleiku
March 8   U.S. Marine Corps combat troops committed
                   to defense of air base at Da Nang
April 28 – May 5   Some 20,000 U.S. troops invade the Domini-
                   can Republic to preempt the possible emer-
                   gence of a pro-Castro government
July 28   President Johnson increases U.S. troop lev-
                   els in Vietnam to 125,000
September 30 – October 1   Indonesian army crushes attempted coup by
                   dissident officers and the Communist Party.
November 25   Army Chief of Staff Joseph Mobutu seizes
                   power in the Congo

1966

February 24   President Nkrumah of Ghana overthrown by
                   a military coup during his absence on an of-
                   ficial visit to the PRC
March 9   President de Gaulle announces France's with-
                   drawal from the NATO military command
March 12   Indonesian army coup takes over power from
                   President Achmed Sukarno, who remains as
                   a figurehead until 1969
March 25 – 27   Coordinated anti–Vietnam War protests in
                   Europe and the U.S., including 63,000 dem-
                   onstrators in Washington, D.C.
June 29   U.S. bombs Hanoi and Haiphong, the two
                   major cities in North Vietnam

August 8	Chinese Communist Party announces start of Cultural Revolution. Red Guards begin officially sanctioned persecution of foreigners and Chinese designated as "reactionary"
October 1	France withdraws from the NATO Military Committee; NATO Headquarters is soon moved from Paris to Brussels
December 1	Grand Coalition of Christian Democrats and Social Democrats takes power in the FRG

1967

January 27	Sixty-seven states including Britain, the U.S., and the Soviet Union sign treaty banning nuclear weapons from outer space
June 5 – 10	Arab-Israeli Six-Day War
June 17	PRC explodes its first hydrogen bomb
June 23 – 25	President Johnson and Premier Kosygin hold Glassboro "Mini-Summit"
July 13	U.S. troop levels in Vietnam are raised to 525,000
September 3	Nguyen Van Thieu elected president in South Vietnam, amid widespread claims of election fraud
September 18	U.S. Secretary of Defense Robert McNamara announces development plans for anti-ballistic missiles (ABM)
October 21	Some 35,000 anti-Vietnam War demonstrators surround U.S. Department of Defense Headquarters, the Pentagon
December 12	NATO formally adopts "flexible response" military doctrine
December 13	U.S. discloses having tested multiple independently targetable re-entry vehicles (MIRV) for its strategic nuclear warheads

1968

January 5	Alexander Dubček elected Czechoslovak Communist Party first secretary

January 20 – February 25	Vietcong Tet Offensive discredits President Johnson's claim that victory is in sight in Vietnam
January 23	North Korea seizes U.S.S *Pueblo*, a spy ship which it claims violated its territorial waters
March 8	Riots in Poland after demonstrations supporting recent Czechoslovak political reforms
March 23	Antonin Novotny removed as Czechoslovak president
March 31	President Johnson announces bombing halt in Vietnam and that he will not seek reelection
May 3 – 5	Dubček visits Moscow to negotiate on the limits of Czechoslovak liberalization
May 13	U.S.-North Vietnamese peace talks begin in Paris
June 27	Czechoslovakia abolishes political censorship
July 1	Britain, U.S., and Soviet Union sign the Nuclear Non-proliferation Treaty. U.S. and Soviet Union announce plans for Strategic Arms Limitation Talks (SALT)
July 29 – August 1	Brezhnev and Soviet Politburo delegation visit Czechoslovakia for negotiations on terms of political reform
August 20	Warsaw Pact forces invade Czechoslovakia
August 24	France explodes hydrogen bomb
August 29	Czechoslovak government announces restoration of orthodox communist controls after Dubček is forced to make concessions in Moscow
September 12	Albania leaves the Warsaw Pact
November 5	Richard Nixon elected U.S. president

1969

March 2	Soviet and PRC forces clash on the Ussuri River
April 17	Dubček replaced as Czechoslovak Communist Party first secretary by Gustav Husak
June 8	Nixon announces major U.S. troop withdraw-

	als and the imminent "Vietnamization" of the war
July 25	On Guam, Nixon announces that U.S. "containment" policy throughout Asia will engage fewer U.S. troops and emphasize indigenous allied forces, armed and trained by the U.S.
August 13	Soviet-PRC border clashes in Xinjiang
September 3	Death of Ho Chi Minh
September 11	Kosygin confers with Zhou Enlai in Beijing on the crisis over border relations
October 21	Willy Brandt elected FRG Chancellor
November 17	SALT begins in Helsinki

1970

January 20	U.S.-PRC dialogue begins via ambassadors in Warsaw
March 19	Brandt meets GDR Premier Willi Stoph at Erfurt in the GDR for talks on mutual FRG-GDR relations
March 25	Britain, France, U.S., and Soviet Union confer on status of Berlin
April 30 – June 29	U.S. and South Vietnamese forces invade Cambodia, intending to destroy North Vietnamese sanctuaries
August 12	Brandt and Kosygin sign Moscow Treaty, extending FRG Ostpolitik
September 28	Death of Egypt's President Nasser
November 3	Salvador Allende sworn in as president of Chile and is Latin America's first democratically elected Marxist head of state
December 7	Brandt extends Ostpolitik further with the Warsaw Treaty between the FRG and Poland
December 20	In Poland, Gomulka is replaced as Communist Party leader by Edward Gierek

1971

| February 11 | Signature of Seabed Treaty by Britain, U.S., Soviet Union and 60 other states |

April 10	U.S. table tennis team arrives by invitation in the PRC
May 3	GDR leader Walter Ulbricht replaced by Erich Honecker, who is considered more open to "détente"
May 27	Egypt's President Anwar Sadat signs friendship treaty with the Soviet Union
July 15	After talks in Beijing between PRC leaders and U.S. National Security Adviser Henry Kissinger, President Nixon announces he will visit the PRC in 1972
August 23	Britain, France, U.S., and Soviet Union conclude Quadripartite Agreement on Berlin, which is signed on September 3; full FRG-GDR transit agreement follows on December 17
November 15	PRC admitted to the UN, replacing the ROC

1972

January 25	Nixon offers U.S. withdrawal from Vietnam in return for cease-fire throughout Indochina
February 21 – 28	Nixon visits Beijing; promises to pursue full U.S.-PRC relations
March 30	Major North Vietnamese offensive into South Vietnam, eventually stopped by heavy U.S. air offensive, including bombing of Hanoi and Haiphong
April 10	Superpowers open Biological Weapons Convention for signature at the UN
May 22 – 26	Nixon-Brezhnev summit in Moscow; SALT I treaty and ABM Treaty are signed
July 18	Sadat expels 17,000 Soviet advisers from Egypt
August 12	Nixon announces the beginning of the withdrawal of U.S. ground combat forces from Vietnam
October 23	U.S. bombing halt in Vietnam
October 26	North Vietnamese Foreign Minister Le Duc

	Tho and Kissinger agree on draft Vietnam peace terms
November 7	Nixon reelected as U.S. president
November 22	Preliminary talks on instituting the Conference on Security and Cooperation in Europe (CSCE) open in Helsinki
December 12	South Vietnamese President Thieu rejects Vietnam peace proposals. North Vietnamese offensive resumes
December 18 – 30	U.S. "Christmas bombing" of Hanoi brings North Vietnam back to negotiations
December 21	FRG and GDR sign Basic Treaty on mutual relations

1973

January 27	Vietnam peace agreement signed in Paris
January 31	U.S.-Soviet Mutual and Balanced Forced Reductions (MBFR) talks begin in Vienna
March 29	Last U.S. forces leave Vietnam
May 17	U.S. Senate starts inquiry into the Watergate affair, a burglary at Democratic Party election headquarters in 1972, traceable to Nixon's staff
May 19	Brezhnev visits FRG, with which he concludes economic and cultural agreements
June 18 – 24	Nixon-Brezhnev summit in Washington, D.C.
September 11	Chilean military junta under General Augusto Pinochet overthrows President Allende. Allende is killed in the fighting
September 18	FRG and GDR join the UN
October 6	Outbreak of Arab-Israeli October War, with Egyptian surprise attack on Israeli positions in the Sinai Peninsula
October 27	Final cease-fire in October War, brokered by Kissinger with Soviet assent; Israel is persuaded to forego complete victory by the U.S. in order to avert the prospect of Soviet intervention on behalf of Egypt

| November 7 | U.S. Congress overrides presidential veto to pass the War Powers Act, which limits executive prerogatives on overseas U.S. troop deployments |
| December 11 | FRG treaty with Czechoslovakia, recognizes 1945 frontier, formally repudiating the 1938 Munich agreement |

1974

April 25	Portuguese dictatorship overthrown by armed forces who pledge political, social reform, and an end to the colonial wars in Angola and Mozambique
May 6	Brandt resigns as FRG Chancellor after his aide Gunter Guillaume is exposed as a GDR spy
May 31	Kissinger finalizes Arab-Israeli cease-fire terms after months of "shuttle diplomacy"
August 8	Richard Nixon resigns as U.S. president rather than face impeachment over the Watergate affair. He is succeeded by Gerald Ford
September 12	Emperor Haile Selassie overthrown in Ethiopia
November 23 – 24	President Ford meets Brezhnev at Vladivostok, where terms of reference for SALT II negotiations are agreed

1975

April 16	Cambodian government falls to Khmer Rouge communist forces
April 30	South Vietnamese capital, Saigon, falls to North Vietnamese forces
June 25	Portugal declares Mozambique independent under Samora Machel
August 1	Helsinki Final Act is signed by 35 states,

	including all the members of NATO and the Warsaw Pact
August 23	Communist Pathet Lao seizes power in Laos
November 11	Portugal declares Angola independent, but the country is divided by civil war

1976

March 15	Egypt breaks its 1971 treaty with the Soviet Union and seeks Western economic aid
June 25	Widespread riots in Poland greet economic austerity measures
September 9	Death of Mao Zedong
November 2	Jimmy Carter elected U.S. president

1977

January 1	Czechoslovak dissidents draft document that will inspire the Charter 77 movement
January 20	Carter's inauguration speech calls for new spirit of unity, trust, and a U.S. foreign policy based on moral exemplarism and human rights
February 27 – March 3	U.S. Secretary of State Cyrus Vance visits Moscow, but is unable to make progress on SALT II
June 30	Carter cancels B-1 strategic bomber
July 28	Somalia invades Ethiopia, starting the Ogaden War
August 21	11th Chinese Communist Party Congress formally rehabilitates Deng Xiao Ping and declares the end of the Cultural Revolution
September 27	Carter and Soviet Foreign Minister Andrei Gromyko discuss draft SALT II treaty terms
November 13	Somalia breaks ties with Soviet Union for supporting Ethiopia in Ogaden War

1978

April 27	Marxist coup in Afghanistan
June 7	Carter speech at the U.S. Naval Academy warns the Soviet Union that détente must be reciprocal
July 13	Albania terminates relations with PRC
October 16	Polish Archbishop of Krakow, Karol Wojtyla, is elected Pope John Paul II
November 6	Shah of Iran declares martial law
December 15	PRC-U.S. diplomatic relations announced
December 25	Vietnam invades Cambodia after months of border tension

1979

January 7	Khmer Rouge driven from power by Vietnamese
January 16	Shah flees Iran during revolution
January 28 – February 5	Deng Xiao Ping visits the U.S. and concludes economic and cultural agreements
February 1	Ayatollah Ruhollah Khomeini returns to Iran from exile in France
February 17	PRC invades Vietnam, but is forced to withdraw by March 15
May 4	Margaret Thatcher, a strongly anti-Soviet conservative, is elected British prime minister
June 2	Pope John Paul II visits Poland, arousing religious and nationalist passions
June 15 – 18	Carter-Brezhnev summit in Vienna; concludes with signature of SALT II treaty
July 17	In Nicaragua, Sandinistas seize power
October 15	Right-wing military coup in El Salvador
November 14	U.S. embassy in Tehran, Iran, is overrun by student demonstrators and American staff are taken hostage
December 10	NATO agrees deployment of modernized U.S. intermediate-range nuclear forces

	(INFs) to Europe in four years time, if the Soviet Union has not agreed to remove its own INFs during this period
December 22 – 28	Soviet invasion of Afghanistan

1980

January 4	President Carter embargoes high technology trade and grain shipments to the Soviet Union and withdraws SALT II treaty from U.S. Senate as sanctions against the Soviet invasion of Afghanistan
January 23	Carter announces the "Carter Doctrine," declaring the U.S. will preserve its access to the Persian Gulf from Soviet encroachment by any means
April 7	U.S. severs diplomatic relations with Iran as the embassy hostage affair continues
April 22	U.S. Olympic Committee announces boycott of 1980 Moscow Olympic Games
April 24	U.S. rescue attempt of Tehran embassy hostages abandoned in failure
May 4	President Tito of Yugoslavia dies
July 27	Exiled Shah of Iran dies
July 31	Carter formulates Presidential Directive 59 (PD-59) on U.S. strategy which includes the notion of fighting nuclear war as a tenable option during a global conflict with the Soviet Union
August 14	Strike at the Lenin Shipyard, Gdansk, Poland, where workers demand the right to organize as an independent union
August 30	Polish government concedes independent union rights
September 6	Polish communist leader Edward Gierek resigns in favor of Stanislaw Kania
September 22	Solidarity, the independent Polish trade union, is formally inaugurated; Iraq invades Iran, initiating an eight-year war

| November 4 | Ronald Reagan elected U.S. president |

1981

January 20	Iran releases U.S. hostages after 444 days
January 24	Solidarity calls national strike for a five-day working week
February 9	General Wojciech Jaruzelski becomes Polish premier
March 2	President Reagan announces U.S. military aid to El Salvador
March 9	Reagan announces U.S. military aid to Afghan Muslim Mujihadeen
April 1	Reagan suspends U.S. economic aid to Nicaragua, claiming the Sandinistas are supporting the insurgents in El Salvador
May 13	Assassination attempt upon Pope John Paul II, later alleged to have originated with the Bulgarian secret service
June 16	U.S. Secetary of State Alexander Haig announces in Beijing that U.S. arms will be sold to the PRC
September 8 – 10	In Poland, Solidarity proclaims the union's national, democratic, and Christian values, calls for union management in industry and for other Warsaw Pact states to allow independent trade unions
September 18	Soviet note warns Polish government to eliminate anti-Soviet activity within its borders
September 22 – 24	Andrei Gromyko proposes nuclear "no first use" pledge by the superpowers to the UN in New York. NATO rejects this, but the U.S. and Soviet Union announce that INF talks will open in Geneva
October 2	President Reagan announces major expansion of U.S. strategic nuclear weapons programs
October 10	Some 250,000 demonstrators in Bonn oppose deployment by NATO of INFs in Europe

October 18	Jaruzelski assumes leadership of the Polish Communist Party
November 18	President Reagan proposes "zero option," the unconditional elimination of all INF weapons
November 30	U.S.-Soviet INF negotiations open in Geneva
December 13	With a Solidarity general strike imminent, Jaruzelski imposes martial law in Poland

1982

May 9	President Reagan proposes Strategic Arms Reduction Talks (START), as mandated in SALT II treaty, which begin on June 29
October 1	FRG Chancellor Helmut Schmidt loses parliamentary no-confidence vote and is succeeded by the Christian Democrat leader, Helmut Kohl
November 10	Death of Soviet leader Leonid Brezhnev. He is succeeded by Yuri Andropov, the former KGB Chairman
December 20	U.S. Congress approves Boland Amendment, banning the Reagan administration from providing aid to the Nicaraguan counterrevolutionaries, the Contras

1983

March 23	Reagan announces the Strategic Defense Initiative (SDI), a space-based strategic nuclear defense system, christened "Star Wars" by the press
July 20	U.S. Congress approves funds for MX mobile ICBM
July 21	Martial law lifted in Poland
September 1	Korean Air Lines Flight 007 shot down in Soviet airspace, provoking Western outrage
October 25	U.S. invades Grenada to avert alleged imminent Cuban-backed coup

October 31 – November 22	U.S. Pershing II and Tomahawk cruise missile INFs deployed to NATO Europe
November 23	Soviet delegation walks out of INF talks in Geneva
December 8	START talks adjourn with no date set for resumption
December 15	MBFR talks on conventional arms control, mandated by the Helsinki Final Act, adjourn with no date set for resumption

1984

February 9	Death of Soviet leader Andropov. He is succeeded by Konstantin Chernenko on February 13
May 8	Soviet Union, followed by the other Warsaw Pact countries, announces it will boycott the 1984 Olympic Games in Los Angeles
November 6	Reagan reelected U.S. president

1985

January 7 – 8	U.S. Secretary of State George Shultz and his Soviet counterpart Andrei Gromyko agree in Geneva to resume START, INF, and ABM talks
March 10	Death of Soviet leader Chernenko
March 11	Mikhail Gorbachev chosen as Soviet Communist Party general secretary
June 11	Gorbachev makes speech to the Soviet Communist Party Central Committee outlining need for economic restructuring
July 2	Gromyko replaced as Soviet foreign minister by Eduard Shevardnadze
November 19 – 21	Reagan-Gorbachev summit in Geneva concentrates on resuming arms control initiatives

1986

January 15	Gorbachev proposes complete elimination of nuclear weapons by the year 2000 and accepts the "zero option" as the basis for INF negotiations
February 25	Gorbachev articulates the principles of "glasnost" and "perestroika" at the 27th Soviet Communist Party Congress and reiterates the need for fundamental economic reform
July 28	At Vladivostok, Gorbachev announces troop withdrawals from Afghanistan and his wish for improved Soviet-PRC relations
October 11 – 12	Reykjavik Summit between Reagan and Gorbachev; agreement is stalled by U.S. refusal to discuss SDI
November 13	President Reagan admits to clandestine U.S. arms sales to Iran
November 25	U.S. Justice Department investigators uncover the NSC's diversion of profits from arms sales to Iran into illegal aid to the Nicaraguan Contras
December 19	Soviet acceptance in principle of U.S. on-site nuclear test inspection in the Soviet Union. Leading Soviet dissident Andrei Sakharov is released from internal exile

1987

February 28	Gorbachev agrees to INF negotiations not linked to SDI
May 5	U.S. Congress opens hearings on Iran-Contra Affair
May 27	NATO defense ministers endorse "double zero" of eliminating INF and short-range nuclear forces
May 29	Warsaw Pact endorses INF, short range nuclear, and conventional force reduction talks with NATO

June 14	In his third visit to Poland, Pope John Paul II arouses widespread pro-Solidarity sentiment
September 15 – 17	Shultz and Shevardnadze begin INF Treaty negotiations in Washington, D.C.
November 2	In criticizing the shortcomings of the Soviet centrally planned economy before party officials, Gorbachev issues a frank denunciation of Stalin
November 18	U.S. Congressional report on Iran-Contra Affair criticizes the Reagan administration's "secrecy, deception, and disdain for the law"
November 19	Contras reject cease-fire offer by the Sandinistas
December 7 – 10	Reagan-Gorbachev summit in Washington, D.C.; INF Treaty is signed

1988

January 28	U.S., Cuban, and Angolan representatives hold peace discussions over the Angolan civil war
February 8	Gorbachev announces Soviet willingness to withdraw from Afghanistan, if an acceptable peace agreement can be reached
March 23	Following a U.S. Congressional vote to cut off all aid, the Contras accept a cease-fire in Nicaragua
April 14	U.S., Soviet Union, Pakistan, and the government of Afghanistan sign Geneva Peace Accords on ending the Afghanistan War
June 28 – July 1	19th All-Union Conference of the Soviet Communist Party approves constitutional reforms including an executive presidency, and an active elected legislature. Perestroika is reaffirmed in the final resolution
June 30	Vietnam begins military evacuation of Cambodia

August 15 – 30	Strike wave in Poland culminates in official negotiations with Solidarity
October 1	Gorbachev assumes Soviet presidency
November 1	Sino-Soviet border agreement
November 8	George H. W. Bush elected U.S. president
November 16	Estonian Soviet Republic declares right of veto over Soviet Union laws
December 7	Gorbachev's speech to UN General Assembly announces deep unilateral Soviet conventional force reductions

1989

January 9	Cuba completes military withdrawal from Angola
January 11	Hungary legalizes noncommunist political parties
January 17 – 19	CSCE convenes in Vienna, proposes NATO-Warsaw Pact negotiations on conventional arms reduction
February 14	Sandinistas accept principle that free Nicaraguan elections should take place by February 1990
February 15	Soviet troops complete withdrawal from Afghanistan
March 6	NATO and the Warsaw Pact begin talks in Vienna on Conventional Forces in Europe (CFE) Treaty
March 12	Demonstrations in Riga for official linguistic primacy of Latvian over Russian in the Latvian Soviet Republic
March 26	Multicandidate Soviet parliamentary elections return a reformist mandate
April 5	Polish government and Solidarity agree on full legal recognition for the union, which will be allowed to participate in forthcoming parliamentary elections
April 9	Georgian nationalist demonstrations in Tblisi crushed by Soviet security troops

June 4	Tiananmen Square demonstrations crushed by PRC military; Solidarity wins every seat it contests in Polish elections
June 16	Imre Nagy ceremonially reinterred in Budapest, Hungary
June 22	Cease-fire declared in Angola
July 7	Warsaw Pact Summit, Bucharest; Gorbachev tells member states they are free to pursue reform in their own ways
August 24	Communist government resigns in Poland; a coalition cabinet is formed under the former Solidarity leader, Tadeusz Mazowiecki
September 10	Hungary opens its border with Austria to GDR citizens with tourist visas
September 18	Hungarian agreement on transition to multi-party democracy; Marxism-Leninism is officially abandoned on October 7
October 1	GDR citizens taking refuge in the FRG's Prague and Warsaw embassies are allowed to leave for the West
October 7	Gorbachev criticizes GDR for lack of reform while attending its 50th anniversary ceremonies
October 16	Mass demonstrations in Leipzig against GDR intransigence
October 18	In GDR, Honecker is replaced by Egon Krenz
October 23	Massive unofficial pro-reform demonstrations in East Berlin
October 27	Warsaw Pact officially denounces the Brezhnev Doctrine
October 28	Mass demonstrations in Prague violently crushed by Czechoslovak security police
November 7 – 9	GDR goverment resigns en masse. New premier Hans Modrow promises relaxed emigration controls and free elections
November 9 – 10	Spontaneous demonstrations at the Berlin Wall prompt the GDR authorities to begin dismantling it

November 10	Bulgarian communist leader Todor Zhivkov resigns in favor of reformist Petar Mladenov
November 17 – 24	Outbreak of "Velvet Revolution" in Czechoslovakia
December 2 – 4	Malta Summit between Bush and Gorbachev declares the end of the Cold War to be in sight
December 10	Czechoslovak President Gustav Husak resigns after appointing a noncommunist coalition government
December 25	After 10 days of civil unrest, Romanian communist dictator Nicolae Ceausescu is arrested and summarily executed

1990

January 12	After negotiations with Lithuania, Gorbachev promises to consider a law permitting Soviet republics to secede from the Soviet Union
January 15	Bulgaria ends communist political monopoly
February 10	In Moscow, FRG Chancellor Kohl concludes economic aid agreement with Gorbachev, in return for the acceptance in principle of FRG-GDR unification
February 26	Sandinistas defeated in Nicaraguan elections by U.S.-funded right wing coalition
March 11	Lithuania declares independence; Gorbachev sends in security troops to restore Soviet control
March 14	Gorbachev announces power of rule by decree
March 25	Estonian parliament votes to secede from the Soviet Union
May 4	Latvian parliament votes to secede from the Soviet Union
May 29	Boris Yeltsin is elected president of the Russian Soviet Federated Socialist Republic
May 30 – June 4	Gorbachev–Bush summit in Washington, D.C.

June 8	Russian Republic legislature declares itself as having domestic jurisdictional primacy over Soviet Union's prerogatives
July 5 – 6	NATO summit in London declares that the Warsaw Pact is no longer an enemy
August 22	Armenia declares independence from the Soviet Union
September 12	After successful discussions between Kohl and Gorbachev in the Soviet Caucasus, Britain, France, U.S., Soviet Union, FRG, and GDR sign a German unification treaty in Moscow
October 3	GDR is dissolved and its territory merged into the FRG
November 19	CFE Treaty is signed in Paris
November 23	Gorbachev proposes "New Union Treaty" between the Soviet Republics
December 9	Lech Walesa, the Solidarity leader, is elected president of Poland
December 20	Shevardnadze resigns as Soviet foreign minister, protesting against Gorbachev's impending dictatorship

1991

January 5	COMECON votes to dissolve itself
January 13 – 29	Soviet forces clash with those of the Baltic states, but are withdrawn under U.S. diplomatic pressure
February 9	Lithuanian referendum affirms independence from Soviet Union
March 31	Warsaw Pact dissolves itself
April 9	Georgia declares independence from Soviet Union
May 21	Collapse of Marxist government of Ethiopia
July 29	In Moscow, Bush and Gorbachev sign START agreement
August 19	Soviet security and armed forces mount coup against Gorbachev

August 21	Soviet coup collapses; Yeltsin rises to power in Russia
August 24	Gorbachev resigns as Soviet Communist Party secretary; Ukraine declares independence
August 29	Soviet Communist Party suspended
November 6	Communist Party abolished in Russia
December 21	Commonwealth of Independent States formed by the Soviet Republics, minus the Baltic states and Georgia
December 25	Soviet Union formally dissolved

Introduction

The European great powers of Great Britain, France, Germany, and Italy were devastated by World War II. By contrast, the United States and the Soviet Union made a huge advance in military power and diplomatic prestige during the war and emerged as superpowers. After 1945 much of the world became divided into two great competing blocs in which the United States championed the West while the Soviet Union represented the East. The conflict was described as a state of cold war and dominated international politics for more than four decades. It came to an end when the Soviet Union dissolved itself in 1991.

BEGINNING OF THE COLD WAR IN EUROPE

Just as World War II revolved around events in Europe, so did the beginning of the Cold War. In 1945 it seemed that the wartime alliance between the United States, Great Britain, and the Soviet Union would continue into peacetime. Despite the show of friendship, however, there was considerable underlying mistrust and disagreement. The British and especially the Americans were historically and ideologically opposed to communism and were suspicious of the extension of Soviet military and political control over Central and Eastern Europe. The Soviets were secretive and defensive. After two German invasions in less than 30 years they equated the control over territory adjacent to their borders as essential for national security.

Indeed, Germany was a particularly divisive issue and was the major factor in precipitating the Cold War in Europe. During World War II the Allies had shared a common aim: subduing Germany militarily. But postwar plans for that country were vague and ill-defined. Cooperation was in evidence as a temporary solution was found in 1945, which placed Germany under joint military occupation and divided the country into four geographical zones to be administered respectively by the United States, Britain, France, and the Soviet Union. The city of Berlin was similarly divided into four separate sectors. Controversy arose, however, over Soviet claims for large reparations from Germany. The United States and Britain agreed in principle, but were reluctant to allow the Soviets to plunder Germany's fragile industrial base. There was also the concern that the Soviets aimed to make all of Germany a communist state. As much by default as calculation, therefore, the Americans and the British adopted a sympathetic attitude toward the defeated enemy and developed a policy of financing the economic rebuilding of western zones as a buffer against perceived Soviet expansion.

The emerging discord between the superpowers could not and would not be confined to Europe as demonstrated in 1946 when President Harry Truman demanded the withdrawal of Soviet troops from Northern Iran. The vigorous American action reflected the growing conviction in Washington that the Soviet Union was no longer an ally but an enemy. The Western Europeans, especially the British, also exerted an important influence on American attitudes. Most notably, the Soviet threat was emphasized by the former British prime minister, Winston Churchill, whose speech at Fulton, Missouri, in March 1946 criticized the Soviets for establishing an "iron curtain" across Eastern Europe. Churchill's warning coincided with the influential ideas of the American diplomat, George Kennan, whose "long telegram" emphasized that Soviet leaders could not be trusted because they were ideologically committed to permanent conflict with the West. Kennan stressed the need to contain Russian expansionism. The term *containment* was widely adopted to describe the aim of American policy in its dealings with the Soviet Union.

The turning point came in 1947 in the eastern Mediterranean after the British government announced that it could no longer maintain a substantial economic and military presence in Greece and Turkey. In effect, Britain's decline presented America with an opportunity to grasp the position of leader of the West, but at the price of abandoning its traditional policy of isolationism in affairs beyond the Western Hemisphere. After internal debate, the Truman administration decided that the challenge would be accepted and that positive action must be taken. In his address to Congress on March 12, 1947, Truman condemned communist aggression and asserted that the United States must be prepared to support the fight for freedom all over the world. The president's speech was referred to as the Truman Doctrine and is often regarded as representing the beginning of the Cold War. It was also in 1947 that the term Cold War first emerged in the United States as a result of a book with that title written by the celebrated American journalist, Walter Lippmann.

For a country as wealthy as the United States it was natuɪ size the use of money to achieve foreign policy objectives. administration believed that a massive program of financial aid ᴠ.ᴜₛ ɪne most effective way to halt the spread of communism in Europe. This idea was articulated by Secretary of State George Marshall in a speech at Harvard University in 1947. While the countries of Western Europe, especially Britain, warmly welcomed the proposed European Recovery Program (ERP), or the Marshall Plan as it became more popularly known, the Soviets felt threatened and accused the United States of a plot to infringe the sovereignty of independent nations. In retaliation the Soviets created the rival Communist Information Bureau. Although the American Congress initially hesitated to fund the Marshall Plan, doubts were dispelled by the communist coup in Czechoslovakia in 1948 that caused a war scare in Washington and highlighted the urgent need for the United States to aid democratic forces in Western Europe. However, the endorsement of the Marshall Plan essentially confirmed that the wartime alliance had finally collapsed, and that Europe was clearly split between the West and the East.

In fact, one of the prime objectives of the Marshall Plan was to boost the economies of the Western zones in Germany. The Soviet leader, Joseph Stalin, sought to counter this by isolating the West's military garrison in Berlin. The imposition of the Berlin Blockade on June 24, 1948, caused consternation in the West where it was interpreted as a calculated move to force a humiliating Western withdrawal from West Berlin. For a few days it even seemed that a full-scale war would break out. But superior Western technology and resources discovered a solution. Salvation for the city and its inhabitants was found in airlifting supplies into the beleaguered city. Almost a year later, on May 12, 1949, Stalin suddenly ended the blockade. The Soviet leader had seriously miscalculated the outcome. Instead of humiliating the West, the failure of the blockade represented a major blow to Soviet military and political prestige. Moreover, it had strengthened anticommunism throughout Western Europe and especially in West Germany. Although the United States, Britain, and France would continue their military occupation, their zones were given political independence in September 1949 with the establishment of the Federal Republic of Germany (West Germany). In October, Stalin retaliated by creating the German Democratic Republic (East Germany). The partition of Germany between East and West provided a foretaste of what would happen to much of the rest of the world during the Cold War.

NATO AND THE WARSAW PACT

By raising the likelihood of war, the Berlin Blockade considerably helped to justify and accelerate the organization of competing military blocs in Europe. Stalin's action was counterproductive in stimulating fears in Western Europe of communist aggression and therefore underlining the urgent need for a Western military alliance. In March 1948, several of the Western European nations formed the Brussels Treaty to provide collective security should a war break out. The members of the pact recognized, however, that a realistic defense against the Soviets required the support of American military power. The Truman administration was sympathetic, but was reluctant to enter into a formal military alliance in peacetime. The sending of American troops to Europe was quite different from exporting dollars under the Marshall Plan. However, the passage in June 1948 of the Vandenberg Resolution by the American Senate indicated that Congress favored some form of American association with the Brussels Treaty, and that a political consensus existed that endorsed the adoption of a positive policy to contain the threat of international communism. The members of the Brussels Treaty were invited to Washington where talks were held to consider and define the extent of America's commitment to the defense of Western Europe. By agreeing to the proviso that an armed attack against any one member would be considered an attack against the whole alliance, the United States gave the military guarantee that the Western Europeans wanted. In April 1949, the North Atlantic Treaty was signed in Washington and led to the establishment of the North Atlantic Treaty Organization (NATO).

In effect, NATO was a logical military complement to the Marshall Plan, but the United States did not initially intend to dominate the alliance. NATO was conceived as a multilateral alliance in which Americans expected the Europeans to assume the main burden in defending themselves. However, this complacent view was soon shattered by the revelation that the Soviets had successfully tested an atomic bomb, and also by communist success in seizing control of Mainland China. Moreover, in 1950 the invasion of South Korea by North Korea raised the possibility of a similar communist assault against West Germany. The fear of external attack was heightened by awareness in the West that the East was greatly superior in conventional forces. A nightmare scenario was envisaged in which Soviet and East European forces would sweep across Central Europe and reach the English Channel within 48 hours. The United States responded by assuming military command of NATO's ground forces, thereby greatly increasing its involvement in the alliance. The Truman administration also proposed the rearmament of West Germany and that country's military participation in NATO. The proposal encountered considerable resistance from some European members, especially France, but was accepted after the United States agreed to fully integrate American troops within NATO's command structure.

Meanwhile, the creation of NATO had motivated Stalin to increase the strength of the Red Army and to accelerate the development of Soviet atomic and thermonuclear bombs. In Churchill's words, a Soviet empire of satellite states stretched in an iron curtain from the Baltic to the Balkans. Although nominally independent, these countries were under Soviet political, economic, and military direction. Economic controls were imposed by the creation of the Council for Mutual Economic Assistance (COMECON). A Soviet counterpart of NATO was also soon in existence although the military alliance known as the Warsaw Treaty Organization (Warsaw Pact) was not officially formed until 1955.

Despite the militarization of the Cold War the superpowers engaged in a war of words and propaganda rather than a "hot" war between themselves during the 1950s. In the United States, the determination to roll back the Iron Curtain and liberate Eastern Europe from communist tyranny was a prominent theme of Dwight D. Eisenhower's successful presidential election campaign of 1952. The leading Republican authority on foreign affairs, John Foster Dulles, declared that the United States must seize the initiative in the Cold War. As secretary of state, however, his actions belied his aggressive rhetoric. Rolling back the Iron Curtain was to be achieved not by military force but by asserting the superior moral example of the free world under the leadership of the United States. The Eisenhower administration adopted a strategy known as the New Look that allowed a significant reduction of expensive conventional forces by substituting strategic air power and the deployment of tactical nuclear weapons. It was a clever strategy – good public relations – and also brought tangible economic benefits. However, it also was instrumental in introducing a balance of terror in which war between NATO and the Warsaw Pact would certainly involve the use of nuclear weapons, and consequently pose the appalling prospect of the annihilation of both sides. If the threat of nuclear holocaust deterred a Soviet invasion of Western Europe, it also prevented the United States from rolling back the Iron Curtain. This was exemplified during the Hungarian Uprising in 1956. As Soviet tanks brutally crushed the resistance of the Hungarians, the Eisenhower administration was unwilling to intervene militarily and thereby implicitly acknowledged that Hungary and the other countries of Eastern Europe were firmly within the Soviet sphere of influence.

KHRUSHCHEV AND KENNEDY

The passivity of the United States during the Hungarian crisis encouraged Soviet diplomacy to adopt a distinct combative tone under the new Soviet leader, Nikita Khrushchev. Furthermore, in October 1957 the Soviet Union delivered a severe blow to American pride by sending the Sputnik around the earth. The age of the intercontinental ballistic missile (ICBM) was inaugurated, and the initial advantage lay with the Soviet Union. In contrast to the secretive Stalin, Khrushchev was an extrovert and eager to proclaim and extol the achievements of communism. In the struggle for peaceful coexistence between capitalism and communism, Khrushchev predicted that the economic and scientific progress of the communist bloc would soon demonstrate the superiority of communism without any need to resort to war.

While Khrushchev's boasts were applauded in the Soviet Union, they carried little conviction in places such as Berlin where the economic prosperity of the western sectors contrasted very favorably with the drab conditions in the eastern sector. But Berlin remained an Achilles' heel of the West. Suddenly in November 1958, Khrushchev created another Berlin crisis by demanding that the Western garrisons be withdrawn from the city within six months. Subsequent diplomatic events demonstrated, however, that Khrushchev did not intend war. A summit meeting of the superpowers was held at Paris in May 1960, but the prospect of agreement was ruled out by the shooting down of an American U-2 spy plane over the Soviet Union. While Khrushchev enjoyed an easy propaganda victory over Eisenhower, his aggressiveness alarmed the West and stimulated the arms race between the superpowers. Since the launch of the Sputnik in 1957 some American military experts had claimed that the Soviets possessed a decisive superiority in missile technology. This concern was a feature of the 1960 presidential election campaign in which the Democratic candidate, John F. Kennedy, charged that a missile gap existed between the United States and the Soviet Union. On assuming the presidency in 1961, Kennedy immediately requested Congress to pass a substantial increase in defense spending to rectify the alleged imbalance in strategic weapons.

The new president also agreed to a personal meeting with Khrushchev at Vienna in June 1961. Prior to the summit, Kennedy had experienced a humiliating setback at the Bay of Pigs in Cuba where a covert operation organized by the Central Intelligence Agency (CIA) was easily defeated by Fidel Castro. At Vienna, Khrushchev tried to browbeat the younger man and threatened to renew the crisis over Berlin. In fact, Berlin was much more of a problem for the communists than for the West. In West Berlin, every day saw the arrival of hundreds of East German refugees intent on traveling to the western sector. Quite unexpectedly, the East German authorities erected a barbed-wire fence during the night of August 12-13, 1961. The fence became the notorious Berlin Wall separating the eastern and western sectors. Kennedy seized the opportunity to condemn a society that felt compelled to build a wall to keep its own people captive. But there was no disposition to resort to war. The crisis was allowed to fade away as both sides acknowledged that the partition of Germany was an undeniable fact.

Khrushchev's bluster was also undermined by evidence that the balance of nuclear weapon superiority was moving decisively against the Soviet Union. There was no missile gap. In fact, under Kennedy, the United States was developing new, advanced weapons systems and appeared to have achieved a first-strike capability. Khrushchev attempted to redress the strategic balance by secretly placing nuclear missiles in Cuba. In October 1962, the world was poised on the edge of nuclear disaster as the two superpowers engaged in diplomatic brinkmanship. Khrushchev's decision to remove the weapons implied to the world that Kennedy had achieved a famous victory. The historical evidence, however, is not so certain. American missiles were also withdrawn from Turkey, and a secret undertaking was given by Kennedy not to invade Cuba. No matter who had won or lost the "missile crisis," it was a disconcerting experience for both Kennedy and Khrushchev. The importance of improving communications was demonstrated by the setting up in June 1963 of a direct hot line between the Kremlin and the White House. A Partial Nuclear Test Ban treaty to outlaw atmospheric tests followed in July 1963.

Kennedy's handling of the Missile Crisis aroused some misgivings among the European members of NATO. Powers such as Britain and France did not like to think of themselves as inferior to the United States and jealously maintained their right to develop their own independent nuclear weapons programs. However, the development of massive Soviet nuclear forces during the 1950s had made Western Europe more dependent than ever on the deterrent of American nuclear weapons. The result was more subordination to the United States, and ironically, a greater feeling of insecurity. Because America was now also in danger of a direct attack from long-range

Soviet missiles, President Charles de Gaulle of France queried whether, in the event of an actual Soviet attack, the United States would defend Western Europe and risk a nuclear exchange that might result in its own destruction. Although the nations of Western Europe continued to regard NATO as fundamental to their security, by the early 1960s the desire to pursue a more independent foreign policy was evident as they sought to improve relations with the Soviet Union and the countries of Eastern Europe.

DISCORD AT THE UNITED NATIONS

The inability of the superpowers to agree over Europe was replicated at the United Nations (UN). As World War II drew to its close the United States had proposed the creation of the United Nations Organization as a means by which the wartime alliance would continue to work together to preserve peace in the postwar world. In order to ensure Soviet membership, various concessions were necessary that included the granting of the power of veto to the five permanent members of the Security Council. Despite early optimism, however, conflict surfaced at the very first meetings of the UN in 1946. Instead of a forum for debate such as the American Congress or the British House of Commons, the UN became an arena for confrontation between the East and West. On occasion, the superpowers consented to the UN serving a useful peacekeeping function, as in Palestine or Kashmir, and member states were asked to contribute troops and military equipment for this purpose. As the frequent use of the Soviet veto demonstrated, however, the raising of cold war issues at the UN resulted more often in diplomatic impasse than constructive dialogue. A change occurred during the late-1950s when the agenda of subjects under discussion was significantly broadened as a result of the acceleration of decolonization. The dissolution of the European colonial empires meant that a large number of new independent nations were created so that the original membership of the UN had almost doubled by 1960. Moreover, the balance of voting power in the General Assembly shifted against the West because a majority of the members now belonged to the "third world" of Africa and Asia.

The American officials who had constructed the UN had envisaged an instrument to promote world peace. But the Soviets were distrustful of an institution that was too similar to the American congress and initially contained a pro-Western majority. Their response was to use the power of veto to ensure that the UN was effectively deprived of real executive power for as long as the Cold War existed. As a result, the UN became primarily an institution to distribute economic and cultural welfare, and a platform for the expression of political propaganda. Where superpower agreement was forthcoming, UN troops continued to maintain agreed cease-fire lines especially in the Middle East and Africa. The notable exception was during the 1950s and 1960s when the UN found itself directly entangled in hot wars in Korea and the Congo.

THE KOREAN WAR

Having defeated Japan almost single-handedly in World War II, the United States rejected the idea of the four-power zonal agreement to administer Germany and refused to allow the Soviets to participate in the military occupation and government of Japan. A similar policy of excluding communist influence was not feasible in China where the rule of the nationalist government headed by Chiang Kai-shek was resisted by the communists under Mao Zedong. Civil war ensued in China until 1949 when the communist forces seized control of the mainland and established the People's Republic of China (PRC). Chiang withdrew to the island of Formosa (Taiwan). Despite possessing limited influence over the outcome of military events on the Chinese mainland, the Truman administration was severely criticized in the United States for losing China. The mood turned into national paranoia when Senator Joseph McCarthy alleged that American inactivity was explained by the fact that communists had infiltrated influential positions in the State Department. The subsequent upsurge of McCarthyism hardened American attitudes toward Communist or Red China. The hostility between the two countries was soon evident in Korea. After Japan's surrender in 1945, the Korean peninsula became divided into two rival states. North of the 38th parallel, the communists under Kim Il Sung dominated North Korea. The southern leader, Syngman Rhee, closely aligned South Korea with the United States. Kim and Rhee publicly denounced the other for causing the division of the country and stated that they would bring about reunification by whatever means were necessary, including the use of force. On June 25, 1950, North Korean forces invaded South Korea. Convinced that the invasion was a deliberate Soviet challenge to the West on a par with the Berlin Blockade, Truman requested an immediate meeting of the Security Council of the UN. At the meeting the American delegation secured the adoption of resolutions calling upon North Korea to withdraw its forces and asked members of the UN to provide troops to drive back the aggressor. Truman replied immediately that the

United States would deploy its military forces on behalf of the UN. Although 16 nations eventually sent troops, the American contribution was by far the biggest and amounted to half the number of combat troops and around 90 percent of air and naval support. The various national contingents were effectively unified under American control and direction.

Initially, the North Koreans almost overran the whole peninsula, but fell just short of achieving total military victory. In September the American commander, General Douglas MacArthur, deftly outflanked the enemy by organizing a surprise and successful amphibious landing at Inchon. The UN forces rapidly crossed the 38th parallel into North Korea and steadily advanced to the border with the People's Republic of China (PRC). Contrary to MacArthur's assessment, China launched a major land offensive in November. A lengthy war of attrition ensued in which the line of battle became settled along the same 38th parallel that had marked the prewar border. The military stalemate was not broken until a new American president, Dwight Eisenhower, took office in 1953. In effect, war-weariness brought all sides to the peace table so that the Panmunjom agreement in July 1953 essentially recognized the existing battle line and prewar borders. Despite three years of war, reunification of Korea was as far away as ever as the North stayed within the communist orbit, while the South remained closely tied with the United States.

The Korean War showed that American officials considered the containment of communism to be a global struggle and not just applicable to Europe. Despite the lack of tangible evidence, the Chinese entry into the war was interpreted in Washington as confirmation that the PRC was a puppet of the Soviet Union. The United States felt justified in its policy of diplomatically isolating Communist China and continued to insist that Taiwan was the legitimate government of China. The war in Korea also radically altered American relations with the other nations of the Far East. The Truman administration concluded defense treaties with Taiwan, Japan, Australia, New Zealand, and the Philippines. In September 1954, President Eisenhower created a formal anticommunist coalition known as the Manila Pact or South-East Asia Treaty Organization (SEATO). In the same year, however, a major communist success occurred in Indochina.

THE VIETNAM WAR

During World War II Japan had seized control of French Indochina. Guerrilla resistance was organized in Vietnam by the Vietminh, a communist movement guided by Ho Chi Minh. At the end of the war in 1945 Vietminh forces entered Hanoi and sought to establish an independent state called the Democratic Republic of Vietnam. However, France was determined to restore Vietnam's colonial status and this sparked the First Indochina War in 1946. Outwardly, France appeared to be winning the war. However, the guerrilla tactics employed by the Vietminh caused a constant drain of lives and money that made the war increasingly unpopular in France. The humiliating surrender at Dien Bien Phu in May 1954 marked the end of France's attempt to hold on to its empire in Indochina.

The Truman administration displayed little interest in Indochina until shaken by the loss of China in 1949 and the outbreak of the Korean War. Beginning in 1950 the United States agreed to a program of financial assistance to France, which steadily increased until it amounted to almost 80 percent of French expenditure on the war. The aid was justified because American officials were anxious over the possible loss of any more Asian countries to communism. This fear gained the name of the "domino theory" after a speech by President Eisenhower in which he suggested that the fall of Indochina could well be followed by similar communist successes in neighboring countries and might ultimately spread to the United States. Despite this alarming scenario, Eisenhower rejected desperate pleas from France for an American air strike to save the French garrison at Dien Bien Phu. The decision was not as momentous as it appeared because the French government had already agreed to join a conference of foreign ministers scheduled to meet at Geneva in July 1954 to discuss peace in Indochina. The Geneva conference confirmed the end of hostilities and the division of Vietnam at the 17th parallel into the separate states of North and South Vietnam.

While not displeased by the end of French colonial rule in Indochina, the Eisenhower administration was disconcerted at the loss of northern Vietnam to communism. In fact, Eisenhower decided that the United States would defeat the domino theory by creating a strong noncommunist nation in the South that would serve as a beacon of freedom in the region. In 1955, American approval was given to Ngo Dinh Diem's establishment of an independent Republic of Vietnam (South Vietnam). Diem was undoubtedly strongly anticommunist, and his repressive rule contributed to the start of the Second Indochina War in 1959. The rebels called themselves the National Liberation Front or Vietcong and declared that their aim was to overthrow Diem and reunify Vietnam.

Although Eisenhower was alarmed by the growing level of violence occurring in South Vietnam, he was more directly concerned over events in

Europe rather than Southeast Asia. However, his successor, John F. Kennedy, regarded Vietnam as an opportunity to implement the fashionable strategy of "flexible response," in which communist guerrillas would be destroyed by American superiority in counterinsurgency operations. Despite official optimism, the initial results were disappointing. More and more American military assistance was required so that the number of American advisers in South Vietnam steadily increased. Kennedy's successor, Lyndon Johnson, sought to punish North Vietnam for its aggression against the South by gradually escalating the fighting on the ground and especially in the air until the enemy was forced to admit defeat. But the cost was enormous in terms of money and men. By 1968, more than 500,000 American servicemen were stationed in South Vietnam and the war was effectively Americanized.

Instead of lowering the enemy's morale, Johnson's policy of escalation stimulated North Vietnamese determination to continue the war. Moreover, an antiwar movement unexpectedly emerged in the United States that steadily grew in numbers and political influence. The turning point came in January 1968 when the Vietcong launched the Tet Offensive and dealt an enormous psychological blow to American confidence about winning the war. Johnson felt compelled to reverse the policy of escalation. However, it was left to his successor, Richard Nixon, to bring an end to American military involvement in Vietnam. The fighting in the South dragged on until an agreement was concluded at Paris in January 1973 that established a cease-fire and allowed American withdrawal disguised in the words of Nixon as peace with honor. Without the continuing military, financial, and political support of the United States, South Vietnam could not survive as an independent country: in 1975, North Vietnamese troops took control of Saigon and brought an end to the second Indochina War by forcibly uniting the two Vietnams. The Vietnam War was a traumatic experience for the United States, and was made the more galling by the fact that both the Soviet Union and Communist China made considerable propaganda gains from America's humiliation while avoiding direct participation in the actual fighting.

THE SUPERPOWERS IN THE MIDDLE EAST

At the end of World War II Great Britain was still regarded as the preeminent foreign power in the Middle East. But British economic and military resources were seriously overextended. Conscious of the region's enormous oil reserves and alarmed that British weakness would provide opportunities for Soviet expansion, the Truman administration chose to become actively involved in the affairs of the Middle East. Special attention was paid to developing friendly relations with oil-rich Saudi Arabia and Iran. More controversial, however, was the development of a close and special relationship between the United States and Israel that aroused Arab hostility and constantly undermined American efforts to appear to be pursuing an even-handed policy toward all the countries in the region.

The role of Egypt was particularly significant. Under the leadership of Gamal Abdel Nasser, Egypt sought to present the region with a successful model of Arab revolutionary nationalism. In terms of foreign policy, Nasser was especially eager to break the tradition of dependence on the West. He negotiated a trade deal with the Soviet Union in 1956 and established diplomatic relations with Communist China. Nasser also nationalized the Anglo-French company that controlled and operated the Suez Canal. In October 1956, British and French forces retaliated by seizing the canal, while Israel simultaneously launched an offensive from the east. President Eisenhower was critical of Nasser, but he would not endorse the use of military force by Britain and France and insisted that those countries terminate their invasion.

The Suez Crisis split the Western allies, boosted the reputation of Nasser, and significantly assisted the rise of Soviet influence in the Arab world. It also marked the replacement of Britain by the United States as the leading Western power in the region. The change was signaled by Eisenhower in a speech on January 5, 1957, outlining what would become known as the Eisenhower Doctrine. But the Cold War perspective was highly misleading. The actions of the superpowers were not directly responsible for the political turbulence of the Middle East. The ruling Arab elites undoubtedly resented foreign interference, but the superpowers were a lesser evil when compared with the threat of revolutionary change and Egyptian hegemony implicit in Nasser's Pan-Arab movement. Nasser, however, complicated matters by looking to the Soviet Union for military and financial assistance. This ensured that the United States expanded its military and financial aid programs to governments that it considered friendly. In the process, the region was entangled in cold war politics. But this did not mean that the nations of the Middle East were transformed into satellites of the superpowers. Increasing oil revenues gave the Arab states not only a significant measure of independence and self-esteem but also the financial resources to prepare for war against Israel and to secure a resolution of the Palestine

Question. The Arab-Israeli conflict and not the Cold War was the central issue that dominated the politics of the region.

CRISIS IN AFRICA

Sub-Saharan African remained firmly on the periphery of events as the Cold War took form in Europe, Asia, and the Middle East. For the two superpowers, the region had traditionally been assigned a low strategic priority. Change occurred beginning in the late 1950s as the process of decolonization gathered momentum. Starting with Ghana in 1957, most of Africa was liberated from European colonial rule within less than a decade. The new states sought to adopt a nonaligned stance in world affairs, but economic weakness and dependence on the export of staple commodities meant that most countries remained closely tied to the economies of their former colonial rulers. For some of the new states the cultivation of relations with the superpowers offered an opportunity for new markets and a means, therefore, of escaping from the state of dependency. But the governments of the United States and the Soviet Union responded cautiously. So long as there was no major disturbance affecting their national interests, they regarded Africa as an area of minor strategic significance.

It was the political crisis in the Congo that thrust Africa temporarily into the center of cold war politics during the early 1960s. Shortly after being granted independence in 1960, the country was plunged into political civil war. The Congolese Prime Minister, Patrice Lumumba, appealed to the UN for military assistance to restore order. Prompted by UN Secretary General Dag Hammarskjöld, the Security Council agreed to dispatch a peacekeeping force. But the superpowers could not keep out of the unfolding crisis. When Lumumba requested military aid from the Soviet Union, American officials feared that a communist coup was imminent and took steps to prevent this from materializing. In September 1960, Lumumba fell from power and was murdered four months later. The event signaled a setback for Soviet influence. Largely financed and equipped by the United States, the UN peacekeeping force was instrumental in restoring public order and allowing pro-Western Congolese leaders to gain political control.

After the end of the Congo Crisis the interest of the superpowers in African affairs soon diminished. The image of a continent on the move was tarnished by frequent changes of government, often by violent military coups. Political instability also engendered poor economic performance so that Western businessmen directed most of their investment not to the poor nations of black Africa, but to the affluent, white-ruled republic of South Africa. The Soviet Union seized the opportunity to condemn the United States for maintaining close relations with South Africa, a nation notorious for its system of apartheid. The war of words was particularly successful for the Soviets in debates on colonialism at the UN. But the Soviets were relatively inexperienced in dealing with African nations and the attempts to extend Soviet influence in Africa had little success during the 1960s. Although the new African states did not hesitate to play off Washington and Moscow to obtain economic and military aid, they wished to preserve their newly won independence and preferred to adopt the policy of nonalignment in world affairs.

REVOLUTION IN LATIN AMERICA

After 1945 the United States sought to maintain its traditional political and military leadership of the Western Hemisphere. A regional system of collective security known as the Rio Treaty was established in 1947 by the Inter-American Treaty for Reciprocal Assistance. Military assistance programs were developed so that the Latin American governments would assume part of the burden of hemispheric defense. While outwardly in favor of democratic governments and elections, the United States found it easier to work with authoritarian regimes that shared America's anticommunist and capitalist ethos. Prominent examples were Fulgencio Batista in Cuba and the Somoza family in Nicaragua. It was a contradiction that belied America's claim to be the champion and protector of the free world.

The Soviet Union had little historical contact with Latin America, and local communist parties were relatively weak in that part of the world. In the era of McCarthyism, however, American officials readily attributed the rise of revolutionary nationalism in Latin America to communist infiltration and subversion. Guatemala was viewed as a test case in the early 1950s because it was feared that local communists aimed to turn the country into a Soviet satellite. In 1954, a small army of Guatemalan political exiles equipped and organized by the CIA staged a successful military coup. Latin American governments were dismayed by America's covert use of armed force to overthrow a legally elected government. They were also disappointed that their cooperative attitude in the Cold War did not result in commensurate economic favors from the United States. In 1961, the

Kennedy administration attempted to remedy affairs by launching the Alliance for Progress.

The desire for a quick victory in the hemispheric battle against communism made the use of covert operations an attractive policy option for American presidents. This was exemplified in the response to the rise to power of Fidel Castro in Cuba. An attempt to overthrow the Cuban leader ended in disastrous failure at the Bay of Pigs in April 1961. The United States was humiliated, while Fidel Castro's prestige was greatly enhanced. Although the Soviets tried to place missiles in Cuba in 1962, to the relief of the United States they did not attempt to integrate Cuba into the Warsaw Pact or join a Soviet system of worldwide alliances. Moreover, the Cuban example of enacting a socialist revolution was not directly copied elsewhere in Latin America during the 1960s. Indeed, the failure of Cuba's attempts to export revolution to the mainland was illustrated by the capture and death of Ché Guevara in Bolivia in 1967.

The United States was successful in preventing a hot war from developing in Latin America. American diplomacy generally opted to use military assistance programs and covert operations to contain communism in the region. To intervene directly with American forces was considered too damaging to America's image in Latin America. However, a close scrutiny was maintained over the danger zone, the region that included the nations of the Caribbean and Central America and was a strategic concern for the United States. In the same way that he was determined not to lose South Vietnam to communism, President Lyndon Johnson would not permit another Cuba in the Caribbean. When political chaos erupted in the Dominican Republic in 1965, he acted decisively by sending more than 20,000 American troops to restore order. The Soviets were critical, but they were impressed and intimidated by Johnson's show of force. They had learned the lesson of the Cuban Missile Crisis, and like the Americans during the putting down of the Hungarian Uprising in 1956, the Soviets had no intention of intervening militarily in America's sphere of influence.

DÉTENTE

Failure to win the Vietnam War brought into question the assumption held since the end of World War II that the United States was indisputably the world's preeminent superpower. Moreover, by the late 1960s the Soviet Union had closed the nuclear gap and boasted a position of parity in nuclear weapons. This brought a change in American policy under Richard Nixon, who was elected president in 1968. Instead of pursuing the confrontational style of Kennedy and Johnson, Nixon chose to seek a relaxation of tensions or détente with the Soviets. The timing appeared opportune because the Soviet leader, Leonid Brezhnev, was eager for more contact with the West especially in terms of trade and investment. The reason lay in the recognition that the economies of the Soviet Union and Eastern Europe had fallen considerably behind those of the West. Furthermore, economic discontent was growing in the satellite countries and was held to be responsible for the emergence of the reform movement in Czechoslovakia in 1968. Nevertheless, while Brezhnev acknowledged the crucial importance of gaining access to Western goods and capital, he had no intention of relaxing Soviet control over Eastern Europe. In 1968, his statement of policy known as the Brezhnev Doctrine had declared that the Soviets would not hesitate to use military force to ensure that the establishment of a communist state was irreversible.

In addition, Brezhnev was suspicious of overtures for détente from an American president who was notorious for his anticommunist views. The initial boost to détente emerged not from Washington or Moscow but from the diplomatic activities of Chancellor Willy Brandt of West Germany. Brandt's policy known as Ostpolitik stressed normalizing West Germany's relations with the Soviet Union and the countries of Eastern Europe including East Germany. Ostpolitik was significant because it meant that, after almost a quarter of a century, West Germany formally accepted the division of Germany into two separate countries and recognized the borders that the Red Army had imposed upon Eastern Europe in 1945.

An unexpected aid to the process of détente between the superpowers was provided by Communist China. Since the late 1950s the Soviet Union and Communist China had competed in an increasingly bitter ideological battle for leadership of the world communist movement. From Eisenhower to Johnson, successive American administrations played no active role in the Sino-Soviet conflict and continued to recognize Taiwan as the legitimate government of China. Responding to suggestions that the Communist Chinese government wanted substantive diplomatic discussions Nixon's national security adviser, Henry Kissinger, secretly visited Beijing in 1971. On Kissinger's return, Nixon astonished the world by announcing that he intended to make an official visit to China. The historic event took place in February 1972, and its highpoint was the personal meeting between Nixon and Mao, an occasion that marked an end to America's long-standing perception of Communist China as an agent of the monolithic communist conspiracy directed from Moscow. China now appeared ironically as an ally to help contain Soviet expansion in Asia. The aim of American diplomacy was, however, not to become ensnared in the Sino-Soviet conflict but to seek a relaxation of tensions simultaneously with both communist powers. Indeed, the possibility that American-Chinese relations were improving had startled the Soviets and made them suddenly very eager to pursue détente with the United States. They were especially eager for Nixon to attend a summit meeting with Brezhnev in Moscow.

The coming together of the two superpower leaders at the Moscow Summit in May 1972 signaled to the world that both sides genuinely wished détente. Further evidence was provided by the signing of the Strategic Arms Limitation Treaty (SALT I) that placed limits on the number of missiles and sought to restrain the massive arms build-up that now threatened the world with nuclear holocaust. The treaty was regarded as a major achievement because discussions over disarmament had regularly engaged the superpowers for almost a decade. Despite the conclusion of the 1963 Partial Nuclear Test Ban Treaty and the 1968 Non-proliferation Treaty, the United States and the Soviet Union had continued to develop and stockpile even more destructive and sophisticated nuclear weapons. Specific talks under the title of Strategic Arms Limitation Talks (SALT) had actually started in November 1969. The fact that they had finally resulted in an arms control treaty was especially gratifying and an indication that the process of détente had made an auspicious beginning.

Both Nixon and Brezhnev enjoyed immediate political benefits from détente. It helped Nixon to win a landslide victory in the 1972 American presidential election. In the Soviet Union, Brezhnev's personal ascendancy within the Politburo was further strengthened. Particularly pleasing to the Soviet leader was the increase in economic cooperation with the West. Détente also presented an opportunity to follow up the achievements made by Ostpolitik toward resolving the broader question of European security. In 1975, the Helsinki Accords gave formal international recognition of existing borders in Eastern Europe. In exchange the Soviets consented to the inclusion of the so-called Basket III provision in which all signatories proclaimed their respect for human rights and political freedoms. The litmus test of détente, however, was whether a new and more definitive arms control treaty to replace SALT I could be successfully negotiated. Progress was stalled, however, by Nixon's dramatic resignation from the presidency in August 1974. The new president, Gerald Ford, expressed his desire to continue the negotiations and met with Brezhnev for this purpose at Vladivostok in November 1974. A draft agreement was approved to form the basis of a new treaty to be known as SALT II. However, in the United

States, traditional mistrust of communism revived and was fueled by rumors that the Soviets were secretly exceeding the limits on nuclear weapons, which had been set down in SALT I. In fact, the SALT II treaty became such a contentious political issue in the United States that Ford decided to delay its submission to the American Senate for ratification until after the 1976 presidential election.

DÉTENTE AND THE THIRD WORLD

The deficiencies of détente were most evident in the heightening of superpower tensions in the Third World. This was especially the case in the Middle East where the regional balance of power had been transformed by Israel's smashing victory over the Arabs in the Six-Day War in 1967. As the principal supplier of economic and military aid to Israel, the United States had long been identified as the protector of Israel. The result was growing anti-Americanism in the Arab world, a development that aided the extension of Soviet influence, especially in Egypt. The demarcation of superpower influence was underscored in 1971 when Anwar el-Sadat, who had succeeded to the Egyptian presidency after Nasser's death, signed a treaty of friendship with the Soviet Union. The need for military assistance made Israel and Egypt appear to be clients of the superpowers, but neither country was an obedient satellite. Both regarded cold war politics as a valuable means to achieve their own national objectives. For Israel, the paramount goal was to ensure national survival and security. The priority of President Sadat was to regain the territories lost to Israel in the 1967 war. The question was not whether but when would another Arab-Israeli war occur? The answer was given on October 6, 1973, the Jewish holy day of Yom Kippur, when Egypt and Syria attacked Israel without warning. Taken by surprise, the Israelis retreated in front of the Egyptian offensive, but they quickly regrouped and inflicted a heavy defeat on the enemy forces.

Although the United States and the Soviet Union sent large amounts of military aid to their respective clients, both superpowers wanted a speedy end to a conflict that they feared might ignite into a full-scale regional war. American and Soviet diplomats cooperated in arranging a cease-fire under the auspices of the UN Security Council. Such action reflected the spirit of détente, but Nixon's latent suspicion of collusion between the Soviet Union and Egypt in starting the war was aroused when Brezhnev implied that Soviet troops were about to be sent to protect Egyptian forces from Israeli attack. In response Nixon issued a state of global alert known as

Defense Condition III that placed American military forces at the highest state of combat readiness in peacetime.

Soviet military intervention did not occur. Nixon's action was premature but its very decisiveness boosted American prestige in the Middle East and resulted in the emergence of the United States as the principal broker in the dispute between Israel and Egypt. A period of shuttle diplomacy ensued in which Secretary of State Henry Kissinger traveled for two years between the capitals of the region. Kissinger was successful in bringing Israel and Egypt together in constructive peace talks although a comprehensive peace settlement did not materialize until 1979. Particularly gratifying for American diplomacy was the dramatic improvement in relations with Egypt, a development that was highlighted in 1976 by Sadat's termination of the 1971 Soviet-Egyptian treaty.

The Soviets responded by turning to Syria and building up that country's military power. In so doing, they undermined the claim that American diplomacy had brought peace to the region because Israel felt more threatened than ever by the implacable hostility of Syria and also by the increasing incidence of terrorism carried out by the Palestinian Liberation Organization (PLO). Moreover, the United States was directly and adversely affected by the retaliatory action of the Organization of Petroleum Exporting Countries (OPEC) whose Arab members had cut back their production of oil as protest against American military support of Israel during the Yom Kippur War. The resulting energy crisis plunged the world economy into recession for much of the 1970s. In the United States, a suspicion existed that the Soviet Union was implicated in the increase of the price of oil and this contributed to growing public criticism of détente.

American concern was also aroused by Soviet activities in Africa. In the Angolan civil war in 1975 the Soviets airlifted weapons and transported more than 20,000 Cuban troops to support the Marxist Popular Movement for the Liberation of Angola. A similar pattern of events took place in East Africa as the Soviets provided financial aid, equipment, and training for the Somali army. However, in the war between Somalia and Ethiopia in 1977, the Soviets chose to support Ethiopia and sent large quantities of military equipment including an airlift of Cuban troops. The subsequent military victory of Ethiopia over Somalia was widely interpreted as a diplomatic triumph for the Soviet Union. The occurrence of Soviet intervention in Africa coincided with the overrunning of South Vietnam in 1975 by North Vietnam and shortly afterward the establishment of communist governments in Cambodia (Kampuchea) and Laos. The result in the United

States was a sense of dismay bordering on humiliation that contributed to the growing disillusionment with détente.

DEMISE OF DÉTENTE

The controversy over détente helped Jimmy Carter to defeat Gerald Ford in the 1976 presidential election. The new president promised an end to America's obsession with cold war politics, but soon found himself closely involved in East-West relations over the issue of arms control. Although he was expected to sign the SALT II agreement made by Ford and Brezhnev at Vladivostok, Carter devised an alternative scheme that included additional reductions. The change annoyed the Soviets and meant that agreement on a new treaty was delayed until Carter met with Brezhnev at the Vienna Summit in 1979. In the meantime, the SALT II treaty continued to arouse so much criticism in the United States that its ratification by the American Senate appeared uncertain.

SALT II was difficult and frustrating, but it was events in Iran and Afghanistan that essentially ended détente between the superpowers. The overthrow in 1979 of the Iranian ruler, Mohammed Reza Shah Pahlavi, was a major blow for American diplomacy in the region. Although the Iranian Revolution was not inspired by communism, it was hostile to the United States. This was made evident when Iranian students occupied the American embassy in Tehran and held 69 Americans hostage. Meanwhile, the Soviet Union invaded Iran's northern neighbor, Afghanistan, in December 1979. The invasion was notably the first time since 1945 that the Red Army had operated beyond the areas occupied during World War II. No doubt, Soviet generals expected a repeat of the successful actions mounted in Hungary in 1956 and Czechoslovakia in 1968, but events demonstrated that they had seriously underestimated the degree of local resistance that the invasion would arouse.

The United Nations condemned the aggression of the Soviet Union against Afghanistan. The Soviets, however, cast their veto in the Security Council to prevent any repetition of the military measures that the UN had taken against North Korea in 1950. But American retaliation was soon forthcoming. President Carter publicly condemned the Soviet invasion and immediately withdrew the SALT II treaty from the Senate. The United States also revived the policy of military containment by establishing a Rapid Deployment Force (RDF) to respond quickly to crises within the region.

Carter's display of American strength and decisiveness signaled a renewal of cold war tensions and the demise of détente.

THE REAGAN DOCTRINE

Despite his tough stance against the Soviets, Carter lost the 1980 presidential election to the even tougher Republican candidate, Ronald Reagan. A staunch anticommunist, Reagan campaigned against détente in favor of a policy of resolving only to negotiate with the Soviet Union from a position of military strength. He also firmly believed that the United States was obligated to act as the leader of the free world. As president, his positive assertion of the superiority of Western values became popularly known as the Reagan Doctrine and was calculated to pose a direct challenge to the Brezhnev Doctrine. With Afghanistan in mind, the president even went so far as to praise in public the activities of freedom fighters who were attempting to overthrow pro-Soviet governments.

Reagan backed up the language of provocation with material aid usually given secretly by the CIA in the form of money and military equipment. This was quietly effective in Afghanistan, but much more public and controversial was the application of the Reagan Doctrine in Central America. Reagan was alarmed by the spread of Cuban and Soviet influence and feared the application of a domino effect in which communism, if unchecked, would expand throughout the region. The result was massive American assistance for the democratic government of El Salvador to defeat the procommunist rebels. A very different policy was pursued in Nicaragua where the aim was not to maintain but to overthrow the Marxist Sandinista government. Reminiscent of Guatemala in 1954 and Cuba in 1961, the CIA recruited and financed an army of guerrillas known as the Contras. Influenced by the Vietnam syndrome, the American Congress was bitterly divided over the issue of Central America. When Congress refused to vote appropriations to aid the Contras, the Reagan administration resorted to covert methods including the diversion of money gained from secret arms sales to Iran. The illegal action was publicly exposed in 1986 and resulted in the Iran-Contra Affair. Without American aid, the Contras agreed to a cease-fire in 1988. Any suggestion of American weakness in retaining control of its backyard was rebutted, however, by Reagan's decisive action in dispatching American troops to intervene in the Caribbean island of Grenada in October 1983.

Reagan's confrontational style was apparent in his relations with the Soviet Union. In order to fulfill his campaign pledge and negotiate from a position of strength he instituted the largest American arms build-up since the scare over the missile gap in the late 1950s. Considerable publicity was attracted to the new weapons system known as the Strategic Defense Initiative (SDI). The idea of Star Wars was extremely ambitious and expensive, but it was not as ridiculous as critics suggested given the ability of American science and technology to have produced a stream of ever more destructive and amazing weapons starting with the atomic bomb in 1945. SDI was certainly regarded with great seriousness and alarm by the Soviets and was placed high on the agenda in ensuing arms talks between the superpowers.

Although rumors circulated that the Reagan administration aimed to build up sufficient military capacity to win a nuclear war against the Soviets, there is no evidence that Reagan regarded war as an objective of American policy. Indeed, soon after becoming president he agreed to enter into arms control negotiations with the Soviets. The talks, which opened at Geneva in November 1981, concerned the disposition in Europe of intermediate-range nuclear forces (INFs). No sooner had the conference commenced than the American delegates startled the Soviets by proposing the zero option, in which American cancellation of the future deployment of new missiles in Western Europe would be matched by the dismantling of existing Soviet INFs. The rejection of the zero option by the Soviets was so predictable that the original proposal was widely regarded at the time to have been a deliberate ploy by Reagan to sabotage the conference. A similar ulterior motive was attributed to his proposal in May 1982 to resume arms talks under the title of Strategic Arms Reduction Talks. The level of mutual distrust on both sides was reminiscent of the dark days of the late 1940s.

THE RISE OF GORBACHEV

Reagan's confrontational style upset the Soviets, but this was only one of the reasons for their unwillingness to enter into constructive arms talks. Soviet diplomacy suffered from aging leadership in the Kremlin and seemed to be in a state of paralysis from the death of Brezhnev in 1982 to the appointment of Mikhail Gorbachev as general secretary in March 1985. Gorbachev's impact was amazing. The new Soviet leader displayed a confident and energetic public persona that captured the international spotlight for the rest of the decade. Dismissing the Brezhnev years as a time of stagnation, Gorbachev boldly declared his intention to transform the Soviet Union by introducing glasnost and perestroika, which would radically reform the political system and the economy. He also recognized that the success of internal reforms was contingent upon significantly reducing the disproportionate share of annual expenditure that was allocated to the military budget. This implied a revolution in Soviet attitudes toward the Cold War because reductions in military spending required improved relations with the West and especially the United States. Gorbachev was keen to travel and meet personally with Western leaders and to impress upon them that they need not fear the Soviet Union. Before becoming general secretary Gorbachev had visited London in December 1984 and had convinced the British prime minister, Margaret Thatcher, that he was a man with whom the West could enter into constructive discussions and do business. President Reagan was intrigued and readily agreed to a summit with the new Soviet leader.

The meeting took place at Geneva in 1985. Although little substantive business was transacted, the summit was regarded as successful because both men established an evident personal rapport. Adept at public relations, Gorbachev went on the offensive in January 1986 and made a speech calling for the elimination of all nuclear weapons by the end of the century. It was now the turn of the Americans to go on the defensive and to respond negatively to a proposal which was so broad and encompassing that it would necessitate the suspension of all research into SDI. Writing personally to Reagan in September, Gorbachev lamented the lack of progress in the arms talks. The result was a hastily arranged summit at Reykjavik in October 1986. Gorbachev saw the meeting as the moment to propose a major breakthrough in arms reductions. Indeed, the two leaders appeared to consent to the elimination of all nuclear weapons. But fundamental differences over SDI prevented the conclusion of what would have been a stupendous agreement.

In what has been described by admirers as an example of diplomatic genius or by critics as weakness, Gorbachev circumvented American intransigence by simply removing SDI from the agenda. In February 1987 he indicated his willingness to negotiate a treaty specifically covering INFs in Europe. Significantly, the major stumbling block of SDI was not mentioned. The INF Treaty was duly signed by Reagan and Gorbachev at the Washington Summit in December 1987 and represented the first nuclear arms agreement to be negotiated between the superpowers for almost a decade. But Gorbachev's efforts to bring about further disarmament continued apace. Without seeking any similar concessions from the West, the

Soviet leader announced in November 1988 substantial cuts in Soviet military forces mainly from troops currently stationed in Eastern Europe. Earlier he had indicated that a Soviet military withdrawal from Afghanistan would be shortly completed. In Africa, Soviet diplomatic pressure resulted in Cuban troops leaving Ethiopia and Angola. In addition, the large financial subsidy allocated to Cuba was considerably reduced in 1991.

THE COLLAPSE OF COMMUNISM

While Gorbachev successfully slashed the military budget and disengaged from the Third World, the Soviet empire of satellite states in Eastern Europe was falling apart and eventually led to the disintegration of the Soviet Union itself in 1991. Ironically, the introduction of radical reforms in the Soviet Union had stimulated movements for similar changes in Eastern Europe. As a result, the authority of local communist bosses was challenged and overthrown. What was unexpected was that the popular uprisings did not lead to the dispatch of Soviet troops to enforce the Brezhnev Doctrine. Indeed, Gorbachev's inaction was interpreted as personal approval of the movements for reform. While this was consistent with a genuine commitment to introduce reform, he did not appear to consider that anticommunist and anti-Soviet governments might emerge in Eastern Europe.

Poland spearheaded the revolt against communist political control. In June 1989, a coalition government was formed that was headed by the first noncommunist prime minister in Eastern Europe for almost 40 years. No Soviet military retaliation was forthcoming. In effect, the Polish Communist Party acceded to popular pressure and peacefully gave up political power. Similar developments occurred in Hungary and Czechoslovakia, but the most notable events took place in Germany. On November 9, the East German government opened the Berlin Wall for the first time since 1961, and in so doing, provided not only East Germans but also the world with a memorable symbol of the collapse of communist authority. It was all the more astonishing because substantial numbers of Soviet troops were currently stationed in East Germany. They simply remained in their barracks as the Wall was broken into pieces.

Presented with an opportunity to determine their political future, the people of East Germany chose reunification with West Germany. The prospect of a powerful united Germany revived memories of the two world wars and evoked particular anxiety in Poland and the Soviet Union. However, satisfactory assurances were forthcoming from the West German government so that the drive toward German reunification gathered remarkable speed and was completed in October 1990. The United States, Soviet Union, Great Britain, and France also formally relinquished their occupation rights and thereby ended an arrangement that had initially been regarded as temporary in 1945, but had lasted for 45 years.

In the West, the political changes in Eastern Europe were observed with a mixture of surprise and bewilderment. Even more inexplicable was the downfall of Gorbachev in 1991. Since coming to power in 1985 Gorbachev's priority had been to implement reforms that would revitalize the Soviet Union. But the Soviet economy remained blighted with chronic mismanagement and inefficiency. While Gorbachev's international prestige soared, at home he was blamed for the country's economic failings and for his unwillingness to grant local autonomy to ethnic groups within the Soviet Union. Gorbachev eventually resigned as general secretary in August 1991. By that time the process of internal disintegration had proceeded to such an extent that the Soviet Union no longer existed as a sovereign entity. On December 8, 1991, the Soviet Union was formally dissolved when 11 of the 15 republics recreated themselves as the Commonwealth of Independent States.

END OF THE COLD WAR

After four decades of cold war politics during which territorial boundaries in Europe had remained virtually fixed, contemporary observers were stunned by the speed and magnitude of the changes taking place in Eastern Europe and the Soviet Union after Gorbachev's rise to power in 1985. Indeed, Gorbachev's commitment to radical reform had initially given cause for optimism that the Soviet economy would be revitalized. But the impact of his reforms spread beyond the Soviet Union and stimulated the people of Eastern Europe to challenge and overturn communist authority. In contrast to the action taken by his predecessors, Gorbachev did not order Soviet military retaliation. He allowed events to take their course in Eastern Europe while at the same effectively withdrawing the Soviet Union from its role as a world superpower. Consequently, the Cold War came to a sudden end not with the explosion of nuclear bombs and missiles, as many experts had feared and even predicted, but as a ship that has passed by quietly in the night. The United States was given victory by default. But it was not a hollow victory. In the late 1940s the Cold War had begun because the superpowers had clashed over Germany and Eastern Europe. By

1991, Germany was reunified and Eastern Europe was finally freed from Soviet political, economic, and military control. The United States had made the greatest contribution to this outcome and it was understandable that Americans should feel triumphant and claim that under their country's leadership, the West had won the Cold War.

The Dictionary

ACHESON, DEAN G. (1893–1971). American diplomat and secretary of state. Acheson was a New Deal lawyer who served briefly at the Treasury Department in 1933 before returning to Franklin D. Roosevelt's (q.v.) administration in 1941 as assistant secretary of state for economic affairs. In this capacity he negotiated Lend Lease terms with Great Britain (q.v.) and helped formulate the Bretton Woods financial agreements. After resigning in August 1945, he was almost immediately recalled by President Harry Truman (q.v.) as under secretary of state. Acheson subsequently oversaw Anglo-American loan negotiations, and in early 1946 headed the Acheson-Lilienthal Committee on international atomic bomb (q.v.) controls prior to the abortive Baruch Plan (q.v.).

During 1946 Acheson became convinced of the need for containment (q.v.) of the Soviet Union, a policy he promoted at the State Department during the lengthy absences of Secretaries James F. Byrnes and then George C. Marshall at the Council of Foreign Ministers (CFM) (qq.v.). He resigned again in June 1947 to return to private legal practice, but in January 1949 was appointed secretary of state, soon achieving closer U.S.-European military relations through the North Atlantic Treaty and the Mutual Defense Assistance Program (qq.v.). He suffered criticism, however, for his alleged neglect of the Chinese civil war, wherein he had previously advocated realistically cordial relations with Mao Zedong (q.v.). Acheson was, nevertheless, the prime mover of NSC-68 (q.v.), a document that recommended global militarized U.S. containment policies. In January 1950, Acheson became further embroiled in controversy for his remarks that unwittingly excluded South Korea from the latter and therefore might tacitly have precipitated the Korean War (q.v.). He served until the end of the Truman administration in January 1953, returning as a senior adviser to Presidents John F. Kennedy and Lyndon B. Johnson (qq.v.).

ADENAUER, KONRAD (1876–1967). West German statesman and chancellor. A prominent German Catholic conservative politician, his self-imposed retirement under the Nazis ended in March 1945 when he was restored as mayor of Cologne by the American military. Adenauer subsequently orchestrated the emergence of the Christian Democratic Union political party, achieving electoral successes in the Länder (states) set up in the western allied zones. Notwithstanding criticism from the Social Democratic Party of his political bias and pragmatic leniency toward ex-Nazis, Adenauer chaired the parliamentary council that in 1948–1949 drafted the "basic law," the constitution for the Federal Republic of Germany (FRG) (q.v.). After federal elections in August 1949, the Christian Democrats aligned with liberals, regional conservatives, East German refugees, and nationalist parties in the new parliament, which narrowly elected Adenauer as federal chancellor.

Adenauer announced friendship with the West, promising denazification, economic reconstruction, and the pursuit of international legitimacy as goals of a single German national state. The FRG accordingly refused to recognize the German Democratic Republic (GDR) (q.v.), set up in the Soviet zone in October 1949, and the Oder-Neisse Line as Germany's frontier with Poland (qq.v.), actions that earned him Eastern bloc condemnation as an aggressive German revanchist. On the other hand, Adenauer worked to bring West Germany into the European Coal and Steel Community (ECSC) and the North Atlantic Treaty Organization (NATO) (qq.v.). Relations with Eastern Europe remained limited meanwhile by the Hallstein Doctrine (q.v.).

Adenauer consolidated his position electorally in 1952 and 1957, buttressed by West Germany's unprecedented postwar economic recovery and extensive welfare state. His prestige was augmented by improved relations with Israel after 1952, by the return of the Saarland from France after a local referendum in 1955, and by his visit to Moscow in 1955 to meet the new Soviet leader, Nikita Khrushchev (q.v.), which initiated West German-Soviet diplomatic relations. After 1958 he also pursued a close relationship with the French president, Charles de Gaulle (q.v.), seeking a Franco-German platform within the emerging European Economic Community (EEC) (q.v.). Adenauer was, however, largely upstaged by Willy Brandt (q.v.) during the 1961 Berlin Crisis (q.v.) during which he related poorly to President John F. Kennedy (q.v.). Electoral reverses soon afterward necessitated a coalition with the Free Democrats who insisted he step down within two years and resign as chancellor in

1963. Adenauer's elder statesman status nevertheless survived and he remained chairman of the Christian Democratic Union until 1966.

AFGHANISTAN. A state in southwest Asia that was a historical buffer between Russian and Western interests, but fell to a coup in April 1978 by the Marxist pro-Soviet People's Democratic Party of Afghanistan (PDPA). Over-ambitious socialist reforms soon provoked a widespread provincial insurrection, which in June 1978 coalesced into an Islamic national salvation front. Beleaguered by chronic factionalism, mass defections, and inexorable territorial losses to Muslim insurgents, the PDPA signed a friendship treaty with the Soviet Union in December 1978. In the following year two Soviet military missions recommended contingency intervention plans that were implemented after an abortive palace-coup in October against the premier, Hafizullah Amin.

On December 22–28, 1979, Soviet forces secured Afghanistan's urban communications centers and borders. The plan was to consolidate and extend the domain of a new PDPA government under Babrak Karmal, but the extent of Afghan resistance was badly underestimated. Moreover, the West perceived this as Soviet opportunism in the Persian Gulf region and the resulting Carter Doctrine (q.v.), economic sanctions, the withdrawal of the SALT II treaty (q.v.), and 1980 Moscow Olympic games boycott effectively ended détente (q.v.). Up to five million Afghan refugees fled to neighboring Pakistan; their border camps provided guerrilla bases and manpower, soon to be equipped under the Reagan Doctrine (q.v.); the PDPA at best held 35 percent of Afghanistan, despite having the support of 116,000 Soviet troops, military aid, improving tactics, and intelligence against diffuse Islamic Mujihadeen forces.

Sustained losses and ephemeral gains in the Afghanistan war alienated domestic Soviet opinion. In March 1986 the new Soviet leader Mikhail Gorbachev (q.v.) publicly favored disengagement, in conjunction with a new Afghan government under the former secret police chief, Mohammed Najibullah, which conceded cultural and administrative regional autonomy. Symbolic Soviet troop reductions were met, however, by increased Chinese, Saudi Arabian, American, and Pakistani aid to respective guerrilla clients. Najibullah nevertheless survived to conclude a peace agreement in Geneva in April 1988 with Pakistan, the Soviet Union, and the United States. Soviet aid continued after military evacuation on February 15, 1989, and Najibullah's renamed Homeland Party held power until April 1992. Deprived of arms by the U.S.-Soviet agreement in September 1991, it fell to an Islamic coalition under the most successful Mujihadeen leader, Ahmad Shah Massud. Over 13,000 Soviet troops and more than one million Afghans died in more than a decade of war.

AGENCY FOR INTERNATIONAL DEVELOPMENT (AID). Agency of the U.S. government mainly concerned in promoting economic relations between the United States and Third World countries. The Agency for International Development was established in 1961 and represented one of several foreign policy initiatives launched by the John F. Kennedy (q.v.) administration to improve American relations with the Third World. AID's function was to coordinate and oversee the formulation and implementation of economic assistance programs. While AID directed money and technical assistance for social and economic needs such as education, health care, and sanitation, these activities were also an integral part of cold war politics because they sought to promote the American image and interests in the Third World at the expense of the Soviet Union. This was particularly evident in the emphasis that AID placed on programs of public safety that resulted in training policemen not so much to maintain public order in their home countries, but to become proficient in counterinsurgency techniques. The association with counterinsurgency meant that AID was often interpreted in Southeast Asia and Latin America as a substitute or cover for the Central Intelligence Agency (CIA) (q.v.). In 1979 AID became a separate division within a new and larger organization called the International Development Cooperation Agency (IDCA).

ALBANIA. Eastern Adriatic state, seized after the Axis withdrawal of November 1944 by communist partisans under Enver Hoxha (q.v.) whose Labor Party (PLA) imposed a totalitarian regime over a diffuse, heterogeneous rural society, which was soon sealed off politically from outside influences. Albania's uncompromising hostility to the West was signaled in October 1946 when it mined two British destroyers in the Corfu Straits, preferring to sever relief ties with the United Nations (UN) (q.v.) rather than accept the ruling of the International Court of Justice on compensation to Great Britain (q.v.). Customs, currency, and industrial ties with Yugoslavia were cut in 1948 in response to attempts at closer federation by Josip Tito (q.v.). After the latter's split with Moscow, Hoxha purged the Labor Party of numerous pro-Yugoslav elements and established his own personality cult modeled on that of Joseph Stalin (q.v.). In 1961, during the Sino-Soviet Split (q.v.), Albania left the Warsaw Pact (q.v.), thereafter acting informally as the representative of the People's Republic of China (PRC) (q.v.) in the UN General Assembly. Hoxha imitated Communist China's disastrous "great leap forward" economic strategy that stressed rapid industrialization and agricultural collectivization. He also announced an Albanian cultural revolution in 1967, with correspondingly rigid ideological controls imposed over every aspect of Albanian life.

Albania remained isolated and extremely underdeveloped even after Hoxha's retirement in 1982. His policies and personality cult were perpetuated by his successor, Ramiz Alia, who vetoed reforms of the type advocated by the new Soviet leader Mikhail Gorbachev (q.v.). Hoxha's death in April 1986 permitted economic overtures to the Federal Republic of Germany (FRG) (q.v.), although the strict control of media outlets limited the extent of popular protest found elsewhere in Eastern Europe in 1989. Indeed, the PLA retained power until its electoral defeat in March 1992, having meanwhile negotiated Albania's entry into the Conference on Security and Cooperation in Europe (CSCE) (q.v.) and the International Monetary Fund (IMF).

ALLENDE GOSSENS, SALVADOR (1908–1973). Chilean Marxist political leader and president. Allende was an unsuccessful presidential candidate for the Socialist Party on three occasions and eventually won a narrow victory in 1970 representing the left-wing coalition Alliance of Popular Unity. In office, Allende introduced radical and controversial measures designed to transform Chile into a socialist state. President Richard Nixon (q.v.) was alarmed by the election of a Marxist and the prospect of communism being established for the first time in a South American country. Particularly worrying was the friendly relationship existing between Allende and Cuba's Fidel Castro (q.v.). Nixon instructed that a policy of economic pressure be pursued to destabilize Allende's government and remove him from office.

In September 1973 General Augusto Pinochet seized power in a military coup during which Allende committed suicide. The new military government declared that Chile had been saved from communism. American complicity in the coup was suspected but could not be proved. While Allende's policies had undeniable popular support in Chile, they also aroused considerable political controversy and opposition. The president's violent death, however, gained him the reputation of a martyr and victim of American imperialism.

ALLIANCE FOR PROGRESS. A major program of social reform and economic development largely funded by the United States and designed to counter the perceived threat of communist expansion in Latin America.

The alliance was proposed by President John F. Kennedy (q.v.) as a peaceful and democratic alternative to the violence and political extremism associated with the Cuban Revolution (q.v.). The Latin American nations welcomed Kennedy's initiative and in August 1961 at a meeting in Uruguay signed the Charter of Punta del Este that formally established the alliance. The United States agreed to provide loans of $20 billion over a period of 10 years.

The degree of American commitment to the program was notably weakened by the assassination of Kennedy in 1963 and by President Lyndon Johnson's (q.v.) growing preoccupation with the Vietnam War (q.v.). Moreover, the goals of social and economic advancement stated in the 1961 Charter proved too ambitious, and in marked contrast to the success of the earlier Marshall Plan (q.v.) in Western Europe, the results of the alliance were disappointing. Unemployment in Latin America actually increased during the 1960s while annual economic growth remained stuck at 1.5 percent and was outstripped by the population explosion. By the early 1970s the program was widely regarded as having failed and it was brought to an end.

ANDROPOV, YURI V. (1914–1984). Soviet political leader and general secretary. Andropov's power base was the State Security Committee or Komitet Gosudarstvennoy Bezopasnosti (KGB) (q.v.), which he led from 1967 until April 1982. Prior to this Andropov had been appointed Soviet ambassador to Hungary in 1953 and had played a crucial role in determining Soviet policy during the 1956 Hungarian Uprising (q.v.). Andropov's reputation as a capable diplomat led to his appointment in 1957 to the Central Committee department for relations with non-Soviet communist parties. He could not avert the Sino-Soviet split, or the departure of Albania from the Warsaw Pact (qq.v.), but did promote Czechoslovakian and Hungarian economic reform programs.

Andropov aligned with Leonid Brezhnev and Alexei Kosygin (qq.v.) in October 1964 to oust Soviet leader Nikita Khrushchev (q.v.). He became chairman of a demoralized KGB in April 1967, joining the Politburo and the Defense Council in May. His main achievement was quelling domestic dissidence without returning to indiscriminate terror through more refined methods of surveillance and coercion, including psychiatric incarceration for intractable dissenters. The KGB also spearheaded anticorruption operations, notably in the Soviet republics, improved its intelligence operations, and enhanced its elite status by patronizing abler young officials. In the 1970s Andropov allied politically with successive

Defense Ministers Andrei Grechko and Dmitri Ustinov, Foreign Minister Andrei Gromyko, and had Mikhail Gorbachev (qq.v.) appointed Politburo agriculture chief in 1980. Their support secured his rise to power, as did KGB anticorruption investigations that neutralized supporters of his rival Konstantin Chernenko (q.v.) as Brezhnev's health declined.

As general secretary, Andropov initiated domestic economic and administrative reforms while seeking renewed détente (q.v.). He sought a summit with President Ronald Reagan (q.v.) and after a Warsaw Pact (q.v.) conference in January 1983 presented extensive arms limitation proposals, including a nonaggression agreement with the North Atlantic Treaty Organization (NATO) (q.v.). He was, however, rebuffed by Reagan. Revived Afghanistan (q.v.) peace talks also proved futile, although border and trade agreements were reached with the People's Republic of China (PRC) (q.v.). In response to the American Strategic Defense Initiative (SDI) and intermediate-range nuclear force (INF) (qq.v.) deployments in Europe, Andropov maintained the costly Soviet military buildup vis-à-vis the West accompanied by efficiency drives in defense industries and agriculture, with the KGB attacking inertia and abuses. In August 1983 Andropov suffered acute kidney failure and made no further public appearances before his death on February 9, 1984.

ANGOLA. A Portuguese colony in southwest Africa that attracted the attention of the superpowers during its struggle for independence. Western interests favored the Frente Nacional de Libertação de Angola (National Front for the Liberation of Angola or FNLA) and União Nacional para a Independencia Total de Angola (National Union for the Total Independence of Angola or UNITA), while Soviet support was directed to Augostinho Neto's (q.v.) Movimento Popular de Libertação de Angola (Popular Movement for the Liberation of Angola or MPLA).

In 1974 Portugal agreed to peace talks that initially excluded the MPLA. The Organization of African Unity (OAU) insisted on all-party negotiations in January 1975, and independence was achieved on November 11. However, FNLA and UNITA forces, with U.S.-sanctioned support from Zaire and South Africa, had already begun to battle the MPLA for territorial supremacy and the capital, Luanda. The MPLA prevailed with the help of airlifted Cuban troops and Soviet-supplied armor and artillery. American intervention was prevented by the Clark Amendment (q.v.). Neto declared nonalignment but the United States refused to recognize his government, which subsequently turned for aid to the Eastern bloc and officially embraced Marxism-Leninism. Overtures from

President Jimmy Carter (q.v.) after 1979 withered under his successor Ronald Reagan (q.v.) who supported renewed UNITA/South African incursions, despite protests from American oil companies such as Gulf and Chevron that operated cordially in Angola under Neto's MPLA successor, Eduardo Dos Santos (q.v.). Cuban forces remained heavily engaged until in early 1988 Soviet leader Mikhail Gorbachev (q.v.) reduced and then terminated essential subsidies, precipitating peace negotiations. These were boycotted by UNITA, despite Cuba's disengagement from Angola in 1989 as a quid pro quo for Namibia's independence from South Africa. Suffering protracted losses, the MPLA accepted revised terms negotiated by African heads of state that admitted UNITA to the Angolan government after a cease-fire in November 1990. The United Nations (UN) (q.v.) oversaw elections in 1992 that produced an emphatic victory for the MPLA, after which UNITA renewed its military opposition, thereby prolonging the Angolan civil war.

ANTI-BALLISTIC MISSILE (ABM). A defensive missile system intended to destroy incoming attacks by enemy intercontinental ballistic missiles (ICBMs) (q.v.). The U.S. Army Air Force began to research ABM feasibility in July 1945, but development did not actually begin until 1957. Progress was later impeded by the skepticism of Defense Secretary Robert McNamara (q.v.), who preferred deterrence (q.v.) for nuclear defense. In addition, practical testing was limited by the 1963 Partial Nuclear Test Ban Treaty (q.v.), while the U.S. Army's interest was diverted by the Vietnam War (q.v.).

The Soviet Union meanwhile had integrated Griffon and Galosh ABMs into its strategic defenses, although their technical limitations led Soviet planners also to favor the security conferred by sophisticated and numerous offensive nuclear weapons. Arguments for ABMs were upheld, however, by the People's Republic of China (PRC) (q.v.), who developed a lesser anti-U.S. strategic capability after 1964. In 1967 President Lyndon Johnson (q.v.) approved a limited city-defense ABM program known as "Sentinel," which his successor, Richard Nixon (q.v.), expanded to cover selected ICBM bases and redesignated "Safeguard." High costs and technical flaws persisted, however, and the system's principal significance was as a bargaining chip in the U.S.-Soviet Strategic Arms Limitation Talks (SALT) (q.v.), which was a by-product yielded by the 1972 Anti-Ballistic Missiles Treaty (q.v.). Limited American facilities permitted by the treaty were closed after the U.S. Congress withdrew funding in October 1975, although a skeleton research program survived to inspire President Ronald Reagan's Strategic Defense Initiative (SDI) (qq.v.) in 1983.

ANTI-BALLISTIC MISSILES TREATY, 1972. A treaty signed by the United States and the Soviet Union in Moscow on May 26, 1972, that limited both sides to 100 anti-ballistic missile (ABM) (q.v.) launchers, deployed within 140 kilometers of one intercontinental ballistic missile (ICBM) (q.v.) base and one strategic nuclear command center. Limits were also placed on guidance, tracking systems, and ABM improvements. The purpose of these limitations was to preserve the offensive "balance of terror" on both sides that was considered essential to deterrence (q.v.). The treaty also affirmed détente (q.v.).

ABM negotiations began in 1969 within the framework of the Strategic Arms Limitation Talks (SALT) (q.v.), but were rendered largely fruitless by American insistence until 1971 on linking ABM with limitations on the number of ICBMs. The Soviet Union, for its part, disingenuously sought ABMs limited to nuclear command centers, knowing the U.S. Congress was likely to cease funding such systems around Washington, D.C. Deadlock was broken by informal discussions between Henry Kissinger and Anatoly Dobrynin (qq.v.). The 1972 treaty was unlimited in duration, with quinquennial review points. It was soon ratified by the U.S. Senate and Supreme Soviet, and in August 1974 was amended to reduce permitted ABM deployments to one base each. In 1985, however, President Ronald Reagan (q.v.) called for a broad interpretation on ABM testing limitations, and in 1986 stated that the treaty should be observed for only a decade longer in order to accommodate his Strategic Defense Initiative (SDI) (q.v.).

ANZUS. Collective security pact between Australia, New Zealand, and the United States. To alleviate concern in Australia and New Zealand over American proposals to restore Japanese independence, the United States entered into a mutual defense treaty with those countries in September 1951. The conclusion of the ANZUS Pact also occurred while the Korean War (q.v.) was taking place and reflected the desire of the Truman (q.v.) administration to build up an anticommunist coalition in the Far East. The pact marked a decline in the influence of Great Britain (q.v.) and a recognition by Australia and New Zealand that the United States was the preeminent military power in the Pacific region. The ties between Australia, New Zealand, and the United States were reaffirmed in 1954 when all three countries became founding members of the South-East Asia Treaty Organization (SEATO) (q.v.).

ARAB-ISRAELI WAR, 1967 (SIX-DAY WAR). A war fought between Israel and Egypt (q.v.), Syria, and Jordan. The war originated with Egypt's President Gamal Abdel Nasser's (q.v.) military buildup along Israel's southern border, his closure of the Straits of Tiran to Israel's shipping, and the announcement on May 30 of a joint Egyptian-Syrian-Jordanian military command, encircling Israel itself. On June 5, Israel responded with decisive military action and launched a preemptive strike that destroyed the Egyptian air force. Israeli airborne and armored offensives then overran the Egyptian army in the Sinai Peninsula, and proceeded to crush Jordanian forces, seize the West Bank of the River Jordan, including Jerusalem's Old City, and finally in the north, take the Golan Heights from Syria.

Two days later, after consulting President Lyndon Johnson on the Hot-Line (qq.v.), the Soviet prime minister, Alexei Kosygin (q.v.), submitted a cease-fire resolution to the Security Council of the United Nations (UN) (q.v.) hoping to avert the utter humiliation of Moscow's Egyptian and Syrian clients. Israel rejected this and the Soviet Union severed diplomatic relations, threatening sanctions. More Hot-Line (q.v.) discussions preceded Johnson pressing Israel into agreeing to a cease-fire on June 10. Superpower naval forces stood by during the conflict, but both hoped to avoid intervention, as affirmed in the subsequent Glassboro "mini-summit" (q.v.). Nonetheless, Soviet weapons and up to 20,000 advisers soon replenished Egyptian and Syrian losses. In October 1967, the United States shipped modern air defense missiles and fighter-bombers to Israel, facilitating an aerial War of Attrition against the Arab countries in 1968.

Meanwhile, Israel rejected UN Security Council Resolution 242 in November 1967, which called for a restoration of the prewar borders as a prelude to creating a Palestinian state, in return for Israel's implicit recognition by the Arab powers. The Palestine Question (q.v.) remained therefore locked in an intractable confrontation, aggravated by the postwar doubling of the Palestinian refugee population, with both superpowers drawn incrementally into arming their respective clients at levels higher than before the Six-Day War.

ARAB-ISRAELI WAR, 1973 (OCTOBER OR YOM KIPPUR WAR). On October 6, 1973, Egypt (q.v.) launched a surprise attack upon Israeli positions along the Suez Canal and in the Sinai Peninsula held since the 1967 Arab-Israeli War (Six-Day War) (q.v.). Syria also attacked the Golan Heights while Israel's forces were largely demobilized for the Yom Kippur religious holiday. Egypt's president, Anwar el-Sadat, aimed for a decisive military success to reverse the June 1967 status quo and assist his plans for diplomatic rapprochement with the United States. Ironically, Sadat's expulsion of Soviet advisers in 1972 was temporarily reversed in February 1973 as he prepared for war against Israel. Moreover, the Soviets colluded in an early United Nations (UN) (q.v.) cease-fire resolution on October 9 to conserve the gains made by the Arab powers. Sadat delayed using this expedient, however, thinking his initial victories presaged Israeli military collapse. In the meantime, the United States airlifted munitions, tanks, and aircraft into Israel to stem its ally's losses. These, combined with information provided by American intelligence, facilitated an overwhelming Israeli counteroffensive against Syria on October 13. The next day Israel pierced Egypt's static positions in the Sinai and drove westward across the Suez Canal to encircle its Third Army. Sadat finally sought terms on October 16.

Anticipating an Egyptian debacle, Israel declined Sadat's offer. In retaliation on October 17 the Arab petroleum states embargoed sales to Israel's western supporters. The escalating crisis prompted Secretary of State Henry Kissinger (q.v.) to visit Moscow where he achieved a mandate for a U.S.-Soviet sponsored cease-fire based on UN Security Council Resolution 338, which Israel rejected on October 22. Sadat then requested a joint superpower peacekeeping force, eliciting unilateral Soviet preparations, which the United States answered with a global nuclear alert and mobilization of its Mediterranean 6th Fleet. Further escalation was averted by Kissinger's threat to reduce arms supplies to Israel and to insist that nonlethal supplies reach beleaguered Egyptian forces. On October 27 a cease-fire was arranged. Kissinger then began "shuttle diplomacy" between the combatant capitals and achieved disengagement terms by May 1974. Sadat received territory in the Sinai and de facto recognition as a party worthy of American interest. Soviet influence was thereafter marginalized to Syria while Egypt formally canceled its friendship treaty in 1976. In return for American economic aid, however, Sadat negotiated a politically costly peace with Israel after 1977. Elsewhere, the Organization of Petroleum Exporting Countries (OPEC), having witnessed the diplomatic potency of the "oil weapon," implemented fourfold price increases by mid-1974, aggravating an international economic recession for the rest of the decade.

ARBENZ GUZMAN, JACOBO (1913–1971). Guatemalan political leader and president. Arbenz was a former army officer who served as defense minister from 1945 to 1950 and was elected president in 1950.

As president, he sought to continue the program of agrarian reform begun by the 1944 Guatemalan Revolution. His expropriation of land owned by the Boston-based United Fruit Company and his personal association with prominent Guatemalan communists provoked the hostility of the Eisenhower (q.v.) administration. A military coup was secretly organized by the Central Intelligence Agency (CIA) (q.v.) that overthrew Arbenz in 1954. He left the country and lived in exile until his death in 1971. Arbenz is an example of a left-wing Latin American leader whose ideas were considered too radical by the U.S. government. American officials considered him a procommunist and decided to remove him from power.

ARMS CONTROL AND DISARMAMENT AGENCY (ACDA). An agency of the U.S. government that was formed in September 1961 as a result of political pressure on then presidential candidate John F. Kennedy (q.v.) by Hubert Humphrey, chairman of the Senate Foreign Relations Disarmament Subcommittee, and after campaign advice from Paul Nitze (q.v.). ACDA helped prepare the 1963 Partial Nuclear Test Ban Treaty (q.v.), but remained largely dormant due to entrenched opposition in American defense circles. In 1969, however, President Richard Nixon (q.v.) used it as his channel for participation in the Strategic Arms Limitation Talks (SALT) (q.v.), primarily to allow National Security Adviser Henry Kissinger (q.v.) to limit the influence of the Departments of State and of Defense. In 1975 ACDA was charged by Congress with monitoring American overseas arms transfers in addition to the implementation of the SALT I treaty (q.v.). Under President Jimmy Carter (q.v.), the agency's liberal character was reinforced with the appointment of détente (q.v.) advocate Paul Warnke as director; it therefore suffered conservative reproach for having contributed to allegedly excessive pro-Soviet concessions in the SALT II treaty (q.v.).

During the Reagan (q.v.) administration ACDA was integrated into mainstream administration efforts to reassert American strategic supremacy. Under its new director, Eugene Rostow (q.v.), its principal mission was to impede arms control agreements in ways contrived to imply Soviet treachery as was the case in the Geneva talks on intermediate-range nuclear forces (INFs) (q.v.), which collapsed in 1983. After 1984 ACDA worked with the Departments of State and Defense to reinterpret the 1972 Anti-Ballistic Missiles (ABM) Treaty (q.v.) sufficiently to justify the Strategic Defense Initiative (SDI) (q.v.). Correspondingly, the agency was largely bypassed in renewed arms control initiatives by

Soviet leader Mikhail Gorbachev (q.v.), although it retained a monitoring role over arms proliferation among Third World powers.

ATOMIC BOMB. Nuclear weapon of mass destruction, using the uranium 235 isotope, which was first tested by the United States at Alamogordo, New Mexico, on July 15, 1945. The atomic bomb was developed and then dropped by B-29 bombers on the Japanese cities of Hiroshima and Nagasaki in early August 1945, immediately killing 80,000 people. A similar number died later from injuries and radiation sickness. Japan's subsequent surrender ended World War II, although controversy remains on whether President Harry Truman (q.v.) used the weapon to intimidate the Soviet leader Joseph Stalin (q.v.). Truman certainly delayed the July 1945 Potsdam Conference (q.v.) until after the Alamogordo tests, but the motivation for the atomic bombing of Japan is far from clear. Stalin publicly played down the weapon's significance, but knew of its potential through spies at Alamogordo. He hurriedly instituted a priority Soviet program under Lavrenti Beria (q.v.). Meanwhile, the American atomic bomb stockpile remained too small to have practical impact. Military planners lacked a coherent nuclear doctrine, much less adequate means of delivery for a decisive strike against the Soviet Union. The American secret nuclear war plan, code-named "Dropshot," did not come into existence until February 1949.

The failure of the 1946 Baruch Plan (q.v.) for international atomic controls nevertheless showed U.S.-Soviet determination to pursue rival military capabilities. In January 1947 Great Britain (q.v.) began its own atomic bomb project. At the same time U.S. nuclear operational planning gathered momentum. The deployment of two B-29 bomber groups to Britain during the 1948–1949 Berlin Crisis (q.v.) invoked the implicit threat of the atomic bomb as a diplomatic counter to Soviet conventional military supremacy in Central Europe. In August 1949 the North Atlantic Treaty (q.v.) powers incorporated American atomic weapons into joint military plans. In that month, however, the Soviet Union successfully tested its first atomic device, radically altering American calculations and prompting Truman to preserve his country's destructive supremacy in January 1950 by authorizing development of the much more powerful hydrogen bomb (q.v.). Possession of the atomic bomb nevertheless remained a sine qua non of world power status. Britain's first weapon was successfully tested in 1952, those of France and the People's Republic of China (PRC) (qq.v.) in 1960 and 1964, respectively.

ATTLEE, CLEMENT (1883–1967). British political leader and prime minister. As the leader of the Labour Party Attlee entered the coalition British war cabinet in 1940. After his party's victory in the 1945 general election, Attlee became prime minister and replaced Winston Churchill (q.v.) as Great Britain's (q.v.) representative at the Potsdam Conference (q.v.). Attlee acted effectively as chairman of a talented and dynamic Labour cabinet whose priority was social and economic reform. In foreign policy he was a liberal internationalist who initially tried to mitigate Anglo-American rivalry with the Soviet Union. In November 1945, while in Washington, D.C., for financial negotiations, he tried in vain to convince President Harry Truman (q.v.) of the benefits of nuclear cooperation with Joseph Stalin (q.v.). In January 1947 his comments on the unwinnability of nuclear war, signaling probable military retrenchment and pro-Soviet conciliation, provoked the threat of mass resignation from the British chiefs of staff. Attlee retracted, thereafter tending to leave relevant policymaking to his ardently anti-Soviet foreign secretary, Ernest Bevin (q.v.). Although during a deep financial crisis he authorized Britain's withdrawal from the Greek Civil War (q.v.), he nevertheless reluctantly authorized the secret development of the British atomic bomb (q.v.).

Attlee subsequently expressed disillusionment with Soviet assimilation policies in Eastern Europe but concerned himself mainly with matters other than the Cold War, most notably Britain's withdrawal from India (q.v.) in August 1947. After Bevin's resignation in March 1951, Attlee's personal interest revived in foreign affairs. Although agreeing to maintain significant British forces in the Korean War (q.v.), Attlee intervened personally with Truman against the extremism of General Douglas MacArthur (q.v.) and opposed American efforts in the United Nations (UN) (q.v.) to brand the People's Republic of China (PRC) (q.v.) an aggressor in the conflict. Moreover, in the 1951 confrontation with Iran (q.v.) over the nationalization of British Petroleum's assets, Attlee ruled out military intervention. Despite major domestic achievements, chiefly in establishing the Welfare State, he narrowly lost the 1951 general election and retired from active politics in 1955.

AUSTRIAN STATE TREATY, 1955. A treaty signed by Great Britain, France (qq.v.), the United States, Soviet Union, and Austria, in Vienna on May 15, 1955. Austria, although part of Hitler's Third Reich after 1938, was designated a German-occupied territory by the Allied powers in November 1943, but was subjected nevertheless to Soviet reparations claims after World War II. Disputes over the latter within the occupying four-power commission in Vienna impeded transition to full Austrian sovereignty, particularly when the conservative Austrian government elected in August 1946 attempted to nationalize industrial assets in the Soviet occupation zone. Talks stagnated and Austria remained under occupation. In February 1955 Soviet Foreign Minister Vyacheslav Molotov (q.v.) proposed that in the light of the recent Paris Agreements, admitting the Federal Republic of Germany (FRG) (q.v.) into the North Atlantic Treaty Organization (NATO) (q.v.), Austrian statehood needed to be guaranteed on the basis of independent neutrality. This was settled in May after conferences in Berlin, Moscow, and Vienna, with Austria officially absolved as a World War II aggressor.

AZERBAIJAN CRISIS, 1946. This northernmost province of Iran (q.v.) was under Soviet occupation during World War II. Under treaty obligations of 1942 with Great Britain (q.v.) and Iran it was to be evacuated six months after the end of the war, a commitment reaffirmed in 1943 at the Teheran Conference (q.v.). However, fleeting American oil interest there in 1944 prompted the Soviet Union not only to demand oil rights of its own, but in response to Iranian parliamentary opposition, to foster Azeri national separatism in a popular front Azerbaijan Democrat Party incorporating northern Iranian communists. At the Potsdam Conference, Joseph Stalin (qq.v.) confirmed the date for Allied withdrawal as March 3, 1946, six months after Japan's rather than Germany's surrender. By December 1945 Soviet-protected separatist provincial governments were established in Azerbaijan and neighboring Iranian Kurdistan. In the process the Red Army disarmed Iranian government forces and sealed off provincial communications.

Great Britain, whose forces were occupying southern Iran, initially favored compromise, to safeguard its extensive oil and other interests, even if this meant that Iran was to be effectively partitioned. The Iranian government, under premier Qavam al-Saltaneh, therefore presented its case to Secretary of State James F. Byrnes (q.v.), who saw it as a vital test of Allied integrity and United Nations (UN) (q.v.) principles. During consultations in Moscow, Stalin was evasive. Iran, therefore, formally complained to the UN Security Council in London in January 1946, where, ironically, British Foreign Secretary Ernest Bevin (q.v.) was the most vigorous antagonist of the Soviet delegate, Andrei Vyshinsky (q.v.). The case was also decisive in convincing President Harry Truman (q.v.) to confront perceived Soviet expansionism. The Soviets nevertheless agreed to negotiate with Qavam, first in Moscow and then in Teheran. Soviet forces remained in Azerbaijan after March 3, 1946, but assurances of American support helped Qavam secure their withdrawal in late April, at the price of northern autonomy and an oil concession to the Soviets.

The affair focused American political attention on the geo-strategic importance of the Near East and the need for anti-Soviet containment (q.v.). Subsequent American military aid to Iran empowered the forcible resumption of central authority over the Azeris in December 1946. The principal separatist leaders were summarily executed, presenting the Soviets with a fait accompli. Moreover, in 1947 Iran's parliament, elected during a communist boycott, refused to ratify the draft Soviet oil concession, completing Moscow's political defeat.

-B-

BAGHDAD PACT. Middle East security organization, formed in 1955 by Great Britain (q.v.), Iraq, Turkey (q.v.), Pakistan, and Iran (q.v.) and known after 1959 as the Central Treaty Organization (CENTO)(q.v.). Since 1947 the United States and Britain had discussed provisions in the region for protecting oil, long-range communications, and wartime air operations against aggression by the Soviet Union. These foundered, however, on Egypt's (q.v.) hostility to British occupation of the Suez Canal zone. In 1953 Secretary of State John Foster Dulles (q.v.) switched American attention to the northern tier states adjacent to the Soviet Union, focusing on Turkey, already a part of the North Atlantic Treaty Organization (NATO) (q.v.) and receiving significant American military aid. This encouraged Iraq, Iran, and Pakistan into cooperation talks with Turkey in 1954, although Britain insisted on coordinating defense arrangements involving Iraq, its most important remaining Arab ally. A Turco-Iraqi accord was signed in Baghdad in February 1955, to which Britain subscribed in April, followed by Pakistan and Iran. In November a council of deputies, secretariat, and military committee were added. The United States attended as an observer whose subsequent role was mainly to finance British arms sales to the other members.

Declining British prestige after the 1956 Suez Crisis (q.v.) undermined the Baghdad Pact's prospects. After 1957 it was largely superseded by the Eisenhower Doctrine (q.v.). Iraq's 1958 revolution necessitated the Pact moving its headquarters from Baghdad to Ankara in October. Iraq withdrew from the Pact in March 1959. Renamed CENTO in August 1959, the Pact existed mainly as a paper entity, particularly after

Britain's withdrawal from east of Suez in 1968, although the end was delayed until February 1979 when the new Islamic Republic of Iran proclaimed nonalignment, soon to be followed by Pakistan.

BANDUNG CONFERENCE, 1955. A meeting of 29 African and Asian states in Bandung, Indonesia (q.v.), from April 18 to April 24, 1955, aimed at establishing cooperation between decolonizing countries independently of either the Western or Eastern blocs. The initiative for the conference came from Prime Minister Jawaharlal Nehru of India (qq.v.) in a joint communiqué with Indonesia, Pakistan, Ceylon, and Burma in April 1954. Attendance criteria were based on loosely defined neutrality. North Korea and South Korea were excluded, as was Israel, in order to accommodate the Arab states. From Sub-Saharan Africa only the Gold Coast, Ethiopia (q.v.), and Liberia attended, although Egypt's President Gamal Abdel Nasser (qq.v.) claimed both African and Middle Eastern credentials. The attendance of the People's Republic of China (PRC) (q.v.) as a Third World rather than Cold War power was vital for Nehru and was achieved by excluding Taiwan (q.v.). Nevertheless, Japan, the Asian South-East Asia Treaty Organization (SEATO) (q.v.) states, and the Baghdad Pact (q.v.) powers attended, as did North Vietnam (q.v.). Anglo-French-American encouragement for resolutions condemning alleged Soviet imperialism was largely unsuccessful. Nehru prevailed, however, in calling for African and Asian mediation as a "moral force" between the superpowers to which PRC Foreign Minister Zhou Enlai (q.v.) acceded, abandoning his initially dogmatic anti-Western rhetoric. The conference adjourned condemning "all forms of colonialism," but also calling for more generous economic aid.

The Bandung Conference signaled the emergence of a Third World agenda discrete from the Cold War and stimulated the nonaligned movement (q.v.). Sino-Indian accord soon proved ephemeral, although the new Soviet leadership under Nikita Khrushchev (q.v.) noted and effectively exploited the potential of nonideological aid and development policies in areas previously remote from Moscow's influence. India, Indonesia, and Egypt became Soviet partners under such expedients. The perceived challenge to containment (q.v.) geopolitics stimulated counterinitiatives from the United States such as the Agency for International Development (AID) (q.v.).

BARRE, MOHAMMED SIAD (1919–1995). Somalian political leader and president. Having served in the British Somaliland colonial police, Siad Barre rose to command the army of independent Somalia (q.v.) in

1966. He mounted a successful military coup in October 1969, after which he gravitated politically to the Soviet Union with whom he signed a treaty of friendship in 1974, forming a superficially Marxist-Leninist Somali Revolutionary Socialist Party in 1976. Siad Barre became disillusioned, however, by the continuing Soviet overtures to his neighbor Ethiopia (q.v.). He attempted to force matters in July 1977 by invading the Ogaden province, thereby augmenting crisis conditions in the Horn of Africa (q.v.). Moscow sided with Ethiopia, however, and on November 13, 1977, Siad Barre terminated relations, closing Somalian ports and airfields to Soviet use, and also expelling numerous East German and Cuban advisers. Subsequent approaches to the United States for aid were only partially successful and inadequate for full-scale war against Ethiopia. Increased American assistance was granted under the Reagan Doctrine (q.v.) and this permitted Siad Barre to continue as president of Somalia. However, aid lapsed after Soviet disengagement from Ethiopia in 1987. Siad Barre fell to a military coup in 1991 and went into exile in Kenya.

BARUCH PLAN. A proposal made by the United States in 1946 for United Nations (UN) (q.v.) control of nuclear information and research. To forestall Soviet demands after October 1945 for a United Nations trusteeship in the Belgian Congo, the world's principal uranium source, Secretary of State James F. Byrnes (q.v.) persuaded Joseph Stalin (q.v.) to endorse the formation of a United Nations Atomic Energy Commission (UNAEC) to control nuclear materials, in which both powers were to have executive equality. In January 1946 a UNAEC charter was drafted by Under Secretary of State Dean Acheson (q.v.) and the American nuclear scientist, David Lilienthal. This envisaged UN nuclear inspections worldwide, a ban on military research, and placed existing atomic bombs (q.v.) under UNAEC control.

The refinement of this charter for UN approval was entrusted in March 1946 to Bernard Baruch, a 74-year-old financier and long-standing policy adviser to successive American presidents. Baruch was influenced by mounting military and congressional skepticism on the trustworthiness of Soviet participation. Consequently, he altered the plan to include a provision to secure speedy punishment of powers violating UNAEC regulations. Moreover, Baruch's staff recommended preliminary inspection of Soviet nuclear research programs before American atomic bombs were put under UNAEC control. Andrei Gromyko (q.v.), the Soviet representative at the UN, proposed the destruction of all American atomic bombs and publication of nuclear research data prior to UNAEC operations. A UN working party convened to reconcile the divergent positions, but in December 1946 the Security Council voted on the Baruch Plan, 10–0 in favor, the Soviet Union and Poland (q.v.) abstained. The UNAEC was thereafter stalled by practical disagreements on inspection and nuclear custodial procedures. A Soviet motion proposing a new international body to uphold a ban on all nuclear weapons was predictably defeated in January 1948. By this time American nuclear war plans with appropriate military capabilities were being developed, while in June 1948 the Soviets began the industrial production of weapons-grade atomic materials, giving top priority to weapons testing.

BATISTA, FULGENCIO (1901–1973). Cuban political leader and president. Batista joined the Cuban army in 1924 and rose to national prominence in the 1933 revolution when he was promoted from sergeant to colonel and shortly afterward became chief of staff of the army. With the support of the military Batista ruled as virtual dictator of Cuba (q.v.), a position that he underscored in 1952 by declaring himself president and suspending the Cuban constitution.

Batista's corrupt and authoritarian rule aroused growing discontent within Cuba, but his staunch anticommunism gained him the support of the U.S. government. The backing of the United States became less certain during the late 1950s and was confirmed by the decision of the Eisenhower (q.v.) administration to suspend shipments of American arms in 1958. An armed rebellion, led by Fidel Castro (q.v.), forced Batista to abdicate power and flee from Cuba on January 1, 1959. He spent the rest of his life in exile.

BAY OF PIGS. A covert operation organized by the Central Intelligence Agency (CIA) (q.v.) to overthrow Fidel Castro (q.v.). In 1960 President Dwight Eisenhower (q.v.) instructed the CIA to prepare a secret military operation to remove Castro from power as it had successfully done against President Jacobo Arbenz (q.v.) of Guatemala (q.v.) in 1954. The CIA set up a base in Guatemala where it recruited and trained a small army of Cuban exiles and opponents of Castro. Code-named Operation Zapata, the plan was to make an amphibious landing at a remote area in the south of Cuba (q.v.), gain a beachhead, and spark off a national uprising against Castro. Although President John F. Kennedy (q.v.) approved the plan in January 1961, he insisted that American military personnel were not to be officially involved in the operation.

The landing took place at the Bay of Pigs on April 17, 1961. The Cuban brigade fought bravely on the beaches, but was outnumbered and quickly overwhelmed by Castro's forces. In the end 114 brigaders died and more than 1,000 were captured. Castro was triumphant and claimed victory over American imperialism. Kennedy was humiliated. The perception that the American president was weak and inexperienced later encouraged Nikita Khrushchev (q.v.) to attempt to place nuclear missiles in Cuba in 1962. The Bay of Pigs also dealt a major blow to the morale and prestige of the CIA. In subsequent interventions in the Caribbean region American presidents came to prefer the use of full-scale military force rather than covert operations. This was exemplified in the Dominican Republic Intervention in 1965 and Grenada Invasion (qq.v.) in 1983. Both occasions involved the direct use of substantial numbers of American troops with tactical air and naval support.

BENEŠ, EDUARD (1884–1948). Czechoslovak politician and president. Beneš was president of the Czechoslovak government-in-exile in London during World War II. Continuing British opaqueness on his country's postwar status led him to pursue a close understanding with the Soviet Union, and in December 1943 he flew to Moscow to sign a treaty of alliance with Joseph Stalin (q.v.). Problems remained, however, over the status of Slovakia, on the governmental participation of Czechoslovak communists under Klement Gottwald (q.v.), and on Soviet wishes to annex the province of Ruthenia. The latter was lost, but in Moscow in March 1945 Beneš negotiated a postwar coalition government, which took office under his presidency on April 4, in Kosice, Slovakia, before finally moving to Prague, which was liberated by Soviet forces on May 9.

Beneš struggled to maintain a political balance between the communists and the other parties, but the former's electoral success in May 1946 allowed it to press forward with state-controlled economic reconstruction and increasing alignment with Soviet interests, particularly in the uranium mining industry. Beneš ultimately failed to effect cooperation against the communists by his own National Socialist Party, the Socialist Party, Catholic parties, and the Slovak Democratic Party. At communist insistence Czechoslovakia was excluded from the European Recovery Program (ERP or Marshall Plan) (q.v.) in 1947 and moved further into the Soviet orbit. Beneš was also denied political support by the army under Ludvik Svoboda (q.v.) and could not prevent the final communist seizure of power in Czechoslovakia in February 1948. His spirit broken, Beneš resigned as president on June 7, 1948, and died after a stroke on September 3, 1948.

BERIA, LAVRENTI (1899–1953). Soviet political leader and chief of the secret police. A Georgian, like his patron Joseph Stalin (q.v.), Beria was involved in the brutal pacification and purging of Soviet Transcaucasia. He was promoted in August 1938 to head the NKVD, the Stalinist secret police organization that was responsible for labor camps, internal security troops, border guards, state security, and counterintelligence. As such Beria was the punitive arm of Stalin's dictatorship, responsible for domestic political purges and exterminating resistance in territories gained in the 1939 Nazi-Soviet Pact, such as the Baltic States and Eastern Poland. During World War II he directed the eastward relocation of Soviet industry and the deportation of ethnic minorities suspected of disloyalty to the Soviet Union. Incidentally, he oversaw the bugging of President Franklin D. Roosevelt's (q.v.) apartments during the Teheran and Yalta Conferences (qq.v.). By 1945 he was acknowledged as the third most powerful Soviet official behind Stalin and Vyacheslav Molotov (q.v.), achieving full Politburo status and the rank of marshal. His security and industrial domain was entrusted that year with the task of developing the Soviet atomic bomb (q.v.).

Beria was the principal advocate of assertive policies in Azerbaijan and Turkey (qq.v.) in 1946, and along with his political ally Georgi Malenkov (q.v.), for severe reparations from Germany, all of which antagonized Great Britain (q.v.) and the United States, helping deepen the Cold War. Having been considered Stalin's likely successor, Beria was suspected of acquiring too much personal power and fell from favor in 1952. His decline was arrested in March 1953 by Stalin's death, after which he hurriedly attempted to widen his power-base by offering domestic and foreign political relaxations, including a cease-fire in the Korean War (q.v.) and overtures to the estranged Yugoslav leader Josip Tito (q.v.). However, the East Berlin Workers' Rising of June 1953 (q.v.) discredited Beria's reforms and provided grounds for his arrest for treason and espionage. Beria was tried and executed on December 23, 1953.

BERLIN BLOCKADE, 1948–1949. Under Allied Four-power administration since July 1945, the former German national capital of Berlin was geographically isolated within the Soviet occupation zone. In 1947 the failure of the Council of Foreign Ministers (CFM) (q.v.) to agree on a German peace treaty resulted in Soviet pressure on the Western-controlled sectors of the city, beginning in January 1948 with disruptions to the running of military trains. Meanwhile, the European Recovery Program (ERP or Marshall Plan) (q.v.) proceeded on the assumption that the British, French, and American occupation zones of Germany, plus their sectors in Berlin, would participate. This was agreed in June and administered by a West German economic council that was effectively a provisional government set up without Soviet consent. A reformed West German currency, freely available in Berlin, was also issued, which the Soviet authorities feared would so marginalize their weak, unreformed zonal currency that the Soviet Union's economic position in Germany might totally collapse. The Western powers agreed to merge Berlin into the eastern currency zone in return for executive powers in Soviet currency administration. The Soviets demanded a reciprocal role in the Ruhr, West Germany's industrial heartland, which the Anglo-Americans refused. Negotiations broke down on June 22, 1948. Two days later Soviet forces closed down Western road and rail links with Berlin.

The Western powers discerned a crucial challenge over Germany's future and on June 27, 1948, began comprehensive aerial supply operations into the city, backed by a counterblockade of the Soviet occupation zone. On July 3 the Soviet authorities offered to lift the blockade if progress toward separate West German statehood was suspended. President Harry Truman (q.v.) refused, reinforcing his position on July 17 by stationing 60 B-29 nuclear bombers in Britain to discourage precipitate Soviet action. A political standoff continued after September 1948 when U.S. General Lucius B. Clay (q.v.) declared the indefinite aerial supply of West Berlin to be feasible. American political opinion meanwhile interpreted the blockade as prima facie Soviet aggression, clearing the way to rapid negotiations for the North Atlantic Treaty (q.v.). Rapid progress was similarly made toward establishing the Federal Republic of Germany (FRG) (q.v.). In January 1949 the Soviet leader, Joseph Stalin (q.v.), attempted renewed dialogue, offering an end to the Berlin Blockade pending the reconvening of the CFM over the German question. The Anglo-Americans, however, did not consent until three days after the finalization of the FRG's Basic Law on May 8, 1949. On May 12 the Soviet authorities reopened all routes into the city. The CFM reconvened on May 25, but predictably reached no new conclusions. The attempted Soviet coercion over Berlin had been wholly counterproductive, rallying American and Western European hostility, and consolidating the position of a separate West German state beyond the perimeter of Soviet interest.

BERLIN CRISIS, 1958. The crisis was precipitated on November 27, 1958, by a Soviet note to Great Britain, France (qq.v.), and the United States demanding negotiations for a settlement within six months of the city's permanent status. Having had the 1958 Rapacki Plan (q.v.) on nuclear disarmament in Central Europe rejected by the West, earlier that month the Soviet Union formally declared Berlin the capital of its satellite, the German Democratic Republic (GDR) (q.v.), to which it would transfer all administrative rights. This was intended to recoup prestige by affirming Soviet security commitments to the Warsaw Pact (q.v.), including the GDR. Were the latter action accepted by the Western powers, de facto recognition of the GDR would be conceded, legitimating the division of Germany despite contrary claims by the Federal Republic of Germany (FRG) (q.v.). Without recognizing the GDR, however, the legal position of the Western powers in West Berlin would become untenable. The Soviets were willing to concede free city status to the latter under the United Nations (UN) (q.v.), but stressed that appropriate retaliation would follow against violations of what it regarded as GDR sovereignty.

On December 31 the Western powers refused to discuss Berlin separately from the entire German question, including free GDR elections, unification, and a formal peace treaty with the prospective single German state. The Soviet leader, Nikita Khrushchev (q.v.), accepted and foreign ministerial talks began in Geneva in May 1959. Interim GDR agency in Berlin, on behalf of the Soviet Union and not as a sovereign entity, was agreed, but the talks ended on August 5, 1959, leaving Berlin's status unresolved.

BERLIN CRISIS, 1961. Deteriorating prospects for a modus vivendi between the German Democratic Republic (GDR) and Federal Republic of Germany (FRG) (qq.v.) in 1960 led to increased migration to the latter by skilled younger workers vital to the GDR economy, mainly through West Berlin, to which access to the GDR remained open under continuing Allied occupation agreements dating from the end of World War II. Determined to shore up his satellite, the Soviet leader, Nikita Khrushchev (q.v.), tried to press a favorable settlement on President John F. Kennedy (q.v.) at the 1961 Vienna Summit (q.v.). He failed, responding with a six-month ultimatum for negotiations, after which the Soviet Union would conclude a full peace treaty with the GDR, rendering the Western occupation of West Berlin, which was not formally part of the FRG, illegal and subject to GDR action. On the advice of former Secretary of State Dean Acheson and Under Secretary of Defense Paul Nitze (qq.v.), Kennedy responded on July 25, 1961, that West Berlin was a symbolically indispensable outpost of freedom, to be defended to the utmost. American reserve forces were partially mobilized and the Berlin garrison reinforced.

Meanwhile, as tensions mounted in July and early August 1961, 50,000 GDR citizens fled via Berlin to the FRG while access yet remained open. After consultations in Moscow with the GDR leader, Walter Ulbricht (q.v.), Khrushchev declared on August 7 that West Berlin was a threat to GDR socialism and would be closed-off pending a final German settlement. Travel restrictions into and out of the city for GDR citizens were gradually tightened until on the night of August 12–13 barbed-wire entanglements and military checkpoints cut all access. In subsequent months the more elaborate Berlin Wall (q.v.) was built. The Soviets and GDR scrupulously observed Allied transit rights that an American military convoy tested on August 19. Fruitless negotiations over Germany's future followed until October 1961 during which Khrushchev withdrew his six-month ultimatum. With the border sealed, however, GDR demographic collapse was averted, effectively stabilizing the division of Germany as a status quo that was preferable to risky superpower antagonism.

BERLIN QUADRIPARTITE AGREEMENT, 1971. Signed on September 3, 1971, by the occupying powers, Great Britain, France (qq.v.), the United States, and the Soviet Union, the agreement defined General Provisions on West Berlin, settling disagreements outstanding since the Berlin Crises of 1958 and 1961 (qq.v.). West Berlin was acknowledged as outside the Federal Republic of Germany (FRG) (q.v.) and remaining under joint Four-power authority. West Germany's ties to West Berlin in matters such as currency, law courts, and private business incorporation were recognized, however, along with free transit for West German citizens and West Berliners to and from the city. Telecommunications between West and East Berlin, disrupted in 1961, were restored. The German Democratic Republic (GDR) (q.v.) was to assume border and transit controls, despite its de jure nonrecognition by West Germany. In a reciprocal concession, West Berlin's separation from the GDR was acknowledged by the opening of a Soviet Consulate General.

The initiative for the agreement originated with West Germany's Ostpolitik (q.v.) that sought improved relations with the Soviets, but with a Berlin settlement as an attached condition. In July 1969 Soviet Foreign Minister Andrei Gromyko (q.v.) accepted this within the broader framework of détente (q.v.), anticipating negotiations as a step toward normalizing relations between West and East Germany, which in turn would help normalize the East-West status quo in Central Europe. Final progress was permitted by the face-saving participation of the GDR in border controls, and by the retirement in May 1971 of the East German leader, Walter Ulbricht (q.v.).

BERLIN WALL. A celebrated and enduring symbol of the Cold War. The Wall was constructed by the German Democratic Republic (GDR) (q.v.) during the 1961 Berlin Crisis as a means of preventing the mass migration of its citizens to the Federal Republic of Germany (FRG) (q.v.). The latter phenomenon was particularly pronounced among younger, skilled, economically productive workers and professionals and was assessed by GDR and Soviet leaders as a fundamental threat to the economic and political viability of the German communist state. The GDR-West Berlin border was closed on the night of August 12–13, 1961, using barbed-wire entanglements, tank traps, and other simple barrier devices. The failure of the occupying powers to settle the city's status by October led to the subsequent construction of a 4.5 meter high concrete wall, 144 kilometers long, with a 100 meter cleared strip on the GDR side, guarded by mines, trip wires, automatic firing devices and 295 watchtowers. Although justified as a defense against capitalist imperialism, the Wall was clearly intended to keep GDR citizens in rather than the West out. Indeed, 79 GDR citizens were killed during attempted escapes.

The Berlin Wall soon became a symbol of Cold War antagonism and the division of Germany. President John F. Kennedy (q.v.) spoke there in June 1963 when he invoked West Berlin as an outpost of world freedom. He was emulated in 1987 by President Ronald Reagan (q.v.). In October 1989, as Soviet authority in Eastern Europe disintegrated, GDR citizens were permitted to circumvent travel restrictions by traveling to the West through Hungary and Czechoslovakia. As an attempt to recoup legitimacy, on November 9, the GDR authorities terminated such restrictions altogether, prompting spontaneous demonstrations by East and West Berliners at the Wall, whose official demolition began the next day. This failed to stem pressure for the GDR's eventual dissolution and absorption into the FRG in 1990.

BEVIN, ERNEST (1881–1951). British diplomat and foreign secretary. A prominent leader of organized labor, Bevin entered Britain's War Cabinet in 1940 as minister of labor. After the Labour Party's general election victory in July 1945, he was appointed foreign secretary by Prime Minister Clement Attlee (q.v.). In office, Bevin relied heavily on his well-known demotic, abrasive style and powerful personality, which along with his visceral anticommunism, were effectively channeled by his senior Foreign Office staff into policies of confrontation with the Soviet Union. His bluff negotiating style recurrently blunted Soviet initiatives in the Council of Foreign Ministers (CFM) (q.v.) and the Security Council of the United Nations (UN) (q.v.). Bevin's main objectives, the preservation of British imperial security focused principally on the Middle East, and preserving the balance of power in Europe against Soviet hegemony, were remarkably consistent with established British diplomatic practice. Despite his articulation of populist principles, Bevin's conduct therefore frequently antagonized the Labour left wing. He also clashed with Attlee, whom he accused in January 1947 of appeasing the Soviet Union. Bevin prevailed after the British military chiefs threatened resignation if assertive policies were not maintained against perceived Soviet expansionism.

Bevin recognized, however, that Great Britain's material weakness necessitated cooperation between the states of Western Europe and with the United States. To this end he was the driving force behind the 1947 Dunkirk Treaty and 1948 Brussels Treaty (qq.v.) that prepared the way for the 1949 North Atlantic Treaty (q.v.). Bevin also played a vital role in the Organization for European Economic Cooperation (OEEC), within which the European Recovery Program (ERP or Marshall Plan) (q.v.) was formulated and administered. Nevertheless, Bevin avoided full economic integration with Europe, also attempting to preserve British global prerogatives independent of the United States. He clashed notably with the Truman (q.v.) administration over the Palestine Question (q.v.). Bevin's final significant act was to secure political support for the implementation of British rearmament for the Korean War (q.v.), which disastrously overextended scarce economic resources and split the Labour Party politically. By March 1951 his seriously deteriorating health compelled Attlee to request that he resign. Bevin died from heart complications five weeks later.

BIDAULT, GEORGES (1899–1983). French diplomat and foreign minister. Bidault was appointed foreign minister in 1944 in the provisional government of Charles de Gaulle (q.v.). In December 1944 he accompanied de Gaulle to Moscow to sign a friendship treaty with the Soviet Union. Disquiet over Poland (q.v.), however, soon determined a pro-Western reorientation of French diplomacy and Bidault's consultations with British Foreign Secretary Anthony Eden (q.v.) in February 1945 secured France's (q.v.) position in the Council of Foreign Ministers (CFM) (q.v.). In May, during the San Francisco Conference (q.v.), Bidault moreover initiated friendly Franco-American dialogue.

In subsequent CFM meetings Bidault treated the anti-Soviet imperatives of Great Britain (q.v.) and the United States as secondary to France's need for anti-German reassurances, prompting recurrent overtures from the Soviet Union. These were definitively rebuffed during protracted economic difficulties in 1947 that raised the possibility of an assumption of power by French communists. Bidault concluded the 1947 Dunkirk Treaty (q.v.) with Britain, and along with Ernest Bevin coordinated meetings in Paris of the Organization for European Economic Cooperation (OEEC) that formulated and later helped administer the European Recovery Program (ERP or Marshall Plan) (q.v.). He also signed the Brussels Treaty (q.v.) on behalf of France. Bidault was out of office until 1953 when he returned as foreign minister, helping negotiate peace terms in the Indochina War (q.v.), but then being forced out again by Pierre Mendès-France (q.v.) for his procolonial stance over Algeria. The latter was Bidault's ultimate downfall. He fled France in 1962 having plotted against de Gaulle with renegade procolonial generals, returning in 1970 to assume elder statesman status on the French Christian Democratic right.

BIERUT, BOLESLAW (1892–1956). Polish communist political leader and president. Bierut was installed in January 1942 as leader of the newly formed Polish Workers' Communist Party. In August 1944 he headed the pro-Soviet Polish provisional government, the Lublin Committee (q.v.), whose sweeping police and quasi-judicial powers eliminated nationalist Polish resistance groups even while Nazi forces remained in Poland (q.v.). In February 1947 he became president of Poland after elections were rigged in favor of his communist-dominated Democratic Front. Thereafter, conservative leaders were imprisoned, leftist parties, labor and youth organizations forcibly merged with the communists into the new United Workers Party over which Bierut became chairman. In 1949 alleged deviationists who proposed a "Polish road to socialism" were purged from the United Workers Party. Ties to the Soviets were reinforced by the appointment of Soviet Marshal Konstantin Rokossovsky (q.v.) as Poland's defense minister and in July 1950 Bierut initiated a Soviet-style six-year economic plan, based on heavy industry and collective agriculture. After the death of his patron Joseph Stalin (q.v.) in March 1953, he resisted Soviet pressure for partial political relaxation, conceding limited party reforms in 1954. Bierut died suddenly on a visit to Moscow in March 1956.

BIOLOGICAL WEAPONS CONVENTION. A convention that was opened for signature by the United Nations (UN) (q.v.) General Assembly in 1972. The document banned the development, stockpiling, and production of biological weapons and followed the submission of identical draft conventions to the UN by the Soviet Union and the United States in September 1971, based on a 1968 British proposal. The con-

vention contributed to the spirit of détente (q.v.) and international cooperation although France and the People's Republic of China (PRC) (qq.v.)
did not ratify it until 1984. By 1991, 110 countries had signed the convention.

BIZONE. The economic fusion of the British and American occupation
zones in Germany, effective from January 1, 1947. It followed the offer
made in July 1946 from Secretary of State James F. Byrnes (q.v.) to join
the American zone economically with those of any of the other Allied
powers. The financially pressured British quickly accepted. By September 1946 a single joint bureaucracy, incorporating officials from the affected German state administrations (Länder), was agreed and a Fusion
Agreement signed on December 2 by Byrnes and the British foreign
secretary, Ernest Bevin (q.v.). The Soviets formally complained that the
Bizone violated the Four-power occupation protocols established at the
1945 Potsdam Conference (q.v.), but after the failure in spring 1947 of
the Council of Foreign Ministers (CFM) (q.v.) to agree on terms for unified German statehood, the Anglo-Americans proceeded to use the
Bizone as the basis for the separate rehabilitation of their respective zones
regardless of Soviet and initial French protests. In January 1948 the
Bizone was extended to include the French occupation zone and entered
the European Recovery Program (ERP or Marshall Plan) (q.v.). In June
the Bizone was furnished with a reformed currency and exchange agreement that conferred economic sovereignty to what was in effect a western German proto-state. The Soviets retaliated by launching the Berlin
Blockade (q.v.).

BOHLEN, CHARLES E. (1904–1974). American diplomat. "Chip"
Bohlen was a Russian specialist and colleague of George Kennan (q.v.),
whose skepticism on prospects for cooperation with the Soviet Union was
solidified by having personally witnessed Joseph Stalin's (q.v.) bloody
political purges of 1938. Although in disagreement with the solicitous
policies of President Franklin D. Roosevelt (q.v.) toward the Soviet
Union, Bohlen was promoted to chief of the State Department's Division of Eastern European Affairs in January 1944. After Roosevelt's death
he formed, along with Kennan and the U.S. ambassador in Moscow, W.
Averell Harriman (q.v.), an anti-Soviet lobby that influenced the new
president, Harry Truman (q.v.). Bohlen continued to advocate stern realistic policies under James F. Byrnes and George C. Marshall (qq.v.)
whom he served as principal adviser on Soviet affairs. His greatest influence was probably as head of the ad hoc State Department "Berlin

Group" that conducted policy toward the 1948–1949 Berlin Blockade (q.v.). He subsequently served as ambassador to France and to the Soviet Union from 1953 to 1957. Having suffered adverse allegations under McCarthyism (q.v.), Bohlen was restricted to largely a functionary role by the Eisenhower (q.v.) administration. After 1959 he continued as an expert adviser, serving again as ambassador in Paris, before retiring in January 1969 and serving briefly as an acting secretary of state in the lame-duck administration of Lyndon Johnson (q.v.).

BOLAND AMENDMENTS. Attempt by the U.S. Congress to restrict the power of the president in foreign affairs. The revelation in the press in 1982 that the Reagan (q.v.) administration was conducting a "secret war" in Nicaragua (q.v.) prompted suspicion in the United States that the country was being dragged into "another Vietnam [War]" (q.v.) The House of Representatives responded in December 1982 with the passage of an amendment to a defense appropriations bill. Named after its sponsor, the Democratic Congressman from Massachusetts, Edward P. Boland, the Boland Amendment prohibited agencies of the federal government connected with intelligence activities from using congressional funds to attempt to overthrow the government of Nicaragua. The amendment expired after one year in December 1983.

A second Boland amendment was passed in October 1984 to prevent the federal government from supporting the paramilitary operations of the Contras in Nicaragua. The passage of a second amendment indicated the depth of congressional hostility to President Ronald Reagan's policy in Nicaragua. The Reagan administration, however, was determined to aid the Contras, and in order to circumvent the restrictions of the Boland Amendment, it resorted to covert methods. This resulted in the Iran-Contra Affair (q.v.) in 1986.

BOMBER GAP. Conclusions drawn in the 1955 U.S. National Intelligence Estimates, reiterated by Senate Armed Services Committee hearings in April 1956, that the Soviets would possess a strategic force of up to 700 bombers by 1959 that would outdo equivalent U.S. Strategic Air Command (SAC) (q.v.) forces, thereby creating a credibility gap in American deterrence (q.v.). Subsequent intelligence reports revealed in 1957 that the bomber gap (q.v.) was an overestimate based on hurried observations of the new Soviet "Bear" bomber at the 1955 Moscow Aviation Day parade. The bomber gap scare nevertheless guaranteed increased resources for Strategic Air Command's (SAC) (q.v.) technically troubled B-52 intercontinental bomber program. In fact, the Soviets were concentrating on missile rather than bomber development for strategic nuclear forces. In October 1957 the Soviets launched their first satellite, the Sputnik (q.v.), which led to American fears of a missile gap (q.v.).

BRANDT, WILLY (1913–1992). West German statesman and chancellor. After living in exile in Norway during the Nazi era, Brandt rose through the ranks of the West Berlin Social Democratic Party to become mayor of the city in 1957. He achieved international prominence for resisting Soviet pressures during the 1961 Berlin Crisis and construction of the Berlin Wall (qq.v.). In 1966 Brandt entered the "grand coalition" formed by the Christian Democratic leader, Kurt Kiesinger, and served as foreign minister. He was chiefly responsible for implementing the Federal Republic of Germany's (FRG) Ostpolitik (q.v.), seeking improved relations with the Soviet bloc, a policy that he extended after becoming West German chancellor in 1969. He rehabilitated the FRG diplomatically by signing the Nuclear Non-proliferation Treaty (q.v.), and in 1970 by concluding the treaties of Moscow and Warsaw (qq.v.) with the Soviet Union and Poland (q.v.), respectively. These did much to allay fears of German revanchism in Eastern Europe, while also opening up extensive trade and investment relations. Brandt's initiatives did much to accelerate détente (q.v.), for which he was awarded the Nobel Peace Prize in 1971. When his chief aide, Gunther Guillaume, was exposed in 1974 as an East German agent, Brandt was forced to resign as chancellor. However, Brandt's international prestige endured, and was maintained by his chairing the North-South Commission that was sponsored by the United Nations (q.v.) and in 1979 produced the "Brandt Report" recommending increased economic assistance for the nations of the Third World.

BREZHNEV, LEONID (1906–1982). Soviet statesman and general secretary. During World War II Brezhnev served as a political commissar in the Ukraine where he directed postwar economic reconstruction. From 1950 to 1954 as chairman of the Moldavian Communist Party he consolidated Soviet power in that newly acquired republic. On becoming a member of the Politburo, Brezhnev was chosen by Nikita Khrushchev (q.v.) to implement plans for radical agricultural expansion in western Siberia. An apparent Khrushchev loyalist, he became Politburo chair in 1960, but subsequently used his office in October 1964 to engineer the overthrow of his patron. In the resulting collective leadership, Brezhnev was general secretary of the Communist Party alongside Alexei Kosygin (q.v.) as prime minister.

Under Brezhnev's leadership the Soviet Union achieved strategic nuclear comparability with the United States in 1970. The Sino-Soviet split (q.v.) deepened, however, while the 1968 Soviet invasion of Czechoslovakia and subsequent Brezhnev Doctrine (qq.v.) asserted Soviet hegemony in Eastern Europe but sacrificed ideological leadership over the Western European communist parties. Moreover, the Soviet economy could not sustain "guns and butter" policies, with both heavy military and civilian spending, so that détente (q.v.) with the United States and constructive responses to West Germany's Ostpolitik (q.v.) were needed. Breakthroughs followed in strategic arms limitation, European security, trade, and economic relations, with the latter covering up serious Soviet weaknesses in agriculture and high technology industries. The Soviet economy was further bolstered by rising oil prices after 1973, permitting Brezhnev to declare the achievement of "developed socialism" based on material parity with the West. Soviet confidence was reflected in continuing rearmament in weapons categories not controlled under détente and in adventurism in areas such as the Horn of Africa and Angola (qq.v.), or using proxies such as Cuba and Vietnam in Nicaragua and Cambodia (qq.v.).

After 1978 Brezhnev's health began to fail and his policies suffered serious reverses. The Soviet economy continued to stagnate while détente collapsed as a result of the ill-considered invasion of Afghanistan (q.v.). Foreign relations deteriorated further in 1981 during the Solidarity crisis in Poland (qq.v.). That year, the 26th Soviet Communist Party Congress set out a reform agenda and called for renewed détente, but the Soviet system was too unresponsive to effect change. By the time of Brezhnev's death in November 1982 a succession struggle had already begun and was won by the reform-minded Yuri Andropov (q.v.).

BREZHNEV DOCTRINE. A principle of Soviet foreign policy that was published in the Soviet Communist Party newspaper *Pravda* on September 26, 1968, to justify the Warsaw Pact invasion of Czechoslovakia (qq.v.). The article, "Sovereignty and the International Obligations of Socialist Countries," asserted the permanent political monopoly of the respective communist parties in the Warsaw Pact states, which were to remain within the pact permanently, under leaders implicitly approved in Moscow. Moreover, should such conditions be jeopardized in any country, it was the fraternal duty of neighboring socialist states to intervene against such threats. The Brezhnev Doctrine elicited charges of Soviet imperialism from the People's Republic of China (PRC) (q.v.), which along with Albania, North Korea, North Vietnam (qq.v.), and Yugoslavia boycotted a socialist unity conference in Moscow in June 1969. Western Europe's communist parties also challenged the principle of Soviet leadership. Nevertheless, the Brezhnev Doctrine operated as a political sword of Damocles within the Warsaw Pact, compelling Poland (q.v.) to crush radicalized labor unrest in 1970 and 1981. Under Mikhail Gorbachev (q.v.), however, it was seen to inhibit the spirit of his reform doctrines, both domestically and in Eastern Europe. The Brezhnev Doctrine, having been informally relaxed sufficiently to permit the introduction of political reforms in Hungary and Poland, was officially denounced on October 25, 1989, clearing the way for the dramatic collapse of communist power in Czechoslovakia, the German Democratic Republic (GDR) (q.v.), and of Nicolae Ceausescu's (q.v.) regime in Romania.

BRITAIN. *See* GREAT BRITAIN.

BRODIE, BERNARD (1910–1978). American international relations scholar and strategic nuclear theorist. Brodie was the first of a generation of civilian strategists who dominated American thinking on nuclear weapons policy throughout the Cold War. In 1946 his book, *The Ultimate Weapon,* anticipated the doctrine of deterrence (q.v.) by asserting that the destructive power of the atomic bomb (q.v.) had transformed the role of the military establishment from winning wars to preventing them. He also envisaged the concept of first strike capability (q.v.) by suggesting that the maximum pre-emptive use of nuclear weapons would be needed to avert the danger of enemy retaliation. While serving as a senior staff analyst at RAND, the U.S. Air Force-sponsored think-tank, Brodie refined and published his ideas in *Strategy in the Missile Age* (1959) and *Escalation and the Nuclear Option* (1966).

BROSIO, MANLIO (1897–1980). Italian politician and diplomat. Brosio served as ambassador to the Soviet Union, Great Britain, the United States, and France between 1947 and 1964. Appointed secretary general of the North Atlantic Treaty Organization (NATO) (q.v.) in 1964, Brosio attempted, in vain, to reconcile divergent French and American perspectives arising from the Vietnam War (q.v.) and concerning the adoption of the flexible response (q.v.) strategy. His overtures were rebuffed by the French president, Charles de Gaulle (q.v.), who withdrew France from NATO's integrated command in 1966. Brosio gave up his NATO post in 1971 and retired from politics in 1976.

BROWN, HAROLD (1927–). American scientist and secretary of defense. A former physicist at the Lawrence Radiation Laboratory in California,

Brown was one of the best and brightest minds who joined the Kennedy (q.v.) administration in 1961. Working under Robert McNamara (q.v.), Brown's qualifications as a scientist and outstanding administrator secured him a number of posts in the Department of Defense including secretary of the Air Force from 1965 to 1969. From 1969 to 1977 Brown was president of the California Institute of Technology. Brown returned to public office in 1977 when he was appointed secretary of defense in the Carter (q.v.) administration. Brown strongly supported arms control and favored the SALT II Treaty (q.v.), but he also believed in building up America's defense capability and was instrumental in promoting the development of the MX missile, Trident submarine, and Stealth bomber.

BRUSSELS TREATY, 1948. A treaty signed by Great Britain, France (qq.v.), Belgium, the Netherlands, and Luxembourg on March 17, 1948, in which they agreed to render each other military aid and assistance if attacked by another state. The treaty originated in a conversation between British Foreign Secretary Ernest Bevin (q.v.) and his French counterpart Georges Bidault (q.v.) in London in December 1947. Bevin also secured the support of Secretary of State George C. Marshall (q.v.) before delivering a major speech on the matter to the House of Commons in which he solicited prospective European defense ties to the United States. Marshall clarified the latter to be possible only if the Europeans initiated their own preliminary collective defense measures. Bevin accordingly attempted to develop the 1947 Dunkirk Treaty with France (qq.v.) into a larger framework. Under the shadow of the February 1948 communist coup in Czechoslovakia (q.v.), the powers concerned convened in Brussels in March, initially projecting a superficial anti-German overtone. The broader significance of the treaty was revealed a week after its signature when Bevin announced that its expansion into a defense treaty to cover the Atlantic Ocean would serve as the basis of negotiations with Canada and the United States in Washington, D.C. The Brussels Treaty therefore served as an important step toward the North Atlantic Treaty (q.v.), which was signed in the American capital little more than a year later.

BRZEZINSKI, ZBIGNIEW (1928–). American diplomat and national security adviser. Born in Poland, Brzezinski emigrated to the United States in 1953 and became a professor of political science at Columbia University specializing in Soviet affairs. From 1973 to 1976 he was director of the Trilateral Commission. In 1977 President Jimmy Carter (q.v.) appointed him national security adviser. Brzezinski was hostile to communism and highly suspicious of the Soviet Union. Consequently, he advised Carter to take a firm line with the Soviets over arms control negotiations and to resist Soviet expansionism in Africa and the Middle East. After the Soviet invasion of Afghanistan (q.v.) Brzezinski was instrumental in helping to formulate Presidential Directive 59 (PD-59) (q.v.) that recommended a major build-up of American military power and war-making capacity. Brzezinski's anti-Soviet ideas were controversial and provoked criticism from Secretary of State Cyrus Vance (q.v.), but his conviction that Western pressure would accelerate the collapse of the Soviet Union was vindicated during the late 1980s.

BULGANIN, NIKOLAI (1895–1975). Soviet political leader and prime minister. Bulganin's early career owed much to the patronage of Joseph Stalin (q.v.) who appointed him armed forces minister in 1947, a member of the Politburo in 1948, and deputy Soviet premier in 1949. In the succession struggle after Stalin's death in 1953, Bulganin aligned with Nikita Khrushchev (q.v.), who installed him as Soviet prime minister in February 1955 in place of the ambitious reformer, Georgi Malenkov (q.v.). That year Bulganin accompanied Khrushchev on tour to Burma, India (q.v.), Yugoslavia, Great Britain (q.v.), and Finland. He cultivated the air of an urbane diplomat and nominally led the Soviet delegation at the 1955 Geneva Summit (q.v.). His support for Khrushchev in the attempted 1957 Politburo coup by the "antiparty group" was noncommittal, and in March 1958 Bulganin was exiled to a minor economic post in Stavropol. He retired in 1960 and disappeared from public life.

BULGARIA. A country in southeast Europe that was invaded by Soviet forces at the end of World War II and remained under communist control throughout the Cold War. In 1946, the communist leader, Georgi Dimitrov, became prime minister. Opposition leaders were imprisoned and a Soviet-style constitution was imposed. Bulgaria became an unwavering Soviet ally, despite briefly flirting with Josip Tito's (q.v.) plans for a Balkan federation in 1948, and with industrialization plans in 1958 based on those of the People's Republic of China (PRC) (q.v.). After Dimitrov's death in 1950, the Stalinist Volko Chervenko assumed power. He was replaced in April 1956 by the more pragmatic Todor Zhivkov who retained office until November 1989. A new constitution in 1971 allowed economic self-management by agrarian peasant groups outside the Communist Party, although Zhivkov's subsequent economic modernization policies were accompanied by the official persecution of Bulgaria's Muslim and ethnic Turkish minorities. However, growing internal criticism and discontent forced his resignation in November 1989, preceding multiparty constitution discussions the following month and the abandonment of communism in 1990.

BUNDY, MCGEORGE (1919–1996). American diplomat and national security adviser. "Mac" Bundy served in army military intelligence during World War II and afterward became a professor of government at Harvard University. Acknowledged as one of the best and brightest minds of his generation, Bundy was offered a choice of positions in the Kennedy (q.v.) administration. He chose to be national security adviser and held this office from 1961 until his resignation in 1966.

It was under Bundy that the influence of the national security adviser and the National Security Council (NSC) (q.v.) was significantly strengthened in the formulation and execution of foreign policy. For example, it was Bundy who first informed President John F. Kennedy in October 1962 that the Soviets were preparing missiles sites in Cuba (q.v.). Bundy was also closely involved in advising President Lyndon Johnson (q.v.) to escalate the war in Vietnam. However, it was growing personal doubt over the direction of American strategy in Vietnam that persuaded Bundy to resign in 1966. Like many other government officials, Bundy's reputation was damaged by the failure of the United States to win the Vietnam War (q.v.).

BUNDY, WILLIAM P. (1917–2000). American diplomat. The older brother of McGeorge (q.v.), Bundy's ability allied with impeccable "eastern establishment" credentials and personal connections ensured a series of government positions beginning with the Central Intelligence Agency (CIA) (q.v.) from 1951 to 1961, the Defense Department from 1961 to 1964, and appointment as assistant secretary of state for Far Eastern Affairs from 1964 to 1969. In the latter post he played a leading role in formulating American strategy in the Vietnam War (q.v.). After leaving government Bundy was editor of the influential periodical, *Foreign Affairs*, from 1972 to 1984.

BUSH, GEORGE H. W. (1924–). American statesman and president. Bush graduated from Yale University and served as a navy pilot during World War II, then he went to Texas to work in the oil industry. Bush jointed the Republican Party and won election to the U.S. House of Representatives in 1966 and 1968. He acquired considerable experience of international affairs by serving as ambassador to the United Nations (UN) (q.v.) from 1971 to 1972, chief liaison officer in Beijing from 1974 to

1975, and director of the Central Intelligence Agency (CIA) (q.v.) from 1976 to 1977. After being elected as vice president in 1980 and 1984 he went on to defeat Michael Dukakis to win the presidential election in 1988.

In contrast to his predecessor, Ronald Reagan (q.v.), whose forceful policy has been credited with significantly contributing to the collapse of the Soviet Union and ending the Cold War, Bush adopted a cautious approach to superpower relations that placed him in the role of an observer rather than a maker of events. Bush wanted friendly relations with the Soviet Union and wished to see the successful implementation of political and economic reforms throughout the communist bloc. He believed, however, that orderly and peaceful change was dependent upon Mikhail Gorbachev (q.v.) remaining in power and that American interference in Eastern Europe would only be counterproductive. The cooperative and friendly relationship that Bush sought with Gorbachev was exemplified in the summit meeting off the coast of Malta (q.v.) in 1989 and the subsequent signing of the Strategic Arms Reduction Treaty (START I) (q.v.) in July 1991.

Bush's strategy was therefore confounded by the overthrow of Gorbachev in August 1991. Nevertheless, he soon established friendly relations with the new Soviet leader, Boris Yeltsin (q.v.). The Bush administration was also successful in assisting the unification of Germany and the setting up of new governments in Eastern Europe. Bush's skill and experience in foreign affairs were most clearly illustrated in his organization and leadership of the United Nations coalition that defeated Iraq in the 1991 Persian Gulf War. The victory brought Bush tremendous popularity in the United States in 1991, but this proved to be only temporary. Bush lost the 1992 presidential election to Bill Clinton largely because his campaign displayed the same mixture of caution and indecisiveness that he had shown in foreign policy during his presidency.

BYRNES, JAMES F. (1879–1972). American diplomat and secretary of state. Byrnes took up a career in law and secured election as a Democrat from South Carolina to the House of Representatives from 1911 to 1925 and the Senate from 1939 to 1941. In 1941 he became an associate justice of the U.S. Supreme Court, but resigned in 1942 to work for the Roosevelt (q.v.) administration in organizing the war effort. In 1945 Byrnes was appointed secretary of state by President Harry Truman (q.v.) and was a significant figure at postwar conferences in which he often clashed with the Soviet foreign minister, Vyacheslav Molotov (q.v.). In September 1946 in an important speech at Stuttgart, Germany, Byrnes stated that American troops would remain in Germany signaling his country's commitment to assist German political and economic recovery. But Byrnes did not always keep Truman fully informed of diplomatic developments and this led to his resignation in 1947 ostensibly on grounds of ill health. Byrnes returned to law practice and later served as governor of South Carolina from 1951 to 1955.

-C-

CAMBODIA. A country in Southeast Asia that was closely affected by the Vietnam War (q.v.). After achieving full independence from France in 1954, Cambodia sought to remain neutral in foreign affairs. It proved difficult, however, for the country to avoid being entangled in the Vietnam War because it shared a common border with South Vietnam. While maintaining friendly relations with the United States and South Vietnam, the Cambodian leader, Prince Norodom Sihanouk (q.v.), also cultivated good diplomatic relations with the People's Republic of China (PRC) (q.v.), and allowed the North Vietnamese to establish military bases on Cambodian territory. In March 1970 Sihanouk was overthrown in a military coup led by General Lon Nol. During the following month President Richard Nixon (q.v.) ordered American and South Vietnamese forces to invade Cambodia with the aim of destroying the North Vietnamese military bases. A political furor erupted in the United States that compelled a speedy withdrawal of American troops from Cambodia. Nixon's action, however, had effectively made Cambodia another battlefield of the Vietnam War. A violent civil war ensued between the pro-American government of Lon Nol and the Khmer Rouge, a communist guerrilla movement that received aid from North Vietnam and China. Lon Nol was defeated by the Khmer Rouge in 1975. Cambodia was proclaimed a communist state and renamed Kampuchea.

CARTER, JIMMY (1924–). American statesman and president. Although a relative political outsider, Jimmy Carter, the governor of Georgia, was elected president in November 1976, reflecting public disillusionment with established politicians over the Watergate scandal and the Vietnam War (q.v.). Carter, however, had gained experience of foreign affairs as a member of the Trilateral Commission, an internationalist think-tank directed by Zbigniew Brzezinski (q.v.), who became his national security adviser. Carter's overtly Christian ethos was manifested in early foreign policy speeches on the primacy of human rights and continuing détente (q.v.). Other foreign policy initiatives included the November 1977 Strategic Arms Limitation Talks (SALT) II Treaty (q.v.) with the Soviet Union that extended strategic nuclear arms controls, the Camp David accords between Egypt (q.v.) and Israel, and the formal recognition of the People's Republic of China (PRC) (q.v.).

Carter suffered Congressional criticisms that he conceded too much to Moscow. These intensified in 1978 when Secretary of Defense Harold Brown (q.v.) initiated extensive cuts in the military budget. In addition, there were fears of Soviet encroachment into Nicaragua (q.v.), and into an "arc of crisis" stretching from Africa to the Middle East. These fears increased in 1979 after the fall of the shah of Iran (q.v.), a principal American ally in the region. In response, Carter authorized a Rapid Deployment Force (RDF) (q.v.) based in the Indian Ocean and in November 1979, the deployment of American intermediate-range nuclear forces (INFs) (q.v.) to Europe.

After the Soviet invasion of Afghanistan (q.v.), Carter formally announced the Carter Doctrine (q.v.) in January 1980 that warned the Soviet Union against further adventurism. He also imposed trade sanctions, declared an American boycott of the 1980 Olympic Games in Moscow, and withdrew the SALT II Treaty from Senate ratification, effectively ending détente. In July 1980 he issued Presidential Directive 59 (PD-59) (q.v.), declaring theater nuclear war-fighting doctrines that superseded more passive deterrence (q.v.) strategies. Despite dramatically increasing American military budgets, Carter failed to elude right-wing criticisms of anti-Soviet weakness. He was also burdened by a deepening economic recession, in part due to the second major round of oil price increases since 1973, brought on by the Middle East crisis. The continuing Iran hostages affair humiliated him further and he was heavily defeated in the November 1980 presidential election by Ronald Reagan (q.v.).

CARTER DOCTRINE. Announced in the State of the Union Address on January 23, 1980, by President Jimmy Carter (q.v.), this doctrine formally warned the Soviet Union after its invasion of Afghanistan (q.v.) that any Soviet attempt to gain control of the Persian Gulf region would constitute a vital threat to American interests and would be repelled, if necessary, by military action. American anxieties had been raised by Soviet opportunism in the Horn of Africa (q.v.), and by the fall of the shah of Iran (q.v.) in 1979 that reiterated Western economic vulnerability to reduced Persian Gulf oil supplies. Carter consequently increased military aid to Pakistan and expanded the Rapid Deployment Force (RDF) (q.v.)

based in the Indian Ocean. To support his policy he withdrew the SALT II treaty (q.v.) from Senate ratification and announced an American boycott of the 1980 Moscow Olympic Games, effectively terminating détente (q.v.).

CASEY, WILLIAM J. (1913–1987). American diplomat and director of the Central Intelligence Agency (CIA) (q.v.). During World War II Casey served in the Office of Strategic Services (OSS). After a career in private business he returned to public service under Presidents Richard Nixon and Gerald Ford (qq.v.) as an adviser on arms control and intelligence activities. In 1980 Casey managed the successful presidential campaign of Ronald Reagan (q.v.) and was rewarded in 1981 with appointment as director of the Central Intelligence Agency (CIA) with, uniquely for the position, cabinet rank. He used the latter to restore budgets and morale at the agency, which he transformed into the executive instrument of the Reagan Doctrine (q.v.), initiating covert operations worldwide against perceived pro-Soviet influences. Casey's often cavalier style bore frequently dubious results, as in the case of attempted counterterrorism in Lebanon and in channeling aid to the Contras in Nicaragua (q.v.). Moreover, his attempts to circumvent Congressional prohibitions on the latter, notably the Boland Amendment (q.v.), precipitated the Iran-Contra Affair (q.v.), investigations of which were imminent when he was forced out of office by a terminal illness in May 1987.

CASTRO, FIDEL (1927–). Cuban communist political leader and president. Fidel Castro began his career of radical political activity while studying law at the University of Havana during the late 1940s. Convinced of the necessity of violent revolution to overthrow the dictatorial rule of Fulgencio Batista (q.v.), he led an armed assault on July 26, 1953, against the Moncada barracks in Santiago de Cuba. The attack was a failure and resulted in Fidel Castro's arrest, imprisonment, and eventual exile. Fidel Castro returned to Cuba (q.v.) in 1956 and organized a guerrilla movement in the mountains of the Sierra Maestra in the southeast of the island. After a precarious beginning the small band of guerrillas gradually gained wider popular support and were able to leave the Sierra Maestra and launch a military offensive against the Cuban army in September 1958. On January 1, 1959, Batista fled from Cuba. Fidel Castro and his forces marched into Havana and took control of the government.

Fidel Castro's rule became a significant element in the Cold War because he was determined to implement the Cuban Revolution (q.v.) and transform Cuba into a socialist society. He was also severely critical of the United States and blamed American imperialism for inflicting economic backwardness not only upon Cuba but the whole of Latin America. President John F. Kennedy (q.v.) responded by denouncing the violence of the Cuban Revolution and advocating the Alliance for Progress (q.v.) as the best way for Latin America to achieve peaceful economic development and social reform. At the same time, the United States attempted to destabilize the Castro regime by conducting covert operations involving acts of sabotage and a military invasion at the Bay of Pigs (q.v.).

Fidel Castro reacted to American hostility by openly describing himself as a Marxist-Leninist. He also entered into close political and economic ties with the Soviet Union so that Cuba was aligned with the communist bloc of nations. In the process, Cuba became heavily dependent upon Soviet economic and military aid. During the Cuban Missile Crisis (q.v.) in 1962 the relationship almost plunged the world into nuclear war. At times it seemed that Fidel Castro had become a puppet of the Soviet Union, but his skill in successfully maintaining Cuba's independence of the United States earned him admiration in Latin America and throughout the Third World. With his beard and cigar and dressed in army fatigues, he cultivated the image of the revolutionary hero and guerrilla fighter.

Although the Soviet Union never entered into a formal military alliance with Castro, his support was useful in serving as a means of challenging American preeminence in Latin America. In this sense, Castro's Cuba was an irritant to the Americans just as West Berlin annoyed the Soviets. Moreover, Castro regularly appeared at international meetings where he criticized American imperialism and offered aid and encouragement to national liberation movements in the Third World. During the 1970s and 1980s Cuban troops were dispatched to Angola and Ethiopia (qq.v.) to fight on behalf of Marxist regimes. The close relationship between Cuba and the Soviet Union was severed in 1991 when Soviet economic and military aid was drastically reduced. Despite the serious economic consequences, Fidel Castro reaffirmed the aims of the Cuban Revolution, called for further sacrifices from the people, and continued to hold on to power.

CEAUSESCU, NICOLAE (1918–1989). Romanian communist, political leader, and president. A junior official under the Stalinist Gheorghe Gheorgiu-Dej (q.v.), Ceausescu became party secretary in the collective leadership formed after the latter's death in 1965. Ceausescu used his position to retire many potential rivals and to build a popular power-base, augmented by calculated departures from Soviet foreign policy strictures. In 1966 he received visits from Tito and Zhou Enlai in addition to Leonid Brezhnev (qq.v.). In 1967 Romania withdrew from the military command of the Warsaw Pact (q.v.) and concluded an economic agreement with the Federal Republic of Germany (FRG) (q.v.). Ceausescu also underscored his independence in 1968 by condemning the Warsaw Pact invasion of Czechoslovakia (q.v.) and was subsequently courted by Western leaders.

After visiting the People's Republic of China (PRC) (q.v.) and North Korea in 1970, Ceausescu constructed a personality cult, with pervasive security apparatus, political and cultural reeducation programs. He also borrowed heavily in the West to finance intensive industrialization that was eventually paid back by exhausting Romania's oil supplies and requisitioning agricultural produce for export. Economic disruption was increased by the enforced relocation of Romania's peasantry to industrial centers. Hardship mounted after 1981, when in response to Western criticisms, Ceausescu decreed economic self-sufficiency and the retirement of Romania's entire $12 billion foreign debt. He also began xenophobic campaigns against Romania's large Hungarian minority while ignoring pressure for reform that intensified after Mikhail Gorbachev (q.v.) visited Bucharest in 1987.

Amid continuing repression, ethnic Hungarians in the city of Timisoara, aware of political change throughout Eastern Europe, staged a mass protest on December 18, 1989, which Romanian troops refused to quell. An attempted rally by Ceausescu in Bucharest on December 21 merely precipitated violent popular dissent and military mutiny. He fled the next day, leaving power to a National Salvation Front. Arrested by traffic police, Ceausescu was returned to Bucharest, charged with genocide, summarily tried and shot on December 25, 1989.

CENTRAL INTELLIGENCE AGENCY (CIA). Agency of the U.S. government responsible for the collection and analysis of secret intelligence. American entry into World War II substantially increased the need for secret service activities and resulted in the establishment of the Office of Strategic Services (OSS) in 1942. The 1947 National Security Act (q.v.) created the Central Intelligence Agency (CIA) to replace the OSS that had been closed down in 1945. The CIA was assigned the function of gathering and analyzing secret intelligence that would be used by the president in the formulation and execution of foreign policy. A second function was the conduct of covert overseas activities involving espionage and counterintelligence.

Like its Soviet counterpart, the KGB (q.v.), the CIA flourished during the Cold War. From its headquarters in Langley, Virginia, the agency collected and analyzed intelligence from a variety of sources including an intensive study of the foreign media, information from overseas agents, and photographic material from U-2 (q.v.) spy planes and satellites orbiting the earth. More controversial has been CIA involvement in covert operations designed to influence domestic political affairs in foreign countries. This activity has ranged from financing anticommunist propaganda to the organization of mercenaries to overthrow governments. At the height of cold war tension in the early 1950s the CIA was regarded in the United States as an important and necessary instrument of American policy. There was general admiration for its success in overthrowing suspected procommunist governments in Iran and Guatemala (qq.v.). The reputation of the CIA was seriously damaged, however, by the failure at the Bay of Pigs (q.v.) in 1961, and by revelations during the 1970s that it had been involved in attempts to assassinate foreign leaders.

Under President Ronald Reagan (q.v.), the CIA became more active in a manner reminiscent of the 1950s, but controversy and scandal were revived over the secret financing of the Contra rebels in Nicaragua (q.v.). Congress attempted to increase its oversight of the CIA by passing the Boland Amendments (q.v.). Largely created and shaped by international conflict between East and West, the CIA approached the end of the Cold War with apprehension and uncertainty as to its future direction and purpose.

CENTRAL TREATY ORGANIZATION (CENTO). *See* BAGHDAD PACT.

CHARTER 77. Czechoslovak dissident organization, formed in January 1977 to seek constructive dialogue with the communist authorities on the fulfillment of their human rights obligations under the United Nations (UN) charter and the Helsinki Final Act (qq.v.). The group's charter demanded nondiscrimination in education and employment, expressive freedoms, and privacy rights. During the following decade it was signed by 1,200 prominent artists, professionals, clerics, and purged former communists. Charter 77 disavowed party political ambitions, lobbying through a 15-member "spokespersons' collective," and gathering international recognition through underground literature, seminars, and cultural events despite systematic persecution. These activities helped channel the public protests that in November 1989 overthrew communist rule in Czechoslovakia's "velvet revolution" (q.v.).

CHERNENKO, KONSTANTIN (1911–1985). Soviet political leader and general secretary. Chernenko's early career was advanced by association with Leonid Brezhnev (q.v.), culminating in 1977 with Politburo membership. Chernenko served essentially as a backroom functionary and emerged as a possible succession candidate by attracting the support of those within the Soviet leadership and the communist party middle bureaucracy who favored the Brezhnev status quo. After the latter's death in 1982, Chernenko was utterly outmaneuvered for the leadership by Yuri Andropov (q.v.), but when Andropov died in February 1984, those who had been threatened by emerging reforms rallied to Chernenko and secured his installation as general secretary.

Chernenko's tenure as general secretary was one of political inertia, caught between party conservatives and reformers, who were gravitating toward Mikhail Gorbachev (q.v.). Chernenko favored returning to economic plans that were focused on heavy industrial expansion and the primacy of the military sector. The latter followed from his inability to restart détente (q.v.) in June 1984, when he offered to resume Strategic Arms Reduction Talks (START) (q.v.) in return for the abandonment of the American Strategic Defense Initiative (SDI) (q.v.) but was rebuffed. After July 1984 Chernenko was gravely ill and virtually incapacitated. Soviet politics were dominated by succession rivalry between Gorbachev and the former Leningrad party secretary Grigori Romanov until Chernenko's death in March 1985.

CHIANG KAI-SHEK (1887–1975). Chinese political leader and president, also known as Jiang Jieshi. From an affluent background, Chiang chose a military career but soon became involved in politics. He took part in the overthrow of the Chinese empire in 1911 and the establishment of the Chinese republic. In 1928 he became leader of the Kuomintang or Nationalist Party and was effectively the ruler of China until 1949. Chiang gained international attention as a result of the Sino-Japanese War (1937–1945). He was particularly admired in the United States where his supporters praised his efforts to defend freedom against the fascist menace of Japan (q.v.). Moreover, Chiang's conversion to Christianity and the fact that his wife had been educated in the United States further enhanced his image as a champion of Western values.

Despite the defeat of Japan in 1945, Chiang's hold on power in China was extremely precarious. In 1949 he was militarily defeated by the communists led by Mao Zedong (q.v.) and sought refuge on the island of Taiwan. Although Chiang exercised autocratic rule in what became the Republic of China (ROC) (q.v.), the United States continued to regard him as an important ally and defender of democracy, this time in the fight against international Communism. Backed by considerable American military and financial assistance, Chiang was able to maintain himself in power in Taiwan until his death in 1975 while at the same time transforming the island into a formidable military stronghold and a bulwark of anticommunism in Southeast Asia.

CHINA, PEOPLE'S REPUBLIC OF (PRC). The communist military victory over the Nationalist government in 1949 resulted in the establishment of the People's Republic of China and marked a dramatic shift in the global balance of power in favor of the Eastern bloc led by the Soviet Union. The new relationship between China and the Soviets was underscored by the visit of Mao Zedong (q.v.) to Moscow in December 1949 and the conclusion of a Sino-Soviet treaty of alliance in 1950. In the United States, there was considerable shock and dismay over what was described as the "loss of China." American support was given to prop up the government of Chiang Kai-shek (q.v.) in Taiwan, while Mainland China was pejoratively called "Communist" or "Red China." The United States refused to grant diplomatic recognition to Communist China and the hostility between the two countries was exemplified in the Korean War (1950–1953), the Quemoy-Matsu Crisis (qq.v.), and Chinese moral and material assistance for national liberation movements in Southeast Asia, especially Vietnam.

Contrary to American assumptions, however, China was not the obedient tool of a monolithic international conspiracy masterminded by the Soviet Union. Beginning in 1956 Chinese communist leaders were severely critical of Soviet ideology and foreign policy. The resulting Sino-Soviet Split (q.v.) took the form of international rivalry and growing tension during the 1960s along the Soviet-Chinese border. Fear of Soviet aggression was a principal reason for China to seek to normalize relations with the United States during the 1970s. Although China remained a communist state, its decision to participate actively in international affairs signified that the world contained a number of centers of power and could no longer be divided simply between Eastern and Western blocs.

CHINA, REPUBLIC OF (ROC). The island of Taiwan, also known as Formosa, lies 100 miles off the coast of China and suddenly acquired importance in the Cold War in 1949 when it became the Republic of China and the refuge of Chiang Kai-shek (q.v.), the leader of the National government. The People's Republic of China (PRC) (q.v.) claimed sovereignty over Taiwan, but the extension of communist control over the island was effectively prevented by the United States who gave Chiang substantial military and financial aid so that the ROC developed a flourishing economy and became a bulwark of anticommunism in the region. The United States also continued to recognize the Republic of China as the legitimate government of the whole of China. Consequently, Taiwan retained the seat of the Republic of China in the Security Council of the United Nations (UN) (q.v.) until 1971.

During the 1960s and 1970s the international status of the ROC was steadily undermined by the decision of various nations to establish full diplomatic relations with Communist China. Formal ties with the United States and Taiwan were broken in 1979 as a result of the American decision to grant diplomatic recognition to the People's Republic of China. Although the American military presence in Taiwan was subsequently reduced, the United States continued to supply the island with weapons for defensive purposes.

CHINESE CULTURAL REVOLUTION. A period of ideological, political, and social turmoil occurring in the People's Republic of China (PRC) (q.v.) from 1966 to 1968. The Cultural Revolution was launched by Mao Zedong (q.v.) in 1966 to restore the revolutionary purity of the Communist Movement. Mao's principal supporters were students who called themselves "Red Guards" and organized mass public demonstrations and attacks on those identified as enemies of Mao and his teachings. A period of intellectual and political persecution ensued in which many prominent Chinese figures were personally humiliated and disgraced. There was also an eruption of violence on a widespread scale resulting in thousands of deaths in all parts of China. In 1968 the Red Guards were disbanded and the army was called in to restore order. In the West, the Cultural Revolution confirmed the popular perception that Chinese communism was ruthless and violent.

CHURCH COMMITTEE. A committee of the U.S. Senate that investigated intelligence activities in 1975–1976. Reflecting the public concern over the expanded power of the president in foreign affairs, the Senate created the Select Committee to Study Governmental Operations with respect to Intelligence Activities in January 1975. The chairman of the committee was the Democratic senator for Idaho, Frank Church. The committee concentrated its investigations particularly on the activities of the Central Intelligence Agency (CIA) (q.v.) and discovered that the

...initely implicated in a number of assassination plots
...ders, most notably Fidel Castro (q.v.).
...onal revelations that were made public by the commit-
...e attempt of the Nixon (q.v.) administration to destabi-
...ist government of Salvador Allende (q.v.) in Chile, and the
illeg.   ...vement of the CIA in espionage within the United States. The
findings of the Church Committee identified serious deficiencies in the
intelligence services and resulted in increased congressional powers to
oversee CIA operations.

CHURCHILL, WINSTON S. (1874–1965). British statesman and prime
minister. Prior to 1940 Churchill had held virtually every major cabinet
post, but had spent a decade out of office and was considered a political
maverick by the Conservative Party. His reemergence was the result of
Great Britain's (q.v.) initial military defeats by Nazi Germany in World
War II. Churchill proved a consummate war leader, aligning Britain
closely with the United States under President Franklin D. Roosevelt
(q.v.). After the Nazi invasion of the Soviet Union in June 1941 he also
deferred his strong anticommunism to ally with Joseph Stalin (q.v.),
forming the Grand Alliance against Hitler that was formally completed
with the entry of the United States into the war in December. Although
the "Big Three" defeated Germany, their pursuit of divergent war aims
ultimately led to the Cold War.

As early as July 1943 Churchill identified likely Anglo-Soviet rivalry
in the Balkans and Near East, but was frustrated in his wish for preemptive Anglo-American advances into Southeast Europe. Moreover, he was
sidelined by Roosevelt at the Teheran Conference (q.v.) in late 1943,
where the latter courted Stalin. Churchill therefore flew to Moscow in
October 1944 to make his own deal with the Soviet leader, which envisaged percentage shares of influence in Greece, Yugoslavia, Bulgaria
(q.v.), and Hungary. Although these arrangements proved relatively durable, differences over Poland soured the Yalta Conference (q.v.) in February 1945; Churchill then pressed for a rapid Anglo-American advance
into Central Europe in order to limit Stalin's gains. He was unsuccessful, but nevertheless gradually persuaded Roosevelt's successor, Harry
Truman (q.v.), on the need for firmer anti-Soviet diplomacy.

Midway through the July 1946 Potsdam Conference (q.v.), Churchill
was electorally defeated, however, and gave way as British prime minister to Clement Attlee (q.v.). Churchill nevertheless influenced the new
foreign secretary, Ernest Bevin (q.v.), to maintain close ties with the

United States and to pursue an anti-Soviet policy to preserve Britain's imperial interests. During a tour of the United States in 1946, Churchill also moved American opinion closer to accepting the idea of a Soviet threat when on March 5 at Fulton, Missouri, he informed an audience including Truman that the Soviet Union had lowered an "iron curtain" (q.v.) across Eastern Europe.

Churchill returned to office as British prime minister in October 1951, and despite his bellicose reputation sought better relations with Stalin and his successors, with whom he repeatedly suggested a summit meeting. By contrast, his assumptions of British superpower status frequently irritated his allies in matters such as relations with the People's Republic of China (PRC), the Korean War, European Defense Community (EDC), nonentry into the European Coal and Steel Community (ECSC) (qq.v.), trade with the Soviet bloc, and German unification. His poor health also convinced many observers that he had clung to power too long. Churchill eventually relinquished office to Anthony Eden (q.v.) in April 1955, still enjoying a popular reputation as Britain's greatest modern statesman.

CLARK AMENDMENT. U.S. Congressional amendment in 1976 to the annual Foreign Aid Appropriations Act, sponsored by Senator Dick Clark of Iowa, and intended to veto funds for covert operations in Angola by the Central Intelligence Agency (CIA) (qq.v.). It reflected American disquiet that the Ford administration was repeating the mistake of the Vietnam War (q.v.) and engaging in a conflict in Angola in which the United States had little tangible interest. The amendment was repealed in 1985, allowing the Central Intelligence Agency to renew aid to the Angolan anti-Marxist leader, Jonas Savimbi (q.v.), within the framework of the Reagan Doctrine (q.v.).

CLAY, LUCIUS D. (1897–1978). American general. Clay served as the U.S. deputy military governor in Germany from 1945 to 1947 and as military governor from 1947 to 1949. After initial cordial relations with his Soviet counterparts, Clay's advocacy for minimum German economic reconstruction as a precondition of reparations deliveries to the Soviets generated friction during meetings in Berlin in late 1945. A definite rift followed in May 1946 when Clay unilaterally broke off negotiations for reparations deliveries from the American occupation zone, an initiative that President Harry Truman (q.v.) endorsed. The American and Soviet zonal authorities consequently embarked on divergent rehabilitation policies. Clay advocated capitalist economic revival as the essential foundation for German democratization. He was also instrumental in creating the Anglo-American Bizone (q.v.), laying the administrative foundations for its development into the Federal Republic of Germany (FRG) (q.v.). He was a member of the American delegation to the 1947 Moscow Council of Foreign Ministers (CFM) (q.v.), which crucially failed to reach terms for a unified Germany. During the resulting 1948–1949 Berlin Blockade (q.v.), Clay supervised the American airlift of supplies into the city, by now overtly calling for a separate West German state as an anticommunist bulwark. Indeed, he delayed his retirement until April 1949 in order to help complete such arrangements.

CLAYTON, WILL (1880–1966). American diplomat. A self-made millionaire, Clayton was recruited into the Office of War Mobilization during World War II. He was appointed assistant secretary of state for economic affairs in 1944 and attended the Potsdam Conference (q.v.). The resultant American-Soviet acrimony persuaded Clayton that sustained American intervention would be needed to preserve liberal capitalism in Europe. He worked to this end as U.S. representative to the United Nations Relief and Reconstruction Administration (UNRRA), helped negotiate a major loan to Great Britain (q.v.) in November 1945, and formulated the aid plan for Greece and Turkey (q.v.), which was administered after March 1947 under the Truman Doctrine (q.v.). Clayton also significantly influenced the formulation in 1947 of the European Recovery Program (ERP or Marshall Plan) (q.v.). His final mission was to complete the General Agreement on Tariffs and Trade (GATT). Clayton retired from the State Department in October 1947, periodically returning to consult on American trade and security policies.

CLIFFORD, CLARK M. (1906–1998). American lawyer and secretary of defense. In May 1946 Clifford rose from the position of naval aide to special counsel for President Harry Truman (q.v.). He distinguished himself in negotiating national rail and coal strike settlements, before submitting an influential report to the president in September 1946, which vindicated official fears of Soviet political intentions and recommended the formal adoption of the policy of containment (q.v.). Clifford drafted the speech announcing the Truman Doctrine (q.v.) to Congress in March 1947, guided the merger of the service departments into a single Department of Defense, and ran Truman's successful 1948 reelection campaign before returning to private legal practice in 1949.

In 1960 Clifford returned to politics to manage the installation of John F. Kennedy's (q.v.) administration, then served on the Foreign Intelligence Advisory Board. He was a skeptic on American commitment to the Vietnam War (q.v.), but continued to serve President Lyndon Johnson (q.v.), who appointed him secretary of defense in January 1968. After the Tet Offensive (q.v.), Clifford limited American troop levels in Vietnam as a prelude to peace talks. He left office in January 1969, although he later served President Jimmy Carter (q.v.) as special envoy to Cyprus and India (q.v.).

COHN, ROY (1927–1986). American lawyer. A precocious U.S. assistant district attorney, Cohn rose to national fame in 1951 as the prosecutor of the atomic spies, Ethel and Julius Rosenberg (q.v.). The following year he was appointed special counsel to Joseph McCarthy (q.v.), chairman of the Senate Investigations Subcommittee on Un-American Activities, achieving notoriety for the hectoring zeal with which he hounded alleged communists from American public life. In 1954 Cohn was forced to resign after revelations that he had attempted to coerce a draft deferment for his companion David Schine. He later developed into an aggressive celebrity lawyer, despite numerous ethics and tax investigations. Cohn died in August 1986 from AIDS-related complications.

COLBY, WILLIAM E. (1920–1996). American intelligence officer and director of the Central Intelligence Agency (CIA) (q.v.). After service in the Office of Strategic Services (OSS) during World War II, Colby joined the CIA in 1950 and specialized in the planning and execution of covert operations. He was influential in directing American policy in South Vietnam and was station chief in Saigon from 1959 to 1962. As director of the Civilian Operations and Rural Developments Supports (CORDS), including Operation Phoenix, Colby's aim was to identify and eliminate Vietcong agents and supporters in South Vietnam. It is estimated that this resulted in the deaths of more than 20,000 suspected Vietcong.

In 1973 Colby was appointed director of the CIA. He responded to the growing public disquiet over the alleged excesses of the agency by appearing before the Church Committee (q.v.) to admit that illegal activities had been carried out in the past including attempts to assassinate foreign leaders. Colby resigned as director of the CIA in 1976. Like many American officials who had been closely involved in policymaking, Colby was personally confused and disillusioned by the inability of the United States to win the Vietnam War (q.v.).

COMMITTEE ON THE PRESENT DANGER. American lobby group set up in December 1950 after discussions by the State-Defense Policy Review Committee, under Paul Nitze (q.v.), to rally influential members of the American scientific, military, political, academic, and media elite behind the high-spending defense programs envisaged by the policy document NSC-68 (q.v.). Having largely achieved its aims, the Committee on the Present Danger disbanded in 1953, but was revived in 1976 by Nitze and Eugene Rostow (q.v.) to oppose détente (q.v.) and the conciliatory internationalism of incoming President Jimmy Carter (q.v.). Its manifesto asserted world domination as an unreconstructed Soviet goal, requiring comprehensive American military superiority in response. In 1980 the committee embraced the presidential candidacy of Ronald Reagan (q.v.), who shared its views and from whose members he chose 32 administration members including Nitze, Eugene Rostow, George Shultz, Jeane Kirkpatrick, and William Casey (qq.v.). Antagonism between the United States and the Soviet Union was duly reinvigorated in the 1980s.

COMMUNIST INFORMATION BUREAU (COMINFORM). An interparty liaison body formed in September 1947 by the communist parties of the Soviet Union, Bulgaria (q.v.), Czechoslovakia, Hungary, Poland (q.v.), Romania, Yugoslavia, France (q.v.), and Italy. The COMINFORM was regarded in the West as a revived version of the Communist International or COMINTERN, which prior to its dissolution in 1943 had effectively controlled the communist parties abroad as instruments of Soviet policy. Although it lacked a standing structure, the COMINFORM signified Moscow's determination to impose bloc discipline in Eastern Europe by conveying related ideological orthodoxies. Moreover, French and Italian communists could be mobilized politically against such developments as the European Recovery Program (ERP or Marshall Plan) (q.v.). However, communist parties in actively disputed spheres such as Germany, China, Greece, Korea, and Indochina were excluded. Moreover, in June 1948 Yugoslavia was expelled for resisting Stalin's will on nonintervention in the Greek Civil War (q.v.). Although the Asian communist parties attended the COMINFORM's 1950 Plenum in Bucharest, the organization failed to develop further. It declined after 1951, when the Italian communist leader, Palmiro Togliatti, refused to become its first secretary general. The COMINFORM was finally dissolved by Nikita Khrushchev (q.v.) in April 1956.

CONFERENCE ON SECURITY AND COOPERATION IN EUROPE (CSCE). Instituted for the East-West discussions that culminated in the 1975 Helsinki Final Act (q.v.), the CSCE included all the European states, except Albania (q.v.), plus the United States and Canada. It was retained as a forum for further discussions, grouped in "baskets," namely, confidence building measures serving Mutual and Balanced Force Reductions (MBFR) (q.v.), economic cooperation, and human rights. The latter dominated CSCE proceedings in the late 1970s, with American attacks on the Soviets holding up progress in other areas. After its meeting in Belgrade in April 1978, the CSCE was essentially dormant, until in 1986, the Soviet leader, Mikhail Gorbachev (q.v.), proposed its revival as the arena within which the Soviets could negotiate for better relations with the West while preserving acceptable security provisions.

As a gesture of good faith, human rights discussions inaugurated renewed CSCE sessions in Vienna in November 1986, preparing the way for Gorbachev to advocate "the Helsinki process" as a pathway toward arms reduction talks while addressing the General Assembly of the United Nations (UN) (q.v.) in December 1988. The CSCE indeed provided the framework for the negotiation of the 1990 Conventional Forces in Europe (CFE) Treaty (q.v.). After the end of the Cold War, however, the CSCE proved redundant as a security forum and was generally disregarded during the crises that followed the final collapse of the Soviet Union in 1991.

CONGO, THE. A state in Central Africa that became independent from Belgium on June 30, 1960. The Congo, however, quickly fell into disorder after army mutinies against remaining Belgian officers were condoned by its radical nationalist prime minister, Patrice Lumumba (q.v.). In July the mineral-rich Congolese province of Katanga seceded under Moise Tshombe (q.v.), prompting Lumumba to request United Nations (UN) (q.v.) troops and to apply additional pressure by appealing for unilateral Soviet support. Lumumba's subsequently volatile discussions with President Dwight Eisenhower (q.v.) and UN Secretary General Dag Hammarskjöld (q.v.) convinced the United States to plan his removal. Central Intelligence Agency (CIA) director Allen Dulles (qq.v.) justified the decision by asserting that Lumumba was another anti-American leader like Fidel Castro (q.v.) and that his rule over one of the West's principal sources of uranium made him a potential threat. Lumumba was overthrown in September by Congo President Joseph Kasavubu (q.v.), backed by his army chief of staff, Joseph Mobutu (q.v.).

On September 20 the Soviet leader, Nikita Khrushchev (q.v.), accused Hammarskjöld of neocolonialism before the UN General Assembly, banging his shoe on the rostrum for emphasis. Nevertheless, UN forces with clandestine CIA support proceeded to crush a rival Congolese government set up by Lumumba's supporters. Lumumba was murdered in

January 1961. In that same year UN operations to recover Katanga began, but were not completed until January 1963. For the next two years further American support for Mobutu's forces was needed to crush Lumumba's supporters in the Eastern Congo who employed Cuban advisers under Ernesto "Ché" Guevara (q.v.). Finally, in November 1965 Mobutu seized full political power with CIA collusion. Mobutu remained until 1997 as a pro-Western, if tyrannical, dictator.

CONTAINMENT. American policy doctrine, originated in George Kennan's long telegram (qq.v.) in February 1946 and expounded in his subsequent X-Article (q.v.). Kennan borrowed heavily from the geopolitical theories of the British geographer, Sir Halford Mackinder, who typified global power politics as a struggle for supremacy between maritime world powers and continental powers, with the latter attempting historically to challenge for global influence by breaking out of the confined interior of the Eurasian landmass and achieving control of the rimland adjacent to the "world ocean." The resulting Anglo-German and Anglo-Russian rivalry in the 19th century implied that U.S.-Soviet relations after World War II would occupy a similar geographic paradigm. Kennan added the observation that Russian states, including the Soviet Union, were geographically, economically, and politically febrile despotisms, compelled to expand outward in order to preempt implosion and internal collapse. Opportunistic Soviet expansionism was therefore inevitable, necessitating an American policy of firm and vigilant containment. Kennan's original formula called for a fluid combination of diplomatic, economic, military, and propaganda efforts around the Soviet perimeter. This indeed influenced American actions during the 1946 Azerbaijan Crisis, the Truman Doctrine, the European Recovery Program (ERP or Marshall Plan), and the North Atlantic Treaty (qq.v.). After 1950, NSC-68 (q.v.) awarded containment a permanent globally militarized character, manifested in Australia–New Zealand–United States Alliance (ANZUS), the U.S. security treaty with Japan, and the Baghdad Pact (qq.v.). Economic imperatives dictated the adoption of massive retaliation (q.v.) in 1953, although the following year, the domino theory (q.v.) drew a front line for containment in Asia whose defense ultimately committed the United States to the Vietnam War (q.v.). President Richard Nixon (q.v.) issued the Guam Doctrine in 1969, which relied on regional proxies in Asia and the Middle East to counter Soviet influence, but this was unsuccessful and his successors resumed active military intervention, notably under the Reagan Doctrine (q.v.). Containment informed and guided American policy at the geo-strategic level throughout the period of the Cold War. That the Soviet Union did finally collapse when deprived of its assertive superpower dynamic under Mikhail Gorbachev (q.v.) may arguably support Kennan's original premise.

CONVENTIONAL FORCES IN EUROPE (CFE) TREATY, 1990. A treaty signed in Paris by the members of the North Atlantic Treaty Organization (NATO) and the Warsaw Pact (qq.v.) on November 19, 1990. Both sides agreed to reduce within four years their armed forces in the area from the Atlantic to the Urals to 20,000 tanks, 30,000 armored combat vehicles, 20,000 artillery pieces, and 6,800 combat aircraft. They would also be subject to on-site verification by each other's inspectors. The CFE Treaty effectively dismantled Soviet offensive capabilities in Central Europe and contributed significantly to ending the Cold War. The initiative for the treaty came from Mikhail Gorbachev (q.v.), speaking in July 1986 at a Warsaw Pact conference in Budapest in favor of conventional arms cuts carried out within the dormant Conference on Security and Cooperation in Europe (CSCE) (q.v.). In December 1988 he announced unilateral Soviet force reductions and partial withdrawals from Eastern Europe to the United Nations (UN) (q.v.) General Assembly in New York. In so doing Gorbachev enacted the principle of asymmetric force reductions by the Soviet Union, which NATO upheld as a precondition for conventional arms control discussions. In March 1989 the Soviet leader was rewarded with corresponding CSCE negotiations in Vienna, with the resulting deadlock being broken the following December in direct talks with President George Bush at the Malta Summit (qq.v.).

COUNCIL FOR MUTUAL ECONOMIC ASSISTANCE (COMECON). Eastern bloc economic organization, established in Moscow in January 1949, comprising the Soviet Union, Bulgaria (q.v.), Czechoslovakia, Hungary, Poland (q.v.), and Romania. Albania (q.v.) joined in April 1949, as did the German Democratic Republic (GDR) (q.v.) in September 1950. Although considered a Soviet response to the European Recovery Program (ERP or Marshall Plan) (q.v.), COMECON at first consisted merely of bilateral trade agreements between its members and was intended largely to serve Soviet reconstruction objectives. After Joseph Stalin's (q.v.) death in 1953 it began to promote systemic cooperation, culminating in 1961 with the adoption of an "International Socialist Division of Labor" in which communist countries specialized in complementary economic sectors. Membership subsequently expanded. Mongolia joined in 1962; Yugoslavia became an associate member in 1965;

and Cuba (q.v.) and Vietnam became full members in 1972 and 1978, respectively. Cooperative agreements followed with Nicaragua in 1983, Mozambique in 1985, Angola, Ethiopia, the People's Democratic Republic of Yemen in 1986, and Afghanistan (qq.v.) in 1987.

In December 1985 Mikhail Gorbachev (q.v.) called an extraordinary session in which he attempted to introduce free-market orientated reforms. These were impeded, however, by divergent member policies. COMECON meetings scheduled for summer 1989 were postponed after further internecine discord on jointly coordinated reforms. The organization reconvened in January 1990, only to have postcommunist member governments accelerate its formal dissolution, which was completed in June 1991.

COUNCIL OF FOREIGN MINISTERS (CFM). Established at the 1945 Potsdam Conference (q.v.), the Council of Foreign Ministers (CFM) comprised the foreign ministers of Great Britain, France, the Republic of China (ROC) (qq.v.), the United States, and the Soviet Union and was charged with drafting the peace treaties intended to conclude World War II formally with Germany and its satellites. The first CFM session was held in London from September 11 to October 2, 1945, but it stalled over Anglo-American objections to Soviet-sponsored communist consolidation in Bulgaria (q.v.) and Romania, to which the Soviets countered by protesting their exclusion from the occupation of Japan (q.v.). Anglo-American-Soviet consultations in Moscow in December 1945 were followed in April 1946 by further CFM sessions in Paris. They led to treaties for Bulgaria (q.v.), Finland, Hungary, Italy, and Romania, which were finally signed in February 1947, after the CFM had approved detailed amendments while meeting in New York in late 1946.

The crucial test of postwar Allied consensus was agreement over Germany and this eluded the CFM at its meeting held in Moscow from March 10 to April 24, 1947. The Truman Doctrine (q.v.) was announced only two days into the sessions, resulting in Soviet intransigence on its demands for German reparations and joint control over the Ruhr industrial district. Moreover, France demanded the transfer of the Saar coalmining district, all of which the United States and Britain vetoed. Indeed, the inclusion of the Anglo-American Bizone (q.v.) in Germany into the subsequent European Recovery Program (ERP or Marshall Plan) (q.v.) was to provoke the 1948–1949 Berlin Blockade (q.v.), which the Soviets ended in return for another CFM meeting intended to reach a final unified German settlement. The meeting was held in Paris in May 1949 and predictably failed. The CFM was next convened in Berlin in January 1954. The Berlin conference did not reach the German settlement desired by the new Soviet leadership, but did agree to meet in April 1954 in Geneva for discussions on Korea and on a cease-fire in the Indochina War (q.v.).

CUBA. The largest island in the Caribbean and a frequent point of conflict in the Cold War. Since the Spanish-American War of 1898 the United States had traditionally exercised a preeminent political and economic influence over Cuba. This was challenged by the rise to power in Cuba of Fidel Castro (q.v.) in 1959. Castro's determination to transform Cuba into a socialist society provoked the hostility of the United States and resulted in the Bay of Pigs (q.v.) and the imposition of a trade embargo. Cuba responded by turning to the Soviet Union for financial and military support and became closely aligned with the communist bloc of nations. The Soviets never entered into a formal military alliance with Cuba, but their attempt to place missiles on the island in 1962 provoked the Cuban Missile Crisis (q.v.) and almost brought about a world nuclear war. Admirers of Fidel Castro claimed that under his rule Cuba remained independent of the United States and provided an enduring symbol of successful defiance to American imperialism. Critics contended that Cuba was a police state in which political and economic rights were brutally suppressed.

CUBAN MISSILE CRISIS. A crisis between the superpowers in October 1962 that threatened to erupt into nuclear war. In 1962, responding to the evident superiority of the United States in strategic weapons, the Soviet leader, Nikita Khrushchev (q.v.), secretly attempted to redress the strategic balance by placing nuclear missiles in Cuba (q.v.). Khrushchev later claimed that his action was "defensive" and intended purely to protect Cuba from an imminent American invasion. But his resort to secrecy and deception conveyed the impression that the missiles were really intended to be "offensive" weapons. Once installed, they would provide the Soviets with the means to threaten the destruction of the principal cities along the eastern seaboard of the United States.

In October 1962 President John F. Kennedy (q.v.) was shocked to learn from American U-2 reconnaissance flights that missile sites were under construction in Cuba. Conscious of the humiliating setback at the Bay of Pigs (q.v.) in 1961, Kennedy believed that he was being tested by Khrushchev. While he was determined to avoid a show of weakness, Kennedy was fearful of instigating a nuclear war. Opinion was divided among his advisers: some recommended air strikes or a military invasion to destroy the missile bases, while others advocated a diplomatic solution. It was believed, however, that the sites were not yet operational and that most of the Soviet military equipment was still at sea en route to Cuba. Kennedy favored therefore the establishment of an American quarantine or naval blockade of Cuba to prevent this equipment from reaching its destination.

A somber mood prevailed at the White House in Washington where American officials were worried that the Soviets might attempt to break through the naval blockade or create a diversion over Berlin (q.v.). The world remained poised on the edge of nuclear disaster until October 28 when Khrushchev sent a telegram agreeing to dismantle the bases. Soviet ships en route to Cuba were turned around. On the surface it seemed that Kennedy had achieved a famous diplomatic victory in forcing Khrushchev to climb down. Indeed, the accusation that he had given in to American nuclear blackmail was damaging to Khrushchev's authority in the Kremlin and contributed to his overthrow in 1964. During the actual 1962 crisis, however, President Kennedy showed no desire to gloat or to humiliate the Soviet leader. In fact, Kennedy had entered into a secret compromise in which he had given Khrushchev an assurance that the United States would not invade Cuba. The president also undertook efforts to withdraw obsolete American Jupiter missiles based in Turkey (q.v.).

Cuba was the country most directly affected by the Cuban Missile Crisis. While Kennedy secured the removal of the Soviet missile sites, he also essentially deprived himself and his successors of the military option to invade the island and overthrow Fidel Castro (q.v.). But the Missile Crisis had involved much more than the present or future condition of Cuba. The world had been taken to the very brink of nuclear war. It was an experience that chastened both Kennedy and Khrushchev. Symbolic of the changed mood was the setting up in 1963 of a direct Hot-Line (q.v.) between the Kremlin and the White House.

CUBAN REVOLUTION. The policy of transforming Cuba (q.v.) from a capitalist to a socialist society was begun by Fidel Castro (q.v.) in 1959 and made Cuba a focal point of the Cold War. The resulting restriction of political rights in Cuba and especially the nationalization of foreign-owned companies provoked the hostility of the U.S. government. In an attempt to destroy the Cuban Revolution, President John F. Kennedy (q.v.) imposed an economic embargo, secured Cuba's expulsion from the Organization of American States (OAS) (q.v.), and engaged in a policy of covert operations to undermine the Castro regime from within Cuba. The survival of the revolution was mainly ensured by the provision of continuing and substantial Soviet economic aid that during the 1980s amounted to more than $5 billion per year.

Some of the policies of the Cuban Revolution were adopted in neighboring Caribbean islands such as Jamaica and Grenada, but they exerted little political impact on the rest of Latin America whose ruling elites were traditionally suspicious of communism and preferred to cooperate with the United States. The notable exception was in Central America where national liberation movements in Nicaragua and El Salvador (qq.v.) acknowledged the importance of links with Cuba. These movements, however, emphasized independence of action and claimed that their inspiration originated from their own national heroes such as César Augusto Sandino and Augustín Farabundo Martí. The sudden withdrawal of Soviet financial subsidies at the end of the Cold War dealt a devastating blow to the Cuban economy and to the claims of Fidel Castro that the Cuban Revolution was successful. Instead of a model for future economic and social development, the revolution appeared inefficient and anachronistic.

CZECHOSLOVAKIA, COMMUNIST SEIZURE OF POWER, 1948. During World War II the Czechoslovak government-in-exile in London under President Eduard Beneš (q.v.) had cordial relations with the Soviet Union. In May 1945 Beneš returned home to become the leader of the ruling National Front. Soviet forces withdrew in July 1945. Constituent assembly elections followed in May 1946. A communist-socialist combination was the largest winner, followed by Beneš's National Socialist Party, the neoconservative People's Party, and the Slovak Democrat Party. The National Front coalition continued with reconstruction policies based on nationalization, land reform, the expulsion and expropriation of Germans, and punitive German reparations. The policies were broadly coincident with Soviet viewpoints. Indeed, in October 1946 a major American loan was canceled after Beneš and his nonparty foreign minister, Jan Masaryk, denounced American plans for German rehabilitation.

Communist influence increased under Klement Gottwald, Rudolf Slansky, and Gustav Husak (qq.v.) through the trade unions and factory councils, emerging into preeminence amid economic hardships during the severe winter of 1947. Fearing a partial reversal of these gains, Gottwald consulted Joseph Stalin (q.v.) on preventing Czechoslovak participation in the European Recovery Program (ERP or Marshall Plan) (q.v.). Belated noncommunist solicitations of American support furnished the pretext for political repression and a full-scale purge in Slovakia, where minor armed skirmishes broke out. Fearing civil war, Beneš approved the repressive measures. In December 1947 the noncommunist parties demanded immediate elections, but were countered by demonstrations organized by the trade unions. The police were meanwhile reorganized under communist control, which on February 13, 1948, provoked the resignation of the other parties from the National Front government in an attempt to precipitate elections. Instead, Beneš yielded to Gottwald's pressure for a fully communist cabinet on February 25, while the army under Defense Minister Ludvik Svoboda (q.v.) confined itself to barracks. The new cabinet won parliamentary approval on March 10. Opposition leaders fled in May after elections that were contrived to produce a communist-dominated National Front victory. Beneš resigned in despair, Masaryk committed suicide, and Gottwald initiated the rapid formulation of a single party regime. Although no Soviet forces participated, the communist seizure of power was seen in the West as a clear indication of Moscow's aggressive intentions to expand international communism, thereby influencing U.S. congressional approval of the Marshall Plan, the Brussels Treaty, and the Vandenberg Resolution (qq.v.).

CZECHOSLOVAKIA, INVASION OF, 1968. On August 21, 1968, Soviet-led Warsaw Pact forces invaded Czechoslovakia in "Operation Danube." The invasion was intended to reimpose conformity with Eastern bloc ideological strictures, which the Soviet leadership felt was threatened by liberalizing reforms introduced by Alexander Dubček (q.v.) during the period known as the "Prague spring." Popular demands for independent political, labor, student, and intellectual organizations were so strong that in May 1968 Dubček was summoned to Moscow and was warned by Leonid Brezhnev (q.v.) to guard against the weakening of communist institutions. Brezhnev visited Czechoslovakia later that month, seeming to reach a modus vivendi in discussions at Karlovy Var. Dubček could not contain events, however, and his party refused a summons in July to a bloc summit in Warsaw. Notwithstanding a declaration of joint principles in early August by Dubček and Brezhnev, an invasion plan was prepared in which Czechoslovak military resistance was to be preempted and vital points throughout the country seized while the antireform party minority under Gustav Husak (q.v.) mounted a coup against Dubček. The latter succeeded despite poorly executed military operations, which were confronted by mass Czechoslovak civil disobedience. A standoff emerged in which Dubček was flown to Moscow for negotiations, along with Husak and the pro-Soviet president, Ludvik Svoboda (q.v.). After promising to remove "rightist" elements, Dubček returned. An uneasy truce followed, with the Soviets attempting self-vindication by proclaiming the Brezhnev Doctrine (q.v.). However, continuing popular dissent necessitated Dubček's final removal in 1969, with firm repression following under Husak's undisputed hegemony.

CZECHOSLOVAKIA, "VELVET REVOLUTION" IN, 1989. Since the Soviet-led invasion of Czechoslovakia in 1968 (q.v.), nascent political opposition to communist rule under Gustav Husak (q.v.) formed around the Catholic church, purged ex-communists, Charter 77 (q.v.), and related groups. Political repression continued until December 1987 when under pressure from the Soviet Union, Husak was replaced by Milos Jakes (q.v.) who embarked on half-hearted reforms. Throughout 1988 the opposition groups became more public, particularly after the 20th anniversary of the invasion. They were rewarded by legitimizing consultations with French President François Mitterand during his visit to Prague in December, notwithstanding violent attempts by Jakes's security police to crush demonstrations. Moreover, Jakes alienated Soviet leader Mikhail Gorbachev (q.v.) by resisting his proposals for the invigoration of the Communist Party by readmitting reformists expelled in the aftermath of 1968.

Mass demonstrations on May Day 1989 inspired by a petition campaign by VONS, a civil rights pressure group led by playwright Vaclav Havel (q.v.), culminated in a mass meeting in Prague's Wenceslas Square on October 28, Czechoslovakia's independence day. This was dispersed by riot police, but 50,000 demonstrators, having observed political reforms in Poland (q.v.), Hungary, and the breach of the Berlin Wall (q.v.), reassembled on November 17, only to be brutally beaten once again by security police. Broadcast by Western TV, news of this massacre spread and on November 19 Civic Forum, a proto-opposition lobby, was formed under Havel's leadership. It demanded a full inquiry into the events of November 17, the resignation of pro-Soviet collaborators in power since 1968, and the release of all political prisoners. Daily demonstrations increased in strength, encouraging dissident news publications, provincial political discussion groups, the support of the church, and labor unions and troops confined to barracks, with Czechoslovak TV defecting from state censorship. Under the threat of a general strike, on November 24 the government began negotiating over the release of political prisoners. Jakes resigned the next day, but the strike proceeded, winning the concession of a new cabinet acceptable to Civic Forum by December 3. Before this, the communist legislature abolished itself, to be replaced by a constitutional assembly under Civic Forum supervision. A new constitution was announced on December 15, 1989, with Havel becoming president on December 26 and multiparty politics restored shortly thereafter.

-D-

DE GASPERI, ALCIDE (1881–1954). Italian political leader and prime minister. De Gasperi was important in bringing political stability to Italy after the end of World War II. As leader of the Christian Democratic Party he ended political cooperation with the Communist Party in 1947 and was successful in presenting the Christian Democrats as an attractive alternative to communism. In foreign affairs, De Gasperi stressed the development of links with the United States. Under his leadership Italy joined the Marshall Plan and the North Atlantic Treaty Organization (qq.v.) and became an integral part of the Western alliance. De Gasperi also favored closer Western European integration and supported the creation of the Council of Europe and the European Coal and Steel Community (ECSC) (q.v.).

DE GAULLE, CHARLES (1890–1970). French statesman and president. De Gaulle was a soldier and politician who led the Free French Movement during World War II and then attempted to restore France's (q.v.) independence, power, and prestige as a victorious ally. Despite American opposition he assumed leadership of the French provisional government in August 1944, demonstrating his country's sovereignty in December by concluding a friendship treaty with the Soviet Union, an act that also helped to improve his relations with the French Communist Party. In January 1946, however, he resigned when it became clear that the French constituent assembly intended to deny him an executive presidency.

De Gaulle returned to office in June 1958 when France faced political implosion during the Algerian War. He secured executive presidential powers under a new constitution and attempted to reestablish French international standing partly to compensate for his controversial decision to abandon Algeria. He argued for tripartisme (q.v.), the formation of a great power security "directorate" with Great Britain (q.v.) and the United States, but was rebuffed by President Dwight Eisenhower (q.v.). Subsequently de Gaulle concentrated on establishing French supremacy within the European Economic Community (EEC) from which Anglo-American influence was to be excluded. He also withdrew France's Mediterranean fleet from North Atlantic Treaty Organization (NATO) (q.v.) command in 1959, ordered NATO nuclear weapons from French soil, and authorized the testing of France's own atomic bomb (q.v.) in 1960, anticipating this as the basis of a fully independent "force de frappe," strategic nuclear striking force.

Moreover, de Gaulle publicly courted the Soviet leader Nikita Khrushchev and the People's Republic of China (PRC) (qq.v.) while also attempting to preserve a distinctively French sphere of influence in postcolonial Africa. He vetoed British entry into the EEC in January 1963, but soon after signed a bilateral cooperation treaty with the Federal Republic of Germany (FRG) (q.v.). Its value was ephemeral, however, as the latter insisted on the primacy of military links with the United States. De Gaulle's frustrations over this factor in Western alliance politics led him to withdraw French forces from NATO command in March 1966. How far de Gaulle's flamboyant gestures bore substantial results is doubtful. Having survived civil unrest in May 1968, he resigned in April 1969 over his failure to reduce the powers of France's upper parliamentary house, ironically shortly after renewing French adherence to the North Atlantic Treaty (q.v.).

DENG XIAO PING (1904–1997). Chinese statesman and communist political leader, also known as Teng Hsiao-ping. Born into an affluent landowning family, Deng joined the Communist Party in 1924 while studying in France. He returned to China in 1926 and worked closely with Mao Zedong (q.v.), participating in the Long March (1934–1935) and subsequently holding various high offices in the government of the People's Republic of China (PRC) (q.v.) after 1949. During the Chinese Cultural Revolution (q.v.) Deng was severely criticized and was temporarily forced into political obscurity. In 1978, however, he took over control of the Communist Party and established himself as the undisputed successor to Mao Zedong, holding power until his death in 1997.

Deng achieved spectacular success in restructuring and revitalizing China's economy and in securing international recognition of China's great power status. In the West, however, Deng's reputation was tarnished by his unwillingness to introduce political reforms and his ruthless suppression of internal discontent at Tiananmen Square in 1989.

DÉTENTE. From time to time during the Cold War, there were distinct periods when relations between the superpowers were friendly rather than hostile. Commentators referred to a "thaw" in the Cold War in the years after Joseph Stalin's (q.v.) death in 1953. During the early 1970s the word "détente" came into popular usage to describe the efforts of President Richard Nixon (q.v.) to secure a relaxation of tensions between the superpowers. Nixon's policy reflected his recognition that the United States was no longer indisputably the world's preeminent superpower and that peace and national security would be best secured by negotiation rather than confrontation. The Soviet leader, Leonid Brezhnev (q.v.), felt flattered at being treated as an equal and saw détente as a valuable means of gaining access to Western technology and capital. The process of improving relations was also assisted by the success of Chancellor Willy Brandt's Ostpolitik (qq.v.) and Nixon's visit to the People's Republic of China (PRC) (q.v.) in 1972.

The high point of détente was the Moscow summit in May 1972 and the signing by Nixon and Brezhnev of the Strategic Arms Limitation Treaty (SALT I) (q.v.). Both leaders considered arms control as the cornerstone of détente and sought to negotiate a more wide-ranging treaty to replace the 1972 agreement. Progress was halted, however, by Nixon's resignation from the presidency in August 1974. Nixon's successor, Gerald Ford (q.v.), met with Brezhnev at Vladivostok in November 1974 and approved the draft of a new treaty to be known as SALT II (q.v.). The proposed arrangement provoked adverse comment in the United States where critics argued that the Soviets were deliberately exploiting détente to their own advantage not only in terms of gaining superiority in nuclear weapons but also to promote communist expansion in the Third World especially in the Middle East, Africa, and Southeast Asia.

The dissatisfaction of the American public with détente partly explained the victory of Jimmy Carter (q.v.) over Gerald Ford in the 1976 presidential election. Superpower relations appeared to improve when Carter and Brezhnev met in Vienna in 1979 and approved a revised SALT II Treaty (q.v.). The treaty once again aroused considerable criticism in the United States and was withdrawn from the Senate by President Carter as a retaliatory measure to show American displeasure at the Soviet invasion of Afghanistan (q.v.) in December 1979. The collapse of détente in 1979 hardly came as a surprise. Despite the public rhetoric emphasizing mutual agreement and cooperation, the reality was that each superpower saw détente as an opportunity and means to gain an advantage over the other.

DETERRENCE. The strategic doctrine formulated by the United States, Great Britain, and the North Atlantic Treaty Organization (NATO) (qq.v.) emphasizing the threat of nuclear retaliation as preemptively dissuading the Soviet Union from initiating offensive military operations against the West because of the massive retaliatory losses to be suffered as a consequence. The feasibility of deterrence was raised in 1952 with the testing of the first American hydrogen bomb (q.v.). The British military chiefs of staff convened soon afterward at the Royal Naval College, Greenwich, and concluded that active defense against thermonuclear attack was impossible. The threat of certain retaliatory annihilation was therefore needed as a psychological inhibitor to potential future Soviet thermonuclear threats. Furthermore, by investing in a deterrent strategic nuclear force, significant economies could be made in the conventional forces deployed worldwide for anti-Soviet containment (q.v.), an argument that appealed to the incoming Republican administration of President Dwight Eisenhower (q.v.). The United States formally adopted deterrence in October 1953 in National Security Council (NSC) (q.v.) memorandum NSC 162/2, which outlined the strategy known as massive retaliation (q.v.). Subsequent evolutionary stages in deterrence doctrines included mutual assured destruction (MAD) and flexible response (qq.v.). The latter doctrine was official NATO policy from 1967 until the end of the Cold War.

DIEM, NGO DINH (1901–1963). South Vietnamese political leader and president. Born into an affluent background, Diem was a Vietnamese patriot who opposed both French colonialism and communism. After a period of self-imposed exile in Europe and the United States, he returned to Vietnam in 1954 to become prime minister, and then, in 1955 president of the newly created Republic of South Vietnam. The Eisenhower (q.v.) administration welcomed Diem's rise to power and regarded him as an important ally in the struggle against the expansion of communism in Southeast Asia. To the communists, Diem was an American puppet and an obstacle to the unification of Vietnam. Diem's patriotism and anticommunism were not in doubt, but he was also personally a tyrant whose nepotism and devout Catholicism exacerbated Vietnamese political, religious, and cultural divisions. His oppressive rule sparked off guerrilla activity in the countryside in 1957 that would later develop into the Vietnam War (q.v.). As Diem's rule became increasingly authoritarian, he lost American support and was overthrown and murdered in a military coup in 1963.

DIEN BIEN PHU. A town in northwest Vietnam that was the location of a decisive battle fought between French and Vietminh (q.v.) forces in 1954. The French commander in Indochina, General Henri Navarre, sought to build a military stronghold at the remote site of Dien Bien Phu with the intention of forcing the Vietminh into a major battle. The Vietminh, led by General Vo Nguyen Giap (q.v.), surrounded the French garrison and launched a series of ground assaults beginning on March 13, 1954. Navarre had seriously underestimated the size of the enemy forces that Giap was able to assemble at Dien Bien Phu. The Vietminh forces numbered more than 70,000 men while the French garrison contained only 13,000 troops. Moreover, Giap possessed sufficient artillery power to shell the adjacent airstrips and thereby prevent the French from airlifting in supplies and reinforcements. In effect, Giap had outmaneuvered the French and placed them in a trap of their own making. As a last resort, the French government appealed to President Dwight Eisenhower (q.v.) for American air strikes to save the beleaguered garrison, but the request was rejected. The garrison eventually surrendered on May 7. The 55 days of battle resulted in 7,500 French killed and wounded with Vietminh casualties estimated at 25,000. The battle marked, however, a major triumph for General Giap and the Vietminh. It was also a humiliating defeat for France and brought a virtual end to the Indochina War (q.v.).

DJILAS, MILOVAN (1911–1995). Montenegrin Yugoslav political leader and dissident. An associate of Josip Tito (q.v.) in the Yugoslav partisan movement during World War II, Djilas visited Moscow in April 1944 to secure Soviet political and military assistance. He was minister without portfolio in Tito's postwar cabinet, helping eliminate anticommunist Yugoslav resistance. However, as Tito's policies toward Trieste, Albania, and the Greek Civil War (qq.v.) created friction with the West and were embarrassing to Joseph Stalin (q.v.), Djilas was summoned again to Moscow in late 1947, where a turbulent dialogue ensued, culminating in Soviet attempts in February 1948 to impose a "treaty of consultation." This was rejected by Tito on the advice of Djilas, resulting in Yugoslavia's expulsion from the COMINFORM (q.v.) in June 1948, and a definitive split with Stalin, which Djilas also expounded on the basis of alleged Soviet departures from pure Marxism. After Tito's rapprochement with the Soviet Union, however, Djilas fell from favor and was imprisoned in 1956. In 1962 he published *Conversations with Stalin,* one of the earliest original studies of Soviet policy during the early Cold War.

DOBRYNIN, ANATOLY (1919–). Soviet diplomat. Dobrynin was appointed Soviet ambassador to the United States in 1962 after having previously worked as an expert adviser on American affairs to Vyacheslav Molotov and Andrei Gromyko (qq.v.). Before his departure for Washington, D.C., Nikita Khrushchev (q.v.) instructed him to establish a confidential channel to President John F. Kennedy (q.v.) which he did, and in the process gained a reputation for urbane, open-handed political realism. Dobrynin's informal exchanges with Robert F. Kennedy (q.v.) during the Cuban Missile Crisis (q.v.) provided what turned out to be crucial opportunities for a final resolution of the affair. Henry Kissinger (q.v.) consulted similarly with Dobrynin during détente (q.v.), as did George Shultz (q.v.) in 1985 when seeking rapprochement between President Ronald Reagan (q.v.) and the new Soviet leader Mikhail Gorbachev (q.v.). Indeed such confidence was placed in Dobrynin's knowledge and experience during this important phase of East-West relations that in March 1986 he was recalled to Moscow to take up the position of secretary for international affairs of the Soviet Communist Party. He continued as a senior policy adviser until his retirement in 1989.

DOMINICAN REPUBLIC INTERVENTION. Island in the Caribbean where the outbreak of political disorder in 1965 resulted in American military intervention. In April 1965 President Lyndon Johnson (q.v.) dispatched more than 20,000 troops to halt the fighting in the civil war, restore order, and prevent the country from becoming "another Cuba" (q.v.). The unilateral intervention aroused heated controversy within the United States and throughout Latin America. Johnson was accused of exaggerating the communist threat and reacting with excessive military force. On the other hand, American troops were withdrawn from the Dominican Republic within six months and a pro-American president was elected in 1966. Moreover, the success of the 1965 intervention demonstrated the effectiveness of quick and decisive American military action in the Caribbean area and compensated to some extent for the earlier disaster at the Bay of Pigs (q.v.) in Cuba in 1961.

DOMINO THEORY. Rationale to justify American resistance against international communism. In April 1954, at a time when the battle of Dien Bien Phu (q.v.) was taking place, President Dwight Eisenhower (q.v.)

outlined the domino theory at a press conference. Implicit in his remarks was that the fall of the Indochina "domino" to the communists would be followed by similar communist successes in neighboring Burma, Thailand, Malaya, and Indonesia (q.v.). After Southeast Asia, communist pressure would extend to Japan (q.v.), Taiwan, and the Philippines. The next dominoes would be Australia, New Zealand, and ultimately the United States itself.

The presumption of the domino theory that the West was facing a communist conspiracy on a global scale was not new and had been the basis of the containment (q.v.) policy adopted by the Truman (q.v.) administration. The domino theory, as stated by Eisenhower, however, possessed a simplicity that appealed to both American officials and their public. It was used by the Eisenhower administration to justify American interventions in the Third World and later became one of the main reasons cited for American involvement in the Vietnam War (q.v.). The fall of South Vietnam to North Vietnam in 1975 did not result, however, in any further communist gains beyond Indochina. Where the domino theory appeared to work was in Europe where the sudden collapse of the Soviet empire of Eastern European satellite nations in 1989–1990 was followed by the disintegration of the Soviet Union in 1991.

DOS SANTOS, JOSÉ EDUARDO (1942–). Angolan Marxist political leader and president. Dos Santos was the successor to Agostinho Neto (q.v.) as leader of the Movimento Popular de Libertação de Angola (Popular Movement for the Liberation of Angola or MPLA), and president of the People's Republic of Angola (q.v.) after 1979. His Marxist regime received significant Soviet and Cuban aid against the forces of Jonas Savimbi's (q.v.) União Nacional para a Independencia Total de Angola (National Union for the Total Independence of Angola or UNITA), which was backed by the United States and South Africa in the Angolan civil war. After 1988 Dos Santos accepted American negotiating terms for the reciprocal disengagement of Cuban and South African troops from Angola, a cease-fire in 1990, and multiparty elections under United Nations (UN) (q.v.) supervision. These elections were won by the MPLA in 1993, after which UNITA resumed fighting, continuing to retard Angola's development, notwithstanding the pragmatic rapprochement that Dos Santos had made with the West.

DUBČEK, ALEXANDER (1921–1992). Czechoslovak communist political leader and president. Dubček returned home in 1938 from exile in the Soviet Union, served in the resistance to Nazi Germany during World

War II, and rose steadily after the war through the Slovakian Communist Party. In August 1955 he underwent political training in Moscow, where he witnessed destalinization under Nikita Khrushchev (q.v.), whose rapprochement with Josip Tito (q.v.) also suggested future opportunities for autonomous communist reforms in Eastern Europe. Dubček returned to Czechoslovakia in 1958, became secretary for industry in 1960, but having had his reform proposals frustrated by the Stalinist leadership of Antonin Novotny (q.v.), he found himself kicked upstairs to the chairmanship of the Slovakian party in 1962.

In 1967, with tacit Soviet toleration, reformist party critics were allowed to dominate a succession of Czechoslovak party conventions, which on January 8, 1968, finally installed Dubček as first secretary. A sweeping "Action Program" followed, leading to the "Prague spring" in which cumulatively bolder liberalization measures eventually provoked the August 1968 Soviet-led invasion of Czechoslovakia (q.v.). Having negotiated a febrile status quo with the Soviets after the invasion, Dubček was precipitately appointed Czechoslovak ambassador to Turkey in April 1969, conceding power to Gustav Husak (q.v.). In June 1970 Dubček was recalled from Turkey and expelled from the party, entering an enforced political retirement that ended on December 28, 1989, during Czechoslovakia's "velvet revolution" (q.v.), when he was named president of the reformed legislature, in effect parliamentary speaker. His death on October 11, 1992, resulted from injuries sustained in a car accident six weeks earlier.

DULLES, ALLEN W. (1893–1969). American diplomat and director of the Central Intelligence Agency (CIA) (q.v.). Like his older brother, John Foster (q.v.), Dulles alternated between private law practice and government service. During World War II Dulles was stationed in Switzerland where he directed the operations of the Office of Strategic Services (OSS). Regarded as an expert on intelligence activities and espionage, he contributed to the founding of the Central Intelligence Agency (CIA) in 1947 and eventually became director in 1953.

During his tenure as director, the CIA greatly expanded its size and activities and was involved in a series of covert operations including the overthrow of the governments of Iran in 1953 and Guatemala (qq.v.) in 1954. But a similar attempt to overthrow Fidel Castro (q.v.) ended in disaster at the Bay of Pigs (q.v.) in 1961. The failure seriously damaged Dulles's reputation and, after a short interval, he resigned as director of the CIA in 1963.

DULLES, JOHN FOSTER (1888–1959). American statesman and secretary of state. Dulles was a successful international lawyer and prominent member of the "eastern establishment" who frequently served in government and undertook special missions on behalf of the president. Indeed, the grandfather of Dulles had served as secretary of state and there were other members of the family including his younger brother, Allen (q.v.), who had diplomatic experience. During the Truman (q.v.) administration Dulles acted as a consultant to the State Department and played a leading role in the conclusion of the peace treaty with Japan (q.v.) in 1951.

Dulles was closely associated with the Republican Party and in the 1952 presidential campaign he campaigned vigorously on behalf of Dwight Eisenhower (q.v.). He was appointed secretary of state in 1953. Dulles was the archetypal "cold warrior" who regarded communism as evil and immoral and was convinced that the Soviets were intent on world conquest. In the 1952 presidential election campaign he advocated liberation and rolling back of the iron curtain (q.v.) in Europe. As secretary of state under Eisenhower, his language remained tough and aggressive but his actions were moderated by the president. Dulles worked very successfully with Eisenhower to contain the expansion of communism by strengthening the North Atlantic Treaty Organization (NATO) (q.v.) and creating the South-East Asia Treaty Organization (SEATO) (q.v.). The uncompromising anticommunism of Dulles reflected an influential element within the Republican Party and would be championed later by Ronald Reagan (q.v.).

DUNKIRK TREATY, 1947. Signed on March 4, 1947, by Great Britain and France (qq.v.), the treaty was precipitated by French concerns over lack of Four-power progress toward a German settlement. The ongoing economic and administrative revival of the Bizone (q.v.) in Germany concerned France's premier Leon Blum sufficiently to have him explore reciprocal security guarantees with Britain during his visit to London in January 1947. However, the British foreign secretary, Ernest Bevin (q.v.), used clauses in the Dunkirk Treaty allowing new signatories to propose a mainly anti-Soviet "Western Union" in January 1948. This additionally embraced Belgium, the Netherlands, and Luxembourg, leading to the March 1948 Brussels Treaty (q.v.), which in turn presaged the April 1949 North Atlantic Treaty (q.v.). The Western Union later became the Western European Union (WEU) in October 1954.

-E-

EAST BERLIN WORKERS' RISING, 1953. A widespread protest in East Berlin against the stringent productivity norms and repressed living standards of the German Democratic Republic (GDR) under Walter Ulbricht (qq.v.). The rising began among construction workers on June 15, 1953. In order to furnish materials for Soviet reconstruction, the GDR's Five-Year plan in 1951 imposed onerous economic demands. Following Joseph Stalin's (q.v.) death in March 1953, Soviet leaders Georgi Malenkov, Vyacheslav Molotov, and Lavrenti Beria (qq.v.) formulated a program known as the "New Course," with administrative decentralization and higher civilian consumption handed down to the GDR's Politburo as policy on June 9, 1953. Ulbricht, however, did not relinquish his grip on the ruling Socialist Unity Party whose official trade union upheld existing austere work norms, provoking the Berlin workers into mass action—a strike. The next day, June 16, 1953, 300,000 GDR workers in key heavy industries also struck, leading the Soviet High Commissioner in Berlin to declare a state of emergency. Soviet troops crushed the strikes and accompanying demonstrations. In all, 21 strikers were killed, 18 executed for treason, and 1,383 injured. Ulbricht's position was reaffirmed and the "New Course" was abandoned in the GDR. The Workers' Rising furnished a pretext for Beria's arrest and facilitated the political advancement in Moscow of Nikita Khrushchev (q.v.).

EDEN, ANTHONY (1897–1977). British statesman and prime minister. A precocious talent in the Conservative Party Eden resigned as foreign secretary in February 1938 over political accommodations with Fascist Italy. He returned to this post during World War II in the coalition cabinet of Winston Churchill (q.v.) and negotiated the 1942 treaty of alliance with the Soviet Union. Eden anticipated postwar tensions with the latter, but at the October 1943 Allied Conference of Foreign Ministers (CFM) was unable to gain American support to preempt the likelihood of a Soviet sphere of influence in Eastern Europe. He subsequently mistrusted the Americans, although he was usually overruled on this by the prime minister.

Eden remained in Churchill's shadow for much of his remaining career. He entered opposition in July 1945 after the Labour Party's election victory, although continuing a friendly correspondence with the new foreign secretary, Ernest Bevin (q.v.). After the 1951 general election he returned to his former post, once more under Churchill, to whom he was regarded as political heir apparent until he became prime minister in April 1955. As foreign minister Eden maintained a pragmatic course over questions such as German unification and thereby antagonized the West German leader, Konrad Adenauer, and U.S. Secretary of State John Foster Dulles (qq.v.). Eden's assumptions of stately primacy further antagonized Dulles during the 1954 Geneva peace talks, which concluded the Indochina War (q.v.). Eden enjoyed a diplomatic triumph in 1954, after the collapse of the European Defense Community (EDC) (q.v.), by persuading the European powers of the North Atlantic Treaty Organization (NATO) (q.v.) to accept West German rearmament under the Paris Agreements (q.v.). Eden's premiership, however, was wrecked by the 1956 Suez Crisis (q.v.) in which he mistakenly presumed unilateral British prerogatives in the Middle East, once again antagonizing the United States at the expense of a fiasco which ended lingering illusions about Anglo-American great power parity. Eden resigned in January 1957 with his already fragile health and his political career irreversibly broken.

EGYPT. Middle East state rendered strategically important by the Suez Canal. After the 1952 Egyptian Revolution, the nationalist leadership of Gamal Abdel Nasser (q.v.) sought nonalignment, negotiating British military withdrawal but also seeking economic aid from Great Britain (q.v.) and the United States. In 1955 Egypt purchased Soviet arms via Czechoslovakia. In retaliation Secretary of State John Foster Dulles (q.v.) terminated aid talks, precipitating the Suez Crisis (q.v.). Having triumphed in the latter, Nasser accepted Soviet economic aid in 1957. Egypt did not become a Soviet satellite but pursued revolutionary pan-Arab nationalist objectives, manifested in a political union with Syria from 1958 to 1961, by a subsequent embroilment in the Yemen Civil War from 1962 to 1967, and finally in the 1967 Arab-Israeli War (Six Day War) (q.v.). Defeat by Israel impelled Egypt closer to the Soviet Union with whom it signed a friendship treaty in 1971, the year after Nasser's death. The new Egyptian leader, Anwar el-Sadat, nevertheless envisaged Western-style capitalist development and sought a position of strength from which to negotiate realignment toward the pro-Israeli United States, by initiating the 1973 Arab-Israeli War (October War or Yom Kippur War) (q.v.).

In 1976 Sadat ended the Soviet friendship treaty and secured economic aid from the United States in return for a peace treaty with Israel, completed in 1979. The unpopularity of the treaty was manifested in

Sadat's assassination in 1981. Profound social problems attributable to capitalist industrialization further generated Muslim radical dissent against the government of Hosni Mubarak, which nevertheless remained a firm ally of the United States.

EISENHOWER, DWIGHT D. (1890–1969). American statesman and president. Eisenhower was a career soldier who proved to be an outstanding staff officer during World War II, rising to become Supreme Allied Commander in Europe with overall responsibility for directing the invasions of North Africa, Italy, and France (q.v.). His outstanding military reputation and wartime experience of working with European leaders resulted in his appointment as the first supreme commander of the North Atlantic Treaty Organization (NATO) (q.v.) in 1950. In 1952 he won the Republican presidential nomination and was elected president. He was reelected for a second term in 1956.

In the 1952 presidential election campaign Eisenhower promised to roll back communism. As president, however, his approach to the Cold War was much less strident and generally sought to improve relations with the Soviet Union. In order to balance the federal budget, he rejected the policy of massive rearmament implicit in NSC-68 (q.v.) and adopted the "New Look" defense strategy (q.v.). This sought to achieve a significant reduction of expensive conventional forces by placing an increased emphasis on strategic air power. Communist aggression would be deterred by the threat of massive retaliation (q.v.) with nuclear weapons. While the New Look was successful in that no major war broke out between the superpowers, it also stimulated the nuclear arms race and led to the development of intercontinental ballistic missiles (ICBMs) (q.v.). Moreover, the limitations of the strategy were demonstrated in crises such as the French request for American air strikes in 1954 at Dien Bien Phu (q.v.) and the 1956 Hungarian Uprising (q.v.) in which Eisenhower chose not to intervene rather than escalate the conflict. However, Eisenhower did act vigorously in the Middle East by proclaiming the Eisenhower Doctrine (q.v.) in 1957. He also warned of the danger of the domino theory (q.v.) in the Far East and built up a powerful anti-Communist coalition in the region that included growing American support for South Vietnam. Under Eisenhower, there was also an expansion of the covert activities of the Central Intelligence Agency (CIA) (q.v.), most notably in overthrowing governments in Iran and Guatemala (qq.v.).

Toward the end of Eisenhower's second administration there was growing criticism in the United States that he appeared weak in comparison with the Soviet leader, Nikita Khrushchev (q.v.). At the Paris summit in 1960 Eisenhower was publicly embarrassed by the revelation that the Soviets had shot down a U-2 (q.v.) spy plane. The image of weakness was heightened during the 1960 presidential election campaign when the Democratic candidate, John F. Kennedy (q.v.), charged that the Eisenhower administration had allowed a missile gap (q.v.) to develop to the advantage of the Soviet Union. Eisenhower countered by including in his farewell speech as president a warning of the danger to freedom of giving too much influence and power to the "military-industrial complex."

EISENHOWER DOCTRINE. In January 1957 President Dwight Eisenhower (q.v.) announced American economic aid and possible military support for Middle East states threatened by international communism. Attempted Soviet patronage of Egypt (q.v.) and its leader Gamal Abdel Nasser (q.v.) contrasted with declining British influence in the region after the Suez Crisis (q.v.) and in March 1957 the U.S. Congress authorized $200 million to support the president's policy. Only Lebanon responded warmly and indeed American marines intervened in the July 1958 Lebanon crisis (q.v.), which followed a pro-Nasser coup in neighboring Syria. After this incident, however, the Eisenhower Doctrine went into abeyance and the idea of long-term commitment to the Arab powers attracted little domestic American interest or support.

EL SALVADOR. A country in Central America that became a focal point of the Cold War during the 1970s and 1980s. Officials in the Reagan (q.v.) administration observed events in Central America primarily in terms of cold war politics. They were alarmed by the guerrilla activities of the Farabundo Martí Liberation Front in El Salvador and regarded the movement as a conspiracy masterminded by the Soviet Union and directly aided by Cuba and Nicaragua (qq.v.). The result was massive American financial and military assistance for the democratic government of El Salvador to suppress the procommunist rebels. In the process, the rebels were denied military victory, but El Salvador came to resemble war-torn South Vietnam (q.v.) during the early 1960s. More than 75,000 Salvadoran civilians were estimated to have been killed in the fighting during the 1980s.

ERHARD, LUDWIG (1897–1977). West German political leader and chancellor. In 1947 Erhard served as chairman of the Bizone (q.v.) currency commission and was later appointed director of economic administration for the German economic council set up by Great Britain, France (qq.v.), and the United States to administer Bizonal participation in the European Recovery Program (ERP or Marshall Plan) (q.v.). A Christian Democrat, Erhard was elected in 1949 to the parliament of the newly formed Federal Republic of Germany (FRG) (q.v.) and was chosen to be economics minister by Chancellor Konrad Adenauer (q.v.). In the 1950s Erhard conceived a "social market economy," which was capitalist but incorporated extensive cooperative protocols between business, labor, and the state. The concept furnished the basis of the West German "economic miracle," earning him international recognition.

In 1963 Erhard succeeded Adenauer as chancellor, promising "moderation and understanding." Notwithstanding the prohibitions of the Hallstein Doctrine (q.v.) he established trade relations with Romania, Bulgaria (q.v.), and Hungary. In 1964 Erhard rebuffed French overtures for a joint "middle way" in international politics independent of the United States. Erhard's "peace note" in March 1966, suggesting nuclear disarmament in Central Europe, was supplemented by offers to the USSR of further economic and security agreements and a final German settlement that evoked a negative response and was overshadowed by France's (q.v.) departure from the North Atlantic Treaty organization (NATO) (q.v.). A domestic recession in 1966 also undermined Erhard's standing, and by the end of the year he had resigned in favor of Kurt Kiesinger (q.v.).

ETHIOPIA. East African state, aligned with the United States until the overthrow of Emperor Haile Selassie in September 1974. The succeeding Derg, or military council, gradually imposed socialist reforms despite widespread political opposition and armed separatism in the northern province of Eritrea. In February 1977 Derg moderates were ousted by the Marxist Haile Mariam Mengistu (q.v.) and American aid was soon terminated, to be replaced by Soviet and Cuban assistance. The latter enabled the Derg to repulse an invasion of the Ogaden province by its neighbor Somalia (q.v.) in July 1977. Prolonged crises followed in the Horn of Africa (q.v.) depriving the Soviets of significant gains as Ethiopia sank into war and suffered a devastating famine in 1984. Despite declaring itself a Marxist-Leninist state in 1987 Ethiopia was deprived of aid by Mikhail Gorbachev (q.v.). Military reverses in Eritrea and the rebel province of Tigré led Mengistu to renounce communism in 1990, but this was not enough to avert his downfall the following year when the capital Addis Ababa was finally occupied by the Tigré People's Liberation Front.

EUROPEAN COAL AND STEEL COMMUNITY (ECSC). In response to the Schuman Plan, a proposal originally made in 1950 by French foreign minister Robert Schuman (q.v.), the governments of Belgium, France, the German Federal Republic (FRG) (qq.v.), Italy, Luxembourg, and the Netherlands signed the treaty of Paris in 1951 out of which the European Coal and Steel Community (ECSC) came into being in 1952. The main purpose was to promote economic recovery of the member states by assisting the development of their respective coal and steel industries. The creation of the ECSC was also greatly influenced by the French diplomat, Jean Monnet (q.v.), who envisaged the organization as a first step toward a politically unified Europe. The ECSC provided an example of successful European cooperation and was merged into the European Community (EC) (q.v.) in 1967.

EUROPEAN COMMUNITY (EC). The European Economic Community (EEC) was founded by the Treaty of Rome of March 1957 and was merged with the European Coal and Steel Community (ECSC) (q.v.) and the European Atomic Energy Community (EURATOM) in 1967, at which point the three were commonly referred to as the European Community (EC). The initial members were Belgium, France, the German Federal Republic (FRG) (qq.v.), Italy, Luxembourg, and the Netherlands. Their principal motive was to promote economic development by reducing trade barriers and harmonizing tariffs among members with the ultimate aim of creating a single economic market. In addition, prominent figures such as Jean Monnet (q.v.) envisaged the eventual formation of a politically unified Europe. The United States initially regarded the move toward European economic cooperation as a valuable means of consolidating the gains of the Marshall Plan (q.v.) and strengthening Western European political stability and resistance against the threat of communist expansion. Especially pleasing was the successful cooperation between France and West Germany that helped to heal the animosities caused by two world wars, and to integrate the FRG within the Western alliance. However, for historical reasons Great Britain (q.v.) felt separate from Europe and was suspicious of the idea of political union. But Britain was impressed by the economic success of the EEC and applied for membership in 1961. Using Britain's special relationship with the United States as justification, President Charles de Gaulle (q.v.) of France vetoed Britain's application. Britain eventually joined the EC in 1973.

The EC was not able to pursue a common diplomatic or defense policy because individual members maintained their own national military forces, and in the case of France and Great Britain, their independent nuclear deterrents. The EC was, therefore, similar to the United Nations (UN) (q.v.) in having a limited and circumscribed role in cold war politics. Nevertheless, the EC was important in assisting economic recovery in Western Europe and thereby helping its members to regain a sense of pride and achievement that assisted the moves toward détente during the 1970s, and by providing a notable example of capitalist success, stimulating the eventual collapse of communist authority in Eastern Europe and the Soviet Union. In 1993 the EC was reorganized as the European Union (EU). The members comprise Belgium, Denmark, the Irish Republic, France, Germany, Great Britain, Greece, Italy, Luxembourg, The Netherlands, Portugal, and Spain. It was envisaged that the EU would be enlarged by the admission of several of the former communist nations of Eastern Europe.

EUROPEAN DEFENSE COMMUNITY (EDC). After the outbreak of the Korean War (q.v.) in 1950 American pressure mounted for the Federal Republic of Germany (FRG) (q.v.) to rearm and contribute directly to the defense of Western Europe. The European members of the North Atlantic Treaty Organization (NATO) (q.v.), however, had misgivings resulting in a proposal by the French prime minister, René Pleven (q.v.), for a combined European army including German troops. On May 26, 1952, France (q.v.), the FRG (q.v.), Italy, Belgium, Luxembourg, and the Netherlands created the European Defense Community (EDC). The EDC had integrated armed forces and a single defense minister accountable to the European assembly and Council of Ministers set up in 1950 by the European Coal and Steel Community (ECSC) (q.v.). However, the controversy over German rearmament was such that in August 1954, the French Chamber of Deputies refused to ratify the EDC treaties. This provoked a critical response from the Eisenhower (q.v.) administration and the threat to reconsider America's commitment to NATO. The result was the FRG's admission into NATO, with its own armed forces under the October 1954 Paris Agreements (q.v.).

EUROPEAN RECOVERY PROGRAM (ERP OR MARSHALL PLAN). American aid program for the economic recovery of Western Europe. The severe winter of January–March 1947 contributed to the opening up of a European "dollar gap" as scarce foreign exchange was diverted away from capital formation into imports of food and fuel, soon exceeding the limited resources of the International Monetary Fund (IMF) and the World Bank, threatening European political as well as economic crisis. Undersecretary of State Will Clayton (q.v.) drafted a relief program, made more urgent by the failure of the Council of Foreign Ministers (CFM) (q.v.) to conclude a German settlement because Anglo-American planners considered German recovery as vital to general European prospects.

On June 5, 1947, in a speech at Harvard University, Secretary of State George C. Marshall (q.v.) announced America's willingness to assist Europe and called on the Europeans themselves to conceive appropriate economic planning institutions. The British foreign secretary, Ernest Bevin (q.v.), and the French foreign minister, Georges Bidault (q.v.), then convened the putative Committee on European Economic Cooperation in Paris (CEEC). Invitations were accepted by the Soviet Union, Poland (q.v.), and Czechoslovakia, but the CEEC's supranational capitalist parameters precluded Soviet participation, and precipitated measures by Moscow to withdraw its two emerging satellites. By late August 1947 a four-year $28 billion program was completed nonetheless, including 16 Western European states and the German Bizone (q.v.), to be administered by the Organization for European Economic Cooperation (OEEC) and the U.S. Economic Cooperation Administration (ECA). President Harry Truman (q.v.) reduced the appropriation for the ERP to $17 billion, which the U.S. Congress finally approved in March 1948, stimulated by the final communist seizure of power in Czechoslovakia (q.v.). Known popularly as the Marshall Plan, the ERP was hugely successful in helping to revive capitalism in Western Europe although without leading to permanent OEEC integration as the United States had hoped. The OEEC's inclusion of the Bizone, which therefore assumed quasi-German state powers, provoked a fundamental rift between the United States and the Soviet Union, which was manifested in the 1948–1949 Berlin Blockade (q.v.) and the formation of a separate Soviet economic sphere in Eastern Europe within the Committee for Mutual Economic Assistance (COMECON) (q.v.).

-F-

FIRST STRIKE CAPABILITY. A strategic concept denoting the ability to wipe out enemy retaliatory forces with a decisive surprise nuclear attack. During the mid-1950s it gained acceptance with U.S. Air Force advocates who criticized deterrence based on massive retaliation (qq.v.) as lacking in credibility if confronted by limited Soviet aggression, for example in Western Europe alone. War-fighting would be necessary in such cases, and this could proceed relatively safely if Soviet strategic forces were eliminated preemptively. In 1960 the American strategic analyst, Herman Kahn (q.v.), fully articulated this concept, which was subsequently facilitated by emerging super-accurate warhead technologies and multiple independently targetable reentry vehicles (MIRVs) (q.v.) and became policy under the Nixon (q.v.) administration. The acquisition by the Soviets of similar warhead technologies in the early 1970s, however, changed the strategic balance again and demanded the creation of a strategic nuclear reserve invulnerable to a Soviet "first strike," preserving deterrence by enabling American thermonuclear retaliation at all times. This capacity became known as a second strike capability (q.v.), and was considered the sine qua non of strategic nuclear security.

FLEXIBLE RESPONSE. A strategic doctrine promoted after 1962 by Secretary of Defense Robert S. McNamara (q.v.), and formally adopted by the North Atlantic Treaty Organization (NATO) (q.v.) in 1967. It assumed a general strengthening of NATO forces below the strategic nuclear level in order to meet Soviet conventional and lesser nuclear aggression in kind, permitting the resolution of diplomatic crisis without immediate resort to all-out nuclear war. Deterrence (q.v.) would be maintained by the threat of escalation to successively more destructive levels of weaponry, compelling the Soviet Union to seek terms had it initiated war, or indeed serving to inhibit risky opportunism. McNamara's thinking was the result of the 1961 Berlin Crisis (q.v.), which caused him to doubt the psychological credibility of massive retaliation (q.v.), in response to geographically or operationally small-scale Soviet military forays. Moreover, President John F. Kennedy (q.v.) was attracted to the idea of using conventional special forces for counterinsurgency operations in areas such as Laos (q.v.), and in the early phase of the Vietnam War (q.v.), where guerrillas clearly were not deterred by the American possession of strategic nuclear weapons.

Under flexible response, NATO's European powers were implicitly to increase their nonnuclear forces for initial conventional defense against Soviet attack, before American nuclear forces needed to engage. This directly contradicted French national strategy based on its own nuclear "force de frappe" or "striking force" deterrent. The result was considerable inter-Allied friction. Indeed, only after French departure from NATO's integrated military command in 1966 could flexible response be implemented. It remained NATO policy until 1991, being superseded by lower levels of operational force after the end of the Cold War.

FORD, GERALD R. (1913–). American political leader and president. After service in the U.S. Navy during World War II, Ford joined the Republican Party and was elected a U.S. Congressman in 1948. In Congress Ford concentrated on domestic politics and rose to become House minority leader in 1965. In 1973 he was chosen by President Richard Nixon (q.v.) to become vice president after the forced resignation of Spiro Agnew. When Nixon resigned in August 1974, Ford became president.

In foreign affairs Ford worked with Secretary of State Henry Kissinger (q.v.) to promote the policy of détente (q.v.) with the Soviet Union. One of his first actions was to meet the Soviet leader, Leonid Brezhnev (q.v.), at the Vladivostok Summit (q.v.) in November 1974. A draft agreement was reached on arms control that was intended to form the basis of a new arms limitation treaty to be known as SALT II (q.v.). The proposed arrangement, however, provoked considerable criticism in the United States where it was condemned as a Soviet maneuver to gain superiority over the United States in nuclear weapons. Further political controversy was aroused by Ford's policy of increasing military aid to pro-American forces in South Vietnam, Cambodia, and Angola (qq.v.). Indeed, Ford felt so vulnerable to domestic criticism in 1976 that he prohibited his staff from using the word détente in his campaign for the presidency. Nevertheless, he still lost the election to Jimmy Carter (q.v.).

FORRESTAL, JAMES V. (1892–1949). American businessman and secretary of defense. An eminent Wall Street financier, Forrestal was recruited into the Roosevelt (q.v.) administration in 1940. He was an able but abrasive administrator who characteristically advocated expanding American armed strength, overseas activity, and anti-Soviet policies. Forrestal firmly advocated the use of the atomic bomb on Japan (qq.v.) in August 1945, and in spring 1946, the dispatch of U.S. Navy forces to Turkey (q.v.) as a show of strength against Soviet pressure for territorial and maritime transit concessions. The following year he was a partisan of the Truman Doctrine (q.v.) and was appointed the first secretary of defense under the provisions of the 1947 National Security Act (q.v.). Forrestal proved ill matched to his new post in which he was challenged by interservice rivalries, cabinet-level budget disputes, and personal estrangement from President Harry Truman (q.v.). His business ties to American oil interests in the Middle East also influenced him toward politically unpopular anti-Zionism. Forrestal resigned in March 1949 suffering acute strain and depression, and shortly afterward committed suicide by jumping from an upper-story window at the U.S. Naval Hospital, Bethesda, Maryland.

FRANCE. Western European power, defeated by Nazi Germany in World War II, liberated in 1944 by the Allies, led by United States and Great Britain (q.v.), to whom it remained allied for postwar security vis-à-vis Germany and the Soviet Union. Nevertheless, French policy also aimed to preserve an independent world role in ways that recurrently challenged its Western allies. Under the leadership of Charles de Gaulle (q.v.), France signed a friendship treaty with the Soviets in December 1944, but accepted British advocacy at the February 1945 Yalta Conference (q.v.) for its admission to the Council of Foreign Ministers (CFM) (q.v.) and permanent membership of the Security Council of the United Nations (UN) (q.v.). Although it initially resisted the Anglo-American rehabilitation of Western Germany, France signed the treaties of Dunkirk, Brussels, and the North Atlantic Treaty (qq.v.), and participated in the European Recovery Program (ERP or Marshall Plan) (q.v.). Moreover, after May 1950 it relied on American military aid in the Indochina War (q.v.).

In 1950 Foreign Minister Robert Schuman (q.v.) settled French anxieties over the rapid economic recovery of the Federal Republic of Germany (FRG) (q.v.) by joining with it in the European Coal and Steel Community (ECSC) (q.v.), which also formed the basis for the European Economic Community (EEC) in 1957. But a related European Defense Community (EDC) (q.v.) foundered in 1954 on French parliamentary objections. French insecurities were augmented moreover by defeat in Indochina, by an anticolonial insurgency in Algeria after 1954, and embroilment in the 1956 Suez Crisis (q.v.). Facing French political disintegration over the Algerian War, de Gaulle returned to power in June 1958 after a 12-year hiatus. He embarked on concerted efforts to restore France's prestige despite having to abandon Algeria in 1962, seeking a "third way" in international politics between the superpowers. Notable exercises of power included testing nuclear weapons in 1960, excluding Britain from the European Economic Community (EEC) (q.v.), concluding a bilateral cooperation treaty with West Germany in 1963, recognizing the People's Republic of China (PRC) in 1964, withdrawing from the North Atlantic Treaty Organization (NATO) in 1966, and refusing to sign the Nuclear Non-proliferation and the Partial Test Ban Treaties (qq.v.).

Although agreeing to British entry to the EEC in 1971, President Georges Pompidou and his successor, Valéry Giscard d'Estaing, continued to uphold France's autonomous world interests, notably in its former African colonies, the Middle East and Eastern Europe, where it cultivated close relations with the Romanian dictator, Nicolae Ceausescu (q.v.). After 1981 President François Mitterand added accelerated efforts to integrate Western Europe politically, as well as economically, to this agenda. Cordial French relations with the United States were accompanied by the opening of preliminary channels to the Soviet leader, Mikhail Gorbachev (q.v.) in 1985. Moreover, Mitterand's 1988 visit to Prague included consultations with dissident leaders that added momentum to the emerging 1989 Czechoslovakian "velvet revolution" (q.v.). France subsequently played a full part in the diplomatic end of the Cold War, while attempting to keep its political distance from ostensible American hegemony.

FUCHS, KLAUS (1911–1988). German nuclear physicist and communist spy. A refugee from Nazi Germany who completed his scientific studies in Britain, Fuchs contributed to early British research on the atomic bomb (q.v.). From the beginning, however, he had passed theoretical data to the GRU (Soviet military intelligence) (q.v.) and continued to do so while working in the United States from 1943 to 1946 on the Manhattan Project, which produced the first practical nuclear weapon. In 1949 Fuchs eventually confessed his espionage to the British Security Service during routine questions concerning his father who lived in the German Democratic Republic (GDR) (q.v.). In 1950 he was sentenced to 14 years in prison. After being paroled in 1959 he returned to the GDR. Fuchs is likely to have helped Soviet atomic bomb research greatly by providing data on plutonium reactions. His exposure hindered future Anglo-American nuclear cooperation, but did lead to the arrest of Ethel and Julius Rosenberg (q.v.), which in turn intensified McCarthyism (q.v.) in the United States.

FULBRIGHT, J. WILLIAM (1905–1995). American politician and chairman of the Senate Foreign Relations Committee. Fulbright was a lawyer and college professor before securing election as a Democrat from Arkansas to the U.S. House of Representatives in 1942 and the Senate in 1944. Fulbright's name became world famous for his sponsorship of a congressional bill in 1946 that provided funds for the exchange of students, scholars, and teachers between the United States and overseas countries. The promotion of educational and cultural contacts was useful propaganda in the Cold War because it presented the United States as an "open" society in contrast to the "closed" Soviet Union.

Fulbright was also prominent in foreign policy as chairman of the Senate Committee on Foreign Relations from 1959 to 1974. Although he initially supported American involvement in the Vietnam War (q.v.) and in 1964 crucially assisted the passage of the Gulf of Tonkin resolution that allowed the United States to take retaliatory military action against North Vietnam, he became a fierce critic of President Lyndon Johnson's (q.v.) policy of escalating the war. Fulbright believed that American leaders had been corrupted by the "arrogance of power."

-G-

GAITHER REPORT. Document reflecting American concern over the nuclear arms race with the Soviet Union in the late 1950s. Reports that the Soviets were successfully developing intercontinental ballistic missiles (ICBMs) (q.v.) prompted President Dwight Eisenhower (q.v.) in 1957 to set up a committee under Rowan Gaither of the Ford Foundation to investigate how the United States should respond. The Gaither Report was similar to NSC-68 (q.v.) in recommending the immediate adoption of a massive program of rearmament. A new development was the emphasis on providing for a national system of civil defense based upon the building of millions of fallout shelters across the United States. President Eisenhower, however, did not accept the pessimistic estimates contained in the Report and decided not to proceed with its main recommendations. Possibly, he was persuaded from information gained from U-2 (q.v.) spy flights that the Soviets were not as advanced in strategic weapons as the Report implied. Nevertheless, parts of the Gaither Report were leaked to the press and gave critics of the Republican administration valuable information with which they accused Eisenhower of allowing the creation of a missile gap (q.v.).

GEHLEN ORGANIZATION. West German intelligence service, named after its founder, former Nazi Major-General Reinhard Gehlen (1902–1979). It was formed under U.S. Army command in 1946 from the remnants of his World War II Foreign Armies East network, which survived throughout Soviet-occupied Eastern Europe and in the Soviet Union itself. In addition, Gehlen persuaded the Americans to reactivate his counterintelligence network inside Germany, claiming an extensive Soviet penetration operation to have already begun there. Under subsequent Central Intelligence Agency (CIA) (q.v.) auspices, located outside

Munich, Gehlen recruited an array of ex-German Army, SS, and anti-Soviet East European personnel for counterintelligence and penetration of the Soviet bloc. In April 1956 the Gehlen Organization was officially transferred to the Federal Republic of Germany (FRG) (q.v.) and became its security and intelligence service. Gehlen retired as its head in 1968, despite earlier embarrassing scandals involving illegal harassment of the press ordered by Defense Minister Franz Josef Strauss (q.v.) and in 1961, the exposure of a deep penetration of his group by Soviet double-agents.

GENEVA SUMMIT, 1955. Convened by the governments of Great Britain, France (qq.v.), the United States, and the Soviet Union, the summit met from July 18 to July 23, 1955. It was the first meeting of its kind since the 1945 Potsdam Conference (q.v.) and was intended to break new ground on a German peace treaty, European military security, disarmament, and East-West political and economic rapprochement. Winston Churchill (q.v.) wanted a summit in 1953, after the death of Joseph Stalin (q.v.), but President Dwight Eisenhower (q.v.) had demurred until the Federal Republic of Germany (FRG) (q.v.) joined the North Atlantic Treaty Organization (NATO) (q.v.) and the new Soviet leadership had demonstrated definitive cooperative overtures. The former was achieved by the October 1954 Paris Agreements (q.v.) and the latter in the May 1955 Austrian State Treaty (q.v.).

At the Geneva Summit, however, intractable differences remained over Germany, despite a joint communiqué on free elections in principle, unification, and German diplomatic sovereignty. Eisenhower's "Open Skies" (q.v.) arms control proposal was also vetoed by Nikita Khrushchev (q.v.). Khrushchev proposed an all-European security treaty, under which American troops would depart the continent. This was rejected by the Western leaders. Therefore little of substance was achieved, notwithstanding the much-celebrated "spirit of Geneva."

GENSCHER, HANS-DIETRICH (1927–). West German politician and foreign minister. Genscher was the leader of the Free Democrat Party and served in the coalition with the Social Democrats as interior minister under Willy Brandt (q.v.), and after 1974, as foreign minister under Helmut Schmidt (q.v.). In 1982, however, he switched allegiance to Helmut Kohl (q.v.) of the Christian Democrats under whom he retained his cabinet post. Genscher upheld Ostpolitik (q.v.), further integration by the European Community (EC) (q.v.) and military links with the United States through the North Atlantic Treaty Organization (NATO) (q.v.). Despite Kohl's reservations, Genscher maintained pragmatic cordiality with the Soviets in the 1980s, making early overtures to Mikhail Gorbachev (q.v.) and at the 1987 Davos World Economic Summit advocating flexible negotiating conditions, which facilitated the landmark intermediate-range nuclear forces (INF) Treaty (q.v.).

Despite "Genscherism" being a German euphemism for slippery politics, Genscher commanded Soviet confidence and was able to procure transit terms in 1989 for the many East German refugees gathered in the Federal German embassy in Prague. This proved a portent of the final collapse of the German Democratic Republic (GDR) (q.v.), after which Genscher reassured Moscow that a unified Germany within NATO would acknowledge the role of the Conference on Security and Cooperation in Europe (CSCE) (q.v.). He also pursued the 1990 Conventional Forces in Europe (CFE) Treaty (q.v.) negotiations enthusiastically and so contributed vitally to ending the Cold War.

GERMAN DEMOCRATIC REPUBLIC (GDR). Established on October 7, 1949, in the Soviet occupation zone of Germany in reaction to the earlier creation of the Federal Republic of Germany (FRG) (q.v.) in the Western Allied occupation zones. The GDR was ruled by the Socialist Unity Party and complemented the Soviet status quo in Eastern Europe, entering the Council for Economic Cooperation (COMECON) (q.v.) in 1950 and the Warsaw Pact (q.v.) in 1955. After 1951 Soviet-style institutions were imposed by the general secretary of the Socialist Unity Party, Walter Ulbricht (q.v.), including an industrial five-year plan, Marxism-Leninism as a compulsory university subject, agricultural collectivization, and a pervasive security apparatus. Many GDR citizens fled west, leading to the closure of the FRG border in 1952. Popular discontent erupted during the 1953 East Berlin Workers' Uprising (q.v.).

Ulbricht resisted destalinization after 1956 but continued to receive Soviet support in the absence of a comprehensive German settlement. Stringent economic five-year and seven-year economic plans were shelved in 1958 and 1959, but large numbers of indispensable skilled workers, technicians, and administrators continued to flee to the FRG via Berlin, which was technically still under Allied control and so eluded GDR border controls. By 1961 Ulbricht faced economic collapse, which was averted only by the construction of the Berlin Wall (q.v.). Limited concessions to domestic living standards followed in 1963, after which the GDR emerged as COMECON's most productive member. Relations with the FRG also improved and diplomatic notes were exchanged in 1967. The GDR, however, remained staunchly pro-Soviet, participating in the 1968 invasion of Czechoslovakia (q.v.) and writing its alliance with the Soviet Union into its constitution in 1974. Nonetheless, in order to reciprocate FRG Ostpolitik and advance détente (qq.v.), the Soviets demanded Ulbricht's replacement in 1971 by Erich Honecker (q.v.).

Honecker concluded the FRG-GDR Basic Agreement in 1972 on de facto mutual recognition. Both states entered the United Nations (UN) (q.v.) in 1973 and signed the Helsinki Final Act (q.v.) in 1975. Honecker also consolidated his position with heavily subsidized consumer programs after November 1971 and attempted high-technology industrialization in 1976. By 1984, however, the GDR was virtually bankrupt, dependent on Western credits, while Honecker refused to initiate reforms demanded by Soviet leader Mikhail Gorbachev (q.v.) in 1987. The Soviets did not intervene against the exodus of GDR citizens westward through the newly opened Hungarian border in summer 1989. Mass demonstrations in Berlin and Leipzig swept Honecker from power on October 18. His successor, Egon Krenz (q.v.), abandoned emigration controls on November 9, and conceded multiparty political participation resulting in the dissolution of the GDR and its formal absorption into the FRG on October 3, 1990.

GERMANY, FEDERAL REPUBLIC OF (FRG). Inaugurated on May 23, 1949, the FRG, more popularly known as West Germany, was formed from nine states (Länder) of the British, French, and American occupation zones of Germany. Quasi-statehood had already emerged under the German economic council, which administered the European Recovery Program (ERP or Marshall Plan) (q.v.) in the Anglo-American Bizone (q.v.), and whose activities provoked the Soviet Berlin Blockade (q.v.) in 1948–1949. The latter merely provided final impetus for West Germany's establishment, and after parliamentary elections in August 1949 Konrad Adenauer (q.v.) became its first federal chancellor. He aligned closely with the United States but also coordinated rapid West German economic recovery with his Western European neighbors, whom he joined in the European Coal and Steel Community (ECSC), and later the European Community (EC) (qq.v.). After the collapse of the European Defense Community (EDC) (q.v.) in 1954, American pressure secured West German rearmament as a member of the North Atlantic Treaty Organization (NATO) (q.v.).

Adenauer also initiated formal relations with the Soviets during his visit to Moscow in September 1955, despite his doctrinaire veto of reunification with the German Democratic Republic (GDR) (q.v.). However, the Hallstein Doctrine (q.v.) impeded West German relations with

Eastern Europe, which were not to improve until Adenauer's resignation in 1963. After 1967 under the guiding influence of Willy Brandt (q.v.) the policy of Ostpolitik (q.v.) sought maximum rapprochement with the Soviet-bloc. A Basic Agreement accorded implicit recognition to the GDR in 1972, permitting both states to enter the United Nations (UN) (q.v.) the next year and to sign the Helsinki Final Act (q.v.) in 1975.

Chancellor Helmut Schmidt (q.v.) subsequently consolidated extensive economic ties with Eastern Europe, while West Germany continued to be the leading Western European industrial economy. Ostpolitik slowed, however, after NATO's decision in 1979 to deploy intermediate-range nuclear forces (INF) (q.v.) on West German soil. Moreover, the latter decision stimulated the emergence of an influential peace movement that was highly critical of West Germany's political links with the United States.

Nonetheless, after October 1982 the new chancellor, Helmut Kohl, persisted in a clearer pro-American course, pushing also for greater European Community integration, while preserving advantageous trade and investment interests in Eastern Europe, mainly through the efforts of Foreign Minister Hans-Dietrich Genscher (q.v.). In 1987 and 1989 West Germany also concluded financial and economic cooperation agreements with the new Soviet leader, Mikhail Gorbachev (q.v.), in return for reduced political controls over the GDR. The latter's collapse in 1989 preceded U.S.-supported negotiations by Kohl with Gorbachev in July 1990 for German unification. A common monetary currency and economic union followed, with a full treaty between the two German states and four Allied powers signed in Moscow on September 12, 1990, permitting the FRG to absorb the GDR on October 3.

GERÖ, ERNÖ (1898–1980). Hungarian communist political leader and first secretary. Gerö reorganized and expanded the Hungarian Communist Party after returning home in December 1944 from exile in the Soviet Union. He served in subsequent postwar coalition governments, dominating the inner circle of the pseudo-popular front Hungarian Working People's Party that brutally imposed a Stalinist system after 1949. In July 1956, at Soviet behest, Gerö was surprisingly appointed first secretary in place of the extreme hardliner Matyas Rakosi (q.v.). Gerö failed, however, in his task of stemming demands for reform and was replaced by the more pragmatic Janos Kadar (q.v.). The 1956 Hungarian Uprising (q.v.) broke out nevertheless, but after it was crushed, Gerö was not rehabilitated. In December 1956, the central committee of the renamed

Hungarian Socialist Workers Party officially blamed misrule by the "Rakosi-Gerö clique" for provoking the rising. Kadar's continuing efforts to establish legitimacy led in August 1962 to formal charges against Cerö, who was stripped of party membership and banished from public life.

GHEORGIU-DEJ, GHEORGHE (1901–1965). Romanian communist political leader and general secretary. In 9144 Gheorgiu-Dej became general secretary of the Romanian Communist Party and energetically expanded his small party via organized labor with promises of radical land reform and advocacy of an antifascist popular front. The latter successfully excluded important centrist and conservative rivals such as the National Peasants Party from politics after 1947. The communists also merged with the socialists to form the Romanian Workers' Party, and in 1948 swept rigged elections to secure complete power. A Soviet-style planned economy, collective farms, and security organs were in place by March 1949, with Gheorgiu-Dej's position thereafter reinforced by repeated purges. He avoided Soviet desalinization mandates in 1955 and 1956 by temporarily resigning the party leadership, but he maintained power through a closed circle of accomplices, including Nicolae Ceausescu (q.v.), who succeeded him after his death in March 1965.

GIAP, VO NGUYEN (1912–). North Vietnamese general and minister of defense. From a peasant background, Giap studied law and jointed the Communist Party during 1930s. He became the commander of the Vietminh (q.v.) forces and in 1945 liberated Hanoi from the Japanese. A master of guerrilla warfare and a brilliant planner and tactician, Giap succeeded in constantly outmaneuvering the French forces during the Indochina War (q.v.) and achieved a celebrated military success at Dien Bien Phu (q.v.) in 1954. His meticulous planning and long-term guerrilla strategy were in evidence during the Vietnam War (q.v.) and resulted in victory over the American and South Vietnamese forces. Giap served as defense minister of the Democratic Republic of Vietnam from 1945 to 1980.

GIEREK, EDWARD (1913–2001). Polish communist political leader and first secretary. Gierek had a reputation as an able economic planner and was suddenly appointed first secretary in December 1970 after a wave of industrial strikes had swept Wladyslaw Gomulka (q.v.) from power. Gierek appeased strikers' delegates with domestic price controls, followed by liberalizing reforms in agriculture and the state security apparatus. He promoted "socialist revival," cultivating youth organizations and the educational and scientific sectors as agencies for the projected technical modernization of the Polish economy. This was financed mainly by credits from France and the Federal Republic of Germany (FRG) (qq.v.), accompanied by a trade agreement with the United States and heavy borrowing from Western banks. The global recession that struck in 1974 resulted in the imposition of an austerity program in 1976 that provoked renewed polish labor unrest. Gierek tried to preempt wider political dissent by effecting a reconciliation with the influential Roman Catholic Church. However, the visit in 1979 of the Polish pope, John Paul II (q.v.), merely provoked further dissidence. Faced with a $15 billion hard currency debt and declining national income in 1980, Gierek raised state economic productivity norms and increased food prices. Resulting strikes were coordinated throughout Poland (q.v.) by what was to become the independent trade union, Solidarity (q.v.). As Poland's crisis deepened, in September 1980 Gierek was replaced as first secretary by Stanislaw Kania.

GLASNOST. Soviet political term meaning "openness" or "frankness" promulgated in February 1986 by Mikhail Gorbachev (q.v.) to imply the tolerance of criticism of the Soviet Union's shortcomings as the prelude to perestroika (q.v.). Initially limited to literary censorship, glasnost was extended after the Chernobyl nuclear disaster in 1986 to include public discussion of social taboos such as drug and alcohol abuse and prostitution. In 1987 poor living standards, inadequate public services, and corruption were exposed, culminating in a Politburo historical commission to inquire into repression by Joseph Stalin (q.v.), which the Soviet authorities had always denied. Under glasnost, "neformaly," i.e., left-wing discussion groups outside the Communist Party, were tolerated after harsh repression in the 1930s. As the pace of restructuring accelerated, many such groups coalesced into "popular front" opposition groups, particularly in the non-Russian Soviet republics. By 1990 the mounting intensity of their criticisms was providing the momentum not only for reform but the very disintegration of the Soviet Union itself.

GLASSBORO "MINI-SUMMIT," 1967. A meeting between the American president, Lyndon Johnson (q.v.), and the Soviet prime minister, Alexei Kosygin (q.v.), held at Glassboro State College, New Jersey, June 23–25, 1967. Taking advantage of the Soviet premier's visit to New York to attend a special session of the United Nations (UN) (q.v.), Johnson invited Kosygin to a personal meeting. A small campus town was chosen as the venue because Kosygin refused to come to Washington so long as the United States was engaged in the Vietnam War (q.v.). Few preparations were made for the "mini-summit" and this was reflected in its lack of substance. However, the fact that the superpower leaders could actually meet and discuss international affairs was regarded as a constructive and hopeful indication that the tensions in the Cold War were easing. The good feeling did not last for very long. Johnson was scheduled to return Kosygin's visit by going to the Soviet Union in October 1968, but he canceled this arrangement as a protest against the Soviet military intervention in Czechoslovakia (q.v.) in August 1968.

GOMULKA, WLADYSLAW (1905–1982). Polish communist political leader and first secretary. Gomulka escaped through German lines in August 1944 to join the Lublin Committee (q.v.) and led the reformed Polish Workers' Party in Nazi-occupied Poland (q.v.). He then served as minister for "recovered territories," supervising the expulsion of the German population from east of the Oder-Neisse Line (q.v.). Although deputy premier, he was eclipsed politically by the Stalinist Boleslaw Bierut (q.v.). Indeed, having advocated a "Polish road to socialism" Gomulka was purged as a deviationist in 1949, jailed from 1952 to 1954, and not reinstated until 1956. After months of Polish labor unrest and demands for political reform, he was appointed party first secretary during the visit to Warsaw in October 1956 by the Soviet leader Nikita Khrushchev (q.v.).

Gomulka began by dismissing Defense Minister Konstantin Rokossovsky (q.v.), rehabilitating church leaders, abolishing collective farms, recognizing workers' councils in industrial management, and renegotiating Red Army occupation rights to preclude political interventions. Having at first relaxed censorship, Gomulka was gradually to reimpose party disciplines. He sought Western economic support, but remained intractably hostile to the Federal Republic of Germany (FRG) and its Ostpolitik (qq.v.). Disappointing Polish economic performance in the mid-1960s was also accompanied by the renewed repression of political critics and by anti-Semitic policies disguised as anti-Zionism. Gomulka failed, however, to contain popular discontent and after violent police tactics failed to break strikes in the industrial cities of Szczecin, Gdynia, and Gdansk, he was removed by his party Politburo in December 1970.

GORBACHEV, MIKHAIL (1931–). Soviet statesman and general secretary. Gorbachev gained full Politburo membership in 1980 and attracted the favor of Yuri Andropov (q.v.). Subsequently, Gorbachev emerged as a prime mover in Andropov's attempted political and administrative reforms, and as his heir apparent, although he was forestalled in the latter role by Konstantin Chernenko (q.v.) after Andropov's death in February 1984. Chernenko's death on March 10, 1985, however, cleared Gorbachev's path to power and he soon promoted sympathetic younger officials, including Foreign Minister Eduard Shevardnadze (q.v.), so that by 1988, two-thirds of the Politburo's members had been replaced.

After the 27th Soviet Communist Party Congress in early 1986, Gorbachev attempted to liberate Soviet economic potential from the stultifying influence of the "nomenklatura," the entrenched party bureaucracy through the processes of glasnost and perestroika (qq.v.). A prerequisite of economic invigoration was to release scarce capital assets from the military-industrial sector without a palpable loss of military security vis-à-vis the West. Gorbachev therefore renewed détente (q.v.), beginning in September 1985 in a summit meeting in Geneva with President Ronald Reagan (q.v.). The later 1986 Reykjavik Summit (q.v.) opened up opportunities for increasingly ambitious arms control agreements resulting in the 1987 Intermediate-range Nuclear Forces (INF) (q.v.) Treaty, in 1988 the revival of Strategic Arms Reduction Talks (START) (q.v.), and the 1990 Conventional Forces in Europe (CFE) Treaty (q.v.). In 1989 Gorbachev withdrew Soviet forces from Afghanistan (q.v.) while reducing aid levels to Third World allies whose activities aggravated the Reagan Doctrine (q.v.). Western approval was also elicited by relaxing domestic Soviet repression, for example in November 1986 with the release from internal exile of the leading dissident Andrei Sakharov (q.v.).

Obdurate resistance to perestroika nevertheless compelled Gorbachev to assume an executive presidency in 1988, reducing Communist Party powers in favor of a standing legislature, elected by multicandidate ballot in spring 1989. Liberalization, however, unleashed powerful latent discontents among workers and non-Russian Soviet nationalities. In May 1989 an aid agreement with the Federal Republic of Germany (FRG) (q.v.) diverted attention from domestic issues but at the expense of relaxing the Brezhnev Doctrine (q.v.) to such an extent that by the end of the year communism in Eastern Europe had collapsed. The decisive abrogation of Soviet military power in the CFE Treaty (q.v.) led the North Atlantic Treaty Organization (NATO) (q.v.) to declare the Cold War officially over in December 1990, leaving Gorbachev to face overwhelming domestic challenges. Inevitable concessions eroded communist power further, alienating many of Gorbachev's most trusted associates and precipitating a coup in August 1991 which resulted in his resignation as general secretary. Despite the failure of his domestic reforms, Gorbachev was arguably the person most responsible for ending the Cold War.

GORSHKOV, SERGEI (1910–1988). Soviet admiral. Although appointed commander-in-chief of the Soviet Navy by Nikita Khrushchev (q.v.) in 1956 to retrench the service, Gorshkov preserved the core of the major surface fleet formed under Joseph Stalin (q.v.) after World War II. The fleet was expanded under Leonid Brezhnev (q.v.) into a service capable of counterfleet sea-denial and antisubmarine operations in every U.S. Navy theater and also contributed submarine-launched missiles to Soviet strategic nuclear forces. The Soviet Navy achieved political parity with land forces and the Strategic Rocket Forces (q.v.) in 1967. It held coordinated global exercises in 1970 and 1975 and provided vital support to the increasing number of Soviet Third World ventures in the 1970s. Gorshkov's 1976 book, *The Sea Power of the State*, entered the Soviet strategic canon. But the huge costs of sea power, including a fleet carrier program, were seen as prohibitive by Mikhail Gorbachev (q.v.), who forced Gorshkov's retirement in 1985. Having achieved unprecedented status under Gorshkov, the Soviet Navy soon entered a period of irreversible decline.

GOTTWALD, KLEMENT (1896–1953). Czechoslovak communist political leader and president. Gottwald headed the Moscow-based Czechoslovak Committee of National Resistance during World War II and was installed as deputy premier in the National Front government of Eduard Benes (q.v.) at Soviet behest in 1945. Gottwald successfully revived the Czechoslovak Communist Party whose electoral success in May 1946 preceded his appointment by President Benes as prime minister. He used his position to extend communist influence in the police, armed forces, and local Czechoslovak national councils. He also enacted orders from Joseph Stalin (q.v.) in 1947 to prevent Czechoslovak participation in the European Recovery Program (ERP or Marshall Plan) (q.v.). Declining communist popularity in late 1947 led Gottwald to plan the February 1948 communist seizure of power in Czechoslovakia (q.v.).

In June 1948 Gottwald became president, having forced Benes to resign for refusing to sign a new constitution establishing state and communist party controls over political and economic life. During the next three years successive purges transformed the civil apparatus and national councils into instruments of communist power. In 1949, Czechoslovakia joined the Council for Mutual Economic Assistance (COMECON) (q.v.) and adopted a Soviet-style five-year plan, which was almost wholly changed two years later to conform with Stalin's military production targets during the Korean War (q.v.). The resulting economic chaos was accompanied by another purge that included Gottwald's close collaborators Ludvig Svoboda and Rudolf Slansky (qq.v.). Ironically, having loyally built Stalin a satellite state, Gottwald died from pneumonia contracted during his attendance at the Soviet dictator's funeral ceremony in March 1953.

GREAT BRITAIN. A Western European power which played a leading role in the Cold War. Along with the United States and the Soviet Union, Great Britain was a member of the "Big Three" wartime alliance that defeated Nazi Germany in World War II. Britain's high prestige and influence in world affairs was symbolized by its wartime leader, Winston Churchill (q.v.) and its prominent role at the Potsdam Conference (q.v.) and at the postwar meetings of foreign ministers, and its permanent membership of the Security Council of the United Nations (UN) (q.v.).

As one of the four powers occupying Germany, Britain was instrumental in cooperating with the United States to defeat the Berlin Blockade (q.v.) and bring about the establishment of the German Federal Republic (FRG) (q.v.). British diplomacy also advocated the containment (q.v.) of communism in Europe and urged the United States to devise a program of economic assistance that became known as the Marshall Plan (q.v.). Although Britain developed and retained its own independent nuclear forces, it promoted the creation of a military alliance to protect Western Europe. This was exemplified in Britain's leading role in the formation of the Brussels Pact and the North Atlantic Treaty Organization (NATO) (qq.v.).

In contrast to the United States and the Soviet Union, Britain lacked the massive economic and material resources to claim the status of a superpower. The Cold War marked, therefore, a period of relative decline for Britain. This was evident in its loss of overseas colonies and its displacement by the superpowers as the preeminent regional power in the Middle East and Africa. The 1956 Suez Crisis (q.v.) was particularly destructive for British prestige in the Arab world. In the 1960s Britain turned increasingly toward Europe and eventually joined the European Community (EC) (q.v.) in 1973. However, British influence in the wider world remained considerable for historic reasons and because Britain enjoyed a special relationship with the United States. The Anglo-American alliance was a major feature of the Cold War and was exemplified in postwar cooperation to rebuild Western Europe, as allies in the Korean War (q.v.), and the close working relationship between President

Ronald Reagan (q.v.) and the British prime minister, Margaret Thatcher (q.v.).

GRECHKO, ANDREI (1903–1976). Soviet general and minister of defense. Grechko served with distinction in the same World War II theater of operations as Nikita Khrushchev and Leonid Brezhnev (qq.v.), both of whom helped to revive and advance his career after the death of Joseph Stalin (q.v.) in 1953. He successively commanded Soviet forces in Germany, Soviet land forces, and Warsaw Pact (q.v.) forces before becoming defense minister in 1967 and a Politburo member in 1972. Although a supporter of détente (q.v.), Grechko supervised a sustained increase and modernization of Soviet military power. His budget exceeded that of the United States after 1971 and was devoted to strategic and intermediate-range nuclear forces (INFs) (q.v.), naval forces, and conventional forces in Europe. He also planned the 1968 invasion of Czechoslovakia (q.v.). By the time of his death in 1976 Grechko had advanced the Soviet Union to an unprecedented position of military comparability with its main rival, the United States, although in a manner that produced alarmist reactions and a subsequent deterioration of East-West relations.

GREEK CIVIL WAR, 1944–1949. A civil conflict which prompted the enunciation of the Truman Doctrine (q.v.) in 1947. German military occupation of Greece during World War II had provoked local guerrilla resistance organized by the procommunist National Liberation Front (Ethnikon Apeleftherotikon Metopon or EAM) and the pro-Western National Democratic Greek Union. After Germany's withdrawal in 1944, civil war erupted between the two factions. Great Britain (q.v.), the traditional great power in the region, was able to bring about a temporary peace in 1945, but the EAM renewed hostilities in October 1946 with encouragement from the neighboring communist regimes of Yugoslavia, Bulgaria, and Albania (qq.v.). In February 1947 the British government secretly informed the Truman administration that it could no longer afford to sustain a substantial economic and military role in Greece.

American officials believed that the EAM was an instrument of communist aggression and was part of a conspiracy masterminded from Moscow to gain control of the Eastern Mediterranean. President Harry Truman subsequently announced the Truman Doctrine (qq.v.) and secured appropriations from the U.S. Congress to dispatch American military supplies and advisers to aid the Greek government against the EAM. The fighting continued until 1949 when a compromise peace was arranged.

The Greek Civil War was an important event in the beginning of the Cold War. American officials interpreted it as part of a communist plot against the West and concluded that assistance was essential to save Greece from communism. Joseph Stalin (q.v.), however, refrained from direct military intervention and thereby cast doubt upon the argument that he was intent upon imposing a communist regime upon Greece.

GRENADA INVASION. A small island in the Caribbean that gained significance in the Cold War as a result of American military intervention in 1983. In October 1983 President Ronald Reagan (q.v.) dispatched more than 7,000 American troops to overthrow the Marxist government and take control of Grenada. This was the first overt instance of direct American military intervention in Latin America since 1965 when President Lyndon Johnson (q.v.) had ordered an invasion of the Dominican Republic (q.v.). Like Johnson, Reagan argued that intervention was necessary to defeat the forces of communism who were attempting to establish a Soviet-Cuban colony that would be used as a military base to export terrorism and undermine democracy throughout the western hemisphere. The Reagan administration also insisted that the operation was not an "invasion" but a "rescue mission" designed to stop an unfriendly government from carrying out a plan to provoke a potential hostage crisis by seizing a group of American medical students resident on the island.

The exact reason for the intervention remained uncertain, but critics were effectively disarmed by its rapid success. Moreover, in keeping with his confrontational style, Reagan demonstrated his determination to uphold the Reagan Doctrine (q.v.) by acting vigorously against perceived communist threats in the Caribbean area.

GROMYKO, ANDREI (1909–1989). Soviet statesman and foreign minister. Gromyko's career began as an economist before he was transferred to the foreign ministry. He became Soviet ambassador to the United States in 1943 and served on the staff of the Teheran, Yalta, and Potsdam Conferences (qq.v.) and the Council of Foreign Ministers (CFM) (q.v.). Gromyko was the permanent Soviet representative at the United Nations (UN) (q.v.) from 1946 to 1948, achieving a reputation for tactical astuteness but ideologically reliable diplomacy. However, his upward rise was interrupted briefly in 1952 when he was shunted sideways as ambassador to London by Andrei Vyshinsky (q.v.).

After Joseph Stalin's (q.v.) death in 1953 Gromyko was restored as deputy foreign minister and then promoted to foreign minister in February 1957. A decade later he emerged as a realistic proponent of détente (q.v.) and in 1972 was promoted to the Soviet Politburo alongside his political allies, Andrei Grechko and Yuri Andropov (qq.v.). Subsequently, his attitude of inscrutable calculation of Soviet state interests produced inveterate skepticism and recrimination in dealings with the assertive administrations of Jimmy Carter and Ronald Reagan (qq.v.). Although Gromyko supported the selection of Mikhail Gorbachev (q.v.) as general secretary of the Soviet Communist Party in 1985, he was moved to the largely ceremonial post of Soviet president, clearing the way for Soviet-U.S. rapprochement. Gromyko retired as Soviet president in 1988.

GROSZ, KAROLI (1930–1996). Hungarian communist political leader and general secretary. While secretary of the Budapest Hungarian Socialist Workers' Party, Grosz emerged as an economic critic of Janos Kadar (q.v.) at the 13th party congress in 1985. Appointed prime minister in June 1987 he was charged with realizing fiscal and limited free-market reforms and abolishing domestic price controls. Grosz forced Kadar to accept similarly reform-minded colleagues as members of an expanded 20-member ruling executive in February 1988, and in May at an extraordinary party conference replaced Kadar as general secretary. Grosz soon extended policies of "socialist pluralism," expanding the nonstate economic sector, tolerating independent labor unions, advocating economic debate outside the party, and in November 1988 discussing multiparty Hungarian politics.

In March 1989 Grosz was assured by Mikhail Gorbachev (q.v.) in Moscow that the Brezhnev Doctrine (q.v.) would not be asserted in Hungary, but he soon found himself outpaced by more radical Hungarian reformers. An officially approved Opposition Roundtable was formed in August 1989, which negotiated for transition to multiparty democracy. Marxism-Leninism was denounced soon after, but in the 1990 elections the renamed Hungarian Socialist Party nevertheless lost to the liberal Democratic Forum, after which Grosz retired from politics.

GROTEWOHL, OTTO (1894–1964). East German socialist political leader and prime minister. Grotewohl was the leader of the Social Democratic Party in the Soviet occupation zone of Germany after May 1945. However, he joined an antifascist coalition with the communists that led to a rift with the Social Democratic Party in the British, French, and American zones. Grotewohl aligned himself closer with the communists and in March 1946 assumed joint chairmanship of the combined Socialist Unity Party. The latter party's association with the Soviet-sponsored administration in Eastern Germany undermined Grotewohl's hope that it could thrive as a nationally popular party. Indeed, as Allied differences on the formation of a single German state became intractable, the Socialist Unity Party was incrementally remodeled to conform to the Soviet communist model. A centrally dominant Politburo was created in January 1949, which assumed quasi-governmental functions over what by October 1949 had become the German Democratic Republic (GDR) (q.v.). Grotewohl became GDR prime minister, although the real power lay with the party bureaucracy under its general secretary, Walter Ulbricht (q.v.). Grotewohl, nevertheless, legitimized the Socialist Unity Party's popular front pretensions and he remained in office until his death in September 1964.

GRU (GLAVNOYE RAZVEDYVATELNOYE UPRAVLENIE). The Soviet military intelligence service that was set up in July 1940 and was initially responsible for signals intelligence (SIGINT). GRU field operations were largely circumscribed by rival bodies within the state security apparatus, although it was highly successful in intelligence gathering against Germany during World War II. Furthermore, from 1958 to 1963 it infiltrated the leading U.S. SIGINT body, the National Security Agency (NSA). Nevertheless, the GRU generally remained a specialized junior partner to the KGB (q.v.), maintaining listening stations in the People's Democratic Republic of Yemen, Cuba (qq.v.), and Vietnam, and operating in support of Soviet forces and advisers in Ethiopia and Afghanistan (qq.v.). After 1981, the GRU also took part alongside the KGB in "Operation Ryan," a global espionage project to discern the likelihood of a preemptive American nuclear first strike (q.v.).

GUATEMALA. A country in Central America that was a focal point of the Cold War during the early 1950s when the Eisenhower (q.v.) administration became concerned by reports of the infiltration of local communists into influential positions in the government of President Jacobo Arbenz (q.v.). Communists were also regarded as instigating the attempts by Arbenz to confiscate land owned by the Boston-based United Fruit Company, the biggest landowner in Guatemala. Fearing that a Soviet satellite state would be created in Central America, President Dwight Eisenhower instructed the Central Intelligence Agency (CIA) (q.v.) to prepare a covert operation to remove Arbenz from power. A small army of Guatemalan political exiles was subsequently recruited, equipped, and trained in Honduras.

In June 1954 a force numbering just over 200 under the command of Colonel Castillo Armas entered Guatemala, and though no significant fighting took place, President Arbenz was persuaded to resign and leave the country. The pro-American Castillo Armas became president. The role of the CIA had been a significant factor in the success of the coup and the experience later emboldened the agency to attempt a similar operation against Fidel Castro in Cuba (qq.v.). This proved, however, much more complex and failed at the Bay of Pigs (q.v.) in April 1961.

GUEVARA, ERNESTO "CHÉ" (1928–1967). Marxist revolutionary hero and guerrilla fighter. Despite his close identification with Cuba and the Cuban Revolution (qq.v.), Guevara was born in Rosario, Argentina. After completing a medical degree at the University of Buenos Aires, he traveled to Guatemala (q.v.) in 1954 and was present during the Central Intelligence Agency's (CIA) (q.v.) operation that overthrew President Jacobo Arbenz (q.v.). Guevara met Fidel Castro (q.v.) in Mexico in 1955 and became one of Castro's closest aides in the struggle to overthrow Fulgencio Batista (q.v.). His Cuban colleagues called him by the nickname of "Ché," an Argentinian term for "buddy."

When Fidel Castro came to power in 1959 he appointed Guevara as minister of industry. Ill-suited to administration and determined to promote armed revolution overseas, Guevara soon gave up governmental office. After spending a short period training guerrilla forces in the Congo in 1965, he returned to South America in 1966 and attempted to organize a guerrilla movement in Bolivia. In 1967 he was captured by Bolivian troops and executed. Guevara's grave was discovered in 1997 and his remains were brought back to be enshrined in Cuba. Despite his failure to arouse popular support for the national liberation movement in Bolivia, "Ché" Guevara acquired legendary status and an international reputation for personal heroism and great skill in conducting guerrilla warfare.

-H-

HAIG, ALEXANDER M., Jr. (1924–). American general and secretary of state. Haig was a career army officer with service in Korea, Europe, and Vietnam before joining the Nixon (q.v.) administration in 1969 as military adviser to Henry Kissinger (q.v.). Haig's administrative skills and experience of military affairs secured his rapid promotion to assistant national security adviser in 1970 and White House chief of staff in 1973. Shortly after President Richard Nixon's resignation in 1974 Haig became supreme allied commander in Europe. Unlike Dwight Eisenhower (q.v.), however, Haig was not able to use this post as a springboard to the American presidency. In 1981 Haig was appointed secretary of state in the Reagan (q.v.) administration. As secretary of state, he advocated a vigorous American response to what he perceived to be Soviet meddling in the Third World especially in El Salvador (q.v.). In the process Haig sought to assert the authority of the State Department in the making of American foreign policy. The result, however, was disagreement with President Ronald Reagan and Haig's resignation in 1982. Haig's career provided an example of the close relationship between the American military and government during the Cold War.

HALLSTEIN DOCTRINE. Foreign policy principle of the Federal Republic of Germany (FRG) (q.v.) that was devised by the deputy foreign minister, Walter Hallstein, and announced by his superior, Heinrich Von Brentano in December 1955. The Hallstein Doctrine declared that the FRG would not have diplomatic relations with states recognizing the German Democratic Republic (GDR) (q.v.). The purpose was to deprive the GDR of international legitimacy, but the principal effect was to preclude FRG relations with Eastern Europe, although Chancellor Konrad Adenauer (q.v.) had already established diplomatic links with the Soviet Union during his visit to Moscow in September 1955. The latter were maintained, although the Hallstein Doctrine impeded further reconciliation until its displacement in the late 1960s by the more pragmatic Ostpolitik (q.v.).

HAMMARSKJÖLD, DAG (1905–1961). Swedish statesman and secretary-general of the United Nations (UN) (q.v.). Hammarskjöld held various financial and diplomatic posts in the Swedish government before he was considered for the post of secretary-general of the UN in April 1953. His Scandinavian nationality made him an acceptable compromise choice and helped him to secure reelection in 1957. Hammarskjöld proved, however, to be an active executive and expanded the role and authority of his office. In an attempt to fulfill the aims of the UN Charter and help to resolve international crises, he was willing to travel all over the world.

While stressing the diplomatic role of the UN, Hammarskjöld also sought to enhance its peacekeeping function. Especially successful was the dispatch of a UN Expeditionary Force to supervise the aftermath of the Suez Crisis (q.v.) in 1956. More controversial, was the involvement of UN military forces in the Congo (q.v.) during which the Soviet Union accused Hammarskjöld of pro-Western bias. In September 1961 he was killed in a plane crash in the Congo (Zaire). Hammarskjöld's tenure of office as secretary-general represented the high point of UN influence in world affairs. However, this had alarmed the great powers who used his death in 1961 to ensure that the authority and powers of future secretaries-general would be limited.

HARRIMAN, W. AVERELL (1891–1986). American financier and diplomat. Harriman inherited a large fortune in railroad and banking interests and chose to enter politics as a Democrat and to hold office in the Roosevelt (q.v.) administration. From 1943 to 1946 he served as American ambassador to the Soviet Union and was one of the advisers who influenced Harry Truman (q.v.) to adopt the policy of containment (q.v.). Harriman was elected governor of New York from 1955 to 1958, but a heavy electoral defeat in 1958 effectively ended his ambitions for state political office.

In 1961, at the age of 70, Harriman joined the Kennedy (q.v.) administration as assistant secretary of state for Far Eastern affairs. During the Johnson (q.v.) administration he acted as an ambassador-at-large. In fact, Lyndon Johnson regarded Harriman's advanced age as an advantage because it denoted vast diplomatic experience and personal acquaintance with many of the world's leaders. In 1968 Harriman headed the American delegation at the Paris Peace Talks with North Vietnam (q.v.). Although Harriman never achieved the highest diplomatic office, he provides an example of a distinguished member of the "eastern establishment" who enjoyed access to and influence with several American presidents.

HAVEL, VACLAV (1936–). Czechoslovak author, playwright, and president. A youthful dissident in the Czechoslovak Writers' Union, Havel campaigned against literary censorship and jointly authored the petition that germinated Charter 77 (q.v.). After his release from prison in April 1978 he helped found VONS (Vybor na Obranu Nespravedlive Stilhangch), a civil rights pressure group, which assumed a prominent role in the Czechoslovak underground political opposition movement. Havel was persistently harassed and imprisoned by the communist authorities between 1978 and 1989, but continued political campaigning. During the 1989 Czechoslovakian "velvet revolution" (q.v.), he was acclaimed as leader of Civic Forum, the umbrella opposition organization that negotiated the transfer of power from the communist regime of Milos Jakes (q.v.). Havel became Czechoslovak president in December 1989 and was confirmed in his position by free elections in June 1990.

HELMS, RICHARD M. (1913–2002). American intelligence officer and director of the Central Intelligence Agency (CIA) (q.v.). Helms pursued a career in secret intelligence first in the Office of Strategic Services (OSS) during World War II and afterward in the CIA. Helms proved to be an outstanding spymaster and efficient bureaucrat who rose to be director of the CIA in 1966. His period as director, however, coincided with growing public criticism of the CIA that resulted in a series of Congressional investigations. Ironically, it was Helms's insistence on distancing the CIA from Richard Nixon's (q.v.) attempt to cover up the Watergate scandal that resulted in his dismissal in 1973. As part of the Congressional backlash against the "imperial presidency," Helms was convicted in 1977 of lying to the Senate four years earlier in hearings on American attempts to overthrow the government of Salvador Allende (q.v.) in Chile. The public disgrace of Helms was an example of the collapse of the Cold War "consensus" which had allowed the president of the United States to use the CIA as his own personal instrument of foreign policy.

HELSINKI FINAL ACT, 1975. Agreement which instituted the Conference on Security and Cooperation in Europe (CSCE) (q.v.) on August 1, 1975, signed by the United States, Canada, and all the European states except Albania (q.v.). It was considered the crowning achievement of détente (q.v.). The "Helsinki process" began in November 1972, stemming from earlier Soviet proposals for an all-European security body. The Final Act recognized Europe's post-1945 borders, included both of the German states, mandated the peaceful resolution of disputes, affirmed human rights, renounced terrorism, and reaffirmed the rule of international law between the signatories. Moreover, advance written notice was to be given of military maneuvers, with observers to be exchanged during the latter, and channels for mutual and balanced force reductions (MBFR) (q.v.) were to be opened. The latter confidence-building measures, however, were to bear little fruit as East-West arms control discussions petered out in the early 1980s. Having remained dormant, the "Helsinki process" provided Mikhail Gorbachev (q.v.) with a means by which he pursued rapprochement with the West after 1985.

HENDERSON, LOY W. (1892–1986). American diplomat. Henderson was a colleague of Charles Bohlen and George Kennan (qq.v.); all of whom served in the Soviet Union prior to World War II and drew negative conclusions on the nature and intentions of the Soviet regime. Henderson served as an expert adviser during the visit to Moscow in August 1942 of Winston Churchill and W. Averell Harriman (qq.v.), but was later reassigned at Soviet behest away from inter-Allied relations. He became American ambassador to Iraq in 1943 and subsequently director of the State Department's Division of Near Eastern Affairs. In this capacity he helped formulate policies of confrontation with the Soviets over the 1946 Azerbaijan Crisis, Turkey, and the Greek Civil War (qq.v.) and drafted the aid program justified by the Truman Doctrine (q.v.) in 1947.

Henderson notably dissented with Truman's pro-Zionist policy and was moved in 1948 to the post of American ambassador to India. However, he quarreled with Prime Minister Jawaharlal Nehru (q.v.) when the latter recognized the People's Republic of China (PRC) (q.v.) and in late 1951 he was transferred to Iran (q.v.) where he helped overthrow Mohammed Mossadegh (q.v.) in August 1953, before returning to Washington, D.C., as deputy undersecretary of state. He retired in 1961.

HERTER, CHRISTIAN A. (1895–1966). American diplomat and secretary of state. Herter entered the foreign service during World War I. After serving in the Harding and Coolidge administrations Herter became a newspaper editor until he was elected as a Republican congressman for Massachusetts from 1943 to 1953 and governor of Massachusetts from 1953 to 1957. While in Congress he backed the bipartisan approach to foreign affairs by leading a delegation to Europe that issued a report in favor of the Marshall Plan (q.v.). In 1957 Herter was appointed under secretary of state and became secretary of state on the death of John Foster Dulles (q.v.) in 1959, a position he held until the end of the Eisenhower (q.v.) administration in 1961. Herter stressed the need for closer ties between the United States and Western Europe. His attempt to improve relations with the Soviet Union was upset, however, by the U-2 (q.v.) incident in 1960.

HILSMAN, ROGER (1919–). American diplomat. Hilsman served with the Office of Strategic Services (OSS) in Burma during World War II. After the war he became a professor of international relations at Princeton University. In 1961 he joined the Kennedy (q.v.) administration as the director of the State Department's Bureau of Intelligence and Research and was promoted in 1963 to assistant secretary of state for Far Eastern affairs. Initially Hilsman was a staunch advocate of counterinsurgency in Vietnam. By 1964, however, his views began to change and he left the Johnson (q.v.) administration. Instead of escalating the war in Vietnam, Hilsman argued for de-escalation of American military involvement and the gradual transfer of the burden of fighting the war to the South Vietnamese. These ideas were expressed in an article published in the journal, *Foreign Affairs*, in 1968 that were influential in shaping the policy of Vietnamization which was adopted by the Nixon (q.v.) administration to end the Vietnam War (q.v.).

HISS, ALGER (1904–1996). American diplomat and communist spy. Hiss was a prominent New Deal liberal who served in the Roosevelt (q.v.) administration in various capacities including the State Department. In 1945 he accompanied President Franklin Roosevelt to the Yalta Conference (q.v.) and acted as secretary-general of the San Francisco conference that organized the United Nations (UN) (q.v.). After leaving the State Department he became president of the Carnegie Endowment for International Peace. In 1948, a senior editor of *Time* magazine, Whittaker Chambers, testified before the House Un-American Activities Committee (HUAC) (q.v.) that he and Hiss had been secret members of a communist spy ring in Washington during the 1930s. The charge seemed preposterous and was vehemently denied by Hiss. Chambers, however, later provided evidence in the form of microfilm of classified material from State Department documents. The statute of limitations prevented Hiss from being tried for espionage, but he was eventually convicted of perjury in 1950 and sentenced to five years in prison.

The Hiss case occurred at a time when the American public was greatly alarmed by the threat of international Communism. Indeed, the revelations made by Chambers appeared to confirm the suspicion of a communist conspiracy directed at the United States and added credibility to the charges against the State Department made by Senator Joseph McCarthy (q.v.). Although Hiss constantly protested his innocence, contemporary opinion generally regarded him as guilty. A principal beneficiary was the congressman from California, Richard Nixon (q.v.), who, as a member of the House Un-American Activities Committee, had been a leading figure in pursuing the investigation of Hiss. Nixon was keen to appear as a tough anticommunist and opponent of the Soviet Union. The publicity attaching to the Hiss case aided Nixon's political rise, but it also earned him the everlasting enmity of leading Democratic politicians.

HO CHI MINH (1890–1969). North Vietnamese communist leader and president. Ho's real name was Nguyen Tat Thanh; however, he adopted a number of aliases to conceal his identity, and in 1942 eventually fixed upon Ho Chi Minh. As a student Ho traveled to Europe and lived in Paris from 1917 to 1924. A dedicated communist, he was one of the original members of the French Communist Party in 1920 and later founded the Indochinese Communist Party in 1930.

When Japan (q.v.) occupied Indochina in 1941, Ho returned to Vietnam and became the political leader of the Vietminh (q.v.). After Japan's surrender in 1945, the Vietminh seized power in Hanoi and proclaimed the Democratic Republic of Vietnam with Ho Chi Minh as president. Although Ho was determined to create a communist society in Vietnam, he was also a Vietnamese nationalist. He was regarded, therefore, not only as the leader but also the symbol and inspiration of the Vietnamese struggle for national liberation from French colonial rule and later from American imperialism. Ho died in 1969 before the end of the Vietnam War (q.v.), but his memory was perpetuated in the renaming of Saigon as Ho Chi Minh City.

HONECKER, ERICH (1912–1994). East German communist political leader and general secretary. After being liberated from Nazi imprisonment by the Red Army, Honecker became leader of the Free German Youth, which subsequently became the youth movement of the German Democratic Republic (GDR) (q.v.). In 1950, Honecker entered the Central Committee of the GDR's ruling Socialist Unity Party. He was promoted to its Politburo in 1958 and replaced Walter Ulbricht (q.v.) as general secretary in 1971 after the latter had resisted Soviet-mandated détente (q.v.). Honecker concluded the 1972 Basic Agreement with the Federal Republic of Germany (FRG) (q.v.), secured GDR membership of the United Nations (UN) (q.v.) in 1973, and signed the Helsinki Final Act in 1975 (q.v.).

In domestic affairs Honecker declared the "unity of economic and social policy," meaning an attempt to construct a model communist society as a tenable alternative to the capitalist FRG. Material advancements did accrue from attempted industrial modernization, but the rigid structures of the Socialist Unity Party and expansive state security apparatus also remained. Amid global recession in the early 1980s, the Soviets also ended subsidies and Honecker was forced in 1983 to seek Western credits, brokered ironically by the FRG. He, nevertheless, resisted pressure for structural reform and in April 1987 openly denounced glasnost and perestroika, then being pursued in the Soviet Union by Mikhail Gorbachev (qq.v.). In September 1987, while visiting the FRG, Honecker also pronounced the division of Germany to be permanent. He was, therefore, isolated from the current of political change evident in Eastern Europe in 1989 and was forced to resign on October 18 by his own Politburo after irrepressible mass public demonstrations for change in Berlin and Leipzig. After the collapse of the GDR he was evacuated to Moscow to avoid FRG prosecution and then sought political exile in Chile.

HORN OF AFRICA. Geo-strategic expression for the region comprising Eritrea, Ethiopia (q.v.), Somalia (q.v.), and Djibouti, which dominates access to the Red Sea, the Gulf of Aden, and the Eastern Indian Ocean. Soviet diplomatic gains in Somalia after 1969 and Ethiopia in 1974 raised American fears for the security of adjacent oil shipment routes. In July 1977, however, war between Somalia and Ethiopia over the disputed province of Ogaden pushed Somalia into the American orbit. Having identified the Horn of Africa as the southern tip of an "arc of crisis" stretching through the Middle East, the United States prepared for possible military intervention by securing the use of port facilities in Somalia in return for arms. Meanwhile, the Soviets reinforced Ethiopia with arms and advisers from the German Democratic Republic (GDR) and Cuba (qq.v.), although the latter were soon more concerned with containing the domestic enemies of Ethiopia's Marxist leader Haile Mariam Mengistu (q.v.). Simmering subnational and ethnic armed conflict throughout the 1980s inhibited both superpowers from deeper intervention in the region. Superpower rivalry ended in 1987 when Mikhail Gorbachev (q.v.) effectively disengaged from Ethiopia. Continuing political disorder in Somalia, however, necessitated a costly, abortive, American-sponsored United Nations (UN) (q.v.) peacekeeping mission in that country in 1991–1992.

HOT-LINE. A direct communications link between the White House in Washington, D.C., and the Kremlin in Moscow. The awareness that the Cuban Missile Crisis (q.v.) in 1962 had almost sparked off a nuclear war was a chastening experience for both John F. Kennedy and Nikita Khrushchev (qq.v.). In an attempt to avoid possible future misunderstanding and miscalculation they agreed on June 20, 1963, to set up a direct Hot-Line for instant teletype communication between the White House and the Kremlin. Messages were not transmitted personally but in code. In fact, the Hot-Line was not the fastest means of communication available. Its importance was that it demonstrated to the world the willingness of both leaders to engage in discussion with each other and was part of a general easing of tensions taking place after the Missile Crisis. The Hot-Line was intended solely for serious emergencies so that its actual use was infrequent. The first known occasion was by the Johnson (q.v.) administration during the 1967 Arab-Israeli War (q.v.). In January 1978 the Hot-Line was upgraded from a teletype printer to become part of a satellite communications system.

HOUSE UN-AMERICAN ACTIVITIES COMMITTEE (HUAC). A committee of the U.S. House of Representatives whose function was to investigate "un-American activities." Established in 1938 primarily to examine charges of profascist activities in the United States, HUAC became better known during the late 1940s for its investigation of alleged communist penetration not only of the American government but also labor unions and the motion-picture industry. Considerable publicity was given to the hearings on communist influence in Hollywood and also to the controversial case of Alger Hiss (q.v.).

HUAC predated McCarthyism (q.v.), but shared many of the latter's characteristics. Its strength arose from deep American unease over the course of the Cold War and the suspicion that foreign policy disasters such as the "loss of China" were caused by the infiltration of communists into influential positions in government and society. But there was also an element of bigotry and bullying that was combined with political self-seeking by members of the committee. Like McCarthyism, HUAC's excesses provoked a backlash in the mid-1950s in which the committee declined in influence and public esteem. In 1969 HUAC changed its name to the Committee on Internal Security. The committee was eventually abolished in 1975.

HOXHA, ENVER (1908–1985). Albanian communist political leader and prime minister. Hoxha emerged from obscurity to establish the Albanian Communist Party in 1941 and subsequently led the antifascist National Liberation Committee of Albania during World War II. In October 1944 he seized power after German forces evacuated the country, taking Soviet Stalinism as his political model. He was rewarded with Soviet recognition in August 1945 and formally declared the People's Republic of Albania (q.v.) in January 1946.

As a loyal Soviet ally, Hoxha broke off relations with Yugoslavia in November 1948, using accusations of Titoism to purge his own party. Albania's geographical isolation from the Soviet bloc permitted Hoxha to continue his dictatorship and defy Moscow's preference for destalinization after 1955. Indeed, he condemned Soviet reforms undertaken by Nikita Khrushchev (q.v.) as "revisionism," and in 1961, during the Sino-Soviet Split (q.v.), he broke completely with the Soviets, preserving external ties only with the People's Republic of China (PRC) (q.v.). In 1966 Hoxha launched an "ideological and cultural revolution" based on Albanian Marxism, seeking to eradicate all traces of the precommunist past and to achieve complete economic self-sufficiency after 1970. In 1976 Hoxha even denounced Mao Zedong (q.v.) and declared Albania's complete political and economic isolation, which continued until his death on April 11, 1985.

HUKBALAHAP INSURGENCY. A guerrilla movement in the Philippines active between 1947 and 1954. The Hukbalahaps (Huks) were mainly drawn from the rural peasantry on the island of Luzon and fought as a guerrilla army against the Japanese during World War II. After 1945 they refused to be disarmed and demanded that the Filipino government enact economic and agrarian reforms. Backed by the United States, the government denounced the Huks as communists and waged a military campaign to destroy the guerrillas. Although sporadic resistance would continue for several years afterward, the insurgency was effectively crushed by 1954. Contrary to American apprehensions, the Huks were not part of an international communist conspiracy orchestrated from Moscow. While some of the Huk leaders expressed communist ideals, they received no material aid from the communist countries. Nevertheless, the United States was suspicious of revolutionary movements in the Third World and aided the Filipino government in suppressing the Huks.

HUNGARIAN UPRISING, 1956. The uprising originated with extensive demands for political reform of the Stalinist regime of Matyas Rakosi (q.v.), following comparable changes in Poland (q.v.) during the summer of 1956. In July a Soviet delegation under Anastas Mikoyan (q.v.) came to Budapest to install a new but equally untenable regime under Ernö Gerö (q.v.). The former premier, Imre Nagy (q.v.), an advocate of a unique Hungarian pathway to socialism, emerged as a popular figurehead whose installation was demanded by mass demonstrations after the similarly inclined Wladyslaw Gomulka (q.v.) was appointed Polish party leader on October 21, 1956. On October 23 Joseph Stalin's (q.v.) statue was toppled by the Budapest crowd, with imminent repression by Gerö preempted by the return of Mikoyan from Moscow. The next day, Janos Kadar (q.v.) was appointed party secretary, with Nagy as premier at the same time as overtly nationalist Hungarian fighters were attacking Soviet troops stationed in the capital. A cease-fire was agreed on October 28 following a general strike and the formation of national councils in the provinces. After further negotiations, Soviet forces began to withdraw from the country, the Hungarian secret police (HVO) was dissolved, a national guard formed, and a multiparty People's Patriotic Government formed under Nagy, who declared the end of single party rule and free elections on October 30. The general strike and widespread protests continued, however, until on November 1 Nagy announced Hungary's withdrawal from the Warsaw Pact (q.v.).

The Soviet Union had already decided that Nagy had lost control of events. On October 31 Soviet troops began to redeploy in and around Hungary for an invasion code named "Operation Whirlwind." Kadar was flown into the Soviet Ukraine to form a countergovernment, which returned to Hungary on November 7, three days after 16 invading Soviet divisions had crushed Hungarian resistance, killing 2,500, with 200,000 refugees taking flight. Nagy was arrested and executed, leaving Kadar to reconstruct the communist state. Western actions were limited to verbal protests, in part due to the contemporaneous outbreak of the Suez Crisis (q.v.).

HUSAK, GUSTAV (1913–1991). Slovakian communist political leader and president. An active resistance member during World War II, Husak was appointed to the postwar coalition Czechoslovakian government as Slovakian interior minister. He chaired the Slovakian Communist Party after 1946 and masterminded the elimination of its main rival, the Slovakian Democratic Party in 1947 on trumped-up conspiracy and treason charges. In 1951, however, he was himself purged as a "bourgeois nationalist" by the Stalinist government of Klement Gottwald (q.v.) and was subsequently jailed until 1960.

Husak was rehabilitated in 1963, but remained outside politics until appointed Czechoslovak deputy premier in April 1968 by Alexander Dubček (q.v.). He worked to implement the latter's Action Program, but was increasingly aligned with President Ludvig Svoboda (q.v.), with whom he worked after the Warsaw Pact (q.v.) invasion of Czechoslovakia (q.v.) in 1968 to help normalize the country's political system to the satisfaction of the Soviet Union. He consolidated his power-base by enforcing numerical Czech/Slovak parity in the national communist leadership in December 1968 and took over Dubček's post in April 1969. By the end of 1970, a thorough purge of Czechoslovak public life removed proreformers, for which he received the personal praise of Leonid Brezhnev (q.v.) at the 14th Czechoslovak Communist Party Congress in 1971. In 1975 Husak also assumed the state presidency, maintaining an orthodox pro-Soviet course despite inexorable economic stagnation, corruption, and repression needed to contain renewed dissent, such as Charter 77 (q.v.). Having resisted meaningful reforms, advocated after 1986 by Mikhail Gorbachev (q.v.), Husak was forced to concede the leadership of the Communist Party in December 1987 to Milos Jakes (q.v.). He continued as head of state and was obliged to appoint a multiparty government on December 10, 1989, during Czechoslovakia's "velvet revolution" (q.v.). Husak retired from public life immediately afterward.

HYDROGEN BOMB. Thermonuclear weapon based on the fusion principle in which massive amounts of energy are released when lighter atoms, hydrogen or its isotope deuterium, fuse, rather than when heavier atoms are split, as in the earlier atomic bomb (q.v.), compared to which the hydrogen bomb is considerably more powerful. A feasibility study on the fusion principle was completed on October 30, 1949, after scientific research in the United States led by Edward Teller and J. Robert Oppenheimer. After the explosion of the first Soviet atomic bomb in August 1949, President Harry Truman (q.v.) was eager to restore American destructive supremacy. He authorized the development of the so-called "super bomb" in January 1950, thereby accelerating production plans after the exposure of the spy Klaus Fuchs (q.v.) aggravated American fears of emergent Soviet thermonuclear capabilities.

In May 1951 test explosions took place at the Pacific Ocean atoll of Eniwetok, followed by a full-scale fusion device, MIKE, on November 11, 1952, which yielded 10 megatons–750 times more powerful than the 1945 Hiroshima explosion. Although use of the hydrogen bomb was seen widely to preclude rational military objectives, its acquisition became a prerequisite for deterrence (q.v.). In 1954 an air-deliverable weapon was tested in the United States. Meanwhile, on August 12, 1954, the first Soviet thermonuclear device, developed under the direction of Andrei Sakharov (q.v.) was tested, followed by a weapon test on November 23, 1955. Great Britain (q.v.) tested its first thermonuclear device in 1957.

-I-

INCHON LANDING. Successful amphibious landing made by United Nations (UN) (q.v.) forces in 1950 during the Korean War (q.v.). The daring operation was conceived and planned by General Douglas MacArthur (q.v.) at a time when the UN and South Korean forces had been pushed back to the southeastern tip of the Korean peninsula known as the Pusan perimeter. MacArthur's aim was to seize the port of Inchon, on the west coast of the peninsula and more than 150 miles behind the North Korean front line. A successful attack would cut off the enemy's supply lines and open the way for a pincer movement by the UN forces.

The landing was carried out on September 15, 1950, with more than 250 ships transporting 70,000 troops. The small number of North Korean defenders at Inchon was surprised and quickly overwhelmed. UN forces entered Seoul, the capital city of South Korea, on September 28. The North Korean army was cut in half, its front line collapsed, and it was soon in headlong retreat. MacArthur's plan had worked to perfection and his already substantial military reputation was elevated even higher.

The Inchon Landing greatly boosted the morale of the UN forces. Instead of imminent defeat, they now perceived the prospect of a stunning military victory over North Korea. However, the entry of the People's Republic of China (PRC) (q.v.) into the Korean War in November 1950 prevented the UN forces from reaping the full reward of the success achieved at Inchon.

INDIA. South Asian power, which after securing independence from Great Britain (q.v.) in August 1947 resisted American overtures and adopted nonalignment in international affairs. Prime Minister Jawaharlal Nehru (q.v.), moreover, recognized the People's Republic of China (PRC) (q.v.) and criticized the United Nations (UN) (q.v.) for pursuing a pro-American policy during the Korean War (qq.v.). In so doing, Nehru provoked a rift with the American ambassador, Loy Henderson (q.v.). Nehru's wish for an independent voice in international affairs was further evinced by his role in convening the 1955 Bandung Conference (q.v.) and in the later nonaligned movement (q.v.). In 1955 he also visited Moscow and later hosted Soviet leaders, Nikolai Bulganin and Nikita Khrushchev (qq.v.), reaching agreement for Soviet economic aid essential to India's industrialization. As a result, the West tended to favor Pakistan more than India, although later in the 1950s and under President John F. Kennedy (q.v.), more generous American assistance was forthcoming to minimize Soviet influence. However, India's value as a military ally was rendered dubious by defeat in its border war with Communist China in 1962. Moreover, Presidents Lyndon Johnson and Richard Nixon (qq.v.) attempted to balance Indo-Pakistani interests that deteriorated into war in 1964 and 1971. In the former conflict Johnson actually welcomed Soviet mediation. Indian relations with the superpowers thereafter fluctuated according to their respective relationships with other Asian states and the impact of the latter on India's position as a developing regional power.

INDOCHINA WAR. A military conflict taking place in the French colony of Indochina between 1946 and 1954, also sometimes referred to as the

"First" Indochina War to distinguish it from the later Vietnam War (q.v.). French control of Indochina was challenged by a communist movement known as the Vietminh and led by Ho Chi Minh (qq.v.). Most of the fighting took the form of guerrilla activity in the countryside. A major conventional battle, however, was fought at Dien Bien Phu (q.v.) in 1954 and resulted in victory for the Vietminh. Peace terms were agreed at the 1954 Geneva Conference providing for French military withdrawal and the division of Indochina into the separate countries of Cambodia, Laos, and North and South Vietnam.

INDONESIA. South East Asian archipelago state that achieved independence from the Netherlands in 1949, and adopted a policy of nonalignment in international affairs under the charismatic presidency of Achmed Sukarno (q.v.). Sukarno hosted the 1955 Bandung Conference (q.v.) and was consequently targeted in Soviet attempts to patronize "anti-imperialist" Third World leaders. In 1956 extensive Soviet military and economic aid programs followed. Moreover, Sukarno tried to co-opt the large Indonesian Communist Party with the result that the U.S. Central Intelligence Agency (CIA) (q.v.) provided arms between 1957 and 1958 for a rebel military government on the Indonesian island of Sumatra. This was crushed, and despite a brief rapprochement with President John F. Kennedy (q.v.), Sukarno drew more than ever on Soviet and communist support for his increasingly autocratic rule.

At the same time Indonesian foreign policy became more volatile. The neighboring Dutch territory of West Irian was seized in 1962. Armed infiltration was also used from 1963 to 1966 to try to break up the Malaysian Federation, which called upon Great Britain (q.v.) for protection. Mounting domestic unrest culminated in October 1965 with the abduction and murder of the Indonesian army chief of staff, with Sukarno's evident assent. In March 1966 the United States supported a military coup under General Suharto that then exterminated the Indonesian Communist Party. After Suharto assumed the Indonesian presidency in 1969, American aid underwrote realignment to the West so that military and economic ties with Moscow were cut in 1970. Indonesia, nevertheless, remained a turbulent and controversial regional power, especially after its invasion of East Timor in 1975 and subsequent serious human rights abuses.

INTERCONTINENTAL BALLISTIC MISSILE (ICBM). Unmanned strategic nuclear delivery system in which a long-range rocket is able to reach targets in the Soviet Union directly from the United States and vice versa. The high speed and small size of ICBM nuclear warheads make active defense impossible, theoretically offering a first strike capability (q.v.) to their possessors. Consequently, after its first hydrogen bomb (q.v.) test in 1954, the United States began work on the Atlas ICBM. In 1957, however, the Soviet launch of Sputnik (q.v.) overtook American efforts and gave rise to fears in the United States of a missile gap (q.v.) that would undermine deterrence (q.v.). ICBM development in the United States therefore received top priority, leading to the production of the Titan missile, and the Minuteman, whose solid fuel propulsion system allowed it to be launched from a fortified subterranean silo, increasing its survivability against Soviet preemptive attack.

American ICBMs were combined in a strategic nuclear triad (q.v.), along with manned bombers and submarine-launched ballistic missiles (SLBMs) (q.v.), all of whose striking power was augmented in the late 1960s by multiple independently targetable re-entry vehicles (MIRVs) (q.v.). After 1964 Soviet defense plans gave similar priority to the Strategic Rocket Forces (q.v.), which achieved destructive parity with the United States in the form of the large and powerful SS-9 ICBM. Notwithstanding the limits imposed by the SALT treaties (qq.v.), both sides developed more sophisticated ICBMs in the late 1970s, including the American MX and the Soviet SS-19, thereby preserving an approximate, if febrile strategic balance.

INTERMEDIATE RANGE BALLISTIC MISSILE (IRBM). Nuclear missiles with a range of between 1,500 and 3,400 miles, first developed by the United States and the Soviet Union during the 1950s. After 1958 American Thor and Jupiter IRBMs were based in Europe and in Turkey (q.v.) in an attempt to bridge the perceived missile gap (q.v.). The liquid-fueled American missiles were an interim measure pending the development of the intercontinental ballistic missile (ICBM) (q.v.) and were scheduled for withdrawal in late 1962.

In the Soviet Union SS-3, SS-4, and SS-5 missiles were provided for the Strategic Rocket Forces (q.v.) during a period of economically motivated conventional force cuts. Soviet ICBM programs, however, were falling behind those of their superpower rival and prompted Nikita Khrushchev (q.v.) to risk deploying IRBMs within striking distance of the United States, precipitating the Cuban Missile Crisis (q.v.). The Soviets subsequently maintained IRBMs in Europe, as did France (q.v.). After 1975 these Soviet units were extensively modernized with the deployment of the SS-20 mobile ballistic missile, leading to the installation of equivalent new American intermediate-range nuclear forces (INFs) (q.v.) in 1983.

INTERMEDIATE-RANGE NUCLEAR FORCES (INF). Term covering intermediate-range ballistic missiles (IRBMs) (q.v.), medium-range ballistic missiles (MRBMs), medium range bombers, and cruise missiles, able to operate within a single geographic theater and not intercontinentally. Intermediate-range nuclear forces (INF) were, therefore, excluded from the SALT treaties (qq.v.), but were a focus of superpower tension after 1975 when the Soviets deployed the mobile SS-20 IRBM, conferring an operational superiority in Europe. In December 1979 the North Atlantic Treaty Organization (NATO) (q.v.) responded with its "twin (or dual) track policy," threatening to deploy the American Pershing II and Tomahawk cruise missiles, but delaying this until 1983 in order to provide time for INF reduction talks.

Negotiations began in Geneva in November 1981, but were immediately stalled by President Ronald Reagan's (q.v.) "zero option," which simply demanded the removal forthwith of all INFs from Europe. This was rejected by the Soviets as one-sided because they would have to dismantle existing forces in being, while the United States was giving up nothing in return. Soviet delegates countered by trying to include British and French strategic forces within the discussions. A deadlock ensued and the talks were eventually suspended in November 1983 shortly after the deployment of American INFs in Europe. Meaningful negotiations were not reopened until the 1986 Reykjavik Summit (q.v.) when Mikhail Gorbachev (q.v.) offered major concessions leading to the 1987 INF Treaty (q.v.).

INF TREATY, 1987. Signed by President Ronald Reagan and the Soviet leader, Mikhail Gorbachev (qq.v.), in Washington, D.C., on December 8, 1987, and formally ratified in Moscow in May 1988. The document eliminated the signatories' intermediate-range nuclear forces (INFs) (q.v.) entirely. INF talks had initially begun at Geneva in 1981 and were resumed in 1985, with reductions proposed again by Gorbachev at the October 1986 Reykjavik Summit (q.v.). Treaty negotiations started in earnest in March 1987 after Gorbachev dropped Soviet preconditions such as the inclusion of British and French nuclear forces and linkage to strategic arms cuts. Gorbachev also accepted global elimination of INFs and an on-site inspection regime to be conducted on American terms. INFs were to be completely destroyed by 1991, effectively fulfilling Reagan's 1981 "zero option." The INF Treaty was a major turning point in East-West relations and indicated the urgency of Gorbachev's need to curtail Soviet military burdens in order to capitalize civilian economic reforms, while preserving an overall balance with the West. Further dramatic Soviet arms reduction initiatives followed that hastened the end of the Cold War.

IRAN. Southwest Asian state which was an early focus of Cold War activity during the 1946 Azerbaijan Crisis (q.v.), thereafter receiving moderate economic and military aid from the United States. In May 1951 the nationalist Iranian government of Mohammed Mossadegh (q.v.) initiated another crisis by nationalizing the assets of the British Petroleum Corporation. The United States vetoed British military intervention, but acceded to an embargo of Iranian oil that plunged Iran into economic crisis. American fears of a coup by the communist Tudeh Party mounted and in August 1953 the Central Intelligence Agency (CIA) (q.v.) enacted a dormant British plan, "Operation Ajax," in which the Iranian army toppled Mossadegh and established the personal rule of Reza Mohammed Shah Pahlavi. The oil controversy was settled in 1954 when Iran also entered the Baghdad Pact (q.v.). In future initiatives, however, such as helping establish the Organization of Petroleum Exporting Countries (OPEC) in 1960, or its trade agreement with the Soviet Union in 1962, Iran often pursued its interests independently of the West.

In 1971 after Great Britain (q.v.) withdrew its forces from the Persian Gulf, President Richard Nixon (q.v.) established closer military relations, envisaging Iran as an effective containment (q.v.) proxy. From 1972 to 1978 Iran imported $19 billion in Western arms, having been promised access to all but nuclear weapons. Iran's military and economic modernization was accompanied, however, by domestic repression and corruption. Moreover, in exercising regional hegemony, the shah antagonized his Arab neighbor, Iraq. During the global recession of 1975–1977, inflationary hardships and industrial dislocation ignited mass opposition, in response to which the shah gave a virtual free hand to his secret police, SAVAK. The CIA entirely failed to appreciate the gravity of Iran's situation prior to the shah's flight in January 1979.

A National Front coalition took power, but was quickly sublimated by the Islamic revolutionary movement of Ayatollah Ruhollah Khomeini (q.v.). Iran was overtaken by anti-American fervor, manifested in the storming of the American embassy in Tehran by revolutionary students demanding the return of the shah for trial. Fifty-two American hostages were held for 444 days, a humiliating experience for the Carter (q.v.) administration. Iran, however, showed a similar hostility toward the Soviet Union and in September 1980, after the outbreak of the Iran-Iraq War, both superpowers agreed not to intervene. U.S.-Iranian antagonism was, nevertheless, to dominate Persian Gulf affairs for the next decade.

IRAN-CONTRA AFFAIR. The controversy originated in March 1984 with the clandestine shipment of arms to counterrevolutionary (Contra) forces in Nicaragua (q.v.) under the terms of the Reagan Doctrine (q.v.). This violated the 1982 Boland Amendment (q.v.), necessitating the use of special channels arranged by Colonel Oliver North, a staff member of the National Security Council (NSC) (q.v.). Simultaneous clandestine arrangements were under way for Israel to ship American-manufactured antitank and antiaircraft missiles to Iran (q.v.), which the NSC hoped would procure the release of American hostages held in Lebanon by Shi'ite Muslim guerrillas. These shipments continued for 15 months after August 1985, generating residual funds, which were diverted to purchase further arms illegally for the Contras.

In November 1986 Lebanese newspapers reported a secret visit to Iran by the NSC director, Robert McFarlane, exposing one side of the affair and severely embarrassing President Ronald Reagan (q.v.). At the same time U.S. Department of Justice investigators uncovered NSC documents which established the link between arms sales to Iran and aid to the Contras. In 1987 joint congressional hearings began which led to the prosecution of McFarlane and North and implicated Director of Central Intelligence William Casey (q.v.). The extent of presidential involvement was also raised. President Reagan, however, successfully denied having knowingly conspired to break the law.

IRON CURTAIN. Popular term used to describe the Soviet policy of cutting off Eastern Europe from contact with the West. The term had been used by German officials during World War II, but it did not attract global attention until it was included by the former British prime minister, Winston Churchill (q.v.), in a celebrated speech which he delivered at Fulton, Missouri, on March 5, 1946. With the deliberate intention of alerting Americans to the dangers of international Communism, Churchill stressed that the Soviet Union had imposed an iron curtain across Europe. The term so aptly conveyed the idea of a divided Europe that it soon entered common usage. In the 1952 American presidential election campaign, the Republicans talked of rolling back the iron curtain. However, the iron curtain remained in place until 1989 when it was metaphorically torn down by the successful revolutions against the communist regimes in Eastern Europe.

-J-

JACKSON-VANIK AMENDMENT. Attempt by the United States Congress to alter the policy of détente (q.v.) pursued by the Nixon (q.v.) administration. Arguing that the latter was giving too many concessions to the Soviet Union, Senator Henry Jackson and Congressman Charles Vanik sponsored an amendment to the 1972 Trade Reform Bill. The Bill proposed to grant the Soviets the status of a most favored nation in trade with the United States. The Jackson-Vanik amendment stated, however, that most favored nation status would only be granted in return for Soviet agreement to lift a recently imposed exit tax on Jewish emigrants wishing to leave the Soviet Union. Secretary of State Henry Kissinger (q.v.) argued that the Amendment would seriously undermine the policy of détente with the Soviet Union. Nevertheless, the Jackson-Vanik Amendment was included in the passage of the Trade Reform Bill in December 1974. The Soviets predictably denounced the Amendment as unacceptable interference in their domestic affairs. The Ford (q.v.) administration, therefore, could not grant most favored nation status to the Soviets. The Jackson-Vanik Amendment illustrated the power of the U.S. Congress and the growing strength of American feeling against the policy of détente with the Soviet Union.

JAKES, MILOS (1922–). Czechoslovak communist political leader. Jakes owed his political advancement to his loyalty to Gustav Husak (q.v.). From 1968 to 1977 Jakes controlled the records of the Czechoslovak Communist Party and supervised the mass dismissal of members considered sympathetic to the disgraced Alexander Dubček (q.v.) after the 1968 Warsaw Pact (q.v.) invasion. In December 1987 Husak named Jakes his successor as first secretary of the Czechoslovak Communist Party. Jakes was, however, unable to staunch the civil dissent that resulted in Czechoslovakia's 1989 "velvet revolution" (q.v.). At first he resisted all efforts to decentralize political power and tried to quell popular demonstrations with police violence. Jakes failed and was removed by the party Central Committee, which then tried last-ditch negotiations with the opposition Civic Forum. The latter's triumph preceded the establishment of democratic government by the end of 1989. In February 1992 Jakes was formally denounced for treasonable conspiracy during the events of 1968.

JAPAN. An important ally of the United States in the cold war politics of the Far East. Defeat in World War II shattered Japan's ambition of imposing its hegemony over East Asia. In 1945 the country was subjected to military occupation and administrative control by the United States and was no longer regarded as a great power. However, Japan's strategic significance was dramatically enhanced by the communist victory in China in 1949 and the outbreak of the Korean War (q.v.) in 1950. The United States now valued Japan as an ally in the Cold War and sought to strengthen that country both economically and militarily in order to contain the spread of Chinese communism. A peace treaty was signed in 1951 to end the American military occupation and restore Japanese independence.

The new government of Japan immediately entered into a bilateral security treaty with the United States to allow the retention of large American military bases, most notably in Okinawa. A period of remarkable economic development began that transformed Japan into one of the world's leading economic powers during the 1960s. Indeed, the Japanese model of economic development proved much more attractive than the example of the People's Republic of China (PRC) (q.v.) to the other nations of the region.

Despite its economic prowess, Japan did not develop an equally powerful military force. To reverse the country's militaristic past, the 1947 Japanese constitution prohibited the acquisition of nuclear weapons and the deployment of troops in overseas wars. A program of rearmament was begun in 1950, but was limited to providing a Self-Defense Force for protection against external aggression. Although regarded as pro-American, Japan did not directly participate in the military crises of the Cold War such as the Vietnam War (q.v.). This meant, however, that Japan found itself occasionally isolated in international affairs and was not consulted over important developments such as President Nixon's (q.v.) visit to China in 1972. On the other hand, Japan had emerged from economic devastation and crushing military defeat in 1945 to become one of the world's most stable and prosperous nations.

JARUZELSKI, WOJCIECH (1923–). Polish general and president. Jaruzelski fought under Soviet command in World War II and then rose systematically to the position of defense minister by 1968. He coordinated Polish military action in the 1968 Warsaw Pact invasion of Czechoslovakia (q.v.) and against the strikes in 1970, which brought down Wladyslaw Gomulka (q.v.). In 1972 he became a full member of the Politburo of the communist Polish United Workers' Party (PUWP), using his position to advance the political careers of his trusted military colleagues.

In 1980, during the government's confrontation with the independent trade union Solidarity (q.v.), Jaruzelski was instrumental in dissuading the Soviets from invading Poland (q.v.) under the terms of the Brezhnev Doctrine (q.v.), by guaranteeing communist rule under martial law if necessary. In February 1981 Jaruzelski was appointed prime minister and when the new PUWP first secretary, Stanislaw Kania, resumed political negotiations with Solidarity in July 1981, he began to plan a military takeover. With Soviet forces on Poland's borders, the coup took place on December 13, 1981. Resulting demonstrations and Solidarity itself were crushed within two weeks. About a fifth of the membership of PUWP was purged with power centralized in a military Committee for National Salvation until December 1982. After this date Jaruzelski retained chairmanship of the ruling Council of State. He attempted to rebuild the PUWP and to maintain domestic austerity to redeem Poland's intractable financial and economic crisis. Full civilian authority was restored in 1986, but with Jaruzelski as first secretary of the PUWP.

After securing Soviet assent, limited free market and price reforms were attempted in 1988, although with inflationary results that provoked renewed labor unrest. By December 1988 Jaruzelski was forced to request round-table discussions with former Solidarity leaders. Partly free elections followed in June 1989 after Mikhail Gorbachev (q.v.) reaffirmed a Soviet policy of nonintervention. Jaruzelski remained as president in a noncommunist government, which by the year's end had dissolved the Polish People's Republic. Jaruzelski retired shortly before presidential elections in 1990, which were won by his adversary, the Solidarity leader, Lech Walesa (q.v.).

JOHN PAUL II (1920–). Polish anticommunist and pope. Karol Wojtyla was cardinal archbishop of Krakow, Poland (q.v.), before his election as Pope John Paul II in September 1978. His subsequent visit to Poland in June 1979 stimulated a religious and nationalist upsurge that galvanized anticommunist opposition. A theological conservative, John Paul II traveled widely all over the world to promote populist Catholic revival, but was hostile to left-wing radicalism particularly among the Latin American clergy. Repeated attempts were made by the United States to cultivate the pope as a counterrevolutionary influence, possibly leading in 1981 to an assassination attempt against him, rumored to have originated with the Bulgarian intelligence service. Nevertheless, during visits to Poland in 1983 and 1987 John Paul II acted as a moderating influence on the communist leader, Wojciech Jaruzelski (q.v.). He also received the

Soviet leader, Mikhail Gorbachev (q.v.), in the Vatican in December 1989. The pope's statesmanlike status was therefore affirmed, with both superpowers acknowledging the need to court his political influence over Catholics worldwide.

JOHNSON, LYNDON B. (1908–1973). World statesman and president. Johnson was a New Deal Democrat who was elected to represent Texas in the U.S. House of Representatives in 1936 and the Senate in 1948. Johnson rose to become an influential figure in Congress and was Senate majority leader from 1955 to 1960. In 1960 he accepted the invitation to become John Kennedy's (q.v.) running mate and was elected vice president. Johnson succeeded to the presidency on November 22, 1963, on the assassination of Kennedy in Dallas.

As president, Johnson concentrated on the construction of what he called "the great society." He wanted to improve the conditions of life for all Americans. Johnson's remarkable political skills were evident in the significant domestic legislation that he persuaded Congress to pass. He was not, however, so successful in international affairs. Johnson was staunchly anticommunist and sought to continue Kennedy's policy of improving relations with the Soviet Union and invited the Soviet leader, Alexei Kosygin (q.v.), to the Glassboro "mini-summit" (q.v.). But relations between the superpowers were soon soured by the Soviet invasion of Czechoslovakia (q.v.) in 1968. In fact, the Soviet action confirmed Johnson's deeply held suspicions of communist leaders. He particularly detested the Cuban leader, Fidel Castro (q.v.), and was determined to resist the expansion of communism in the western hemisphere. This was exemplified in the decision to send American troops to intervene in the Dominican Republic (q.v.) in 1965.

Johnson's greatest self-imposed challenge and ultimate disaster was in attempting to defeat the communists in the Vietnam War (q.v.). Intent on punishing Communist North Vietnam for its aggression against South Vietnam, Johnson deliberately escalated the fighting on the ground and in the air. Bombing raids were ordered against North Vietnam and thousands of American combat troops were dispatched to fight the Vietcong in South Vietnam. Johnson confidently viewed the conflict in Vietnam as a "limited" war in which America's greatly superior power would quickly prevail. The enemy, however, proved to be much more formidable than he had anticipated and it was the United States that soon found the cost of escalation unacceptable. The turning point came in January 1968 when the Vietcong launched the Tet Offensive (q.v.). Johnson subsequently announced that the policy of escalation would be reversed and that he would seek a negotiated end to the war.

Johnson's Vietnam policy was highly controversial. Instead of projecting American power and leadership, it conveyed an image of military incompetence and provoked discontent among America's allies in the North Atlantic Treaty Organization (NATO) (q.v.). Serious political and social divisions also emerged within the United States. Large antiwar demonstrations were staged in which the president was a frequent target of criticism as protesters chanted: "Hey, hey, LBJ, how many kids have you killed today?" The collapse of Johnson's political prestige and standing was so evident that he withdrew his candidacy for the 1968 presidential election. On giving up the presidency, Johnson retired from public life.

-K-

KADAR, JANOS (1912–1989). Hungarian communist political leader and first secretary. Kadar was active in the Hungarian underground during World War II and was therefore marginalized by the "Muscovites" who returned from the Soviet Union to rule postwar Hungary under Matyas Rakosi (q.v.). Having been imprisoned between 1951–1954, Kadar was elevated to the Politburo of the Hungarian Workers' Party during Soviet-mandated reforms in July 1956. On October 25, 1956, he was promoted to first secretary, ruling in conjunction with premier Imre Nagy (q.v.). During the Hungarian Uprising (q.v.), Nagy's loss of political control was preceded by Kadar flying secretly to the Ukraine where he formed a countergovernment that took power after the Soviet invasion of November 4, 1956.

Kadar then attempted to construct a new Hungarian Socialist Workers' Party (HSWP), which denounced the 1956 rising as a fascist counterrevolution but also sought legitimacy by purging former Stalinist Hungarian leaders. Nagy was executed in 1958, after which Kadar succeeded in building a well-run economy with semi-autonomous management, supplementary free-market activities in industry and agriculture, coordinated after 1968 under the "New Economic Mechanism." In contrast to the rest of the satellite countries, Hungary maintained comparatively high living standards throughout the 1970s and notably gained entry into the International Monetary Fund (IMF) and World Bank in 1982. Kadar also recruited a pragmatic, technocratic HSWP leadership, whose mixed-economy experimental models were praised by Mikhail Gorbachev (q.v.). Hungarian currency convertibility in 1986, however, brought problems such as inflation, unemployment, and financial deficits. In May 1988, an emergency HSWP conference was convened to effect radical countermeasures. Its first deed was to retire Kadar, followed by decentralizing concessions to the private economic sector that presaged the virtual abandonment of communism in Hungary.

KAHN, HERMAN (1922–1983). American mathematician and theoretical nuclear strategist. In 1948 Kahn became an analyst for the RAND Corporation, the U.S. Air Force-sponsored think-tank, specializing in behavioral and mathematical models for projected nuclear war-fighting. He left RAND in 1961, founded the Hudson Institute, and proceeded to publish his ideas on deterrence (q.v.). These concentrated on the calculated application of conventional and nuclear forces in differing combinations and at different locations for varying political objectives. His books, *On Thermonuclear War* (1960), *Thinking About the Unthinkable* (1962), and *On Escalation: Metaphors and Scenarios* (1965), greatly influenced the emerging strategic doctrine of flexible response (q.v.) that was adopted officially by the North Atlantic Treaty Organization (NATO) (q.v.) in 1967.

KASAVUBU, JOSEPH (1913–1969). Congolese political leader and president. On the country's achieving independence from Belgium in June 1960, Kasavubu became president of the Congo (q.v.). He was confronted almost immediately with the secession of the southeastern province of Katanga under Moise Tshombe (q.v.), and a terminal rift with Congo Prime Minister Patrice Lumumba (q.v.). Kasavubu became politically dependent on his military commander, Joseph Désiré Mobutu (q.v.), who also enjoyed the confidence of the U.S. Central Intelligence Agency (CIA) (q.v.) as a stabilizing pro-Western force. Kasavubu was significant, however, as a legitimizing figurehead for the United Nations (UN) (q.v.) intervention on behalf of the central government during the subsequent Congolese civil war. UN forces withdrew in 1964, after which Mobutu's army received direct American and Belgian aid. Having outlived his usefulness, Kasavubu was overthrown by Mobutu in November 1965.

KENNAN, GEORGE F. (1904–). American diplomat who originated the doctrine of containment (q.v.). Kennan was a foreign service officer who specialized on Soviet affairs. While serving as chargé d'affaires at the American embassy in Moscow he wrote the famous long telegram (q.v.) in 1946. He returned to Washington, D.C., to head the State Department's

Policy Planning Staff from 1947 to 1949 and was widely acknowledged to be the author of the doctrine of containment. Kennan retired from the State Department in 1950 although he later served briefly as ambassador to the Soviet Union in 1952 and Yugoslavia from 1961 to 1963. After leaving the foreign service, Kennan became a leading authority on the Cold War and expressed his ideas in numerous books, articles, and lectures. He was particularly critical of the influence of the military upon American diplomacy and warned of the dangers to peace of the arms race in nuclear weapons. His view that containment would ultimately result in victory for the West and that it would also be essentially a political struggle was vindicated by the collapse of the Soviet Union and the end of the Cold War.

KENNEDY, JOHN F. (1917–1963). World statesman and president. Kennedy was educated at Harvard University and served in the U.S. Navy during World War II. After the war he joined the Democratic Party and was elected to represent Massachusetts in the U.S. House of Representatives in 1946 and the Senate in 1952. In 1960 Kennedy defeated Richard Nixon (q.v.) in the presidential election. A prominent feature of Kennedy's election campaign was his criticism of the Eisenhower (q.v.) administration for showing diplomatic weakness in the Cold War and allowing the development of an unfavorable missile gap (q.v.) between the United States and the Soviet Union.

As president, Kennedy carried out his promise to provide vigorous leadership to contain the expansion of International Communism. He made a number of impressive public speeches including the inaugural presidential address in 1961 in which he eloquently stated that America would "pay any price" and "bear any burden" to preserve and promote world freedom. Kennedy talked of "winning the minds" of the people of the Third World in the battle between democracy and communism. Programs designed to achieve this were the Alliance for Progress and the Agency for International Development (AID) (qq.v.).

In practice, however, Kennedy's policies generally emphasized military means rather than persuasion. He was particularly attracted to the strategy of sending American military equipment and advisers to help friendly governments defeat suspected communist insurgency. This was carried out openly in countries such as South Vietnam (q.v.), but secret or covert operations were conducted elsewhere, most notably in Cuba (q.v.). Kennedy's presidency was also marked by a substantial increase in American military spending. Instead of giving America greater security, the build-up in weapons stimulated the arms race with the Soviet Union and heightened the risk of nuclear war and destruction.

During his first six months in office, Kennedy experienced a series of diplomatic setbacks in the Cold War. In April 1961 a covert operation organized by the Central Intelligence Agency (CIA) to overthrow Fidel Castro (qq.v.) ended in disaster at the Bay of Pigs (q.v.) in Cuba. The summit meeting between Kennedy and Nikita Khrushchev (q.v.) at Vienna in June 1961 worsened rather than improved superpower relations. The creation of the Berlin Wall (q.v.) in August was regarded by Kennedy as a deliberate maneuver by Khrushchev to test the strength of the West. However, Kennedy's public declaration that the Western powers would defend West Berlin demonstrated qualities of firmness and leadership that compared highly favorably to what proved to be Khrushchev's empty threats to force the West to withdraw. Similarly, Kennedy's firmness and diplomatic skill during the Cuban Missile Crisis (q.v.) in 1962 was considered a personal triumph for the American president.

Kennedy did not seek to humiliate Khrushchev over the crises in Berlin and Cuba. Indeed, the very real prospect of nuclear war breaking out during the Cuban Missile Crisis persuaded Kennedy to seek improved relations with the Soviet Union. In 1963 a Hot-Line (q.v.) was opened between Washington and Moscow to provide a means of direct communication at times of crisis. Agreement was also reached on a Partial Nuclear Test Ban Treaty (q.v.). It is argued by admirers of Kennedy that the policy of improved relations between the superpowers was seriously interrupted by his assassination on November 22, 1963. They point out that he was determined to reduce international tensions and reverse the policy of American military involvement in Southeast Asia. Others contend, however, that the president's idealistic and forceful approach to international affairs stimulated conflict rather than accommodation with the Soviet Union.

KENNEDY, ROBERT F. (1925–1968). American politician and attorney general. During the 1950s "Bobby" Kennedy managed the political campaigns that won his older brother's election to the U.S. Senate in 1952 and the presidency in 1960. In the John F. Kennedy (q.v.) administration, Robert Kennedy served as attorney general. He was also his brother's closest confidant and personal adviser. This influence included foreign affairs and was illustrated during the Cuban Missile Crisis (q.v.) in 1962 when he argued effectively against launching a preemptive

American air strike against the missile sites. In 1964 Kennedy resigned the post of attorney general and was elected senator for New York. In 1968 he declared himself a presidential candidate and conducted a campaign that was sharply critical of President Lyndon Johnson's (q.v.) policy of escalating the Vietnam War (q.v.). During the campaign in June 1968, Robert Kennedy was assassinated.

KHOMEINI, RUHOLLAH (1902–1989). Iranian religious and political leader. Khomeini led the Shi'ite Muslim opposition to the secularizing regime of Reza Mohammed Shah Pahlavi in Iran (q.v.). Exiled in 1964 to Iraq and later to France (q.v.), he returned to Iran in February 1979 after the shah's fall. Khomeini's massive prestige and popularity permitted him to develop a populist Muslim revolutionary movement, which was not only virulently anti-American and anticommunist, but also hostile to secular and dynastic governments in neighboring states. On November 4, 1979, pro-Khomeini demonstrators sacked the American embassy in Tehran, subsequently detaining 52 American hostages for 444 days, inflicting terminal political and electoral damage on President Jimmy Carter (q.v.).

American strategic anxieties in the Persian Gulf, expressed in the 1980 Carter Doctrine (q.v.), were aggravated by Khomeini's general encouragement of Muslim revolutionaries, although such actions notably undermined the pro-Soviet government of Afghanistan (q.v.). The Islamic Republic of Iran, declared on December 3, 1979, therefore introduced a powerful indigenous Muslim influence into Middle East politics, which significantly departed from the bipolar superpower paradigm of the Cold War. The United States and the Soviet Union agreed not to seek advantage at the expense of the other in the 1980–1988 Iran-Iraq War. Instead both superpowers attempted consensually to minimize the political challenge of a new elementally militant indigenous ideology to the febrile regional status quo.

KHRUSHCHEV, NIKITA (1894–1971). Soviet statesman and general secretary. During the 1930s Khrushchev was loyal to Joseph Stalin (q.v.) and was rewarded with rapid advancement into the Soviet Politburo. In World War II he was first secretary of the Ukrainian Communist Party, where he supervised postwar industrial and agricultural reconstruction. Although his sometimes-unorthodox organizational methods attracted criticism, Khrushchev returned to Moscow in 1949 to enter a Stalinist inner-circle that also included Lavrenti Beria, Georgi Malenkov, and Nikolai Bulganin (qq.v.). After Stalin's death in 1953, Khrushchev emerged because he seemed a political conservative. He used his position as first secretary of the Soviet Communist Party to broaden his power-base and ally himself politically to the military under Georgi Zhukov (q.v.). Beria was removed and executed, and after an interlude of joint leadership, Malenkov was ousted as premier in February 1955 after which Khrushchev emerged as the uncontested Soviet leader.

Khrushchev's tenure was notable for a doctrinal shift from the idea of an inevitable war with the Western capitalist system to more protracted economic, diplomatic, and ideological competition. The latter was first articulated as "peaceful coexistence" by Malenkov and then greatly expanded. Domestically, this entailed a bold expansion of Soviet agriculture, with initially impressive results. Khrushchev also diverted resources from the military-industrial sector into civilian housing and light consumer industries aimed to create a more appealing Soviet way of life as a plausible alternative to capitalism. The operative political factor in economic reform was destalinization, which resulted in dismantling the state terror apparatus and decentralizing the Soviet bureaucracy. Significant reform was heralded at the 20th Congress of the Soviet Communist Party in February 1956, when Khrushchev's "secret speech" regaled delegates with an unprecedented denunciation of Stalin's errors and brutality. Many of Stalin's purge victims were reinstated and official censorship relaxed. Leadership changes also followed in many Soviet satellite states, although Khrushchev's "revisionism" led ultimately to the Sino-Soviet Split (q.v.).

In foreign policy, Khrushchev sought new opportunities by a combination of conciliation, generous foreign aid initiatives, and flamboyant personal diplomacy. He pursued rapprochement in 1954 with the estranged Yugoslav communist leader, Josip Tito (q.v.), relinquished military bases in Finland and China, followed in 1955 with the Austrian State Treaty, Geneva Summit, and recognition for the Federal Republic of Germany (FRG) (qq.v.). Soviet security interests were reconfigured within the Warsaw Pact (q.v.), permitting Poland (q.v.) to destalinize in 1956, although Imre Nagy's (q.v.) declaration of neutrality prompted the crushing of the Hungarian Uprising (q.v.). Khrushchev, nevertheless, had great success attracting decolonizing states such as India, Egypt, Indonesia, and Cuba (qq.v.).

In 1957 Khrushchev survived an attempted coup by the Politburo. He subsequently replaced Zhukov as defense minister and imposed closer party controls over the military, taking advantage of the prestige generated by the launch of Sputnik (q.v.). In 1958 Khrushchev also assumed the title of premier, although mounting problems in industry and agriculture, resulting from unrealistic planning and poorly implemented reorganization, put him under increasing domestic pressure. As a result his diplomacy became chaotically bellicose during the 1958 and 1961 Berlin Crises, the 1960 U-2 Affair, the 1961 Vienna Summit, and 1962 Cuban Missile Crisis (qq.v.). Internal bureaucratic conflict, a string of harvest failures after 1960, resistance to military spending cuts, and rising consumer prices further undermined his position. He also alienated his middle-rank communist support by trying to introduce regular reelections to party posts. In October 1964 the Politburo forced his retirement, replacing him with his former protégés, Leonid Brezhnev and Alexei Kosygin (qq.v.).

KIESINGER, KURT (1904–1988). West German political leader and chancellor. Kiesinger became secretary of the conservative Christian Democratic Union despite having been a Nazi prior to 1945. He was favored by Konrad Adenauer (q.v.) whom he accompanied to Moscow as chair of the parliamentary foreign affairs committee in 1955. Kiesinger also served as justice minister and state prime minister of Baden-Württemburg, returning to federal politics in 1966 to rescue the Christian Democrats from electoral defeat following the decline in popularity of Chancellor Ludwig Erhard (q.v.). In the "grand coalition" with the Social Democrats that followed, Kiesinger held the office of chancellor. He assigned the foreign ministry to Willy Brandt (q.v.), whom he reluctantly permitted to initiate Ostpolitik (q.v.), which resulted in an historic rapprochement between the Federal Republic of Germany (FRG) (q.v.) and the Soviet bloc. Kiesinger suffered electoral defeat in 1969 and conceded power to Brandt.

KIM IL SUNG (1912–1994). North Korean communist political leader and president. Kim joined the Korean Communist Party in 1931 and for a number of years lived mostly in the Soviet Union and China. He returned to Korea with the Soviet occupation forces in 1945 and became president of the Democratic People's Republic of Korea in 1948. Intent on reunifying North and South Korea, Kim invaded South Korea in 1950 and precipitated the Korean War (q.v.). Despite the failure of his invasion, Kim constantly proclaimed his ambition to reunify Korea. His maintenance of North Korea on a permanent war footing, including the development of nuclear weapons in the late 1980s, resulted in international isolation and unfriendly relations not only with South Korea and the United States, but also lost him the support of the Soviet Union and the People's Republic of China (PRC) (q.v.).

KIRKPATRICK, JEANE J. (1926–). American political scientist and diplomat. A professor of political science at Georgetown University, Kirkpatrick was an active member of the Democratic Party who became disillusioned with the foreign policy of President Jimmy Carter (q.v.). She believed that the United States should properly seek to maintain right-wing "authoritarian" governments in power and oppose left-wing "totalitarian" regimes. In her opinion, Carter had failed to make this distinction with the result that he had allowed the overthrow of pro-Western governments in Nicaragua and Iran (qq.v.).

Kirkpatrick's views attracted the attention of the Republican presidential candidate, Ronald Reagan (q.v.), who invited her to become his foreign policy adviser during the 1980 presidential election. In 1981 Reagan appointed Kirkpatrick American ambassador to the United Nations (UN) (q.v.), a post she held until 1985. Kirkpatrick's strident anti-communism and combative personal style were influential both in shaping and exemplifying the policy that became known as the Reagan Doctrine (q.v.).

KISSINGER, HENRY A. (1923–). American statesman and secretary of state. Born in Germany, Kissinger came to the United States as a refugee from the Nazis in 1938. He was educated at Harvard University and served in the U.S. Army during World War II. After the war Kissinger became a professor of government at Harvard and earned an international reputation as an expert on nuclear weapons and foreign policy. Although he frequently acted as a consultant to the State Department, Kissinger did not actually hold a government office until he was appointed national security adviser by President Richard Nixon (q.v.) in 1969.

Recognizing that the United States was no longer the preeminent superpower, Kissinger worked with Nixon to launch important initiatives in foreign policy, most notably the pursuit of détente (q.v.) with the Soviet Union. The desire for cooperation rather than confrontation was reflected in a series of summit meetings between Nixon and Leonid Brezhnev (q.v.) and the conclusion of arms control agreements in 1972. Another significant diplomatic achievement for Nixon and Kissinger was the "opening" to the People's Republic of China (PRC) (q.v.) that was exemplified by the president's visit to Beijing and his meeting with Mao Zedong (q.v.) in 1972. In the affairs of the Middle East Kissinger took a more visible role when he engaged in "shuttle diplomacy" traveling between the various capitals of the region in an effort to broker a peace settlement after the Arab-Israeli War of 1973 (q.v.).

Kissinger's diplomatic activities gained considerable publicity and earned him the status of an international celebrity. For his contribution toward ending the Vietnam War (q.v.) he was awarded the Nobel Peace Prize in 1973. However, there was criticism in the United States that the policy of détente had given too many concessions to the Soviet Union. Moreover, like so many other American leaders, Kissinger could not escape being implicated in the blame for America's perceived failure to win the Vietnam War. Kissinger argued that the effectiveness of American foreign policy was undermined by domestic pressures such as the Watergate political crisis and the failure of the U.S. Congress to pass funds to aid pro-Western forces in South Vietnam, Cambodia, and Angola (qq.v.). Kissinger left office in 1977 but continued to act as an influential consultant, writer, and lecturer on foreign policy.

KOHL, HELMUT (1930–). West German political leader and chancellor. Kohl was a member of the Christian Democratic Union and replaced Helmut Schmidt (q.v.) as chancellor in October 1982. He allowed his Free Democrat coalition partner, Foreign Minister Hans-Dietrich Genscher (q.v.) to maintain cordial relations with the Soviet Union and the German Democratic Republic (GDR) (q.v.), but openly preferred closer ties with the United States and the European Community (EC) (q.v.). Kohl, nonetheless, authorized financial aid to the GDR in 1983 and courted Mikhail Gorbachev (q.v.) after 1985 for cooperative political and economic relations.

Under Kohl's leadership, the Federal Republic of Germany (FRG) (q.v.) seemed inexorably to be assuming a centrally influential position in European and wider international affairs. From this position, after the fall of the Berlin Wall (q.v.) in 1989 Kohl commanded the political dialogue on a new FRG-GDR relationship and visited Moscow in January 1990, gaining Soviet assent for German unification talks. In June 1990 Kohl clarified with President George Bush (q.v.) that the unified Germany would remain in the North Atlantic Treaty Organization (NATO) (q.v.). Despite British and French reservations, the way was therefore cleared for "two plus four" unification negotiations, concluded in the Soviet Caucasus on July 15, 1990. A treaty followed in Moscow in September and the GDR was formally absorbed into the FRG on October 3, 1990. Kohl and the Christian Democrats swept state and federal elections in January 1991 and he remained chancellor until his electoral defeat in 1998.

KGB (KOMITET GOSUDARSTVENNOY BEZOPASNOSTI). The KGB or the Soviet Committee of State Security was the principal Soviet foreign intelligence and domestic security service. It was reformed in 1954 as a state committee accountable to the Politburo rather than the independent ministry, which had been the bailiwick of Lavrenti Beria (q.v.), the chief agent of political terror under Joseph Stalin (q.v.). Like its predecessors, the GRU (q.v.), NKVD, and MGB, the KGB evolved into a state within the state. It ran foreign intelligence, internal security and counterintelligence, border troops, economic and industrial espionage, protected Soviet officials and installations, monitored dissidents, maintained transport security, communications and cryptography, military counterintelligence, and political archives. Probably one-third of Soviet diplomatic employees were KGB agents.

The first KGB chairman, Ivan Serov, personally supervised the crushing of the 1956 Hungarian Uprising (q.v.). His successors Alexander Shelepin (1958–1961) and Vladimir Semichastny (1961–1967) attempted to shed the KGB's brutal reputation by recruiting elite university graduates and youth workers from the Communist Party. The KGB cooperated with Leonid Brezhnev (q.v.) in toppling Nikita Khrushchev (q.v.) in 1964 and reached the peak of its influence after May 1967 when Yuri Andropov (q.v.) became its chairman. The KGB provided him with an optimum power-base, which was also the best informed and most critically aware organ of the Soviet state. It supported Mikhail Gorbachev's (q.v.) political ascent, but eventually the chaotic impact of his reforms led the KGB chairman, Vladimir Kryuchkov, to join the August 1991 coup that precipitated the final collapse of the Soviet Union. Nevertheless, powerful former-KGB elements retained an important role in post-Soviet Russian politics.

KOREA, NORTH. *See* KOREAN WAR.

KOREA, SOUTH. *See* KOREAN WAR.

KOREAN AIR LINES (KAL) FLIGHT 007. Incident reflecting the low point of relations between the United States and the Soviet Union during the 1980s. On September 1, 1983, Korean Air Lines (KAL) Flight 007, flying from Alaska to South Korea, strayed off course and penetrated Soviet airspace over Siberia. A Soviet military plane shot down the civilian airliner with the loss of life of all 269 crew and passengers. At first, the Soviets denied that the incident had actually taken place and later, after acknowledging that it had occurred, alleged that the plane was involved in espionage for the United States. President Ronald Reagan (q.v.) countered by condemning the shooting down as "a crime against humanity" and indicative of the inherently evil nature of communism. The incident was useful for Reagan because it appeared to vindicate his policy of rejecting détente (q.v.) on the ground that the Soviets could not be trusted to keep to any agreement.

KOREAN WAR. A major conventional war taking place in the Korean peninsula from 1950 to 1953. At the end of World War II in 1945 the Korean peninsula was arbitrarily divided at the 38th parallel by the United States and the Soviet Union. The temporary division soon became fixed and separated the country into two antagonistic rival states. The communists were dominant in the North and formed the Democratic People's Republic of Korea (North Korea) with the Marxist revolutionary, Kim Il Sung (q.v.), as its leader. In the South, the Republic of Korea (South Korea) was headed by Syngman Rhee (q.v.), who stressed close relations with the United States. The tensions of the Cold War in Europe were replicated in Korea as Kim and Rhee vilified each other for causing the division of the country. Both leaders declared that they would bring about reunification by whatever means were necessary, including the use of force. A state of undeclared civil war ensued.

On June 25, 1950, Kim Il Sung launched a surprise and well-prepared invasion of South Korea designed to liberate the South and thereby reunify the two Koreas. But Kim miscalculated in believing that the United States would remain passive as North Korean forces absorbed the whole peninsula. Although the Soviet Union carefully avoided direct military involvement in the war, the Truman (q.v.) administration was convinced that the invasion was masterminded from Moscow and that its real purpose was to test the resolve of the West.

Assisted by the fortuitous absence of the Soviet representative at the United Nations (UN) (q.v.), the United States secured the passage of UN resolutions calling upon North Korea to withdraw its forces from South Korea and asking UN members to supply troops to drive back the invaders. On June 27, 1950, President Harry Truman announced that the United States would deploy its military forces on behalf of the UN. Although 16 nations eventually sent troops, the American contribution was so much the largest—amounting to half the number of combat troops and 80 to 90 percent of air and naval support—that the various contingents were unified under American control and direction. One of America's most senior generals, Douglas MacArthur (q.v.), was appointed as commander of the UN forces.

During the first weeks of fighting, the North Koreans virtually overran the whole peninsula, but were unable to achieve complete military victory. In September, MacArthur brilliantly outflanked the enemy by making an amphibious landing at Inchon (q.v.). The North Korean forces were cut in half and were soon in headlong retreat. The UN forces proceeded to cross the 38th parallel and steadily advanced to the Yalu River, which marked the North Korean border with the People's Republic of China (PRC) (q.v.). The original mission to resist aggression was thereby deliberately changed to include the conquest of North Korea. MacArthur confidently predicted that neither the Soviet Union nor China would join the war, but he was proved grievously wrong with respect to China when that country launched a major offensive involving 200,000 troops in November 1950. It was now the turn of the UN forces to retreat. MacArthur advocated retaliatory air strikes against China, but Truman refused to expand the war beyond Korea and removed MacArthur from his command in April 1951.

By deliberately limiting the war, Truman abandoned the goal of seeking total victory over North Korea and indicated that he was willing to accept a territorial settlement that broadly reflected the prewar status quo. The result was a prolonged and costly war of attrition in which the lines of battle moved back and forth until both sides consolidated their respective positions close to the same 38th parallel that had marked the prewar border. The military stalemate was broken by the new American president, Dwight Eisenhower (q.v.) who, shortly after assuming office in 1953, made it known that he was prepared to use atomic weapons against China. This threat combined with the evident war-weariness on all sides to bring about a cease-fire signed at Panmunjom in July 1953. The agreement essentially recognized the existing battle line and prewar borders. Although provision was made for future conferences to discuss reunification, the politics of the Cold War ensured that the peninsula would remain divided at the 38th parallel. North Korea stayed firmly within the communist orbit, while South Korea remained closely tied to the United States.

Almost 34,000 Americans died in the Korean War while the number of Koreans and Chinese killed, injured, and missing numbered more than three million. Since the country still remained divided at the 38th parallel, the fighting appeared to have achieved little except wreak further destruction upon an already unfortunate people. Moreover, the Korean War hardened rather than moderated cold war hostilities in the Far East. Whether the People's Republic of China acted independently or was manipulated by the Soviets into joining the war, the consequences for subsequent Sino-American relations were disastrous. The United States concluded that Communist China was its principal enemy in the Far East and proceeded to attempt to isolate that country both diplomatically and economically. Another round of military conflict would take place not in Korea but farther to the south of the continent in Southeast Asia.

KOSYGIN, ALEXEI (1904–1980). Soviet political leader and prime minister. Kosygin was chief executive of Leningrad during World War II and entered the Politburo in 1948, holding ministerial positions in finance and light industry. He stood by Nikita Khrushchev (q.v.) during the abortive 1957 coup and was promoted to deputy prime minister in 1958. In October 1964 amid mounting economic and political difficulties, Kosygin united with Leonid Brezhnev (q.v.) to force Khrushchev's retirement. Kosygin became prime minister, assuming primary responsibility for diplomatic relations and the nonagricultural economy. In the latter, he restored professional centralized ministries in 1965, with flexible prices, limited free-market incentives, and managerial autonomy in 1966. However, he alienated vested middle-rank interests that accordingly gravitated toward Brezhnev, helping the latter to achieve overall political preeminence.

Kosygin achieved prominence in foreign policy during the 1967 Glassboro "mini-summit" (q.v.) with President Lyndon Johnson (q.v.). After the 1969 Ussuri River Incident (q.v.) he also held crisis-management talks with the Chinese foreign minister, Zhou Enlai (q.v.). During the era of détente (q.v.), however, Kosygin was eclipsed by Brezhnev, although he preserved his position as prime minister and remained a member of the Politburo until retirement due to ill health in 1980.

KRENZ, EGON (1937–). East German communist politician and general secretary. Krenz rose through the Free German Youth organization to the Central Committee of the Socialist Unity Party in 1973 and the Politburo in 1983. He succeeded Erich Honecker (q.v.) as general secretary on October 18, 1989, hoping to avert complete political collapse of the German Democratic Republic (GDR) (q.v.) amid mass civil dissent and the flight of thousands of GDR citizens westward through the newly opened borders of Poland (q.v.), Hungary, and Czechoslovakia (q.v.).

Krenz visited Moscow for consultations on November 1, 1989, but was denied practical assistance by the Soviet leader, Mikhail Gorbachev (q.v.). On November 9, he attempted to salvage his position by relaxing emigration controls, which led only to the spontaneous public demolition of the Berlin Wall (q.v.), emphasizing his lack of effective authority. In subsequent negotiations for a modus vivendi with West German Chancellor Helmut Kohl (q.v.), Krenz was undercut by his prime minister, Hans Modrow, who precipitately raised the question of German reunification. Abandoned by his colleagues and bloc partners, Krenz was removed from the leadership of the Socialist Unity Party on December 3, 1989, and was expelled from the renamed Party of Democratic Socialism on January 21, 1990. The GDR's collapse continued nonetheless prior to its assimilation by the Federal Republic of Germany (FRG) (q.v.) in October 1990.

-L-

LAIRD, MELVIN R. (1922–). American politician and secretary of defense. Laird was elected as a Republican Congressman from Wisconsin in 1953. His long service on the Defense Subcommittee of the House Appropriations Committee gained Laird a reputation as an expert on defense matters. In 1969 he was appointed secretary of defense in the Nixon (q.v.) administration. Laird favored speedy American military disengagement from the Vietnam War (q.v.) and advocated the strategy of "Vietnamization" in which the South Vietnamese army would assume the burden of fighting the Vietcong. But he was also a "cold warrior" and firmly believed that the United States must be a strong military power. After leaving office in 1972 Laird openly criticized the policy of détente (q.v.) and especially the strategic arms limitation treaty (SALT II) (q.v.) that he argued had given too many advantages to the Soviet Union.

LANSDALE, EDWARD G. (1908–1987). American general and specialist in covert operations. An Air Force officer, Lansdale served in the Office of Strategic Services (OSS) during World War II and became an expert in counterinsurgency. In the early 1950s he was assigned to the government of the Philippines to help suppress the Hukbalahap Insurgency (q.v.). In 1954 Lansdale was appointed head of the Central Intelligence Agency's (CIA) (q.v.) military mission in Saigon and began a 10-year personal association with South Vietnam. During this period he organized propaganda campaigns and directed sabotage operations against the communists. In between tours of duty in South Vietnam, Lansdale was chosen by President John F. Kennedy (q.v.) to direct Operation Mongoose, a secret project of sabotage and infiltration designed to bring down the government of Fidel Castro in Cuba (qq.v.) in 1962. Although much of his work was conducted in secrecy, Lansdale acquired a legendary reputation as an American role model that was used by

William J. Lederer and Eugene Burdick as the basis for the character of Colonel Edwin Hillendale in their novel, *The Ugly American.*

LAOS. A country in Southeast Asia that became entangled in the politics of the Cold War. After achieving independence from France in 1954, Laos chose to pursue a neutral foreign policy. The country, however, was split between pro-Western interests backed by the Laotian army versus a communist guerrilla movement known as the Pathet Lao that was receiving support from Ho Chi Minh and the Vietminh (qq.v.). The United States provided aid to the Laotian army while the Soviet Union and North Vietnam backed the Pathet Lao. Civil war erupted in 1958 and continued intermittently throughout the period of the Vietnam War (q.v.) from 1964 to 1973. Parts of the Ho Chi Minh Trail lay in Laos so that the country became an important staging post for the movement of North Vietnamese military equipment and troops to South Vietnam. Consequently, Laos experienced American bombing raids and an incursion by the South Vietnamese army in 1971. The Laotian civil war ended in 1974 with victory for the Pathet Lao and the establishment of a communist government.

LEBANON CRISIS, 1958. In 1958 the unification of Egypt and Syria in the United Arab Republic (UAR) encouraged political demonstrations against the Maronite Christian-dominated pro-Western government of Lebanon, headed by Prime Minister Camille Chamoun. In May 1958 his forces clashed with Muslim Lebanese supporters of the Egyptian president, Gamal Abdel Nasser (q.v.). The United States feared a political collapse that would favor the UAR and its patron, the Soviet Union. Chamoun invoked the Eisenhower Doctrine (q.v.) to request American military intervention on his behalf. The State Department procrastinated, however, trusting in mediation by United Nations (UN) Secretary-General Dag Hammarskjöld (qq.v.). Events came to a head on July 14, 1958, when a nationalist military coup succeeded in Iraq. Eisenhower consulted with British Prime Minister Harold Macmillan (q.v.) and the next day, in "Operation Blue Bat," American marines landed to occupy Beirut and keep Chamoun in power. British paratroopers were also airlifted into Jordan to support King Hussein while units of the American Seventh Fleet took up positions outside the Persian Gulf. The Lebanon Crisis soon ended and the intervention forces withdrew before the end of the year.

LEHMAN, JOHN (1942–). American strategist and secretary of the navy. From 1969 to 1977 Lehman served on the staff of the National Security Council (NSC) (q.v.) and the Arms Control and Disarmament Agency

LIE, TRYGVIE • 199

(ACDA) (q.v.). In 1981 he was appointed secretary of the navy by President Ronald Reagan (q.v.) and issued the "Lehman Doctrine." This was a policy directive for the construction of an American fleet consisting of 600 major units that was dedicated to global power projection against indefinite Soviet challenges. Moreover, Lehman oversaw the "forward maritime strategy," which planned for preemptive striking operations against the Soviet Northern Fleet's bases in the Soviet Union in the approach to a possible future war. This strategy was adopted officially by the North Atlantic Treaty Organization (NATO) (q.v.) and contributed greatly to increasing tensions between the United States and the Soviets. After his resignation in 1987, Lehman continued as an advocate of aggressive development of American sea power.

LEMAY, CURTIS E. (1906–1990). American general and commander of the U.S. Strategic Air Command. LeMay was the architect of the American bombing offensive against Germany and Japan during World War II. Throughout the 1950s and early 1960s he stressed the absolute importance of strategic air power and the necessity of maintaining the American air force at a high level of strength. During the Cuban Missile Crisis (q.v.) he urged a preemptive air strike on the missile sites in Cuba (q.v.). Even more notorious was LeMay's hawkish position on the Vietnam War (q.v.) and his public statements during the 1968 presidential election campaign urging that American air power be used to "bomb them [the North Vietnamese] back into the stone age."

LIE, TRYGVIE (1896–1968). Norwegian diplomat and the first secretary-general of the United Nations (UN) (q.v.). Lie was foreign minister in Norway's government-in-exile during World War II and led the Norwegian delegation to the United Nations' San Francisco Conference (q.v.) in April 1945. A moderate socialist and politically acceptable to both superpowers, Lie became UN secretary-general in February 1946. He set up the UN Secretariat in New York, although suffering increasing Soviet criticism of his apparent pro-American leanings. This trend reached its nadir during the Korean War (q.v.), when Lie precipitately declared North Korea the aggressor, providing grounds for UN military intervention. He was consequently boycotted by the UN's communist members. Moreover, Lie consented at American behest to institute loyalty investigations of UN staff, an action that was associated with McCarthyism (q.v.). With the UN in mounting disarray Lie resigned in November 1952 and was succeeded by Dag Hammarskjöld (q.v.).

LINKAGE. Complex diplomatic bargaining strategy articulated by Henry Kissinger (q.v.), under which Soviet cooperation on peace negotiations in the Vietnam War (q.v.) could be secured by offering reciprocal inducements in apparently unrelated areas of interest, such as strategic nuclear arms control. After appointment to the Nixon (q.v.) administration as national security adviser in 1969, Kissinger pursued this course and in the process opened diverse opportunities for U.S.-Soviet dialogue, which were to coalesce into the process of détente (q.v.).

LIPPMANN, WALTER (1889–1974). American newspaper columnist and writer on foreign affairs. Lippmann was one of the founders of the *New Republic* in 1914 and became a celebrated syndicated columnist. Adopting what became known as the "realist" approach to foreign affairs, Lippmann was critical of the policy of global containment (q.v.) that he believed was too ambitious and would overextend American resources. In a series of articles in 1947 he warned that America was in danger of entering into a prolonged cold war with the Soviet Union. Although Lippmann did not actually invent the term cold war, he was responsible for bringing it to public attention in the United States. Lippmann was credited with immense knowledge of the Washington foreign policy establishment. Consequently, his views were highly respected in Washington, and he was frequently consulted by presidents and policymakers.

LISBON CONFERENCE, 1952. A meeting in February 1952 of the Council of the North Atlantic Treaty Organization (NATO) (q.v.) to discuss alliance rearmament during a period of intensified tensions with the Soviet Union. Influenced by the American document NSC-68 (q.v.), the conference called for 98 divisions, plus 7,000 combat aircraft, to be available at 30 days notice for deployment in Europe by 1954. Not only did this reaffirm the need for rearmament by the Federal Republic of Germany (FRG) (q.v.), which the United States wanted, but it threatened to impose a large burden on the fragile economies of Western Europe. In July 1952 the British military chiefs of staff devised an alternative, based on strategic nuclear deterrence (q.v.). This appealed to the incoming Eisenhower (q.v.) administration whose New Look defense strategy (q.v.) abandoned the costly targets set at Lisbon in favor of massive retaliation (q.v.).

LODGE, HENRY CABOT (1902–1985). American diplomat. Lodge followed the example of a famous grandfather and became a prominent Repuolican politician and authority on foreign affairs. He was elected senator for Massachusetts from 1936 to 1944 and 1947 to 1953. During the Eisenhower (q.v.) administration Lodge served as head of the American delegation to the United Nations (UN) (q.v.). In 1960 Lodge accepted the Republican vice-presidential nomination, but was defeated in the election. Lodge served as American ambassador to South Vietnam from 1963 to 1964 and from 1965 to 1967. The fact that he was a Republican accepting appointments from Democratic presidents indicated the bipartisan nature of political support for American involvement in the Vietnam War (q.v.). In 1969 Lodge headed the American delegation at the Paris peace talks on Vietnam.

LONDON DECLARATION, 1990. Made by the North Atlantic Treaty Organization (NATO) (q.v.) on July 6, 1990, following a report delivered by President George Bush (q.v.) on his meeting in Washington, D.C., in June with the Soviet leader, Mikhail Gorbachev (q.v.). The latter had produced the Strategic Arms Reduction Talks (START) (q.v.) treaty and terms of reference for the Conventional Forces in Europe (CFE) (q.v.) treaty. NATO therefore declared its intention to abandon flexible response (q.v.), which was based on the declaratory first-use of nuclear weapons during a European war. Such weapons would now be regarded as a last military resort. American and Soviet short-range nuclear forces would also be withdrawn from Europe. NATO forces would disengage from forward positions along Warsaw Pact (q.v.) frontiers and Gorbachev would be invited to address NATO prior to the establishment of permanent Warsaw Pact (q.v.) diplomatic representation at NATO headquarters. Finally, NATO and the Warsaw Pact should make a joint resolution stating that both were "no longer adversaries."

LONG TELEGRAM. An important diplomatic dispatch written by George Kennan (q.v.) in 1946. The American chargé d'affaires in Moscow, George Kennan, believed that officials in the Truman (q.v.) administration did not truly understand the mentality of the Soviet leaders. In order to gain the attention of his superiors at the State Department, Kennan dispatched in February 1946 an 8,000-word critique of Soviet policy that became known as the long telegram. In it he warned of the danger of "acting chummy" with the Soviets and explained that their leaders could not be trusted because they were Marxist-Leninists and committed to the belief that war with capitalism was inevitable. The analysis was timely and welcomed in Washington where it reinforced the already strong anti-Soviet prejudices of American officials and was used to justify the adoption of the policy of containment (q.v.).

LOVETT, ROBERT A. (1895–1986). American financier and secretary of defense. Lovett was a prominent member of the "eastern establishment" who combined careers in banking and law with regular periods of service in government. During World War II he served under Secretary of War Henry Stimson and developed an expertise in diplomatic and strategic affairs. Lovett also established a close working relationship with Army Chief of Staff George Marshall (q.v.) that continued after the war when the latter became secretary of state and later secretary of defense.

Lovett was one of the original cold warriors in that he was actively involved in developing the doctrine of containment (q.v.), preparing the Marshall Plan (q.v.) and assisting the creation of the North Atlantic Treaty Organization (NATO) (q.v.). In 1951 he succeeded Marshall as secretary of defense and held this office until the end of the Truman (q.v.) administration in 1953. Despite never again holding a post in government, Lovett continued to act as an influential adviser on foreign affairs. In 1960 President-elect John F. Kennedy (q.v.) offered him the position of either secretary of state or secretary of defense. Lovett declined and suggested Dean Rusk and Robert McNamara (qq.v.). During the Cuban Missile Crisis (q.v.) in 1962 Lovett was a member of ExComm, President Kennedy's inner circle of policy advisers.

LUBLIN COMMITTEE. The communist-dominated provisional government of Poland (q.v.) that was formed in Moscow in July 1944 from leftist refugee elements. The Committee was installed in the Polish province of Lublin, the first to fall to the Red Army that month as Nazi forces retreated. This so-called "Polish National Liberation Committee" provided the platform on which Joseph Stalin (q.v.) sought to reconstitute postwar Polish politics. With the interior ministry under communist control, the Lublin Committee's police and judicial powers provided cover for the Soviet elimination of nationalist resistance groups who were loyal to Poland's government-in-exile in London. When the latter refused to accept pro-Soviet revisions of Poland's eastern border, the Soviets recognized the Lublin Committee as the sole legitimate Polish government. At the Yalta Conference (q.v.) in February 1945, Stalin was persuaded, however, to agree in principle to free Polish elections open to all antifascist parties, and an expanded interim government to incorporate some "London Poles." Nevertheless, the Lublin Committee had already firmly established the political preconditions within Poland through which ultimate communist influence could be assured.

LUMUMBA, PATRICE (1925–1961). Congolese political leader and prime minister. A colonial civil servant and trade unionist in the Belgian

Congo, Lumumba founded in 1958 the Mouvement National Congolais, which was strongly influenced by the pan-African ideas of Ghana's leader, Kwame Nkrumah (q.v.). In June 1960 Lumumba became the first prime minister of the independent Congo (q.v.) forming an uneasy partnership with President Joseph Kasavubu (q.v.). In the developing Congo Crisis, which followed widespread army mutinies and the secession of the province of Katanga under Moise Tshombe (q.v.), Lumumba appealed to the United Nations (UN) (q.v.) for military assistance in restoring order. He also unilaterally contacted the Soviet Union. Fearing the extension of communist influence, the United States and Belgium urged Kasavubu to dismiss the prime minister. In September 1960 Lumumba was arrested by the Congolese army under Joseph Désiré Mobutu (q.v.). After a failed escape attempt, Lumumba was flown to Katanga in January 1961, handed over to rebel troops, and killed.

-M-

MACARTHUR, DOUGLAS (1880–1964). American general who played a leading and controversial role in the postwar occupation of Japan and the Korean War (qq.v.). MacArthur was the son of a general and similarly enjoyed a distinguished military career. Promoted to general in World War I, he held various high offices in the Army before retiring in 1935. Recalled to active duty in 1941 he directed the successful Pacific campaign against Japan. In 1945 MacArthur was appointed supreme commander of Allied forces in Japan. Acting as a virtual dictator, he proceeded not only to disarm Japan but also introduced reforms designed to transform the country's political and economic system.

In June 1950 President Harry Truman (q.v.) placed MacArthur in command of the United Nations (UN) (q.v.) forces with the task of repelling the North Korean invasion of South Korea. MacArthur executed a brilliant amphibious landing at Inchon (q.v.) that outflanked the enemy and forced its retreat from South Korea. However, the general's prediction that the People's Republic of China (PRC) (q.v.) would not enter the war proved grievously wrong. In pursuit of total victory MacArthur wished to conquer North Korea and recommended that the war include direct attacks upon China. But Truman refused to expand the war beyond Korea and removed MacArthur from his command in April 1951.

On his return to the United States, MacArthur was given a hero's welcome. This was partly a tribute to his outstanding military career, but it also reflected criticism of the Truman administration for pursuing a weak policy in Asia and being soft on communism. But the "Truman-MacArthur controversy" was short-lived. Despite an attempt to make the general a political candidate in the 1952 presidential election, MacArthur lacked political support and soon disappeared from public attention.

MCCARTHY, JOSEPH R. (1908–1957). American politician whose anticommunist campaign created the term McCarthyism (q.v.). McCarthy pursued a career in law before going into politics and winning election in 1946 as the Republican senator for Wisconsin. The senator sprang to national prominence in February 1950 when he made a speech at Wheeling, West Virginia, in which he claimed that he possessed the names of known communists who were currently employed in the State Department. McCarthy was unable to substantiate his charges, but his speech had an amazing impact on American public opinion and for the brief period from 1950 to 1953 McCarthy was arguably the most powerful politician in the United States. Reelected to the Senate in 1952 he used his position as chairman of the Senate subcommittee on investigations to intensify his campaign to identify and remove communists from public office. McCarthy drew support from genuine American concern and confusion over the emergence of the Cold War, but his style of bullying and harassing witnesses eventually proved counterproductive. In 1954 he was censured by the Senate and his political influence rapidly diminished.

MCCARTHYISM. A movement in the United States that exerted considerable influence on American foreign policy in the Cold War. Public concern over loyalty and un-American activities predated the Cold War. During the 1930s fear of profascist infiltration resulted in the creation of the House Un-American Activities Committee (HUAC) (q.v.). Suspicion of communist subversion grew during the late 1940s and was fueled in February 1950 by Senator Joseph McCarthy's (q.v.) speech at Wheeling, West Virginia, in which he charged that the State Department was "infested" with communists. McCarthy's allegations of disloyalty and treason in government were never substantiated, but they appeared to provide an explanation to Americans who were perplexed by the "loss of China" to communism and reports that the Soviet Union had developed its own atomic bomb 10 years ahead of American predictions. Moreover, the sudden outbreak of the Korean War (q.v.) in June 1950 seemed to give further weight to McCarthy's charges.

In an atmosphere of virtual hysteria the public demanded the discovery and removal of communists and their sympathizers from positions in American government and public life. McCarthy conducted hearings in the Senate that were broadcast live on radio and television. He became so much the symbol of the anticommunist campaign that it was named after him. McCarthyism was justified in seeking to detect spies and traitors, but it was discredited by its excesses and became associated with sensationalism, bigotry, and intimidation. It was especially destructive within the State Department and brought about the dismissal and resignation of several hundred officials. Indeed, McCarthyism was one of the major factors in the decision of the United States not to establish diplomatic relations with the People's Republic of China (PRC) (q.v.). Although the era of McCarthyism came to an end in the mid-1950s its legacy endured through the 1980s and was illustrated by the unwillingness of American political leaders to be seen to be soft on communism.

MCCLOY, JOHN J. (1895–1989). American lawyer and diplomat. McCloy was an international lawyer who served as under secretary of war from 1941 to 1945 and was a member of the American delegation to the Potsdam Conference (q.v.). He urged a policy of reconstruction in Germany after World War II, and after serving as the president of the World Bank, was appointed American high commissioner to the newly formed Federal Republic of Germany (FRG) (q.v.) in 1949. This was a civilian post superseding the outgoing American military governor, Lucius Clay (q.v.). McCloy's main tasks were to administer aid to the FRG from the European Recovery Program (ERP or Marshall Plan) (q.v.) and liaise with Federal German Chancellor Konrad Adenauer (q.v.) during the consolidation of the emerging U.S.-FRG alliance. McCloy attempted to sidestep attendant controversies over German rearmament by encouraging the European Defense Community (EDC) (q.v.), over which he brokered Franco-German agreement. In 1952 he stepped down to assume the presidency of the Chase Manhattan Bank, but nevertheless continued to be an advocate of close relations between the United States and West Germany.

MCCONE, JOHN A. (1902–1991). American businessman and director of the Central Intelligence Agency (CIA) (q.v.). McCone made his fortune in the steel and shipbuilding industries during World War II. A staunch Republican, he served in the Eisenhower (q.v.) administration as undersecretary of defense and chairman of the Atomic Energy Commission. McCone was appointed director of CIA by President John F. Kennedy (q.v.) in November 1961. The fact that McCone was a Republican and had no direct association with the CIA was considered a positive political advantage because it maintained the bipartisan approach to foreign policy. But McCone was also Kennedy's personal choice and his appointment underscored the president's powerful influence over the CIA. As director, McCone placed greater emphasis on intelligence gathering than covert operations. This proved invaluable to President Kennedy in providing information during the Cuban Missile Crisis (q.v.) in 1962.

President Lyndon Johnson (q.v.), however, was not so receptive to the generally pessimistic tone of CIA reports on the situation in Vietnam (q.v.). McCone resigned as director in April 1965 and returned to private business. The resignation demonstrated the power of the president in the making of American policy during the Cold War. Like Allen Dulles (q.v.) in 1961, McCone had effectively lost the confidence of the president and had to be replaced.

MACMILLAN, HAROLD (1894–1986). British statesman and prime minister. A prominent member of the Conservative Party, Macmillan succeeded Anthony Eden (q.v.) as prime minister in January 1957 in the aftermath of the Suez Crisis (q.v.). Macmillan tried to rehabilitate Great Britain (q.v.) as a world power mainly through close relations with U.S. presidents Dwight Eisenhower and John F. Kennedy (qq.v.). Anglo-American cooperation was evident in the 1958 Lebanon Crisis (q.v.) and in rejecting French President de Gaulle's attempt to establish tripartisme (qq.v.) in Western security affairs. In 1962, at Nassau in the Bahamas, Macmillan obtained American Polaris missiles from Kennedy to permit the continuation of Britain's strategic nuclear forces. Macmillan's period as prime minister was marked by rising domestic prosperity, notwithstanding inexorable retreat as a colonial power and increasing dependency on the United States. The latter factor led de Gaulle to veto British membership of the European Economic Community (EEC) (q.v.) in January 1963. Macmillan's government was also shaken by the Profumo Affair in 1963, a sex scandal with damaging security implications that contributed further to British political self-doubt. By the time of Macmillan's resignation in October 1963, Britain was beset by significant balance of payments problems, which were further to erode its great power vitality during the coming decade.

MCNAMARA, ROBERT S. (1916–). American business executive and secretary of defense. After serving in the U.S. Air Force during World War II, McNamara took up a business career and eventually rose to become president of Ford Motor Company. President John F. Kennedy (q.v.) appointed McNamara as secretary of defense in 1961 primarily for his reputation for efficiency and proven organizational skills. McNamara presided over a radical reorganization of the Defense Department and a military build-up that included significant developments in missile and submarine technology.

McNamara was also an advocate of defeating communist insurgency by flexible military response and regarded South Vietnam as a highly suitable opportunity to put this strategy into effect. His hawkish views were influential in persuading both Kennedy and Lyndon Johnson (q.v.) to increase American military involvement in the Vietnam War (q.v.). During the Johnson administration McNamara and the Defense Department were placed by the president in virtual charge of the American prosecution of the war. By 1967, however, McNamara's optimism had turned to pessimism and he recommended a reversal of the policy of escalation. In 1968 he resigned his cabinet post and became president of the World Bank, a position he retained until 1981. During the 1980s McNamara became a prominent critic of nuclear weapons and later revealed that he had long considered that American military involvement in the Vietnam War had been a grievous mistake.

MALAYAN EMERGENCY. Communist insurgency in the British colony of Malaya from February 1948 to July 1960. It was led by Chin Peng, the secretary general of the Malayan Communist Party and the former leader of Malayan resistance to Japanese occupation during World War II. Chin Peng reactivated his organization, renamed as the Malayan Races Liberation Army (MRLA) to fight the British, using classical guerrilla strategies modeled after those used in China by Mao Zedong (q.v.). Outlying mines and plantations would be attacked, gradually creating liberated areas, which were to be merged by further fighting before final offensives against urban and administrative centers. In April 1950 Great Britain (q.v.) was forced by initial MRLA successes to mount full military counteroperations, eventually using 30,000 British and Commonwealth troops, 30 air squadrons, and a significant police and intelligence network against about 9,000 MRLA guerrillas.

Unjust comparisons have been made between British success in Malaya compared with French and American failures in the Indochina and the Vietnam Wars (qq.v.). MRLA forces were overwhelmingly ethnic Chinese, easily distinguished from a largely hostile Malay Muslim population. Moreover, the MRLA was geographically isolated from Soviet or Chinese support. Britain carefully avoided indiscriminate reaction, indeed moving Malaya to independence in 1957 under cooperative native élites. Britain also conducted a successful "hearts and minds" propaganda campaign against the Malayan Communist Party, whose peasant Chinese supporters were separated in fortified "new villages" from the MRLA. By 1954 most British operations consisted of eradicating isolated, nomadic MRLA units, a process completed by autumn 1959.

MALENKOV, GEORGI (1902–1988). Soviet political leader and prime minister. Malenkov was personal secretary to Joseph Stalin (q.v.) during the great purges of the 1930s, and secretary of the Central Committee of the Soviet Communist Party from 1939 to 1953. He was also deputy premier and part of Stalin's inner circle, including Lavrenti Beria, Vyacheslav Molotov, and Nikita Khrushchev (qq.v.). After Stalin's death in 1953 Malenkov became prime minister, although he surrendered the party secretaryship to Khrushchev, prior to collaborating with him to topple Beria in the ensuing struggle for power.

Malenkov was a political innovator who advocated economic decentralization, higher civilian living standards, and "peaceful coexistence" with the capitalist system. The latter envisaged nonmilitary competition with the West, having acknowledged the ultimate futility of a war for supremacy, which was bound to employ strategic nuclear weapons. Nevertheless, Malenkov remained unpopular within the party where he was regarded as an overmighty former sycophant of Stalin. Khrushchev forced him to resign as prime minister in February 1955, before ironically proceeding to implement most of Malenkov's proposed reforms. Malenkov was finally demoted from the Politburo in July 1957, having taken part in the unsuccessful plot to remove Khrushchev as first secretary. In 1964 he was expelled from the Communist Party and thereafter lived in obscurity.

MALINOVSKY, RODION (1898–1967). Soviet general and minister of defense. Malinovsky commanded Soviet forces at Stalingrad in World War II and was appointed defense minister by Nikita Khrushchev (q.v.) in 1957, replacing the dangerously popular Georgi Zhukov (q.v.). Malinovsky kept up a cautious rearguard resistance against Khrushchev's attempted reduction of Soviet conventional forces in favor of less costly nuclear weapons. Instead of Western-style deterrence (q.v.), he advocated "all arms" war-fighting doctrines, which incorporated the Soviet Strategic Rocket Forces (q.v.) into the active war plans of the ground and air forces. Malinovsky was able to build up the latter after the fall of Khrushchev in 1964 and died in office in 1967.

MALTA SUMMIT, 1989. A meeting between President George Bush (q.v.) and the Soviet leader, Mikhail Gorbachev (q.v.), held on December 2–3,1989, on the Soviet cruise ship *Maxim Gorky* outside Valetta Harbor, Malta. It was the first direct consultation between the leaders of the United States and the Soviet Union after the collapse of communism in Eastern Europe. During the summit Bush pressed for renewed Strategic Arms Reduction Talks (START) (q.v.) and negotiations for a Conventional Forces in Europe (CFE) treaty (q.v.). Tentative discussions on the possibility of German reunification were also accompanied by offers of American economic aid. Bush obtained a pledge from Gorbachev to end Soviet military aid to Nicaragua (q.v.), although the Soviet leader was refused a reciprocal American commitment to improve relations with Cuba (q.v.). Gorbachev added, nonetheless, that the Soviet Union would never start a war with the United States, and in the press conference concluding the summit, both leaders spoke openly of a new era in international relations and an imminent ending of the Cold War.

MANSFIELD AMENDMENTS. Attempts by the U.S. Senate to reduce American military involvement in the Cold War. From 1966 to 1973 Senate Majority Leader Mike Mansfield of Montana sponsored a series of amendments that he attached to bills in the Senate. The purpose was to bring about cuts in defense spending by significantly reducing the number of American troops serving in Europe. Mansfield argued that it was the responsibility of the European members of the North Atlantic Treaty Organization (NATO) (q.v.) to make up the shortfall and thereby ensure a more equitable sharing of the financial burden of defending Western Europe. The Mansfield Amendments reflected traditional American isolationism and suspicion of foreign entanglements. They also coincided with domestic political controversy over the Vietnam War (q.v.) and were influenced by the desire of Congress to check the expanding power of the "imperial presidency." The fundamental significance attached to the defense of Western Europe in American cold war strategy and the desire not to weaken NATO ensured, however, that the amendments were regularly defeated.

MAO ZEDONG (1893–1976). Chinese statesman and chairman, also known as Mao Tse-tung. From a peasant background, Mao was trained as a teacher. In 1921 he was prominent in helping to establish the Chinese Communist Party. In order to escape the political repression of the Nationalist government, Mao led the Chinese communists in 1934–1935 on the Long March covering 6,000 miles. Successfully pursuing the tactics of guerrilla warfare against both the Nationalist government of Chiang Kai-shek (q.v.) and the Japanese invading army, Mao progressively built up mass popular support for the communist movement by winning the trust and admiration of the peasants.

In 1949 Mao overthrew the Nationalists and established the People's Republic of China (PRC) (q.v.) in October 1949. Known popularly as "Chairman Mao," he ruled Mainland China until his death in 1976. In terms of the Cold War, Mao was a cult figure and inspiration for national liberation movements throughout the Third World. As such, he was considered the inveterate enemy of international capitalism and the United States, a power he once contemptuously described as "a paper tiger." However, Mao's belief in the inevitability of war with the capitalist powers also caused friction with the Soviet Union and resulted in the Sino-Soviet Split (q.v.). Mao was criticized for being dogmatic but his ability to act pragmatically was indicated in 1971 by his invitation to President Richard Nixon (q.v.) to visit China. The meeting with the American president in Beijing in 1972 exemplified Mao's standing as a world statesman and his achievement in securing America's recognition of Communist China as a world power.

MARSHALL, GEORGE C. (1880–1959). American general and secretary of state. A career army officer, Marshall rose to the rank of general and served as Army chief of staff during World War II. Marshall became one of many prominent examples of military men who were appointed by the president to high government office or a special overseas mission during the Cold War. During World War II he accompanied Franklin Roosevelt (q.v.) to the summit meetings of the Big Three. In 1945 President Harry Truman (q.v.) chose Marshall to go to China on a mission to try and resolve the differences between Chiang Kai-shek and Mao Zedong (qq.v.). In 1947 Marshall became secretary of state and proposed the European Recovery Program (ERP) (q.v.) to promote the economic recovery of Europe. The program became popularly known as the Marshall Plan and its success provided an enduring tribute to Marshall's great skill as a diplomat and statesman as well as a soldier.

MARSHALL PLAN. See EUROPEAN RECOVERY PROGRAM.

MASSIVE RETALIATION. American and North Atlantic Treaty Organization (NATO) (q.v.) doctrine of strategic nuclear deterrence (q.v.). The term originated in a speech on January 12, 1954, made by Secretary of State John Foster Dulles (q.v.) to the Council on Foreign Relations, New York. Dulles asserted that any Soviet military attack on American interests would be countered by a full-scale thermonuclear offensive against the territory and cities of the Soviet Union. The intent of this policy was to intimidate Moscow to a point where it would not dare use its overwhelming more numerous conventional forces against the West for fear of the consequences. Moreover, the United States would be relieved of the need to maintain the costly conventional forces required to counter a Soviet attack in kind. This was in essence the Eisenhower (q.v.) administration's New Look defense strategy (q.v.) of October 1953, adopted by NATO two years later. The question of its psychological credibility after the Soviets developed their own thermonuclear weapons gave rise in the 1960s to the revised strategy of flexible response (q.v.).

MENDÈS-FRANCE, PIERRE (1907–1982). French political leader and prime minister. During World War II Mendès-France joined the Free French movement of Charles de Gaulle (q.v.) and served as national economics minister in the postwar French provisional government. He was a vociferous parliamentary critic of the Indochina War (q.v.) and became prime minister in June 1954 after France's final defeat. Mendès-France initiated French research on the atomic bomb (q.v.) and, after the parliamentary rejection of the European Defense Community (EDC) (q.v.), endorsed the October 1954 Paris Agreements (q.v.) that admitted the Federal Republic of Germany (FRG) into the North Atlantic Treaty Organization (NATO) (qq.v.). After resigning as prime minister in February 1955, Mendès-France became a notable opponent of de Gaulle after the latter's return to power in 1958. In that year Mendès-France was expelled from the Radical Party after a much-publicized meeting in Moscow with Nikita Khrushchev (q.v.), but was to help establish the reconstructed French Socialist Party from fragmented moderate leftists, retaining his role as senior opposition leader to de Gaulle.

MENGISTU, HAILE MARIAM (1937–). Ethiopian Marxist political leader and president. Mengistu was a prominent member of the Derg, the military council that overthrew Emperor Haile Selassie in September 1974. As vice-president and leader of the Derg executive he conducted widespread political purges in conjunction with sweeping socialist reforms in Ethiopia (q.v.) from 1975 to 1976. His methods provoked violent clashes with other socialist and labor organizations, and the Derg tried to oust him in December 1976. He mounted a successful countercoup in February 1977, crushing his opponents with such brutality that the United States canceled economic aid to Ethiopia on humanitarian grounds. In May 1977 Mengistu subsequently visited Moscow and aligned himself with the Soviet Union. Military aid from the latter and also from the German Democratic Republic (GDR) and Cuba (qq.v.) was vital to his defeat of Somalia (q.v.) in the Ogaden War, which began in July 1977, and in campaigns against insurgents in the northern province of Eritrea. This relationship, nevertheless, provoked considerable American fears for strategic security in the Horn of Africa (q.v.). The construction of a Marxist-Leninist state in Ethiopia began in August 1979 and was declared complete in 1987, notwithstanding intractable economic hardships, famine, war, and civil dissension. In 1990 the withdrawal of Soviet aid led Mengistu to abandon communism. He was overthrown in 1991 and forced into exile.

MIKOYAN, ANASTAS (1895–1978). Soviet political leader and president. Appointed to the Politburo in 1935, Mikoyan served as an expert in food production, distribution, and foreign trade. In 1953 he aligned himself politically with Nikita Khrushchev (q.v.) and introduced the latter's "secret speech" criticizing Joseph Stalin (q.v.) at the 20th Soviet Communist Party Congress in 1956. As Soviet deputy premier he flew to Budapest in June 1956 to oversee the removal of the Hungarian Stalinist leader, Matyas Rakosi (q.v.), and returned in October for talks with Imre Nagy (q.v.) that nevertheless failed to stem the Hungarian Uprising (q.v.).

Mikoyan was rumored to have opposed Soviet military intervention in Hungary. Moreover, he ardently advocated "peaceful coexistence" with the West, to which he frequently traveled as a roving ambassador, in addition to recurrent visits to non-Soviet communist leaders. He supported Khrushchev during the abortive Politburo coup in 1957, but having been removed to the largely ceremonial post of president of the Supreme Soviet in July 1964, Mikoyan was a passive observer when Leonid Brezhnev and Alexei Kosygin (qq.v.) took power in the following October. Mikoyan was, nevertheless, forced to relinquish his office in December 1965 and left the Politburo in April 1966.

MILITARY INTELLIGENCE (MI6). British counterpart of the American Central Intelligence Agency (CIA) (q.v.) and the Soviet KGB (q.v.), also known as the Secret Intelligence Service (SIS). MI6 is a secret agency of the British government whose function is to gather military intelligence and conduct espionage and counterespionage. It has usually worked very closely with the CIA. In contrast to the CIA, however, MI6 has lacked the financial resources and political direction to engage in large-scale paramilitary covert operations. Another branch of British military intelligence is MI5, the Security Service, which is similar to the

American Federal Bureau of Investigation (FBI) and is concerned with internal security and counterespionage activities within Great Britain (q.v.).

MISSILE GAP. An allegedly imminent Soviet superiority over the United States in intercontinental ballistic missiles (ICBMs) (q.v.), implied in the 1957 Gaither Report (q.v.), seemingly vindicated later in the year by the launch of Sputnik (q.v.). If true, this would have conferred a Soviet first strike capability (q.v.) over the United States, undermining the credibility of the strategy of deterrence (q.v.). Similar to the chimerical bomber gap (q.v.) of 1955, American commentators asserted that the missile gap needed to be closed with accelerated American ICBM programs. President Dwight Eisenhower (q.v.) consequently prioritized the Minuteman ICBM and the Polaris submarine-launched ballistic missile (SLBM) (q.v.). Nevertheless, the inflated image of Soviet ICBM capabilities projected by Nikita Khrushchev (q.v.) ensured that 1960 presidential candidate John F. Kennedy (q.v.) made the missile gap a vital campaign issue. After his election Kennedy devoted even greater resources than Eisenhower to strategic nuclear arms procurement, confronting the Soviet Union with a missile gap of its own. Embarrassing Soviet ICBM deficiencies influenced Khrushchev into taking high-risk policies, which precipitated the 1962 Cuban Missile Crisis (q.v.).

MOBUTU, JOSEPH DÉSIRÉ (1930–1997). Congolese/Zairian military leader and president, also known as Mobutu Sese Sekou. In July 1960, after a series of violent mutinies threatened the government of Patrice Lumumba (q.v.), Mobutu rose from noncommissioned rank in the Belgian colonial force publique to become chief of the army staff in the newly independent Congo (q.v.). In September 1960 he sided, however, with President Joseph Kasavubu (q.v.) against Lumumba, whom his forces arrested before handing him over to rebel forces in the separatist province of Katanga where he was killed. Thereafter, Mobutu, with Belgian and American support, held the balance of power in Congolese politics. Kasavubu came to terms with Katanga's leader Moise Tshombe (q.v.) in 1964 after four years of civil war, but in November 1965, Mobutu himself took power. His personal dictatorship soon prevailed, needing periodic American and French intervention to maintain itself, in return for which he was a staunch supporter of Western initiatives in surrounding African states. Notwithstanding its extreme brutality and corruption, Mobutu's rule continued until May 1997 when his regime collapsed and he fled into exile.

MOLOTOV, VYACHESLAV (1890–1986). Soviet diplomat and foreign minister. Appointed chairman of the Soviet Council of Ministers by Joseph Stalin (q.v.) in 1930, Molotov built the powerful complex of state ministries that allowed his patron to consolidate power. Molotov became foreign minister in May 1939, concluding the nonaggression pact with Nazi Germany in August, which effectively enabled Hitler to launch World War II. Molotov remained as Stalin's closest foreign policy aide during the war against Germany, conducting ministerial-level relations with Great Britain (q.v.) and the United States. He attended the Teheran, Yalta, and San Francisco conferences (qq.v.). Before the latter in April 1945, President Harry Truman (q.v.) berated him over alleged Soviet violation of Allied agreements in Poland (q.v.). This celebrated episode signaled the rapid deterioration of American/Soviet relations, which in turn gave rise to the Cold War.

Molotov doggedly upheld Soviet interests in the Council of Foreign Ministers (CFM) (q.v.), which could not agree to acceptable terms for a postwar settlement in Germany. While attending the Committee for European Economic Cooperation (CEEC) in Paris in July 1947, he decisively rejected terms for Soviet participation in the European Recovery Program (ERP or Marshall Plan) (q.v.), effectively presaging the partition of Europe into separate capitalist and Soviet spheres. In 1949, however, he was removed from government and party office as a result of his wife's alleged political dissidence. He returned to favor shortly before Stalin's death, after which he regained the foreign ministry as the price of his support for Georgi Malenkov (q.v.) within a new collective leadership. Molotov, nevertheless, remained a doctrinaire Stalinist, out of step with Malenkov, Nikita Khrushchev, Nikolai Bulganin, and Anastas Mikoyan (qq.v.). He was removed as foreign minister again in 1956, and demoted from the Politburo in 1957 having conspired in vain with Malenkov to remove Khrushchev. Molotov was appointed ambassador to Mongolia before being fully denounced in October 1961 and expelled from the Communist Party in 1964.

MONNET, JEAN (1888–1979). French business leader and politician. During World War II Monnet joined the Free French movement of Charles de Gaulle and used his international contacts to provide vital channels to otherwise unavailable American material assistance. De Gaulle, however, dropped him after France's (q.v.) liberation from the Nazis in 1944. Monnet returned to French government in December 1945 as director of "the Plan," a six-year state-led economic reconstruction scheme, which was eventually capitalized by the European Recovery

Program (ERP or Marshall Plan) (q.v.). Monnet also realized the necessity of political and economic cooperation with the rapidly emerging
Federal Republic of Germany (FRG) (q.v.) and he conceived the outline
of what was to become the European Coal and Steel Community (ECSC)
(q.v.), whose coordinating High Authority he chaired. Having shaped one
of the institutional foundations of capitalist recovery in Western Europe,
Monnet also sought to promote political integration and was the progeni-
tor of the European Defense Community (EDC) (q.v.), although this
scheme was rejected in 1954 by the French parliament.

MOSCOW TREATY, 1970. Signed on August 12, 1970, by Willy Brandt
and Alexei Kosygin (qq.v.) on behalf of the Federal Republic of Germany
(FRG) (q.v.) and the Soviet Union. The treaty was an important affirma-
tion of détente and Ostpolitik (qq.v.), which recognized Europe's post-
1945 frontiers, including the Oder-Neisse Line and the FRG border with
the German Democratic Republic (GDR) (qq.v.). Significant FRG-Soviet
trade and aid relations followed as did a similar Treaty of Warsaw between the FRG and Poland, the Quadripartite Agreement on Berlin, and
the Conference on Security and Cooperation in Europe (CSCE) (qq.v.).
It also eroded the Hallstein Doctrine (q.v.) and, although its preamble
alluded to a single common solution of the German question, it also
paved the way to the 1972 Basic Treaty between the FRG and GDR.

MOSSADEGH, MOHAMMED (1882–1967). Iranian nationalist politician and prime minister. Mossadegh was a leading critic of British and
Soviet occupation policies in Iran (q.v.) during World War II. In October 1944 he orchestrated parliamentary legislation against new foreign
oil concessions that obstructed Soviet plans in the north of the country
and so contributed to the 1946 Azerbaijan Crisis (q.v.).

In March 1951 Mossadegh drafted a bill for the nationalization of the
British Anglo-Iranian Oil Company (AIOC, now BP), to popular Iranian
acclaim. He became Iran's prime minister the same month, with AIOC's
assets being seized finally in June. Although British Prime Minister
Clement Attlee (q.v.) was also dubious about the efficacy of military
action, the United States crucially vetoed British intervention. It assented,
however, to an embargo of Iranian petroleum products, which had severe domestic economic consequences for Iran. Reza Mohammed Shah
Pahlavi attempted to remove Mossadegh in July 1952, but the latter's
National Front government was swept back into power after only a week
by massive popular demonstrations. Continuing economic distress, however, augmented the revolutionary momentum of the communist Tudeh

Party. In August 1953 the Central Intelligence Agency's (CIA) (q.v.) chief of operations for the Middle East, Kermit Roosevelt (q.v.), revived a dormant British plan for a coup by royalist military officers to topple Mossadegh in favor of personal rule by the shah. This succeeded, the oil crisis was resolved, and Iran was assimilated as an ally of the United States.

MOZAMBIQUE. East African state that became independent from Portugal on June 25, 1975, after a 13-year guerrilla war by the Frente de Libertação de Moçambique (Mozambique Liberation Front or FRELIMO) led by Samora Machel. In 1977 at its 3rd Party Congress, FRELIMO declared itself Marxist-Leninist and began to extend its political framework in conjunction with ambitious social, educational, and economic modernization plans, which challenged many indigenous structures and traditions. Mozambique joined the Non-Aligned Movement (q.v.) and aided African liberation struggles in neighboring Rhodesia and South Africa. After successive South African invasions of Mozambique, in 1981 Machel concluded aid and trade agreements with the Soviet Union and its allies. South African and American intelligence organizations therefore sponsored the self-styled Resistência Nacional Moçambicana (Mozambique National Resistance or RENAMO), a counterrevolutionary group rooted in rural resistance to FRELIMO reform programs. A protracted and widely destructive civil war followed.

After the 1984 Nkomati Accords with South Africa, Mozambique pursued a largely successful political and economic rapprochement with the United States, Great Britain (q.v.), and Western Europe. Nevertheless, with funds from private right-wing American sources, and clandestine help from the South African defense ministry, RENAMO continued its activities. Moreover, Machel's death in an air crash in 1986 was likely to have resulted from South African fire. The Mozambican civil war continued even after peace accords were signed in Rome in December 1990.

MULTI-LATERAL FORCE (MLF). Joint strategic nuclear force for the North Atlantic Treaty Organization (NATO) (q.v.), proposed by the Kennedy (q.v.) administration in 1962 as a way of containing unilateral Western European nuclear ambitions. The MLF was to operate American-manufactured Polaris missiles in a flotilla of submarines and cruisers manned by joint NATO crews. Indeed, the sale of Polaris to Great Britain (q.v.) in November 1962 was intended by Kennedy to serve as the basis for such a force. Genuine enthusiasm for the MLF, however, came only from the Federal Republic of Germany (FRG) (q.v.). Britain sought unilateral deterrence (q.v.) forces, as did France under President Charles de Gaulle (qq.v.), which insisted on its own nuclear weapons programs. The MLF petered out in 1964 after insuperable disagreements on its command and control. At the administrative level, NATO, nevertheless, maintained a combined Nuclear Planning Group.

MULTIPLE INDEPENDENTLY TARGETABLE RE-ENTRY VEHICLE (MIRV). Strategic nuclear delivery system, enabling a single missile to launch many warheads against separate targets after atmospheric reentry during suborbital flight. Initially conceived by the United States as a preemptive countermeasure against Soviet anti-ballistic missiles (ABMs) (q.v.), MIRVs were first deployed in the Minuteman III and submarine-launched Poseidon missiles, with levels of improved accuracy that conferred a potential first strike capability (q.v.) against Soviet missile bases. Related "counter force" doctrines were adopted by Secretary of Defense James Schlesinger (q.v.) in 1974. The Soviets, however, soon developed their own MIRVs, including virtually invulnerable submarine-launched systems. MIRV restrictions were included in the SALT II Treaty (q.v.), whose eventual nonratification by the United States preceded continuing MIRV technical refinements by both superpowers for the duration of the Cold War, preserving deterrence (q.v.) by allowing both sides to maintain certain offensive capabilities.

MUSKIE, EDMUND S. (1914–1996). American politician and secretary of state. Muskie was a Democratic senator from Maine and served on the Senate Foreign Relations Committee until he was appointed secretary of state by President Jimmy Carter (q.v.) in April 1980. Muskie vacillated between tough anti-Soviet rhetoric on Afghanistan and Poland (qq.v.) and a conciliatory tone on renewing détente (q.v.) with particular regard to ratifying the SALT II Treaty (q.v.). In September 1980 he met the Soviet foreign minister, Andrei Gromyko (q.v.), in New York to agree on joint abstention from the Iran-Iraq War. Muskie also attacked what he considered the bellicose foreign policy proposals of Ronald Reagan (q.v.) during the 1980 presidential election campaign. Muskie left office in January 1981. He later served on the Tower Commission that investigated the Iran-Contra Affair (q.v.) in 1987.

MUTUAL AND BALANCED FORCE REDUCTIONS (MBFR). Conventional force reduction talks between the North Atlantic Treaty Organization (NATO) and the Warsaw Pact (qq.v.). They were proposed by NATO in June 1968 and finally convened in Vienna in October 1973 after having been accepted by the Soviet leader, Leonid Brezhnev (q.v.), during wider negotiations leading to détente (q.v.). MBFR talks, however, were continually deadlocked over categorical terms of reference and became a diplomatic shuttlecock subject to suspension and prevarication by both participants. MBFR was superseded by Mikhail Gorbachev's (q.v.) proposal of unilateral Soviet conventional force cuts to the General Assembly of the United Nations (UN) (q.v.) in December 1988. The MBFR process was formally completed in February 1990 prior to the opening of fresh negotiations for the Conventional Forces in Europe (CFE) treaty (q.v.).

MUTUAL ASSURED DESTRUCTION (MAD). American strategic nuclear doctrine. In 1962 Secretary of Defense Robert McNamara (q.v.) coined the term "assured destruction" to describe the minimum threat needed to maintain a credible strategy of deterrence (q.v.) against the Soviet Union. In effect, this meant possessing the capability to exterminate no less than a third of the enemy's population in an American retaliatory nuclear attack. The imminent acquisition of intercontinental ballistic missiles (ICBMs) by the Soviet Strategic Rocket Forces (qq.v.) led in 1964 to the modification of this principle to mutual assured destruction. The implication was that reciprocal annihilation capabilities would inhibit either superpower from initiating general war, and therefore deterrence would be maintained through a "balance of terror." By contriving the unfortunate acronym MAD, this doctrine played into the hands of antinuclear critics.

MUTUAL DEFENSE ASSISTANCE PROGRAM (MDAP). American military aid program for the European signatories of the North Atlantic Treaty (q.v.), put to Congress by President Harry Truman (q.v.) in July 1949. It envisaged $1.4 billion to permit the states concerned to buy American arms needed for the minimum credible defense against possible Soviet attack. This sum represented a 10 percent increase in American defense expenditure and provoked Congressional resistance. However, Congress quickly approved the MDAP in September 1949 after Truman announced that the Soviet Union had successfully tested its first atomic bomb (q.v.). The MDAP was supplemented in December 1951 by the Mutual Security Agency, which superseded the Economic Cooperation Administration (ECA) set up by the European Recovery Program (ERP or Marshall Plan) (q.v.). American financial aid to Europe thereafter facilitated extensive weapons purchases, training, and base construction.

-N-

NAGY, IMRE (1896–1958). Hungarian communist politician and prime minister. Nagy returned to Hungary in 1945 after having been exiled in Moscow during World War II. He served under Matyas Rakosi (q.v.) as agriculture minister before retiring into academic life in 1948 after opposing enforced agricultural collectivization on the Soviet model. He was recalled in July 1953 during a temporary round of Soviet-mandated reforms, replacing Rakosi as prime minister and announcing a "new course" based on economic decentralization and reduced political repression. Rakosi, nevertheless, stayed on as first secretary of the ruling Hungarian Workers' Party and was able to have Nagy branded a "right-wing deviationist" culminating in his expulsion from the party in 1954.

During the Hungarian Uprising (q.v.) the party Central Committee reappointed Nagy prime minister on October 24, 1956. Faced with widespread civil insurrection, he abolished the state security police, appointed a coalition cabinet, and promised multiparty elections. Having seemingly negotiated a Soviet military withdrawal from the country, Nagy announced Hungary's neutrality in international affairs, and on November 2, its withdrawal from the Warsaw Pact (q.v.). The latter move furnished the pretext for a full-scale Soviet invasion on November 4. Nagy took refuge in the Yugoslavian embassy in Budapest. Despite having been promised safe conduct from the city, he was arrested in transit and taken to Romania. In June 1958 Nagy was tried in secret and executed on charges of counterrevolutionary armed uprising.

NASSER, GAMAL ABDEL (1918–1970). Egyptian nationalist political leader and president. Nasser was the most dynamic of the leaders of the military coup that toppled the Egyptian monarchy in July 1952. He gradually assumed complete power, becoming president in 1956 and eliminating his military and civilian political opponents en route. His foreign policy was first to dissolve Egypt's virtual dependency on Great Britain (q.v.) and then to promote Egypt as the focal point of pan-Arab nationalist revolution throughout the Middle East. He eschewed the Baghdad Pact (q.v.) and in 1955 concluded modern-arms transfers from the Soviet Union via its satellite, Czechoslovakia. Despite Nasser's wish for nonalignment in the Cold War, the purchase of arms from Czechoslovakia led to the rupturing of economic aid talks with Britain and the United States, to which Nasser responded by nationalizing the Suez Canal in July 1956, thereby initiating the Suez Crisis (q.v.).

Having emerged ascendant from the latter, Nasser's radical appeal sufficiently alarmed the United States to formulate the Eisenhower Doctrine (q.v.) in 1957. Soon afterward, Nasser accepted Soviet economic aid, although he adamantly maintained his political independence, crushing the Egyptian Communist Party, forming the United Arab Republic with Syria in 1958 and further advocating Arab unity, with hostility to Israel as common cause. He clashed with U.S.-supported Saudi Arabia in the Yemen civil war, which proved a costly failure, and in spring 1967 he attempted to recoup prestige by provoking the Israelis. The result was the 1967 Arab-Israeli War (Six Day War) (q.v.) in which Egypt was routed. Nasser's prestige never recovered. For defense he became more dependent than ever on Soviet arms and advisers, and within the Arab world his influence was diminished by the Saudis. Having ended a futile "war of attrition" with Israel, Nasser died suddenly of a heart attack in September 1970.

NATIONAL SECURITY ACT, 1947. Act of Congress designed to make the executive branch of the United States government better informed and more efficient in its exercise of diplomatic and military policy. Passed by Congress in July 1947, the National Security Act reflected the rise of the United States to the status of world superpower and the recognition of American political leaders that the country must become actively involved in world affairs. The principal purpose of the act was to improve the flow of information and advice to the president by creating the National Security Council (NSC) to advise on foreign policy and the Central Intelligence Agency (CIA) (qq.v.) to gather and interpret foreign "intelligence." The CIA was also assigned the function of undertaking overseas covert operations. In addition, the armed services were united within a new Department of Defense whose headquarters were located in the Pentagon just outside Washington, D.C. A civilian would serve as secretary of defense in order to preserve civilian control of the military.

NATIONAL SECURITY COUNCIL (NSC). One of the principal foreign policy instruments of the president of the United States. The National Security Council was established by the National Security Act (q.v.) of 1947. The main function of the NSC is to advise the president on matters relating to national security. When it meets as a council its members include the president, the vice president, the secretaries of state and defense, the director of the Central Intelligence Agency (CIA,) and the chair of the Joint Chiefs of Staff (JCS). A permanent NSC staff has also come into being and is headed by the special assistant to the president for national security affairs or more popularly known as the national security adviser.

Initially, under President Harry Truman (q.v.) the NSC was mainly regarded as a means of bringing together the various agencies of the government involved in foreign policy and also of preparing comprehensive studies of diplomatic issues. However, the NSC steadily increased its influence over the making of foreign policy as a result of the growth of its own permanent staff and the fact that the national security adviser usually possessed an office in the White House that provided direct access to the president. The power of the NSC was most evident during the Nixon (q.v.) administration when Henry Kissinger (q.v.) served as national security adviser.

NSC-68. One of the most important and influential internal documents analyzing American relations with the Soviet Union at the beginning of the Cold War. In January 1950, at a time of concern caused by the report that the Soviets had developed an atomic bomb (q.v.) and the shock of the "loss of China," President Harry Truman (q.v.) requested a comprehensive review of America's armed forces to be prepared for discussion by the National Security Council (q.v.). National Security Memorandum 68, also known as NSC-68, was completed in April 1950 and was the work of the State Department's Policy Planning Staff headed by Paul Nitze (q.v.). Starting with the premise that the Soviet Union actively sought world domination, NSC-68 argued that the military power of the United States was currently inadequate to prevent this. The report concluded that the United States must undertake an enormous military effort on a scale commensurate with wartime rearmament.

It was considered unlikely that Congress would readily agree to a massive increase in the annual defense budget. But the timing of NSC-68 was fortuitous in that the sudden outbreak of the Korean War (q.v.) in June 1950 appeared to confirm the report's warning of communist aggressiveness. Consequently, the anticipated Congressional opposition to the recommendations contained in NSC-68 was subdued and large defense appropriations were quickly secured. NSC-68 was therefore highly significant in providing a rationale for American rearmament in the early 1950s.

NEHRU, JAWAHARLAL (1889–1964). Indian political leader and prime minister. The first prime minister of India (q.v.) after independence was secured from Great Britain (q.v.) in August 1947, Nehru declared himself democratic, socialist, and chose to remain within the British Commonwealth. He rebuffed American attempts to co-opt him as a model noncommunist Asian leader, exercising his neutrality in the Cold War by recognizing the People's Republic of China (PRC) (q.v.). He incurred further American displeasure by criticizing United Nations (UN) (q.v.) actions during the Korean War (q.v.), and by accepting considerable Soviet industrial aid prior to his visit to Moscow in July 1955. He was also critical of the South-East Asia Treaty Organization (SEATO) and the Baghdad Pact (qq.v.), particularly as the latter furnished Western military aid to his hostile neighbor Pakistan.

Nehru advocated political independence for decolonizing powers from either superpower bloc and was a driving force behind the 1955 Bandung Conference and the subsequent Non-Aligned Movement (qq.v.). In the latter he became a rival of Communist China and its charismatic foreign minister Zhou Enlai (q.v.). Indeed, after suffering an embarrassing defeat by Communist China in the 1962 Indo-Chinese Border War, Nehru made overtures to President John F. Kennedy (q.v.), although he continued to preclude an Indo-American military alliance up to his death in 1964.

NETO, AGOSTINHO (1922–1979). Angolan Marxist political leader and president. Neto was trained as a doctor in Portugal where he was imprisoned for opposing the right-wing dictator, Antonio Salazar. Neto returned to his native Angola (q.v.) in 1959 and opened a free medical practice in the capital, Luanda. He also opposed Portuguese colonial rule and in 1962 fled from detention to the Congo (q.v.) where he formed the neo-Marxist Movimento Popular de Libertação de Angola or People's Movement for the Liberation of Angola (MPLA). MPLA guerrilla operations contributed to the achievement of Angolan independence in November 1975 and Neto became the country's president. However, the MPLA was immediately engaged in civil war by its anti-Marxist rivals, the Frente Nacional de Libertação de Angola or National Front for the Liberation of Angola (FNLA), and the União Nacional para a Independencia Total de Angola or National Union for the Total Independence of Angola (UNITA) under Jonas Savimbi (q.v.). With substantial military aid from the Soviet Union, the German Democratic Republic (GDR) and Cuba (qq.v.), Neto was victorious, although UNITA survived under South African patronage, and with clandestine American support. Neto began to construct a socialist system in Angola, but he fell victim to cancer from which he died in a Moscow hospital in September 1979.

NEUTRON BOMB (ENHANCED RADIATION WEAPON OR ERW). Battlefield nuclear weapon, researched after 1973 by the U.S. Army within the provisions of the strategy of flexible response (q.v.). It was intended to release neutrons lethal to all living matter, including Soviet troops, but with minimal heat and blast. Surrounding buildings and "hard" economic assets would therefore suffer minimal damage. The Nuclear Planning Group of the North Atlantic Treaty Organization (NATO) (q.v.) began discussion on deployment of the neutron bomb in 1976, but its semiclandestine funding provoked objections in the U.S. Congress. In the Federal Republic of Germany (FRG) (q.v.), where the weapon was most likely to be used in wartime, there were also widespread objections to the evident cynicism of a device that seemingly spared property but killed enormous numbers of people. Similar public protests emerged in the Netherlands and Great Britain (q.v.), prompting a concerted diplomatic effort by National Security Adviser Zbigniew Brzezinski (q.v.) to overcome European resistance. Neverless, on April 7, 1978, when President Jimmy Carter (q.v.) deferred the neutron bomb's production indefinitely. This decision provoked concerted right-wing attacks on Carter, which undermined the credibility of his leadership among the American public.

"NEW LOOK" DEFENSE STRATEGY. Adopted by the Eisenhower (q.v.) administration in October 1953 and elucidated in the document NSC-162/2. It proposed that, instead of maintaining the costly conventional forces needed to meet likely Soviet aggression in kind, the United States should rely on deterrence (q.v.) through strategic nuclear forces that could annihilate the Soviet Union directly if it ever dared to start a war. Made feasible by the hydrogen bomb (q.v.), this strategy had first been mooted in July 1952 by the British military chiefs of staff as an alternative to the demanding peacetime rearmament goals set at the Lisbon Conference (q.v.). Described colloquially as massive retaliation (q.v.), the "New Look" strategy facilitated extensive cuts in the conventional American defense budget. However, it also significantly advanced the importance of manned bombers and missiles, and consequently, stimulated rather than reduced the arms race between the superpowers.

NGO DINH DIEM. See DIEM, NGO DINH.

NICARAGUA. A country in Central America in which the overthrow of the dictator, Anastasio Somoza, in 1979 resulted in the rise to power of the Sandinista National Liberation Front (Frente Sandinista de Liberación Nacional or FSLN). The Sandinistas (q.v.) were openly Marxist and admired the Cuban Revolution (q.v.). They did not wish, however, to break off relations with the United States or align with the communist bloc.

The Reagan (q.v.) administration was hostile and sought to destabilize the Sandinistas by applying a combination of external economic pressure and internal civil disorder. The Central Intelligence Agency (CIA) (q.v.) organized and financed an army of counterrevolutionary guerrillas known as the "Contras" who operated from bases in neighboring Honduras and Costa Rica. The Contras gained little military success and remained heavily dependent upon American financial assistance.

Influenced by the "Vietnam syndrome," American political opinion was sharply divided over the issue of Nicaragua. The fear of being sucked into "another Vietnam [War]" (q.v.) not only ruled out the use of American combat troops in Central America but also seriously restricted the amount of financial support that Congress would vote to assist the Contras. This prompted the Reagan administration to resort to covert methods of funding the Contras and led to the Iran-Contra Affair (q.v.). The withdrawal of American material support compelled the Contras to agree to a cease-fire in 1988. The Sandinistas eventually lost power after being defeated in national elections held in 1990.

NITZE, PAUL (1907–2004). American diplomat and expert on arms control. Nitze was a successful financier who made significant profits out of timely investments in pharmaceuticals during World War II and served in the U.S. Foreign Economic Administration, and the Strategic Bombing Survey. In 1947 he became assistant to Under Secretary of State Will Clayton (q.v.), whom he helped draft the European Recovery Program (ERP or Marshall Plan) (q.v.). In 1949 he moved to the State Department's Policy Planning Staff, succeeding George Kennan (q.v.) as director in January 1950. Unlike Kennan, Nitze ardently supported the development of the hydrogen bomb (q.v.) and incorporated his views on the danger of imminent Soviet aggression and the need for global American military power in the policy document NSC-68 (q.v.), of which he was the principal author.

Nitze left office in January 1953 despite offers to continue from the incoming administration of Dwight Eisenhower (q.v.). Nevertheless, he retained considerable influence outside government, helping to draft the Gaither Report (q.v.) in 1958 and acting as John F. Kennedy's (q.v.) foreign policy adviser during the 1960 presidential election campaign. During the Cuban Missile Crisis (q.v.) in 1962 Nitze was a member of Kennedy's Executive Committee. He served as secretary of the navy from 1963 to 1967, as deputy secretary of defense from 1967 to 1969, and in 1969 led the American delegation at the Strategic Arms Limitation Talks (SALT) (q.v.).

Nitze was skeptical on détente (q.v.) over which he frequently clashed with Henry Kissinger (q.v.). His continuing anti-Soviet animus drove him to participate in the revived Committee on the Present Danger (q.v.) in 1976, which greatly influenced President Ronald Reagan (q.v.), whom Nitze served as principal negotiator with the Soviets on intermediate-range nuclear forces (INFs) (q.v.) and as an adviser at the 1986 Reykjavik Summit (q.v.). Nitze also assisted Secretary of State George Shultz (q.v.) to conclude the INF Treaty (q.v.) and resume Strategic Arms Reduction Talks (START) (q.v.). He retired from government in 1989.

NIXON, RICHARD M. (1913–1994). American statesman and president. Nixon was a small-town Californian attorney, who after service in the U.S. Navy during World War II was elected as a U.S. Congressman. He served on the House Un-American Activities Committee (HUAC) (q.v.), achieving national prominence pursuing the case of Alger Hiss (q.v.). Nixon was elected U.S. senator in 1950 and was the presidential running mate of Dwight Eisenhower (q.v.) in 1952, notwithstanding potentially damaging questions on the propriety of his finances. As vice president he severed ties with anticommunist Senator Joseph McCarthy (q.v.), acting principally as a roving goodwill ambassador for the administration. Nixon was narrowly defeated in the 1960 presidential election by John F. Kennedy (q.v.), but he eventually returned in 1968 and prevailed over a Democratic Party demoralized and divided by the Vietnam War (q.v.).

The priority of the Nixon administration was to extricate the United States from Vietnam through the diplomatic strategy of linkage (q.v.), proposed by National Security Adviser Henry Kissinger (q.v.), which led in turn to détente (q.v.) and yielded considerable progress in arms control and European security agreements with the Soviet Union. Furthermore, Nixon authorized diplomatic contact with the People's Republic of China (PRC) (q.v.), which he visited in 1972. In 1969 at Guam he outlined the "Nixon Doctrine" under which American troop levels in Vietnam would be reduced, although military aid would continue, thereby enabling South Vietnam to defend itself. This became the model for American relations with Third World client states for most of the 1970s. Nevertheless, Nixon seemingly expanded the Vietnam War in 1970 by having American and South Vietnamese forces invade neighboring Cambodia (q.v.). However, the imminence of a peace agreement in 1972 secured his reelection by a landslide majority and American troops disengaged fully from Vietnam in March 1973.

Despite continuing successes in détente and in responding to a burgeoning economic recession, Nixon's presidency was severely undermined by the Watergate Scandal, in which his office attempted to cover-
up its illegal clandestine surveillance of the 1972 Democratic Party
presidential election headquarters. This culminated in Nixon's resignation, under threat of Congressional impeachment, in August 1974. The
scandal aggravated American public doubt over an over-mighty executive branch and along with the dawning reality of defeat in Vietnam,
sapped American confidence. Nixon was pardoned by his successor
Gerald Ford (q.v.), but retired from public life in disgrace. In his later
years he reemerged as an occasional political commentator and expert
on foreign affairs.

NKRUMAH, KWAME (1909–1972). Ghanaian political leader and president. Educated in the United States and Great Britain (q.v.) where he was
strongly influenced by the ideas of pan-Africanism and Marxism,
Nkrumah returned in 1947 to his native Gold Coast, a British colony, with
a radical commitment to decolonization throughout Africa. He attempted
to mobilize the emerging Gold Coast proletariat, but in so doing split with
the established nationalist party, the United Gold Coast Convention, in
1949, forming instead the Convention People's Party. The latter adopted
civil disobedience and strikes to dislodge British rule and Nkrumah was
consequently jailed. The British soon realized, however, that his cooperation was indispensable to an orderly transfer of power and released
him. Nkrumah became Gold Coast prime minister in 1952 and president
of the renamed Ghana, which became independent in 1957 as black
Africa's first postcolonial state.

Nkrumah began ambitious development programs, supported independence struggles elsewhere in Africa, and was a driving force behind
the founding of the Organization of African Unity (OAU) in 1963. After 1960 falling commodity prices and deteriorating terms of trade with
the West impelled him toward cooperation with the Soviet Union. Nikita
Khrushchev (q.v.) notably agreed to fund the vital Volta Dam hydroelec-
tricity project. In adverse economic circumstances, Nkrumah also accrued
quasi-dictatorial powers, culminating in the declaration of a single-party
state and his presidency for life in 1964, backed by internal security services trained by the Soviet KGB (q.v.). Concerned by the prospect of
increased Soviet influence in Africa, Britain and the United States supported a military coup in 1966 that ousted Nkrumah while he was visiting the People's Republic of China (PRC) (q.v.) for economic aid negotiations.

NON-ALIGNED MOVEMENT. Originated in the 1955 Bandung Conference (q.v.) and in subsequent consultations between Josip Tito, Gamal Abdel Nasser, and Jawaharlal Nehru (qq.v.) in 1956, the first summit of "nonaligned" or leaders who were militarily unaffiliated with either superpower, took place in Belgrade, Yugoslavia, in September 1961. Its intention was to promote the security and development of Third World states outside channels still dominated by the former colonial powers and the two superpowers. Twenty-five South American, African, Middle Eastern, and Asian leaders, plus Tito, attended the summit. Although it lacked permanent status, the Non-Aligned Movement encouraged the formation in 1964 of the United Nations (UN) (q.v.) Conference on Trade and Development (UNCTAD), held further summits, and by the time of its 1983 meeting in New Delhi, India (q.v.), had 101 members. These included states as radical as Cuba (q.v.) and as conservative as Saudi Arabia, who participated under the auspices of the Non-Aligned Coordinating Bureau (NACB). The bureau's main role was to facilitate consultations and resolutions intended to notify and influence the great powers on matters of collective concern to the membership.

NORTH ATLANTIC TREATY, 1949. Signed on April 4, 1949, in Washington, D.C., by the United States, Great Britain, France (qq.v.), Belgium, Luxembourg, the Netherlands, Denmark, Norway, Iceland, Italy, Portugal, and Canada. Its most important provision was Article 5 that stated that any attack against a signatory would be regarded as an attack upon all, implying the commitment of American military power to collective defense against an aggressor. This was clearly aimed at the Soviet Union whose seemingly belligerent initiation of the 1948–1949 Berlin Blockade (q.v.) was the catalyst for formal transatlantic security negotiations. An initial framework was provided by the 1948 Brussels Treaty (q.v.) with American participation encouraged by the Vandenberg Resolution (q.v.). The treaty's terms were limited geographically in Article 6 to the signatories' territories in the North Atlantic area, north of the Tropic of Cancer, avoiding an American commitment to defend European colonies. The treaty, nevertheless, provided the foundation of Western European military security for the duration of the Cold War. In January 1950 it acquired an integrated administrative and command structure, the North Atlantic Treaty Organization (NATO) (q.v.), and was signed additionally by Greece and Turkey (q.v.) in 1952, the Federal Republic of Germany (FRG) (q.v.) in 1954, and Spain in 1982.

NORTH ATLANTIC TREATY ORGANIZATION (NATO). Institutional structure formed in January 1950 by the signatories of the North

Atlantic Treaty (q.v.), under Article 9 that empowered them to consider measures for its implementation. A supervisory North Atlantic Council and a Defense Committee were formed by the members' foreign and defense ministers, respectively. In addition, the NATO Military Committee with an Anglo-American-French Standing Group was formed, composed of each member's military chiefs of staff. The outbreak of the Korean War (q.v.) precipitated further joint planning provisions, embodied after 1951 in Supreme Headquarters Allied Powers Europe (SHAPE) and Supreme Allied Commander Atlantic (SACLANT), both under American command, with Commander-in-Chief Channel (CINCHAN) assigned to the British.

In 1952 at the Lisbon Conference (q.v.), a civilian bureaucracy under a secretary general was formed to administer supply, finance, and procurement policy. Greece and Turkey (q.v.) were also admitted as members at Lisbon, as was the Federal Republic of Germany (FRG) (q.v.) under the 1954 Paris Agreements (q.v.), after American pressure following the collapse of the European Defense Community (EDC) (q.v.). Having failed, however, to meet the demanding conventional rearmament goals set at Lisbon, NATO adopted American strategies based on the use of nuclear weapons, massive retaliation (q.v.) in 1956, and flexible response (q.v.) in 1967. Prior to the latter, France (q.v.) withdrew from the NATO military command, although still subscribing to the North Atlantic Treaty. Spain joined in 1982, although it also withdrew its forces from NATO military command in 1986.

Other NATO controversies included "burden sharing" that was used by American critics, notably in the form of the Mansfield Amendments (q.v.), to accuse the Western European allies of providing inadequate resources while enjoying American protection. Moreover, in 1979 the "twin track" decision to employ American intermediate-range nuclear forces (INFs) (q.v.) to Europe provoked widespread European alarm. In the era of the Reagan Doctrine (q.v.), the United States frequently asked its sometimes skeptical NATO allies to provide forces "out of area." Nevertheless, NATO successfully endured for the duration of the Cold War and ultimately served as a negotiating party with the Warsaw Pact (q.v.) in the Conventional Forces in Europe (CFE) Treaty (q.v.) that brought the conflict effectively to a close. Indeed, by the end of the 1990s NATO was negotiating membership with former Eastern bloc states and establishing cooperative relations with Russia.

NOVOTNY, ANTONIN (1904–1975). Czechoslovak communist political leader and president. After his release from a Nazi concentration camp in 1945, Novotny was appointed to the Central Committee of the Czecho-slovak Communist Party in 1946, and to the party secretariat in 1951, shortly before it was purged by its Stalinist leader, Klement Gottwald (q.v.). Novotny succeeded Gottwald as party first secretary in 1953 and became Czechoslovakian president in 1957. He remained on good terms with the Soviet leader, Nikita Khrushchev (q.v.), despite continuing destalinization in the Soviet Union. After the latter's fall in 1964, Novotny was forced to make liberalizing economic reforms to reverse industrial and agricultural stagnation in what had once been the most developed member of the Council for Mutual Economic Assistance (COMECON) (q.v.). But his resistance to political change frustrated the growing reformist lobby within his party and he was replaced as first secretary in January 1968 by Alexander Dubček (q.v.), then as president by Ludvig Svoboda (q.v.) in March, and finally deprived of party membership in June. Considered an administrative liability, Novotny was not rehabilitated after the 1968 Warsaw Pact (q.v.) invasion of Czechoslovakia (q.v.), although in 1971 his membership of the Communist Party was perfunctorily restored.

NUCLEAR NON-PROLIFERATION TREATY, 1968. Signed on July 1, 1968, and entered into force on March 5, 1970, the treaty bound Great Britain (q.v.), the United States, and the Soviet Union not to transfer existing nuclear weapons to nonnuclear weapons states. Moreover, the nonnuclear weapons states signing the treaty, notably Japan and the Federal Republic of Germany (FRG) (qq.v.), agreed neither to acquire nor develop such capabilities. By 1970, 98 states had signed the treaty, although France and the People's Republic of China (PRC) (qq.v.) did not. Furthermore, India (q.v.), Pakistan, Israel, Brazil, South Africa, and Argentina were nonsignatories who were suspected of subsequently attempting to develop nuclear weapons. The treaty, nevertheless, reinforced the move toward détente (q.v.) by reassuring the Soviets about limits on future West German military power. Ironically in 1992, after the Cold War was over, France and Communist China finally acceded to the treaty.

NUCLEAR OPTIONS. Principle first investigated in 1961 by Secretary of Defense Robert McNamara (q.v.) that sought to expand the types and uses of nuclear weapons available to American policymakers in order to maximize the latitude for diplomatic maneuvering in the event of war with the Soviet Union. Existing deterrence (q.v.) doctrines emphasized all-out destruction, but McNamara sought means whereby Soviet military targets could be attacked selectively in order to influence negotiations. A reserve capacity for "assured destruction" would remain in the event that the Soviets did not conform to American expectations. In June 1962 McNamara outlined his policy at the University of Michigan, although it fell into abeyance after the Cuban Missile Crisis (q.v.).

In January 1974, however, Secretary of Defense James Schlesinger (q.v.) announced a strategic "counterforce" doctrine in which highly accurate American nuclear warheads could be deployed selectively against Soviet missile bases, thereby reducing the likelihood of escalation to a full nuclear exchange if deterrence failed. Nuclear war-fighting against the Soviets therefore became implicitly feasible to American planners, who now assumed that the annihilation of American cities in wartime was not a foregone conclusion. This logic was affirmed by President Jimmy Carter (q.v.), whose Presidential Directive PD-59 (q.v.) envisaged a war plan based on a prolonged set of limited nuclear exchanges, restricted geographically to the European theater, and only striking at high-value military targets while avoiding Soviet population centers.

-O-

ODER-NEISSE LINE. Post-1945 border between Germany and Poland (q.v.), drawn along the Oder and Neisse rivers. The subject was discussed by Winston Churchill and Joseph Stalin (qq.v.) at the Teheran Conference (q.v.) in 1943. The pre-World War II border was to be moved westward thereby awarding the territories of Posen, Silesia, and Eastern Pomerania to Poland, an arrangement that would also divide East Prussia with the Soviet Union, displacing seven million Germans in the process. This was mainly to compensate Poland for significant territorial losses to the Soviet Union, which insisted on the restoration of the "Curzon Line," the 1920 Polish-Soviet boundary that had been adjusted in 1921.

At the Yalta Conference (q.v.) in February 1945 the westernmost branch of the Neisse was affirmed as the new boundary, from behind which, as agreed at the July 1945 Potsdam Conference (q.v.), the German population was to be expelled and its property confiscated. However, the absence of a full peace treaty between the Allies and a single recognized German state meant that the new border was never fully ratified. The German Democratic Republic (GDR) (q.v.) was forced to do so in the 1950 Görlitz Agreement with Poland, but the Federal Republic of Germany (FRG) (q.v.) under Chancellor Konrad Adenauer (q.v.) refused, largely because the latter's political constituency included influential Eastern German refugee political parties. Adenauer's claim to Germany's 1937 territories led to persistent Soviet charges that he was an aggressive revanchist. Indeed, the recognition of the Oder-Neisse Line by Willy Brandt in the 1970 Treaties of Moscow and Warsaw (qq.v.) was a vital precondition for the success of both Ostpolitik and détente (qq.v.). Correspondingly, it was an integral feature of the 1975 Helsinki Final Act (q.v.).

OFFICE OF STRATEGIC SERVICES (OSS). *See* CENTRAL INTELLIGENCE AGENCY.

OGARKOV, NIKOLAI (1917–1994). Soviet general. Ogarkov was chief of the Soviet General Staff from 1977 to 1984. He maintained that Western imperialism was an aggressive threat to the Soviet Union regardless of détente (q.v.) and that the armed forces should therefore be given unquestioned industrial and technological primacy within the Soviet planned economy. His particular concern was that technologically advanced American and other Western weapons systems portended an operational revolution in warfare in the 1980s that would render massive Soviet conventional forces obsolescent. He therefore advocated increased defense spending in direct juxtaposition to the economic reform strategies being advanced by Yuri Andropov (q.v.). Despite the latter's death in 1984, Ogarkov was transferred from his posts as chief of staff and deputy defense minister in September 1984. Under Mikhail Gorbachev (q.v.), "new military thinking" was decreed, shifting to a passive defense posture with relative military security preserved by greater East-West arms control. Ogarkov conducted a journalistic campaign against the latter doctrine and in 1989 was dismissed from the Central Committee of the Soviet Communist Party.

OPEN SKIES. Proposal on arms control made by President Dwight Eisenhower (q.v.) in 1955. At the Geneva summit in July 1955 Eisenhower suggested that each nuclear power should permit regular aerial photography of the other's territory. He argued that this would diminish the risk of war and mark an important step toward general disarmament. The proposal was accepted by Great Britain and France (qq.v.), but dismissed by the Soviet Union as a blatant American attempt to discover Soviet military secrets. Eisenhower had expected a Soviet refusal. In fact, his offer was part of the long-running propaganda battle conducted between the two superpowers in which the Americans condemned the Soviets for war-mongering and vice versa. The failure of the proposal also underscored the secretiveness of the Soviets and their opposition to verification. This was a regular stumbling block in all discussions over arms control throughout the Cold War. A form of "open skies" was actually implemented unilaterally by the United States in 1956 when U-2 (q.v.) spy planes began to fly across the Soviet Union to film military installations.

ORGANIZATION OF AMERICAN STATES (OAS). A regional organization of the nations of the western hemisphere. The OAS was created in 1948 in accordance with article 52 of the Charter of the United Nations (UN) (q.v.) that allowed member states to enter into separate regional organizations to deal with local security problems. By ensuring that inter-American disputes would be first submitted to the OAS rather than the UN, the United States sought to insulate Latin America from external political influence and interference. On several occasions during the Cold War, for example the intervention in Guatemala (q.v.) in 1954 and the imposition of economic sanctions upon Cuba (q.v.) in 1962, the United States used the OAS as an instrument to endorse and ratify its Latin American policies. The impotence of the OAS was visibly demonstrated in the Dominican Republic in 1965 and Grenada (qq.v.) in 1983 when American military intervention took place unilaterally and without any consultation with the governments of Latin America.

OSTPOLITIK. Foreign policy reorientation by the Federal Republic of Germany (FRG) (q.v.) embracing improved relations with Eastern Europe. It was conceived and expounded by Egon Bahr, Willy Brandt's (q.v.) chief policy planner at the West German foreign ministry from 1966 to 1969. Ostpolitik proposed abandoning the Hallstein Doctrine (q.v.) and seeking a modus vivendi with the Soviet bloc, even including the German Democratic Republic (GDR) (q.v.). In part this reflected strained relations with the United States during the Vietnam War (q.v.), with Bahr seeking a way to depend less for security on high American military force levels via greater consensus on mutually acceptable European security principles. Moreover, having experienced a partial economic recession in 1965–1966, West Germany was eager to reopen access to traditional German trade and investment locations in Central and Eastern Europe.

When Brandt became chancellor in 1969, Ostpolitik was officially adopted and led to the 1970 Treaties of Moscow and Warsaw (qq.v.), the 1971 Quadripartite agreement on Berlin, the 1972 Basic Treaty with the GDR, and in 1973 to treaties with Bulgaria (q.v.), Czechoslovakia, and Hungary, all accompanied by an increase in aid and trade relations. Fur-

thermore, Ostpolitik permitted the Conference on Security and Cooperation in Europe (CSCE) (q.v.) to progress toward agreement on the
Helsinki Final Act (q.v.) in 1975. Notwithstanding subsequently poor
U.S.-Soviet relations, Ostpolitik remained the basis for pragmatic and
constructive relations between West Germany and the Soviet Union and
its allies for the remainder of the Cold War.

-P-

PALESTINE LIBERATION ORGANIZATION (PLO). See PALES-
TINE QUESTION.

PALESTINE QUESTION. The creation of the state of Israel in 1948 resulted in the displacement of hundreds of thousands of Palestinian refugees. The determination of the Israelis to maintain and expand the territory under their control was matched by an equal resolve by the Arabs
to regain the land lost by the Palestinians. In the ensuing bitter struggle
the Israelis recorded a stunning military victory in the Arab-Israeli War
of 1967 (q.v.) but lost political advantages in the Arab-Israeli War of 1973
(q.v.). Both sides in the conflict sought to exploit cold war politics to their
own benefit by looking to the superpowers for diplomatic and material
support. The United States regarded Israel as an outpost of Western values
in the region and became that country's principal supplier of military and
economic aid. The Soviet Union backed the Arab cause and cultivated
close relations notably with Egypt (q.v.) and Syria. After the 1973 War,
in an attempt to counter Israel's military successes on the battlefield, the
Arab governments resorted to using their economic power in the form
of driving up the world price of oil. More militant elements such as the
Palestine Liberation Organization (PLO), which was formed in 1964,
adopted organized terrorism as the preferred method of forcing Israel to
grant concessions. Despite several attempts by American presidents and
diplomats, especially Henry Kissinger (q.v.), to broker a durable peace
agreement, the Palestine Question remained unresolved at the end of the
Cold War.

PARIS AGREEMENTS, 1954. Concluded on October 23, 1954, after preliminary discussions in London, between Belgium, Great Britain (q.v.),
Canada, France (q.v.), the Federal Republic of Germany (FRG) (q.v.),
Italy, Luxembourg, the Netherlands, and the United States. After the
collapse of the European Defense Community (EDC) (q.v.), and subse-

quent American criticisms of its European allies, British Foreign Secretary Anthony Eden (q.v.) proposed negotiations between West Germany and the Brussels Treaty (q.v.) powers to agree to terms for West German rearmament and entry into the North Atlantic Treaty Organization (NATO) (q.v.). Nine-power talks, also including Canada and the United States, followed and resulted in the enlargement of the Brussels Treaty into the Western European Union (WEU), including Italy and West Germany. The WEU was to supervise West German rearmament, particularly to prevent it from acquiring nuclear weapons. Furthermore, to reassure France, Britain undertook to maintain four army divisions and a tactical air force on West German territory for indefinite renewable 20-year periods. West Germany entered NATO operationally under these conditions in May 1955.

PARTIAL NUCLEAR TEST BAN TREATY, 1963. Signed on August 5, 1963, in Moscow by Great Britain (q.v.), the United States, and the Soviet Union, the treaty prohibited the testing of nuclear weapons in the open atmosphere, in outer space, or under water. It was the final result of deliberations that began in Geneva in 1958 and involved a tripartite expert commission investigating the dangers of atmospheric nuclear tests. Shortly after the 1961 Berlin Crisis (q.v.), however, the Soviet Union announced its resumption of such tests, raising tensions in the nuclear arms race and leading the United States to follow suit shortly afterward. A test ban treaty remained under discussion in 1962, but not until after the chastening effect of the Cuban Missile Crisis (q.v.) did the Soviet leader, Nikita Khrushchev (q.v.), respond positively to overtures for a final agreement made by President John F. Kennedy (q.v.). Intensive negotiations began in January 1963 and were completed in August. Rather than a complete ban on nuclear testing, they agreed upon a compromise partial ban that permitted underground testing and excluded the intractable question of the on-site inspection of each side's test facilities by the other. The treaty, nevertheless, suggested potential for détente (q.v.) after a period of acrimonious superpower relations.

PEOPLE'S REPUBLIC OF CHINA (PRC). See CHINA, PEOPLE'S REPUBLIC OF.

PERESTROIKA. Soviet political term meaning "restructuring" promulgated in conjunction with glasnost (q.v.) by Mikhail Gorbachev (q.v.) at the 25th Congress of the Soviet Communist Party in February 1986. Initially, perestroika concentrated on senior party and government personnel changes, followed in 1987 by experimental decentralization in state industrial management and in 1988, under a policy of "socialist pluralism," land leases to private farmers. However, inertia and resistance by middle-level bureaucrats led Gorbachev to introduce significant constitutional changes at the 19th Conference of the Soviet Communist Party in July 1988. He retrenched the powers of the party Central Committee and assumed an executive presidency, answerable to a new assembly, the Chamber of People's Deputies that was elected in spring 1989 by a virtually unprecedented multicandidate poll. By cultivating a support-base outside the established party, Gorbachev was able to enforce mass resignations from its Central Committee in April 1989 and in October he ended the "nomenklatura" system of standing official party lists for state appointments. Increased investment in light industry, agriculture, and housing, partly financed by military budget cuts, was also intended to garner public support for reform. Nonetheless, in July 1989 miners' strikes in the Ukraine revealed that, without traditional Soviet political controls, pervasive public discontents could undermine the government's authority. This was especially marked in the non-Russian Soviet republics.

In November 1989 Gorbachev published *The Socialist Idea and Revolutionary Perestroika* that called for reform initiatives outside the Communist Party but within the Soviet polity. However, the divergent political forces thereby unleashed soon overwhelmed the debilitated administrative system. By mid-1990 questions such as independence for non-Russian Soviet republics, disestablishing the Communist Party, the free press, private property, continuing economic fragmentation, and Gorbachev's attempts to preserve the Soviet Union by assuming greater personal power at the expense of immediate reform revealed a burgeoning Soviet terminal malaise. Gorbachev's attempted solution was the "New Union Treaty" of April 1991 that conferred extensive federal autonomy to the republics. Political conservatives vainly attempted to arrest this de facto dissolution of the Soviet Union by the abortive military and KGB (q.v.) coup of August 1991.

PLEVEN, RENÉ (1901–1993). French socialist politician and prime minister. Pleven was appointed defense minister under Georges Bidault (q.v.) between October 1949 and June 1950, with responsibility for resolving the Indochina War (q.v.) and securing France's (q.v.) participation in the North Atlantic Treaty Organization (NATO) (q.v.). He became prime minister in July 1950 shortly after the outbreak of the Korean War (q.v.).

Although Pleven resisted American pressure for rearmament by the Federal Republic of Germany (FRG) (q.v.), he acted on the suggestion of Jean Monnet (q.v.), and endorsed the formation of German units under what became known as the Pleven Plan for a European Defense Community (EDC) (q.v.). Great Britain (q.v.) and the United States accepted this principle in January 1951, but rejected Pleven's proposal for a tripartite NATO ruling council, or tripartisme (q.v.).

Pleven's first cabinet fell in February 1951 and after a second brief prime ministership he returned to the defense ministry from March 1952 to June 1954. He authorized initial atomic bomb (q.v.) research later extended by Pierre Mendès-France and Charles de Gaulle (qq.v.), but also presided over France's final defeat in the Indochina War (q.v.) and was unable to secure parliamentary ratification for the EDC. During the Algerian crisis Pleven rebuffed solicitations to form a new centrist party as part of an effort to save the French Fourth Republic. After de Gaulle's return to power in June 1958, Pleven became a critical outsider in French governmental politics.

POLAND. Eastern European state that furnished a vital geo-strategic corridor between Germany and the Soviet Union. Joseph Stalin (q.v.), therefore, considered a controlling interest in Poland's affairs as vital to Soviet security after World War II and he pursued this consistently at the wartime Teheran and Yalta Conferences (qq.v.). The Polish government-in-exile in London was strongly anti-Soviet, however, so that Moscow set up its own Polish National Liberation Committee, or the Lublin Committee (q.v.), under the Stalinist exile Boleslaw Bierut (q.v.), which imposed political control in areas of Poland liberated from Nazi occupation by the Red Army. This process was seen by President Harry Truman (q.v.) to have violated protocols agreed at Yalta for democratic political reconstruction and was a cause of friction that contributed to the outbreak of the Cold War. In fact, precise terms had been left vague by Truman's predecessor, Franklin D. Roosevelt (q.v.), whose priority had been to co-opt the Soviets into the postwar United Nations (UN) (q.v.) even if that necessitated making concessions over Poland.

A compromise coalition that grafted "London Poles" into the Lublin Committee status quo was eventually agreed, although elections in April 1946 were effectively rigged to secure Bierut's ascendancy. This lasted until 1956 when destalinization took place under Wladyslaw Gomulka (q.v.). The latter process depended on unswerving Polish loyalty to the Warsaw Pact (q.v.). Gomulka fell from power in 1970 during widespread labor disturbances resulting from attempted economic austerity measures. His replacement, Edward Gierek (q.v.), was hardly more successful. His inability to stem the independent trade union Solidarity (q.v.) in 1980, or popular nationalism inspired by the election of a Polish pope, John Paul II (q.v.), necessitated a military coup in 1981 by General Wojciech Jaruzelski (q.v.) in order to avoid a Soviet invasion under the terms of the Brezhnev Doctrine (q.v.). The coup provided rich propaganda for President Ronald Reagan (q.v.). Nevertheless, pluralistic political reforms eventually followed at the behest of the Soviet leader, Mikhail Gorbachev (q.v.), culminating in partly free elections in June 1989. A Solidarity-led coalition government under Tadeusz Mazowiecki took power in August 1989 and was followed in 1990 by the election of Lech Walesa (q.v.) as president. In 1991 Poland dissolved its alliance with the Soviet Union.

POTSDAM CONFERENCE, 1945. A summit meeting of the victorious "Big Three" powers held at Potsdam, near Berlin, from July 17 to August 2, 1945. The United States was represented by President Harry Truman (q.v.), the Soviet Union by Premier Joseph Stalin (q.v.), and Great Britain (q.v.) at first by Prime Minister Winston Churchill (q.v.) and later by the newly elected prime minister, Clement Attlee (q.v.), who replaced Churchill on July 27. The summit took place two months after the defeat of Germany. Its main purpose was to consider how to implement the decisions made at the Yalta Conference (q.v.), but it also provided an opportunity for the British and Soviet leaders to have a personal meeting with the new American president.

Truman had succeeded Franklin D. Roosevelt (q.v.) on the latter's death in April. The new president had limited experience of international affairs and was reputed to be strongly anticommunist. At Potsdam, however, the atmosphere was outwardly cordial and all leaders affirmed a common desire to pursue postwar cooperation in order to preserve peace and avoid a third world war. Much of the actual business of the conference revolved around Germany and included arrangements for that country's zonal partition and government, disarmament, denazification, provision for reparations, and provisional recognition of the Oder-Neisse line (q.v.) as the territorial border with Poland (q.v.). The work of drawing up definitive peace treaties with the defeated enemy countries was assigned to the foreign ministers who set up a Council of Foreign Ministers (CFM) (q.v.) to organize a series of future meetings for this purpose.

The conference was notable for Truman's veiled reference to the atomic bomb (q.v.) when he mentioned privately to Stalin that the United States had come into possession of a powerful new weapon. While some historians have interpreted this as a calculated American threat, and arguably marking the start of the Cold War, Stalin did not appear to be troubled by Truman's remark, and indeed, confirmed that the Soviets would enter the war against Japan (q.v.) as had been agreed earlier at the Yalta Conference. The Soviets did join the war, but serious difficulties between East and West quickly emerged over Poland and Germany. By 1947 the friendly feeling that had been apparent at the Potsdam Conference was replaced by the tension and hostility of the Cold War.

PRESIDENTIAL DIRECTIVE 59 (PD-59). An influential statement redefining American defense strategy in 1980. The perception that the Soviet Union had built up not only a very powerful nuclear arsenal but also the capability to target its weapons more accurately motivated President Jimmy Carter (q.v.) to reconsider American defense strategy. Studies carried out in 1979 by the National Security Council (NSC) (q.v.) and the Department of Defense resulted in PD-59 that was signed by President Jimmy Carter on July 25, 1980. Reflecting the views of national security adviser Zbigniew Brzezinski and Secretary of Defense Harold Brown (qq.v.), PD-59 stated that the United States must be fully prepared for the contingency of fighting a protracted nuclear or nonnuclear conflict with the Soviet Union. In effect, PD-59 was endorsing the "counterforce" nuclear strategy proposed by Secretary of Defense James Schlesinger (q.v.) in 1974, but the political support for the implementation of PD-59 resulted in a substantial increase in American defense spending.

The Carter administration claimed that the strategy was merely enhancing the ability of the United States to deter war. The Soviet Union argued, however, that the United States was seeking to gain the ability to win a nuclear war by achieving absolute superiority in nuclear weapons. Soviet suspicions of American motives were heightened by the election to the American presidency of Ronald Reagan (q.v.) in 1980. Reagan embarked on a major build-up of American military power that was consistent with the recommendations contained in PD-59.

-Q-

QADDAFI, MUAMMAR AL (1942–). Libyan revolutionary leader and president. Qaddafi led a military coup in 1969 that overthrew the pro-

Western monarchy of Idris al-Senussi, and was nominated president of the Libyan Arab Republic. He secured the removal of British and American military bases in Libya, incrementally nationalized Western oil holdings, and signed a cooperation agreement with the Soviet Union in March 1972. Soviet arms deliveries began in May 1974, with an official visit in 1975 by the Soviet premier, Alexei Kosygin (q.v.). Libya, however, did not become a mere client state. Qaddafi developed a highly idiosyncratic program of Arab socialism that began to dissolve formal political structures in Libya, abolished private property, and embraced Muslim and Maoist principles in his manifesto, *The Green Book*. Qaddafi was also uncompromisingly anti-Zionist and violently confrontational with neighboring Arab and African states that he considered to be impeding revolution.

Relations between Libya and the United States steadily deteriorated particularly when Qaddafi began to use military expertise provided by pro-Soviet Syria, the German Democratic Republic (GDR), and Cuba (qq.v.) to train guerrillas whom he was suspected of encouraging and assisting to attack "imperialist" targets in Israel, Ireland, Germany, and Italy, often with civilian casualties. In April 1986 American airborne reprisals followed, while Qaddafi was ostracized internationally after the bombing of Pan-Am flight 103 over Lockerbie, Scotland, in 1988, was traced to Libyan agents. His activities were further circumscribed by falling oil revenues in the late 1980s and by abandonment as a Soviet ally under Mikhail Gorbachev (q.v.).

QUEMOY-MATSU CRISIS. The control of the two islands, situated in the Taiwan Strait and only a few miles from the Chinese mainland, created a crisis between the United States and the People's Republic of China (PRC) (q.v.) that threatened to erupt into war in 1954–1955 and 1958. The offshore islands had been retained and strongly fortified by the Republic of China (ROC) (q.v.) after 1949. In 1954–1955 and again in 1958 Communist China asserted its claim to the islands by launching artillery bombardments from bases on the mainland. Determined to resist the loss of territory in Southeast Asia to communist aggression, the Eisenhower (q.v.) administration entered into a defense treaty by which the United States gave a formal pledge to protect the ROC. When the PRC resumed its bombardment of Quemoy in 1958 President Dwight Eisenhower moved powerful American naval forces to the area. The result was and ending of the Bombardment and in 1959 the holding of negotiations between the United States and Communist China to defuse crisis.

-R-

RAKOSI, MATYAS (1892–1971). Hungarian communist politician and prime minister. Rakosi spent World War II in the Soviet Union and returned to Hungary in April 1945 to become first secretary of the Hungarian Communist Party, working in conjunction with Ernö Gerö (q.v.) to achieve power via a Popular Front coalition with the Peasant, Smallholders', and Social Democratic parties. By 1948 the latter parties had either been eliminated or forcibly merged with the communists into the Hungarian Workers' Party. On the grounds of their alleged sympathy for Yugoslavian communist leader Josip Tito (q.v.), many of Rakosi's rivals, including Foreign Minister Laszlo Rajk, were executed or, like Janos Kadar (q.v.), imprisoned.

After the death of Joseph Stalin (q.v.) in March 1953, Rakosi was forced to step down as Hungarian prime minister, a post he had assumed in 1952. He was able to return to full power in 1954 during a period of political uncertainty in Moscow. By 1956, however, the adoption of destalinization in the Soviet Union put overwhelming pressure on Rakosi's position. Popular demands for change were intensified in June 1956 after a new government took power in Poland (q.v.) and the next month, under instructions from Anastas Mikoyan (q.v.), Rakosi was replaced by Gerö. Rakosi went into exile in the Soviet Union and was later officially blamed for violations of "socialist legality" that provoked the 1956 Hungarian Uprising (q.v.). The regime of Janos Kadar sought to gain further legitimacy by formally expelling Rakosi from the Hungarian Socialist Workers' Party in 1962.

RAPACKI PLAN. Proposal for a nuclear-free zone in Central Europe put to the United Nations (UN) (q.v.) by the Polish foreign minister, Adam Rapacki, on October 2, 1957. The plan called for the removal of all nuclear weapons from the Federal Republic of Germany (FRG), German Democratic Republic (GDR), Poland, and Czechoslovakia (qq.v.). It followed abortive arms control and disengagement discussions in 1956 by the British prime minister, Anthony Eden (q.v.), and his Soviet counterpart Nikolai Bulganin (q.v.). The Rapacki Plan was certainly authorized by the Soviet leader, Nikita Khrushchev (q.v.), pursuant to his policy of "peaceful co-existence" with the capitalist powers. It was summarily rejected by the Eisenhower (q.v.) administration and by the North Atlantic Treaty Organization's (NATO) (q.v.) Supreme Allied Commander Europe, General Lauris Norstad, as a one-sided contrivance intended to dislocate NATO theater nuclear forces needed to counter overwhelming

Soviet conventional strength. Moreover, West German Chancellor Konrad Adenauer (q.v.) rejected the Rapacki Plan because it assumed tacit recognition of the GDR, thereby violating the Hallstein Doctrine (q.v.). Indeed, in March 1958, the West German Parliament effectively quashed Rapacki's proposal when it approved German forces acquiring tactical nuclear weapons under American supervision.

RAPID DEPLOYMENT FORCE (RDF). Since the end of World War II the United States had sought to protect Iran (q.v.) from communist expansion and to cultivate a close military relationship with that country. The overthrow of the shah in February 1979 and the Soviet invasion of neighboring Afghanistan (q.v.) in December 1979 compelled the Carter (q.v.) administration to reconsider its strategy for the Persian Gulf region. It was decided to implement earlier plans to create a force of 100,000 troops drawn from the army and marine corps that would be locally based so that it could respond quickly to crises occurring within the region. The Rapid Deployment Joint Task Force or "RDF" was in place by the spring of 1981. The RDF was intended to represent a deterrent to Soviet aggression in the region and signified the determination of the United States to revive the policy of military containment (q.v.) that had been discredited by the Vietnam War (q.v.).

REAGAN, RONALD W. (1911–2004). American statesman and president. Reagan was a well-known Hollywood film star before entering politics and winning election as governor of California in 1966. After two failed attempts to win the Republican presidential nomination in 1968 and 1976, he was successful in 1980 and went on to defeat Jimmy Carter (q.v.) in the presidential election. In his first term as president, Reagan was able to lower federal taxes, reduce inflation, and stimulate economic recovery. This greatly contributed to his landslide re-election victory in 1984.

During the 1980s Reagan exerted a considerable personal impact on cold war politics. He took office in 1981 holding strong views about America's duty to act as the leader of the "free world." In what came to be known as the "Reagan Doctrine" (q.v.) he pledged support for those fighting against the tyranny of communism. Reagan was especially distrustful of the Soviet Union and during his first presidential term he denounced that country as "an evil empire." He condemned the shooting down of Korean Air Lines (KAL) Flight 007 (1.v.) in 1983 as "a crime against humanity" and cited the incident as a vindication of his abandonment of the policy pursued by his predecessors during the 1970s of seeking détente (q.v.) with the Soviets.

Reagan adopted an aggressive and confrontational diplomatic style that was reinforced by a massive military build-up. A number of new weapons systems were developed of which the most ambitious and controversial was the Strategic Defense Initiative (SDI) (q.v.). The aim of SDI was to set up weapons in outer space that would provide a protective shield to defend the United States from missile attack. Reagan claimed that SDI promoted world peace, but Soviet officials argued that the United States was seeking to achieve sufficient military power to win a nuclear war against the Soviets. The implementation of the Reagan Doctrine also aroused controversy, especially the covert support that the Reagan administration gave to the Contras in Nicaragua (q.v.).

Despite his anticommunist rhetoric, Reagan did not seek nuclear war. He was also a pragmatic politician who was aware of the need to reduce the huge deficits in the American budget arising from the policy of increasing military spending. Consequently, Reagan was prepared to meet with the Soviet leader, Mikhail Gorbachev (q.v.), to discuss an agreement that would lead to substantial reductions in nuclear weapons. Ironically, Reagan's anticommunist image was extremely useful in deflecting domestic criticism that he was hypocritically engaging in détente or that he might be seeking to appease the Soviets. The first summit meeting of the two superpower leaders was held at Geneva in November 1985. Subsequent summits were held at Reykjavik (1986), Washington, D.C. (1987), and Moscow (1988) (qq.v.). The Moscow meeting was notable because it marked the formal signing of the ratification documents of the treaty on intermediate and shorter-range missiles (INF Treaty) (q.v.), the first nuclear arms agreement to be negotiated between the superpowers since SALT II (q.v.) in 1979.

During Reagan's presidency the United States recaptured the sense of national self-confidence and international purpose that had been severely undermined by the traumatic experiences of the Vietnam War (q.v.) and the Watergate political scandal. Reagan was also successful in achieving a substantial military build-up that, his admirers argued, had frightened the Soviets into unilaterally offering concessions on nuclear arms control and withdrawing from overseas military commitments, most notably in Afghanistan (q.v.). Indeed, Reagan's supporters claimed that it was his determined and farsighted leadership that had primarily been responsible for bringing about the collapse of the Soviet Union and the end of the Cold War.

REAGAN DOCTRINE. A popular term used to describe the anticommunist policy of the Reagan (q.v.) administration. Speeches expressing hostility to communism and criticism of the Soviet Union were principal features of Ronald Reagan's presidency. In 1985 he publicly praised the activities of "freedom fighters" who were seeking to overturn pro-Soviet regimes in the Third World, especially in Afghanistan and Nicaragua (qq.v.). The president's positive assertion of the universality of Western democracy and morality became popularly known as the "Reagan Doctrine." By seeking to liberate peoples under communist control the doctrine was calculated to pose a direct challenge to the contention of the Brezhnev Doctrine (q.v.) that the establishment of a communist state could not be reversed. Reagan, however, was mindful of the lessons of the Vietnam War (q.v.) and did not intend direct American military intervention as had occurred in Vietnam. Instead he preferred "low-intensity conflict" that mainly involved the Central Intelligence Agency (CIA) (q.v.) in covertly equipping and funding anticommunist forces in Central America, Africa, the Middle East, and Southeast Asia. The retreat of the Soviet Union from its military commitments in these regions in 1989–1990 was interpreted by Reagan's admirers as a victory for the Reagan Doctrine.

REYKJAVIK SUMMIT, 1986. A summit meeting of the two superpower leaders, Ronald Reagan and Mikhail Gorbachev (qq.v.), held in Reykjavik, Iceland, on October 11–12, 1986. Reagan and Gorbachev had met previously in Geneva in November 1985. The Reykjavik summit was a brief and informal meeting that was hastily arranged at Gorbachev's initiative and reflected the Soviet leader's desire to persuade Reagan to accept a major breakthrough in arms reductions. It seemed that his efforts would be crowned with astounding success when it was leaked to the press that the two leaders had consented to an agreement to eliminate all nuclear weapons. But the mood of optimism quickly collapsed when Reagan insisted that the United States must continue the development of the Strategic Defense Initiative (SDI) (q.v.).

Despite the contemporary perception that the meeting had been a failure, it was generally believed that a crucial step forward had been taken in that the Soviets finally recognized SDI to be nonnegotiable and that to insist on its termination merely prevented agreement on other substantive issues. This was confirmed in February 1987 when Gorbachev indicated his willingness to negotiate an agreement covering intermediate and shorter-range nuclear forces (INFs) (q.v.) in Europe. Significantly, SDI was not mentioned. The discussions at Reykjavik were therefore important in facilitating the negotiation of the INF treaty (q.v.) that Reagan and Gorbachev signed at the Washington, D.C., summit in

December 1987, the first nuclear arms agreement to be concluded between the superpowers for almost a decade.

RHEE, SYNGMAN (1875–1965). South Korean political leader and president. A dedicated Korean nationalist, Rhee was a political exile for most of his life. A good deal of this time was spent in the United States where Rhee received a Ph.D. from Princeton and gained a number of influential supporters. In 1945 he returned to Korea and was elected president of the Republic of Korea (South Korea) in 1948. Rhee was in office during the Korean War (q.v.) and was reelected president of South Korea in 1952, 1956, and 1960. His staunch anticommunism gained him praise and support from the United States, but his inflexible character and increasingly authoritarian rule provoked political discontent and mass demonstrations. In 1960 Rhee suddenly resigned as president and left the country.

RICKOVER, HYMAN G. (1900–1986). American admiral. As a naval officer Rickover was attached to the atomic bomb (q.v.) program, then to the U.S. Atomic Energy Commission, and finally became head of the U.S. Navy's nuclear reactor division. He innovated the procurement of nuclear-powered vessels for the navy, beginning in 1954 with the submarine USS *Nautilus,* and then submarine-launched ballistic missiles (SLBMs) (q.v.) that guaranteed a vital role for the navy in implementing the strategy of deterrence (q.v.). He retired from active duty in 1964, but remained as an official consultant on strategic and procurement issues. Rickover was forced into complete retirement in 1981 by Secretary of the Navy John Lehman (q.v.), whose plans for the expansion of the conventional fleet he criticized as wasteful and operationally unsound.

RIDGWAY, MATHEW B. (1895–1993). American general. A distinguished airborne commander in World War II, Ridgway was appointed in December 1950 to command the demoralized U.S. Eighth Army during the Korean War (q.v.). Facing massive counteroffensives by Chinese People's Liberation Army troops, Ridgway successfully rallied the overextended United Nations (UN) (q.v.) forces. In April 1951 he took command of UN forces after the controversial dismissal of General Douglas MacArthur by President Harry Truman (qq.v.). He stabilized the front in Korea before appointment in May 1952 as the North Atlantic Treaty Organization's (NATO) (q.v.) Supreme Allied Commander Europe, and in 1953 as U.S. Army chief of staff. Ridgway disagreed, however, with the "New Look" (q.v.) strategy adopted by President Dwight Eisenhower (q.v.) and accepted early retirement. He continued, nevertheless, as a commentator on military affairs and in 1968 was appointed by President Lyndon Johnson (q.v.) to an expert advisory panel on strategy in the Vietnam War (q.v.). Ridgway advocated significant reductions in American forces in South Vietnam, thus presaging eventual American withdrawal from that conflict.

RIO TREATY (RIO PACT). A collective security arrangement to protect the nations of the western hemisphere. The Rio Treaty was formally known as the Inter-American Treaty for Reciprocal Assistance and was signed by the United States and 20 Latin American countries in Rio de Janeiro, Brazil, in September 1947. The treaty was significant because it marked the first time in its history that the United States had entered into a military alliance during peacetime. Article three of the treaty foreshadowed the North Atlantic Treaty Organization (NATO) (q.v.) by providing that an armed attack against any American state shall be considered as an attack against all the American states. In effect, like NATO, the military power of the United States provided a guarantee to defend the signatories of the Rio Pact. The treaty was formally invoked by President John F. Kennedy (q.v.) during the Cuban Missile Crisis (q.v.) in 1962.

ROKOSSOVSKY, KONSTANTIN (1896–1968). Soviet general and Polish defense minister. Rokossovsky served in the Soviet army during World War II and commanded the First Byelorussian Front that entered Poland (q.v.) in June 1944. He halted his advance before reaching the capital, Warsaw, in August, allowing the Nazis to annihilate noncommunist resistance forces who had risen in the city. Before advancing into Germany in January 1945, Rokossovsky's forces enabled the Lublin Committee (q.v.) to consolidate its power. He returned to Poland after the German surrender to reconstitute its armed forces on Soviet lines and in 1949 was appointed Polish defense minister. Inevitably, he was identified as the principal agent of Joseph Stalin (q.v.) in Poland and was removed from office in 1956 by Wladyslaw Gomulka (q.v.). Rokossovsky retired in 1960 after having served briefly as deputy Soviet defense minister under Rodion Malinovsky (q.v.).

ROOSEVELT, FRANKLIN D. (1882–1945). American statesman and president. Born into an affluent background in Hyde Park, New York, Roosevelt was educated at Harvard University and Columbia Law School. He became active in politics as a member of the Democratic

Party and served as assistant secretary of the navy in the administration of Woodrow Wilson (1913–1919). After contracting polio in 1921 he briefly retired from politics before returning to become governor of New York in 1928 and then was successfully elected president on four successive occasions in 1932, 1936, 1940, and 1944.

As president, Roosevelt was admired for his personal magnetism and political shrewdness. In domestic affairs, he launched the New Deal to combat the massive economic and social problems caused by the Great Depression of the 1930s. In foreign affairs, he favored an internationalist role for the United States, but felt politically constrained by the strength of isolationist sentiment. The attack on Pearl Harbor by Japan (q.v.) in 1941, however, plunged the United States into World War II and presented Roosevelt with an opportunity to influence and shape world affairs. Although he never lost sight of the main objective of leading the Allies to military victory in Europe and the Far East, Roosevelt also sought to establish a framework of international institutions, most notably the United Nations Organization (UN) (q.v.), to promote and guarantee peace and prosperity for all nations in the postwar world

Roosevelt believed that his vision of the future required not only the active participation and leadership of the United States but also the cooperation of other great powers, especially the Soviet Union. During World War II he had placed great emphasis on cultivating a close personal relationship with the Soviet leader, Joseph Stalin (q.v.), and for this reason had traveled long distances to summit conferences at Teheran in 1943 and Yalta (qq.v.) in 1945. Roosevelt died, however, on April 12, 1945, only a few weeks before the end of the war in Europe. His hope that the wartime alliance between the United States and the Soviet Union would continue into peacetime was not realized.

Critics argued that Roosevelt was partly responsible for the outbreak of the Cold War because he had been too naive and trusting. By allowing Eastern Europe and parts of Asia to fall under Soviet control, he had merely encouraged the Soviets to make further demands on the West. Supporters of Roosevelt's foreign policy have replied that Eastern Europe in 1945 was firmly under the control of the Red Army and that the United States had little direct influence to exert on the disposition of territory in that region. In their view Roosevelt's stress on improving relations between the United States and the Soviet Union had brought military success in World War II and provided the best means of promoting peace and freedom in the postwar world. The continuation of this policy was prevented by the sudden death of the president in 1945.

ROOSEVELT, KERMIT (1916–). American intelligence agent. He served in the Central Intelligence Agency (CIA) (q.v.) as director of Middle East operations and refined and implemented Operation Ajax, the military overthrow of Iran's Prime Minister Mohammed Mossadegh (qq.v.) in August 1953. The coup was intended to preempt a future seizure of power by the Iranian communist Tudeh Party and established the personal rule of Reza Mohammed Sha Pahlavi as an ally of the United States.

ROSENBERT, ETHEL. (1918–1953) AND JULIUS (1921–1953). American husband and wife who were convicted of spying for the Soviet Union. In 1949 the United States was shocked to learn that the Soviets had successfully tested an atomic bomb (q.v.) and that America's monopoly of atomic weapons had suddenly come to an end. Americans believed that the Soviet achievement could only be explained by espionage. Amid a background of virtual public hysteria Julius and Ethel Rosenberg came under investigation. During World War II Julius Rosenberg had served as an engineer in the U.S. Army Signal Corps. He had also been a member of the Communist Party. Ethel Rosenberg was implicated because her brother was an army sergeant who had worked at Los Alamos, New Mexico, where the first atomic bomb had been developed in 1945. The Rosenbergs were arrested in 1950 and convicted in 1951 for passing classified information on the bomb to the Soviet Union. They were executed in 1953.

The imposition of the death penalty stimulated considerable public controversy in the United States. Supports of the Rosenbergs argued that they were victims of the hatred and unreasoning fear unleashed by McCarthyism (q.v.). In refusing pleas for clemency in 1953, President Dwight Eisenhower (q.v.) described them as secret agents and traitors who had worked for the Soviet Union against the United States.

ROSTOW, EUGENE V. (1913–2002). American lawyer and diplomat. Rostow was the older brother of Walt and combined a career of professor of law at Yale from 1944 to 1984 with a series of posts serving several presidential administrations. After acting as a consultant at the State Department during World War II, he worked on the economic reconstruction of Europe before becoming under secretary of state for political affairs from 1966 to 1969. Rostow joined with Paul Nitze (q.v.) in 1976 to form the Committee on the Present Danger (q.v.) with the aim of warning America of its vulnerability to Soviet nuclear attack and that a major military build-up was necessary to counter this threat. Though a

Democrat, Rostow's views on strategic issues were very much in keeping with those of the Republican leader, Ronald Reagan (q.v.), and he served in the Reagan administration as director of the Arms Control and Disarmament Agency (ACDA) (q.v.) from 1981 to 1983.

ROSTOW, WALT W. (1916–2003). American political scientist and national security adviser. Born in New York and educated at Yale, Rostow followed his older brother, Eugene, into the federal government during World War II and served in the Office of Strategic Services (OSS) selecting targets in Nazi-occupied Europe for Allied strategic bombing. After the war Rostow became professor of economic history at the Massachusetts Institute of Technology. A friend and adviser of John F. Kennedy (q.v.), he was appointed in 1961 as deputy to the national security adviser, McGeorge Bundy (q.v.). Rostow succeeded Bundy as national security adviser in April 1966, a position he held to the end of the Johnson (q.v.) administration in January 1969.

Rostow was strongly anticommunist and was regarded as one of the leading "hawks" on the Vietnam War (q.v.). His visit to South Vietnam with General Maxwell Taylor (q.v.) in 1961 was influential in persuading Kennedy to increase the number of American military advisers in that country. President Lyndon Johnson's use of air power to escalate the war also reflected Rostow's optimistic belief in the effectiveness of strategic bombing that he had gained from his wartime service at OSS. Like Johnson, however, Rostow's career and reputation were blighted by the failure of the United States to win the Vietnam War.

RUSK, DEAN (1909–1994). American diplomat and secretary of state. Rust was educated at Davidson College and served in the U.S. Army during World War II. AFter the war he held various positions in the defense and state departments including assistant secretary of state for Far Eastern affairs from 1950 to 1952. Rusk's tenure of office at the State Department coincided with the outbreak of the Korean War (q.v.), an event that convinced him that the West must resolutely resist communist aggression in Asia. In 1952 he left the State Department and became president of the Rockefeller Foundation.

Rust returned to office in 1961 when President John F. Kennedy (q.v.) appointed him secretary of state. Although overshadowed in the Kennedy administration by MacGeorge Bundy and Robert McNamara (qq.v.), Rust proved to be a capable diplomat and loyal servant to both Kennedy and Lyndon Johnson (q.v.). Rusk was consistent in recommending that the West stand firm against communist aggression. During the 1962

Cuban Missile Crisis (q.v.) he became famous for his description of the conflict as each side standing "eyeball to eyeball." Rusk adopted a consistently hawkish view on the Vietnam War (q.v.) and was one of the few advisers who argued against Johnson's decision to reverse the policy of escalation after the Tet Offensive (q.v.) in 1968. With the end of the Johnson presidency in 1969, Rusk left the State Department and became professor of international law at the University of Georgia. His eight years as secretary of state was the longest period of any incumbent in that office during the Cold War.

-S-

SAKHAROV, ANDREI (1921–1989). Soviet nuclear scientist and political dissident. Sakharov was the youngest inductee into the Soviet Academy of Sciences in 1953 and led research on the development of the Soviet hydrogen bomb (q.v.). He advocated arms control and was said to have influenced Nikita Khrushchev (q.v.) in favor of concluding the 1963 Partial Nuclear Test Ban Treaty (q.v.). Sakharov also lobbied for the removal of ideological strictures from Soviet science and publicly argued against the revival of Stalinism after the overthrow of Khrushchev in 1964. During the 1970s he used the underground press to publish his views on the increasing danger of nuclear war. Overseas acclaim followed in the award of the Nobel Prize for Peace in 1975. Finally, his condemnation of the Soviet invasion of Afghanistan (q.v.) led to internal exile from Moscow, providing a cause célèbre for the Reagan (q.v.) administration. Sakharov's personal integrity was beyond doubt and he was rehabilitated in 1986 by Mikhail Gorbachev (q.v.). In 1989 only a short time before his death he was elected to the Soviet Chamber of People's Deputies.

SALT (STRATEGIC ARMS LIMITATION TALKS). Nuclear arms control negotiations between the United States and the Soviet Union that began in Helsinki on November 17, 1969. Earlier overtures for SALT between the American Secretary of Defense, Robert McNamara (q.v.), and the Soviet Ambassador to the United States, Anatoly Dobrynin (q.v.), had taken place in May 1967. American negotiators wished to limit Soviet anti-ballistic missile (ABM) (q.v.) development, while the Soviets focused on American offensive forces, mainly multiple independently targetable re-entry vehicles (MIRVs) (q.v.). Progress was therefore slow until in June 1968, the Soviet foreign minister, Andrei Gromyko (q.v.), declared Soviet willingness to discuss both issues.

Since 1964 the Soviet Union had invested heavily in intercontinental ballistic missiles (ICBMs) (q.v.), aiming to achieve parity with the United States. But Soviet ICBMs were threatened with obsolescence by improved American warhead and targeting technologies. Moreover, it was imperative for the Soviets that they limit the costs of any probable strategic arms race. However, dialogue with the Americans stalled after the 1968 Warsaw Pact invasion of Czechoslovakia (q.v.) and was not resumed until January 1969 when Richard Nixon (q.v.) became president.

After the talks officially opened at Helsinki in November 1969, continuous sessions were later held in Vienna. Progress was slow, but was assisted by an increasing desire on both sides to reach agreement. Direct discussions between Nixon and Leonid Brezhnev (q.v.) eventually convened in May 1972 and these ironed out remaining differences on permitted numbers of submarine-launched nuclear missiles (SLBMs) (q.v.). The SALT I Treaty (q.v.), which was signed by the two leaders on May 26, 1972, outlined an interim set of limitations pending subsequent progress to a further treaty on reduced forces.

SALT I TREATY, 1972. Signed on May 26, 1972, by U.S. President Richard Nixon and the Soviet leader, Leonid Brezhnev (qq.v.), along with the Anti-Ballistic Missiles (ABM) Treaty (q.v.), after almost three years of Strategic Arms Limitation Talks (SALT) (q.v.). The document was formally titled "Interim Agreement on Certain Measures With Respect to the Limitation of Strategic Offensive Arms" and was an important manifestation of détente (q.v.). It froze inventories on both sides of fixed intercontinental ballistic missile (ICBM) (q.v.) launchers on land after July 1, 1972, and submarine-launched ballistic missile (SLBM) (q.v.) launchers immediately. Existing systems could be modernized or replaced, implying that launchers could be fitted with more numerous multiple independently targetable re-entry vehicles (MIRVs) (q.v.). The signatories acknowledged that the strategic arms race was not ended and agreed to pursue more complete agreements in future talks.

The treaty's protocols limited the United States to 710 SLBM launchers in up to 44 submarines and the Soviets to 950 SLBM launchers in up to 62 submarines. In effect, the United States was limited to 1,054 ICBM launchers, and the Soviets to 1,600. However, the Americans possessed more MIRVs than the Soviets, while the Soviets continued to replace their own missiles with new variants with greater capacity or "throw weight." Furthermore, bomber aircraft were not included in the treaty.

The SALT I Treaty was intended, however, to facilitate progress to more comprehensive agreements, which indeed emerged under the SALT II Treaty (q.v.).

SALT II TREATY, 1979. Signed by U.S. President Jimmy Carter and the Soviet leader, Leonid Brezhnev (qq.v.), in Vienna on June 18, 1979, after negotiations codified by the 1974 Vladivostok Summit (q.v.). Two years of discussions in Geneva, starting in January 1975, had foundered upon Soviet resistance to limiting the carrying capacity, or throw weight, of strategic nuclear missiles and American refusal to prohibit the development of emerging technologies such as more powerful submarine-launched ballistic missiles (SLBMs), multiple independently targetable re-entry vehicles (MIRVs), the neutron bomb, mobile land-based intercontinental ballistic missiles (ICBMs) (qq.v.), new heavy bomber aircraft, and cruise missiles.

Carter launched a new initiative in March 1977, which his conservative opponents denounced as containing too many concessions. In the final treaty both sides were limited to 2,400 strategic launchers of all kinds, including ICBMs, SLBMs, and bombers capable of launching nuclear missiles at a range greater than 600 kilometers. Within this limit each side was permitted 1,320 launchers with MIRV. No increase in throw weight over existing missiles was allowed and each side was to test only one more type of light ICBM. Cruise missiles were to be limited in range to 600 kilometers and were not to have MIRV. These terms were to be enacted by September 1981 and were to last until 1985, by which time Strategic Arms Reduction Talks (START) (q.v.) were intended to have achieved more far-reaching controls.

The SALT II Treaty provoked controversy in the United States because it allowed heavier Soviet missiles to be updated with MIRV. The new long-range Soviet "Backfire" bomber was also excluded. American critics argued that the agreement opened a "window of vulnerability" in the United States to a Soviet first strike (q.v.), which deployed decisively superior destructive power. The U.S. Senate was therefore unlikely to have ratified the treaty without the inclusion of significant amendments. Meanwhile, the embattled Carter administration withdrew the treaty in retaliation against the Soviet invasion of Afghanistan (q.v.).

SANDINISTAS. The popular name generally given to the Sandinista National Liberation Front (Frente Sandinista de Liberación Nacional or FSLN) that ruled Nicaragua (q.v.) from 1979 to 1990. The FSLN was established in 1961 and took the name "Sandinista" from César Augusto

Sandino, a celebrated Nicaragua nationalist and anti-American hero of the 1920s and 1930s. The Sandinistas fought a guerrilla campaign against the authoritarian rule of Anastasio Somoza and eventually took power in 1979. The intention to implement radical political changes in Nicaragua based on the model of the Cuban Revolution (q.v.) aroused the hostitlity of the United States. The Reagan (q.v.) administration feared that a communist beachhead was being established in Nicaragua that, if unchecked, would lead to pro-American regimes falling like dominoes throughout the region. A policy of destagilizing the Sandinista government was persued. This included a combination of economic pressure and the financing of "Contras" to promote internal disorder. The Contras made little military impact on the Sandinistas who retained effective control of the army. The Sandinistas eventually lowt power after being defeated in national elections held in 1990.

SAN FRANCISCO CONFERENCE, 1945. An international conference that led to the creation of the United Nations (UN) (q.v.). During World War II the leaders of the Big Three agreed to discuss the formation of a new international organization to promote world peace in the postwar world. Preliminary meetings to draw up a draft charter were held in 1944 at Dumbarton Oaks in Washington, D. C. In contrast to the arrangements at the end of World War I, it was decided to devote a separate conference to the question of establishing a new world body to be know as the United Nations Organization. The conference was attended by 50 nations and opened in San Francisco on April 25, 1945. The UN Charter was formally approved on June 26. The holding of the conference at San Franscico allowed the U.S. government to take the leading role and showed the importance attached by the United States to the new organization. However, friction between American and Soviet delegates was also evident at San Francisco and indicated that the future sessions of the United Nations would be marked by conflict as much as cooperation.

SAVIMBI, JONAS. (1934–2002). Angolan political leader. In 1964 Savimbi founded the União Nacional para a Independencia Total de Angola or National Union for the Total Independence of Angola (UNITA), which was rooted in the Ovimbundu people of southern Angola (q.v.). After the collapse of Portuguese colonialism and the granting of Angolan independence in November 1975, Savimbi led UNITA in a civil war against the ruling Soviet-backed Marxist Movimento Popular de Libertação de Angola or People's Movement for the Liberation of Angola (MPLA) under Agostinho Neto (q.v.). Savimbi suffered initial defeat by strong Cuban-supported MPLA forces, but coming within the provisions of the Reagan Doctrine (q.v.), his fortunes were revived by covert American and South African support in the 1980s. In 1990 with the Cold War in abeyance, the United Nations (UN) (q.v.) supervised a cease-fire and subsequent elections. In 1993, however, Savimbi was defeated in the elections and resumed fighting with continuing destructive effect.

SCHELLING, THOMAS (1921–). American strategic nuclear theorist. Schelling was trained as an economist and taught at Yale and Harvard Universities. His 1964 work *Arms and Influence* discussed nuclear weapons as a usable tool in superpower diplomacy. He introduced complex models based on "game theory," which included psychological matrices anticipating enemy responses to likely punishment and reward as a basis for nuclear planning. Along with Herman Kahn (q.v.), he led the abstract debate on rationally controllable nuc lear war, suggesting how the United States could bargain with the Soviet Union in wartime by threatening it with operational escalation to greater levels of nuclear destruction. Schelling also divided nuclear weapons into discrete categories, such as tactical, theater, strategic, etc., and his ideas on arms control greatly influenced the negotiating framework within which discussions took place between the United States and Soviet Union.

SCHLESINGER, JAMES (1929–). American strategic nuclear theorist and secretary of defense. Schlesinger was employed by the RAND Corporation, the influential U.S. Air Force-sponsored think-Tank, as a stra-tegic nuclear theorist. U.S. President Richard Nixon (q.v.) appointed him chair of the U.S. Atomic Energy Commission in 1969, and briefly in 1973 as director of the Central Intelligence Agency (CIA) (q.v.) before making him secretar of defense from 1973 to 1975. In the latter post he developed the Schlesinger Doctrine of war-fighting in which nuclear options (q.v.) would be used if deterrence (q.v.) failed. Schlesinger also adopted a strategic nuclear targeting policy called "counter force" based on an effective first strike capability (q.v.) against Soviet military bases. An all-out Soviet counterstrike would still be deterred by an impregnable American retaliatory force of submarine-launched ballistic missiles (SLBMs) (q.v.). Schlesinger later served President Jimmy Carter (q.v.) as secretary of energy, and in this post advocated expanding the testing of nuclear weapons.

SCHMIDT, HELMUT (1918–). West German political leader and chancellor. Schmidt was a prominent member of the Social Democratic Party who played a vital role in brokering the 1966 "grand coalition" between his party and the Christian Democratic Union. He was appointed defense minister by Chancellor Willy Brandt (q.v.) in 1969, was moved in 1971 to the ministry of economics and finance and succeeded Brandt as chancellor in May 1974. Schmidt maintained Ostpolitik (q.v.) and also used the economic influence of the Federal Republic of Germany (FRG) (q.v.) to accelerate Western European political integration, while at the same time seeking to encourage a collectively more equal relationship with the United States.

Schmidt's relationship with President Jimmy Carter (q.v.) encountered difficulties, particularly over West German reluctance to reduce important economic links to the Soviet Union after the latter's invasion of Afghanistan (q.v.) in 1979, and on negotiating strategies with Moscow over intermediate-range nuclear forces (INFs) (q.v.) in Europe. He further antagonized the United States by refusing to impose anti-Soviet economic sanctions during the suppression of political dissent in Poland (q.v.) and by openly criticizing the aggressive policies of U.S. President Ronald Reagan (q.v.). Schmidt relinquished the chancellorship in October 1982 after failing to win a parliamentary vote of confidence.

SCHUMACHER, KURT (1895–1952). German political leader. A prominent member of the Social Democratic Party, Schumacher had been imprisoned by the Nazis in the Dachau concentration camp during World War II. After the end of the war he revived his party in the British occupation zone and strenuously resisted efforts by Otto Grotewohl (q.v.) to form a popular front with the German communists. When this occurred in April 1946, Schumacher responded by forming a breakaway section of the Social Democratic Party outside the Soviet zone. It became the leading party of the anti-Soviet German left, standing for pacifistic socialist reconstruction, and also opposing the politically conservative revival of Germany being pursued by Konrad Adenauer (q.v.) and the Christian Democratic Union under American patronage.

Schumacher attempted to impede the formation of the Federal Republic of Germany (FRG) (q.v.). He also attacked Adenauer's unequivocal alignment with the West and denounced American pressure for West German rearmament after 1950. His uncompromising stance helped confine his party to permanent opposition status during the 1950s. Schumacher, who had been seriously wounded in World War I and whose health had collapsed in Dachau, fell seriously ill in December 1951 but continued in political life until shortly before his death in August 1952.

SCHUMAN, ROBERT (1886–1963). French politician and prime minister. Schuman began his political career as a member of the center-right Popular Republican Movement party. He became French finance minister in 1946 and prime minister the following year. He faced a mounting economic crisis and political confrontation with the communists and affiliated trade unions, which he assuaged during two brief, troubled terms in office. In July 1948 Schuman became foreign minister and helped negotiate the North Atlantic Treaty (q.v.). He was unable, however, to deflect American enthusiasm for creating the Federal Republic of Germany (FRG) (q.v.), whose rapid economic recovery he determined to sublimate within supranational European institutions. In May 1950 he endorsed what became known as the Schuman Plan. Despite its name, the plan was drafted in fact by Jean Monnet (q.v.) and resulted in the creation in 1952 of the European Coal and Steel Community (ECSC) (q.v.) within which West German dynamism would be harnessed to market and planning structures designed to guarantee reciprocal economic benefits not only for France (q.v.) but also for all its Western European members.

SEABED TREATY, 1971. A treaty that was opened for signature by the United Nations (UN) (q.v.) on February 11, 1971, and was subscribed to by 63 states including the United States, Soviet Union, and Great Britain (q.v.). The treaty arose from a draft Soviet resolution to the UN in June 1968 banning fixed military installations from the ocean floor, along with limits on patrolling by nuclear submarines. The Soviet purpose was clearly to restrict deployment by the United States of submarine-launched ballistic missiles (SLBMs) (q.v.) and fixed antisubmarine detection equipment. The United States responded in May 1969 with a narrower draft, banning fixed nuclear weapons from the ocean floor, as the basis for negotiations. The final document applied this restriction in areas more than 12 miles from the signatories' coastlines and was a limited arms control gesture typical of the incremental approach of the superpowers to détente (q.v.).

SHANGHAI COMMUNIQUÉ, 1972. Public statement marking the beginning of diplomatic rapprochement between the United States and the People's Republic of China (PRC) (q.v.). The Communiqué came at the end of President Richard Nixon's (q.v.) historic visit to China in February 1972 and was signed by Nixon and the Chinese prime minister, Zhou Enlai (q.v.). After more than two decades of hostility between the two countries, it was agreed that both governments would set up their own liaison office in each other's capital. Full diplomatic relations were established in 1979.

SHEVARDNADZE, EDUARD (1928–). Soviet politician and foreign minister. Shevardnadze was promoted under Leonid Brezhnev (q.v.) within the notoriously corrupt and impenetrable Georgian Communist Party, which he led after 1972. In 1985 he was appointed Soviet foreign minister by Mikhail Gorbachev (q.v.), having achieved a reputation in Georgia for capable, innovative administration influenced by the mixed-economy experiments of Hungary's Janos Kadar (q.v.). He was mistrusted, however, in the foreign ministry, whose officials regarded him as Gorbachev's politically appointed factotum and attempted to resist rapprochement with the West in favor of the cautious and dogmatic diplomatic practices perfected by Andrei Gromyko (q.v.).

In July 1988 Shevardnadze formally instructed his officials to divorce diplomacy from ideology and to press enthusiastically for greater Soviet arms reductions, the gradual abandonment of the Brezhnev Doctrine (q.v.) in Eastern Europe, and for faster Soviet domestic reform. In so doing he exposed himself to hostile criticisms from which the increasingly embattled Gorbachev declined to protect him. Their relationship deteriorated badly after April 1989 when Gorbachev approved the violent suppression of nationalist demonstrations in Georgia. Shevardnadze openly criticized Gorbachev's new executive presidency and finally resigned in December 1990, having been embarrassed during a foreign ministers' meeting in Houston, Texas, when he was informed for the first time about Soviet troop deployments that seemingly violated the recently signed Conventional Forces in Europe (CFE) Treaty (q.v.). After the collapse of the Soviet Union, Shevardnadze became president of the independent state of Georgia.

SHULTZ, GEORGE P. (1920–). American diplomat and secretary of state. After teaching industrial relations at the University of Chicago, Shultz served in the Nixon administration as secretary of labor from 1969 to 1970, director of the Office of Management and Budget from 1970 to 1972, and secretary of the treasury from 1972 to 1974. After a period of working as president of the Bechtel Corporation Shultz returned to public office in 1982 when he was appointed secretary of state in the Reagan administration.

Like Ronald Reagan (q.v.), Shultz was strongly anticommunist and endorsed the policy of supporting anti-Soviet movements in the Third World. Shultz, however, favored diplomacy rather than confrontation with the Soviet Union and worked with Reagan to secure arms control agreements. Despite criticism that he was too cautious, Shultz enjoyed a reputation for integrity and professionalism. These qualities enabled him to retain Reagan's confidence and to hold the office of secretary of state for more than six years.

SIHANOUK, NORODOM (1922–). Cambodian political leader and head of state. Born into the royal family, Sihanouk became king of Cambodia (q.v.) from 1941 to 1953 and again in 1993. During the intervening period he served in various capacities as prime minister and head of state. Sihanouk was typical of many Third World leaders who represented small nations surrounded by powerful neighbors and affected by the politics of the Cold War. Sihanouk similarly sought to maintain his country's independence by pursuing a neutralist policy. Although Sihanouk kept Cambodia from becoming directly involved in the Vietnam War (q.v.), he permitted the North Vietnamese to set up military bases within Cambodian territory. In 1970 he was overthrown by a military coup and sought refuge in the People's Republic of China (PRC) (q.v.). Although Sihanouk later returned to Cambodia and continued to play a prominent role in politics, he was never able to regain the personal prestige and influence that he had enjoyed prior to 1970.

SINO-SOVIET SPLIT. A serious rift in relations between the Soviet Union and the People's Republic of China (PRC) (q.v.) that was suspected but only definitively revealed on July 16, 1960, with the announcement that Soviet advisers and aid experts were to leave the PRC within the month. Despite their 1950 friendship treaty, relations between the Soviets and Communist China had been strained since the death of Joseph Stalin (q.v.) in 1953. The Chinese criticized the subsequent Soviet policy of "peaceful coexistence" with the capitalist world, and Moscow's overtures to "bourgeois" nationalist leaders in decolonizing Asia and Africa. The Chinese leader, Mao Zedong (q.v.), also attacked the "secret speech" that Nikita Khrushchev (q.v.) had made in 1956 and that had served as the prelude to destalinization.

Mao embarked instead on the "great leap forward," an ambitious economic program of rapid industrialization and agricultural collectivization that turned away from the Soviet model. Indeed, he alluded to China as being the leader of the international communist movement. Economic failures, however, aroused domestic Chinese dissent, which in July 1959 Khrushchev seemed to endorse when he accused Mao of "petit bourgeois fanaticism." Soviet aid to China's atomic bomb (q.v.)

program was ended soon afterward. In retaliation Chinese political journals openly condemned Soviet leaders as "revisionist" in cultivating relations with the Western imperialists. The Soviet Union withdrew its aid and advisers after an acrimonious international communist conference in Bucharest in June 1960.

Sino-Soviet relations continued to deteriorate throughout the 1960s. In 1961 Mao supported Albania's (q.v.) withdrawal from the Warsaw Pact (q.v.). In 1962 the Soviets remained neutral in China's border war with India (q.v.). Although Zhou Enlai and Alexei Kosygin (qq.v.) coordinated policy during the early part of the Vietnam War (q.v.), China condemned the 1968 Warsaw Pact invasion of Czechoslovakia (q.v.) as "Soviet imperialism." In the immediate aftermath of the 1969 Ussuri River Incident (q.v.), both sides were particularly antipathetic and this ironically facilitated American rapprochement with Communist China after 1971.

SLANSKY, RUDOLF (1901–1952). Czechoslovak communist politician. Slansky was exiled to the Soviet Union in 1939. He participated in Slovakian resistance to the Nazis in 1944 and became general secretary of the Czechoslovak Communist Party, which he represented at the founding of the Communist Information Bureau (COMINFORM) (q.v.) in September 1947. A loyal Stalinist colleague of Klement Gottwald (q.v.), Slansky took command of the party's People's Militia during the February 1948 communist seizure of power in Czechoslovakia (q.v.). He subsequently headed the party security and control commission, which proceeded to purge all heterogeneous influences from Czechoslovak public life.

In January 1950 Slansky returned from briefings in Moscow with a Soviet-style economic plan for Czechoslovakia. The first task was to condemn opponents as "bourgeois nationalists" and to secure their removal from office. Among those removed was Gustav Husak (q.v.). Slansky then established a national security ministry, which implemented repeated purges, culminating in that of his entire party in January 1951. In July, however, Joseph Stalin (q.v.) ordered the purging of Slansky himself. Slansky was arrested in November 1951 and executed for antistate conspiracy in December 1952.

SOKOLOVSKY, VASSILY (1897–1968). Soviet general and strategic nuclear theorist. Sokolovsky served as the Soviet representative on the Allied Control Commission in Berlin during the Berlin Blockade (q.v.), and as chief of the Soviet General Staff from 1953 to 1960. He supervised the reduction of Soviet conventional forces under Nikita Khrushchev (q.v.) although his periodic resistance to the extent of this process probably led to his retirement. Nevertheless, his 1962 book, *Military Strategy,* emphasized the central role of nuclear weapons in modern war and became the seminal work on Soviet strategy and doctrine. Rather than emphasizing deterrence (q.v.), as in the West, the Soviet armed forces were regarded as a political instrument whose utility depended on their ability to secure victory in war. Sokolovsky's ideas were used to justify a rapid and extensive build-up of Soviet nuclear weapons in conjunction with large conventional forces. Both would operate together from the outset if war was selected as a means of achieving Soviet state goals.

SOLIDARITY. Noncommunist Polish trade union, formally established on September 22, 1980. Unofficial labor activism in Poland (q.v.) had been influential in removing Wladyslaw Gomulka (q.v.) in 1970 and re-emerged in 1976 in protest against austerity measures imposed by Edward Gierek (q.v.). In July 1980 food price increases provoked strikes in the industrial centers of Silesia, Szczecin, and notably in Gdansk where an interfactory strike committee was formed under Lech Walesa (q.v.). The latter provided the framework for Solidarity in the coming months, forcing the government to accord recognition in the September 1980 Gdansk Agreements.

In November 1980 further Solidarity action affirmed the right to strike, in return for recognizing the political monopoly of the communist United Workers' Party. Throughout 1981, however, deepening economic hardships led Solidarity to demand unionization beyond heavy industry, administrative independence, and relaxed political censorship. Solidarity's first national congress in September 1981 made no mention of socialism and resolved to pursue what it called national, Christian, and democratic values, calling for similar movements to be formed elsewhere in Eastern Europe. Under Soviet pressure, the Polish prime minister, General Wojciech Jaruzelski (q.v.), attempted to reimpose restrictions on Solidarity, to which it responded by calling a general strike. Before this could take place, Jaruzelski imposed martial law on December 12, 1981, quickly crushing the union. Solidarity was formally made illegal in October 1982, after a summer of demonstrations, which were often violently suppressed. The union, nevertheless, maintained an underground Provisional National Committee, which resumed open activity in 1987, organized successful strikes in 1988, and entered negotiations in early 1989 for extensive political reforms. Solidarity's legality was restored in April 1989. It soon formed a Civic Committee, in effect a political party that did well enough in national elections in June 1989 to compel the formation of a coalition government in which the communists held a bare minority.

SOLZHENITSYN, ALEKSANDR (1918–). Soviet author and political dissident. A decorated officer in World War II, Solzhenitsyn was arrested in April 1945 while on active duty and exiled internally until 1957 for having made remarks critical of Joseph Stalin (q.v.). After his rehabilitation, two works, *One Day in the Life of Ivan Denisovich* (1962) and *The Gulag Archipelago* (1973–1978), drew worldwide attention to the harshness of the Soviet penal labor system. Solzhenitsyn was nominated for the 1964 Lenin Prize and won the 1970 Nobel Prize for Literature, but was expelled from the Soviet Union in 1974 after the publication of the first volume of *The Gulag Archipelago*. He was hailed as a celebrity in the West where his misfortunes provided abundant propaganda for interests hostile to détente (q.v.). While his writings continued to stress the fundamental malevolence of the Soviet system, he also denounced Western materialism from the perspective of highly spiritual Russian Orthodox mysticism, believing that alleged declining moral values would lead to eventual capitulation to communism. After a period of residence in the United States Solzhenitsyn returned to Russia in 1994 after having been fully exonerated of treason by the post-Soviet authorities.

SOMALIA. A country in the Horn of Africa (q.v.) that was formed in 1960 from the territories of Italian and British Somaliland. Somalia inherited significant boundary disputes with its American-backed neighbor, Ethiopia (q.v.), and after 1963 it sought military aid from the Soviet Union. After 1969 the regime of Major General Mohammed Siad Barre (q.v.) sought even closer ties with Moscow, culminating in a Treaty of Friendship in 1974 and the adoption of Soviet-style party institutions two years later. However, Soviet patronage of the new Marxist Ethiopian government created friction that Somalia attempted to resolve in July 1977 with a full-scale military invasion of the contested Ogaden province.

Soviet preference for Ethiopia led to a termination of Somalian-Soviet relations, the expulsion of numerous Cuban and East German technical advisers, and Siad Barre's offer in 1979 of air and naval facilities to win the favor of the United States. Nevertheless, American military aid was only forthcoming after the election of Ronald Reagan (q.v.). A decade of political instability degenerated into violent anarchy after Siad Barre's fall to a military coup in 1991.

SOUTH-EAST ASIA TREATY ORGANIZATION (SEATO). A military alliance organized by the United States to provide collective security against the expansion of communism in Southeast Asia and the Pacific. A succession of crises over Taiwan, Korea, and Indochina (qq.v.) motivated the Eisenhower (q.v.) administration in 1954 to create an anticommunist coalition known as the Manila Pact or South-East Asia Treaty Organization (SEATO). Intended as a Far Eastern counterpart to the North Atlantic Treaty Organization (NATO) (q.v.), the new regional defense organization comprised the United States, Great Britain, France (qq.v.), Australia, New Zealand, Pakistan, Thailand, and the Philippines. In contrast to NATO, however, the treaty did not provide for an automatic commitment by its signatories to use force to resist aggression. The members of SEATO simply agreed to confer in the event of any perceived threat to the peace of the region. Consequently, SEATO approved the actions of its members in sending troops to fight in South Vietnam, but did not officially engage in the Vietnam War (q.v.). The limits of the alliance were also underscored by its failure to include among its members leading regional powers such as India and Indonesia (qq.v.). After American military withdrawal from South Vietnam, the alliance was deemed to have no more utility and was disbanded in 1977.

SPAAK, PAUL-HENRI (1899–1972). Belgian foreign minister and secretary general of the North Atlantic Treaty Organization (NATO) (q.v.). Spaak was the main architect of "Benelux," the postwar political and economic alignment of Belgium, the Netherlands, and Luxembourg. He was also active in promoting the economic recovery of Western Europe as chairman of the Organization for European Economic Cooperation (OEEC), which was set up to administer the European Recovery Program (ERP or Marshall Plan) (q.v.). As Belgian foreign minister he played a vital role in formulating the 1948 Brussels Treaty (q.v.). Spaak was the inaugural chairman in 1950 of the Council of Europe, and as such was pivotal in realizing Robert Schuman's (q.v.) plan for the European Coal and Steel Community (ECSC) (q.v.) and for advancing plans for the European Defense Community (EDC) (q.v.).

Spaak served as secretary general of the North Atlantic Treaty Organization (NATO) from 1957 to 1961, then returned as Belgian foreign minister and assumed a liaison role with the United States and United Nations (UN) (q.v.) during the crisis in the Congo (q.v.). He retired from politics in 1966.

SPUTNIK. Soviet artificial satellite that was launched on October 4, 1957. It was the first such device to orbit the earth and passed three times over the United States. Soviet leader Nikita Khrushchev (q.v.) maximized the propaganda value that the sputnik gave to apparent Soviet technological advances. Moreover, his rocket scientists made overt references to imminent intercontinental ballistic missile (ICBM) (q.v.) production, while on October 6, 1957, the Soviets also tested a powerful hydrogen bomb (q.v.). In the United States concern was expressed about the existence of a missile gap (q.v.). This was used to justify a sustained build-up of American strategic weapons that rapidly outstripped real Soviet capabilities and pushed Khrushchev into the actions that precipitated the 1962 Cuban Missile Crisis (q.v.).

STALIN, JOSEPH (1879–1953). Soviet statesman and general secretary. After 1926 Stalin established an impregnable personal dictatorship in the Soviet Union by exploiting his powers as general secretary of the Soviet Communist Party, and in the 1930s by brutally exterminating his real and imagined rivals and critics during the great purges. He ordered the rapid industrialization of the Soviet Union via a highly centralized collectivist state, permeated by his own personality cult and sustained by institutionalized political terror. In August 1939 a nonaggression pact was concluded with Nazi Germany, but the Soviet Union was attacked in June 1941, casting it into a unlikely alliance with Great Britain (q.v.) and the United States. As a member of the "Big Three," alongside President Franklin D. Roosevelt and British Prime Minister Winston Churchill (qq.v.), Stalin was ultimately victorious in World War II. Disagreements, however, were soon to lead to the Cold War.

In many respects Stalin sublimated ideology to practical politics. At the Teheran, Yalta, and Potsdam Conferences (qq.v.), he obtained considerable latitude to control affairs in Eastern Europe, particularly in Poland (q.v.), which his military forces occupied. In October 1944 he agreed with Churchill that Britain should possess a majority influence in Greece and an equal interest with the Soviets in Yugoslavia. Although American policy opposed spheres of influence, Roosevelt made ambiguous concessions to the emerging status quo in order to preserve Soviet adherence to United Nations (UN) (q.v.) paramountcy in international security affairs. President Harry Truman (q.v.), however, increasingly sought to resolve outstanding questions on clear pro-American ideological lines. Stalin responded in a significant speech in Moscow on February 9, 1946, which affirmed the doctrine of irreconcilable conflict between socialism and capitalist imperialism, and the inevitability of a decisive war between the two systems. He correspondingly imposed unambiguous political controls in areas under Soviet military occupation, mainly by promoting disproportionate communist influence in the anti-fascist coalition governments provisionally set up in Eastern Europe during the aftermath of the defeat of the Nazis. This process was consolidated by the creation of the Communist Information Bureau (COMINFORM) (q.v.), which after September 1947 coordinated communist activities as a bloc.

Despite outward appearances, Stalin's position was strategically and economically weak. Large Soviet occupation forces were maintained in Eastern Europe to ease the demographic burden on the war-damaged industry and agriculture of the Soviet Union. The urgency given to Soviet atomic bomb (q.v.) research after August 1945 indicated another source of insecurity. The Soviets also demanded punitive political terms for reconstituting Germany, whose rapid revival Stalin greatly feared. These were unacceptable to the Western allies in the Council of Foreign Ministers (CFM) (q.v.). The decision of the West to proceed with the separate reconstruction of the Bizone (q.v.), in conjunction with the European Recovery Program (ERP or Marshall Plan) (q.v.) further stimulated the Soviets to preclude capitalist penetration of its Eastern European sphere. This process culminated in the 1948–1949 Berlin Blockade (q.v.), which was intended to disrupt Western progress to creating the Federal Republic of Germany (FRG) (q.v.), but merely served as a final pretext for the creation of the FRG. Moreover, Stalin's crude methods precipitated the formation of an integrated Western military alliance, with the signature of the North Atlantic Treaty (q.v.) in April 1949.

Beyond the limits of Soviet military occupation Stalin's political opportunism was also easily rebuffed, as in the 1946 Azerbaijan Crisis, in Turkey, and in the Greek Civil War (qq.v.). His relative indifference to events in Greece also alienated Yugoslavia's communist leader, Josip Tito (q.v.), prompting a serious rift to which Stalin responded by purging Titoist sympathizers, real or imagined, in the remaining satellite states. Elsewhere, Stalin's diplomacy was pragmatically cautious. In August 1945 he recognized Chiang Kai-Shek's Republic of China (ROC) (qq.v.) and did not support the Chinese communists systematically until Mao Zedong (q.v.) seized power in 1949.

Notwithstanding the Soviet acquisition of nuclear weapons in 1949, Stalin's final years witnessed further diplomatic frustration. In 1950 he was drawn into supporting Kim Il Sung's launch of the Korean War (qq.v.), which merely served to globalize the American strategy of anti-

Soviet containment (q.v.). Nevertheless, by the time of his death in March 1953 the Soviet Union was regarded as a superpower, and in terms of military power, was surpassed only by the United States. His successors soon reformed his undiluted totalitarianism in pursuit of more dynamic political and economic opportunities.

STRATEGIC AIR COMMAND (SAC). United States Air Force (USAF) command, primarily responsible for strategic nuclear operations. The Strategic Air Command originated with an inquiry in September 1945 under General Carl Spaatz into the military implications of the atomic bomb (q.v.). A core nuclear bomber force was set up in September 1946 and rapidly expanded under General Curtis LeMay (q.v.) in 1947, after the establishment of the USAF as a service branch fully separate from the U.S. Army. With the development of the hydrogen bomb (q.v.), SAC assumed responsibility for the "New Look" defense strategy (q.v.) of President Dwight Eisenhower (q.v.). It became the most lavishly funded of the American service commands, accumulating a massive force of B-47 and B-52 long range bombers, supplemented after 1955 with inter-mediate-range ballistic missiles (IRBMs) (q.v.) and later with intercontinental ballistic missiles (ICBMs) (q.v.). The vulnerability of SAC to a Soviet first strike capability (q.v.) led President John F. Kennedy (q.v.) to authorize a triad (q.v.) force structure that also included submarine-launched ballistic missiles (SLBMs) (q.v.) under U.S. Navy command, and also the doctrine of flexible response (q.v.). Nevertheless, SAC retained its mission as the foundation of the strategy of deterrence (q.v.) for the duration of the Cold War.

STRATEGIC ARMS LIMITATION TALKS. *See* SALT.

STRATEGIC ARMS REDUCTION TALKS (START). Mandated in the unratified SALT II Treaty (q.v.), these discussions between the United States and the Soviet Union were formally proposed by U.S. President Ronald Reagan (q.v.) on November 18, 1981, and began in Geneva on June 29, 1982. Progress was limited, however, by the conflicting aims of the participants. The Americans sought to redress what they considered pro-Soviet imbalances in the SALT II Treaty by reducing missile numbers, throw weight, and achieving sublimits on land-based missiles. The Soviets focused instead on limiting the new and more advanced American weapons technologies such as mobile launchers, cruise missiles, more accurate multiple independently targetable re-entry vehicles (MIRVs), and the space-based Strategic Defense Initiative (SDI) (qq.v.). Indeed, when American intermediate-range nuclear forces (INFs) (q.v.)

were deployed to Europe in November 1983, the Soviets broke off START. In March 1985 Mikhail Gorbachev (q.v.) resumed talks. He soon offered a 50 percent reduction in strategic arms, which Reagan rejected because it was linked to the termination of SDI. Progress was revitalized, however, during the 1989 Malta Summit (q.v.), with START resuming in Washington, D.C., in May 1990 on the basis of 6,000 warheads to be retained by each side. A full agreement followed in July 1991, in which that number of warheads was to be installed in 1,600 launchers each with sublimits on launcher types and a reduction of heavier Soviet missiles by one-half. Air-launched missiles were also limited, as were nuclear tests. In addition, extensive on-site inspection and data exchanges were agreed in order to guarantee overall strategic nuclear force reductions of about one-third by either party.

STRATEGIC DEFENSE INITIATIVE (SDI). American space-based ballistic missile defense program that was first announced by President Ronald Reagan (q.v.) in a national televised address on March 23, 1983. SDI entailed an initial five-year $25 billion research study and was intended to lead to a defense system in outer space capable of destroying an incoming Soviet strategic nuclear attack on the United States. Such a prospect undermined the "balance of terror" on which mutual deterrence (q.v.) rested, because American immunity to Soviet retaliation would make the capability to launch a "first strike" (q.v.) theoretically tenable as a military option. The Soviet Union, therefore, strongly objected to SDI, fearing itself to be economically incapable of countering what many analysts skeptically dubbed "Star Wars."

In March 1985 Mikhail Gorbachev (q.v.) reopened the Strategic Arms Reductions Talks (START) (q.v.) in the forlorn hope of achieving the termination of SDI. In practice, however, the program faced profound technical difficulties, and although President George Bush (q.v.) maintained funding, SDI was reduced in scope to protecting America's retaliatory intercontinental ballistic missile (ICBM) (q.v.) forces. Moreover, the 1991 Missile Defense Act reaffirmed the 1972 Anti-Ballistic Missiles (ABM) Treaty (q.v.) and further retreated from Reagan's initial concept by asserting that the purpose of SDI was only to defend against non-Soviet nuclear missile attack.

STRATEGIC ROCKET FORCES. Soviet strategic nuclear service branch, constituted in December 1959 to operate all missiles with a range above 1,000 kilometers. Under Nikita Khrushchev (q.v.) nuclear weapons of all types were emphasized in Soviet military doctrine, but he publicized decisive long-range capabilities to justify extensive conventional force cuts. Nevertheless, by 1964 the Strategic Rocket Forces deployed only the SS-4 and SS-5 intermediate-range ballistic missiles (IRBMs) (q.v.), which were capable of only reaching European targets. This deficiency explained Khrushchev's gamble in 1962 that led to the Cuban Missile Crisis (q.v.). After Khrushchev's fall in 1964, top priority was given to the deployment of intercontinental ballistic missiles (ICBMs) (q.v.). By 1969 over 1,200 single warhead "heavy" SS-9 and SS-11s were in service, permitting negotiation from a relative position of strength during the Strategic Arms Limitation Talks (SALT) (q.v.).

Soviet strategic doctrine was to achieve such a favorable "correlation of forces" that in wartime the United States would not contemplate launching a "first strike" (q.v.) on the Soviet Union. Correspondingly, conventional and intermediate-range nuclear forces (INFs) (q.v.) could be used decisively, if needed, for victorious but limited operations in Europe. The former presumption required technological comparability with the American Strategic Air Command (SAC) (q.v.) forces and after 1975 Soviet ICBMs such as the SS-18 and SS-19 combined heavy throw weight with multiple independently targetable re-entry vehicles (MIRVs) (q.v.). In surviving under the SALT II Treaty (q.v.), the latter, along with the mobile SS-24 ICBM aroused American fears of overall Soviet strategic superiority, and stimulated a renewed strategic nuclear arms race under Presidents Jimmy Carter and Ronald Reagan (qq.v.) that ended only with the 1991 Strategic Arms Reductions Talks (START) (q.v.) agreement.

STRAUSS, FRANZ JOSEF (1915–1988). West German political leader and defense minister. Strauss was a co-founder and leader after 1961 of the Christian Social Union, the Bavarian conservative party that aligned in federal politics with the Christian Democratic Union. From 1953 to 1956 Strauss served Konrad Adenauer (q.v.) as minister without portfolio, and until 1962 as defense minister, a post in which he built up the strength of the West German army, the Bundeswehr. He was forced to resign, however, after illegally using state security powers to raid the offices of the magazine *Der Spiegel,* and to detain its staff, who were investigating the affairs of his ministry.

In 1966 Strauss was recalled to participate in the "grand coalition" as finance minister under Chancellor Kurt Kiesinger (q.v.). He opposed Ostpolitik (q.v.) and ran unsuccessfully for chancellor in 1980 against Helmut Schmidt (q.v.). Although he subsequently abandoned federal politics, Strauss retained the post of Bavarian state prime minister and continued to be an influential political figure in West Germany.

SUBMARINE-LAUNCHED BALLISTIC MISSILE (SLBM). Strategic nuclear delivery system, housed in a submarine, and deployed far from the controlling state's territory. Intended to be immune to an enemy first strike capability (q.v.), the SLBM is a virtual guarantor of deterrence (q.v.). In 1958 the Polaris SLBM program began in the United States in response to the Gaither Report (q.v.), and was expanded and refined under President John F. Kennedy (q.v.) and his secretary of defense, Robert McNamara (q.v.). By 1969 Polaris A-3 SLBMs could strike the Soviet Union from a radius encompassing the Indian Ocean, requiring the Soviets to maintain a naval presence there and to improve their antisubmarine forces. In 1972 the U.S. Navy deployed Poseidon, a SLBM with multiple independently targetable re-entry vehicles (MIRVs) (q.v.). Equivalent Soviet forces entered service in 1974. After 1969 Great Britain (q.v.) deployed Polaris, purchased from the United States. France (q.v.) also developed its own SLBM. Although numerical limits on SLBMs were included in the SALT II Treaty (q.v.), in the 1980s the American Trident D-5, also bought by Britain, further increased the range, payload, and accuracy of SLBMs. Soviet comparability was maintained by the development of Delta and Typhoon class submarines.

SUEZ CRISIS, 1956. On July 26, 1956, Egypt's leader, Gamal Abdel Nasser (qq.v.) nationalized the Suez Canal in reaction to the decision of Great Britain (q.v.) and the United States to terminate talks on economic aid. The waterway was Anglo-French owned and a vital strategic and financial asset whose seizure greatly damaged the prestige of Britain and France (q.v.) in the Middle East. Moreover, Nasser had begun to support nationalist guerrillas in the French territory of Algeria, to promote anti-British radicalism throughout the region and Palestinian incursions into Israel. The Suez Canal issue was seen as a final provocation in London, Paris, and Tel Aviv, and as futile negotiations between Nasser and a hastily formed Suez Canal Users Association dragged on, joint Anglo-French-Israeli military action against Egypt was secretly planned in October 1956.

"Operation Musketeer" began with an Israeli invasion of the Sinai Peninsula on October 29, 1956, followed by an Anglo-French invasion of the Suez Canal zone on November 4, ostensibly for peacekeeping purposes after Nasser rejected transparently unacceptable cease-fire terms.

The plan had been kept secret from President Dwight Eisenhower (q.v.), and despite its military success, severely embarrassed the American president when he sought moral credibility in denouncing the Soviet suppression of the 1956 Hungarian Uprising (q.v.). Nikita Khrushchev's (q.v.) voluble support for Egypt also increased Soviet diplomatic prestige in the Middle East. Therefore, after Britain suffered an Arab oil embargo, Eisenhower refused to make dollar funds available to the British for alternative petroleum purchases. A dramatic run on the pound followed, forcing the British to accept a cease-fire unilaterally on November 6, without consulting the French. Having had its inability to act as an independent world power fully exposed, Britain was humiliated. United Nations (UN) (q.v.) forces supervised disengagement by the end of December 1956 and in January 1957, the British prime minister, Anthony Eden (q.v.) resigned, his political career having been destroyed. The Suez Crisis enhanced the prestige of Nasser in the Arab world while dividing the Western alliance and boosting the reputation of the Soviet Union as an anti-imperialist and a friend of the Arab nations.

SUKARNO, ACHMED (1901–1970). Indonesian political leader and president. A prominent nationalist, Sukarno opposed the restoration of Dutch colonial rule after 1945 and was elected the first president of the new Republic of Indonesia (q.v.) in 1949. The Eisenhower (q.v.) administration was suspicious of Sukarno because he favored a policy of Indonesian nonalignment in international affairs and was instrumental in organizing the Bandung Conference (q.v.) attended by nonaligned nations in 1955. There was also concern that Sukarno was too tolerant of the Indonesian Communist Party. Hoping to remove Sukarno from power, the Central Intelligence Agency (CIA) (q.v.) secretly supported an attempted military coup in 1958. On this occasion the revolt was unsuccessful, but Sukarno was later overthrown by a military rebellion in 1966.

SVOBODA, LUDVIK (1895–1979). Czechoslovak general and president. Svoboda commanded exiled Czechoslovak forces in the Soviet Union during World War II. President Eduard Beneš (q.v.) made him defense minister in April 1945 and he successfully integrated air and armored units that had fought under Great Britain (q.v.) with his own troops, prior to the withdrawal of Soviet forces from the country by the end of the year. In office, Svoboda was a moderate who tempered communist administrative and economic initiatives. He was dismissed as defense minister and stripped of his army rank in the purge of 1950.

On March 22, 1968, after the enforced resignation of the Stalinist Antonin Novotny (q.v.) during the "Prague spring," Svoboda was elected president of Czechoslovakia by its reformist National Assembly. During the subsequent 1968 Warsaw Pact invasion (q.v.), rather than defending his country's integrity, he interceded between the Soviet leader Leonid Brezhnev (q.v.) and the Czechoslovak party secretary Alexander Dubček (q.v.). Under the regime of Gustav Husak (q.v.) that gradually emerged, Svoboda remained president, was appointed to the party Politburo, and participated in Dubček's removal from public life in 1970. Svoboda thereafter served as a figurehead helping to legitimize pro-Soviet rule until his retirement in 1975.

-T-

TAIWAN. *See* CHINA, REPUBLIC OF (ROC).

TAYLOR, MAXWELL D. (1901–1987). American general and chairman of the Joint Chiefs of Staff (JCS). Taylor served with distinction in World War II as commander of the 101st Airborne Division. As the first American general to set foot in France during the Allied invasion in 1944, he acquired the status of a war hero. After World War II Taylor served in various key positions ranging from superintendent of West Point from 1945 to 1949, military governor of Berlin from 1949 to 1951, commander of the Eighth Army in the Korean War (q.v.), and army chief of staff from 1955 to 1959.

Known for his advocacy of countering communist military threats with flexible response (q.v.) rather than massive retaliation (q.v.), Taylor was given the opportunity to put his ideas into practice when he was appointed in 1961 as President John F. Kennedy's (q.v.) personal military adviser and later as chairman of the Joint Chiefs of Staff from 1962 to 1964. Kennedy sent Taylor on two fact-finding missions to South Vietnam (q.v.) with Walt Rostow (q.v.) in 1961 and with Robert McNamara (q.v.) in 1963. The resulting Taylor-Rostow and Taylor-McNamara Reports were highly influential in expanding America's military role in Vietnam. From 1964 to 1965 Taylor served as American ambassador to South Vietnam. Although a supporter of Lyndon Johnson's (q.v.) policy of escalating the fighting, he became increasingly alarmed by the extent to which the war was being "Americanized." Taylor was typical of those American officials whose initial optimism was later confounded by the inability of the United States to win the Vietnam War (q.v.).

TEAM B. An expert panel appointed in 1976 to criticize findings by the Central Intelligence Agency (CIA) (q.v.) that conservative Republican politicians were considered to have seriously underestimated Soviet military power and hostile intentions. It arose from Deputy Secretary of Defense Robert Ellsworth's proposal in January 1976 to solicit "competitive analysis" from outside the agency, and was approved by incoming Director of Central Intelligence, George H. W. Bush (q.v.). Team B was chaired by the right-wing Yale historian, Richard Pipes, and it routinely inflated official estimates of the Soviet threat to American security, proceeding from the assumption that the ruble-dollar exchange rate had been underestimated in calculations of the Soviet defense budget. At a time of American public doubt on the need for aggressive military policies, Team B and bodies such as the Committee on the Present Danger (q.v.) generated contradictory fears, which undermined confidence in détente (q.v.) and supported the bellicose admonitions of presidential candidate Ronald Reagan (q.v.) in his 1980 election campaign.

TEHERAN CONFERENCE, 1943. A meeting between the Soviet leader, Joseph Stalin, President Franklin D. Roosevelt, and the British Prime Minister, Winston Churchill (qq.v.), in Teheran, Iran, from November 28 to December 1, 1943. The meeting was intended to coordinate Allied strategy against Nazi Germany before the concluding stages of World War II and to consider features of the postwar political settlement. Stalin won approval for the retention of Baltic, Polish, and Romanian territories gained under the terms of his 1939 nonaggression pact with Nazi Germany, with Poland (q.v.) to be compensated by transfers of German territory. The Anglo-Americans also agreed to invade Western Europe in May 1944, and the Soviets to join the war against Japan (q.v.) three months after Germany's defeat. The postwar organization of the United Nations (UN) (q.v.) was also discussed.

The Teheran Conference was notable for Roosevelt's courting of Stalin, somewhat at Churchill's expense. In the process it is argued that the Soviet Union was misled into anticipating American assent for a Soviet sphere of influence in Eastern Europe in return for general conformity with Roosevelt's internationalist plans. The latter's successor Harry S. Truman (q.v.) sharply disabused Stalin of these notions and the resulting acrimony was a major stimulus of the Cold War. The Teheran Conference may be seen therefore as the first round of superpower diplomatic maneuvering for the securing of postwar interest.

TET OFFENSIVE. A surprise Vietcong assault on American military bases in 1968 that proved to be a turning point in the Vietnam War (q.v.). At a time when the U.S. government claimed that it was winning the war in Vietnam, the communist forces known as the Vietcong launched the Tet Offensive on January 31, 1968, to coincide with the lunar new year's holiday. The surprise attack was beaten back with heavy losses for the Vietcong, but not before television pictures had shown Vietcong soldiers actually attacking the American embassy in Saigon, the capital city of South Vietnam. Consequently, Tet severely undermined American confidence about winning the war and was one of the principal reasons why President Lyndon Johnson (q.v.) decided to reduce the scale of American military involvement in South Vietnam and seek a negotiated settlement to end the war.

THATCHER, MARGARET H. (1925–). British political leader and prime minister. Educated at the University of Oxford, Thatcher joined the Conservative Party and was elected to the House of Commons in 1959. After serving as minister of education and science from 1970 to 1974 in the government of Edward Heath, she became leader of the Conservative Party in 1975 and prime minister in 1979. Thatcher led her party to further victories in the British general elections of 1983 and 1987 and remained prime minister until her resignation in 1990.

Thatcher's right-wing views and hostility to communism earned her the nickname of the "iron lady" and made her a natural ally of President Ronald Reagan (q.v.). Indeed, the close diplomatic relationship between Thatcher and Reagan was a feature of the 1980s and greatly enhanced Thatcher's international prominence and influence. The Anglo-American special relationship was helpful to Britain during the Falkland Islands war in 1982 and to the United States when it resolved to launch a bombing raid on Libya in 1986. Thatcher's influential role in cold war politics was underscored by Mikhail Gorbachev's (q.v.) visit to London in 1984. Her report that the West could "do business" with Gorbachev was an important factor in persuading Reagan to enter into constructive discussions with the new Soviet leader.

TITO, JOSIP (1892–1980). Yugoslav politician and communist general secretary. During World War II Tito led Partisan resistance to the Nazis and their Yugoslav allies. By late 1943, with British support, he controlled most of central Bosnia and western Serbia, defeating German, Serbian nationalist Chetniks, and collaborationist Croat forces. A Croat himself, leading mainly Montenegrins and Bosnian Serbs, Tito eradicated heterogeneous nationalist groups mercilessly after the German withdrawal from the Balkans in September 1944. He had flown to Moscow shortly before this to negotiate with Joseph Stalin (q.v.) for crucial Soviet military intervention that helped him seize the Yugoslavian capital Belgrade. The Red Army, however, quickly moved on into Hungary. Tito was therefore not placed under direct Soviet occupation and declared his own Yugoslav Republic in March 1945. He reconquered the remainder of the country himself and negotiated from a position of indomitable strength with royalists exiled in London.

Despite the conclusion of a 20-year Soviet-Yugoslavian friendship treaty in April 1945, Tito's aggressive initiatives over Trieste (q.v.), for a communist-controlled Balkan Federation, and for aid to the communists in the Greek Civil War (q.v.) received little support from Stalin. Indeed, differences over the latter led to Yugoslavia's expulsion from the Communist Information Bureau (COMINFORM) (q.v.) in June 1948 that was followed by a bitter political estrangement from the Soviet Union.

Although Tito succeeded in attracting some British and American military and economic aid in 1949, and notwithstanding his hostility to Soviet political domination, he remained unwaveringly communist in ideology. In 1955 he began a rapprochement with Stalin's successors, but this was soon to end after the Soviet suppression of the 1956 Hungarian Uprising (q.v.) and execution in 1958 of Imre Nagy (q.v.). Tito then pursued association with the Non-Aligned Movement (q.v.) that formalized its existence with a summit held in Belgrade in 1961. Despite moderate economic success, Tito's state became troubled by recrudescent disputes between Yugoslavia's several nationalities. A federal constitution in 1974 gave devolved governmental powers to the latter but Yugoslavian statehood depended largely on Tito's personal prestige and power. Political disintegration began inexorably after his death in 1980.

TOURÉ, SÉKOU (1922–1984). Guinean political leader and president. An anticolonialist labor leader in the French territory of Guinea, West Africa, Touré rejected attempts to maintain devolved Guinean union with France (q.v.) and insisted on complete independence. This was obtained after a popular referendum in September 1958, after which Touré became Guinea's first president. Deprived of French economic aid, Touré formed a political union with Ghana, under Kwame Nkrumah (q.v.), which Mali joined in 1960, and which subsequently sought Soviet development assistance. Moreover, Touré adopted Marxist doctrines and assumed despotic powers.

Ties with Western economic interests were maintained, but after 1969 the Soviets had the leading role in Guinea's military, industrial, and infrastructural modernization. In return Soviet forces were allowed to use Guinean air and port facilities, ostensibly for its own protection after an abortive invasion in 1970 by dissident exiles and Portuguese mercenaries. However, Touré canceled Soviet privileges in 1978 prior to an expedient economic realignment with France and the United States. Touré died in 1984 during emergency heart surgery.

TRIAD. American strategic nuclear force structure proposed in 1962 by Secretary of Defense Robert McNamara (q.v.). In order to guarantee deterrence (q.v.), American retaliatory power had to be invulnerable to a Soviet first strike capability (q.v.). This would be achieved by diversifying American forces into a "Triad" consisting of first, manned bombers, mainly B-52s armed with Hound Dog missiles; second, intercontinental ballistic missiles (ICBMs) (q.v.) including the Minuteman solid-fuel missile, protected in a hardened underground silo; and third, submarine-launched ballistic missiles (SLBMs) (q.v.), which could evade detection and so launch a "second strike" against the Soviets even if the United States itself was annihilated. The latter weapons particularly upheld the "assured destruction" of any assailant, and the strategic nuclear triad was retained as a security principle by the United States for the remainder of the Cold War.

TRIESTE. Northern Adriatic city, claimed by Italy and Yugoslavia, but temporarily occupied in April 1945 by converging British Commonwealth forces and Yugoslav communist partisans. Josip Tito (q.v.) was rebuffed in his demand for control of the city by the British commander, Field Marshal Sir Harold Alexander. Great Britain asserted military governorship that was soon reinforced by American troops, although the surrounding countryside remained under Yugoslav control and a number of skirmishes ensued. A significant military clash was averted by a diplomatic note from President Harry Truman (q.v.) to the Soviet leader, Joseph Stalin (q.v.), whose wish for a favorable peace treaty with Italy led him to restrain Tito. A treaty was concluded on September 15, 1947, by the Council of Foreign Ministers (CFM) (q.v.), but without resolving Trieste's status. It remained a "free territory" under joint Anglo-American and Yugoslav jurisdiction until the de facto territorial lines were legitimized in October 1954. The city itself went to Italy and the hinterland was incorporated into Yugoslavia.

TRILATERALISM. Ideas that influenced the foreign policy of President Jimmy Carter (q.v.). The Trilateral Commission was a private think-tank that was established in New York in 1973 by the American banker, David Rockefeller. Under the direction of Zbigniew Brzezinski (q.v.) the Commission affirmed the "trilateral" nature of the Western alliance by bringing together government officials, business executives, and scholars from the United States, Western Europe, and Japan (q.v.) to study and discuss international affairs.

A notable member of the Commission was the governor of Georgia, Jimmy Carter. After his election as president in 1976 Carter appointed a number of American members of the Commission to his administration including Brzezinski as national security adviser and Cyrus Vance (q.v.) as secretary of state. But the attempt to pursue a "trilateral" foreign policy was seriously undermined by the existence of competing national interests within the Western alliance. For example, Carter's criticism of the Organization of Petroleum Exporting Countries (OPEC) for raising oil prices and his proposals for retaliation against the Soviet Union for invading Afghanistan (q.v.) provoked conflict rather than cooperation between the United States and its allies in Western Europe and Japan.

TRIPARTISME. French political doctrine for the control of Western security affairs by a tripartite American-Franco-British "directorate." On September 17, 1958, President Charles de Gaulle (q.v.) submitted this proposal formally to President Dwight Eisenhower and the British Prime Minister, Harold Macmillan (qq.v.), specifying that the North Atlantic Treaty Organization (NATO) (q.v.) would assume subordinate status to the tripartite directorate. De Gaulle's motives reflected a desire to retain French military primacy within Western Europe over the Federal Republic of Germany (FRG) (q.v.), obtain collective security protection for French interests beyond the geographic limits applied in the North Atlantic Treaty (q.v.), and give France (q.v.) a voice in Western strategic nuclear policy outside NATO. Although de Gaulle implied that France would revise its alliance relationships if the proposal was not adopted, a rejection followed nonetheless from Eisenhower on October 20, 1958. It was also strongly denounced by NATO Secretary General Paul-Henri Spaak (q.v.). De Gaulle later revealed that he fully expected to be rebuffed, but that he sought to make clear that French diplomatic and military initiatives were fully autonomous from the United States, Great Britain (q.v.), and NATO. This was further underscored in 1966 when France withdrew from the alliance's integrated command.

TRUMAN, HARRY S. (1884–1972). American statesman and president. Born in Missouri, Truman became active in the local politics of Kansas City and was elected Democratic senator for Missouri in 1934. Elected to the vice presidency in 1944, he succeeded to the presidency on Franklin Roosevelt's (q.v.) death in April 1945. Despite his long experience of American politics, Truman was conscious that he lacked knowledge of international affairs. He loathed communism, however, and believed that the Soviet Union was bent on world conquest and had to be resisted.

Whereas Roosevelt had carefully cultivated a friendly personal relationship with Joseph Stalin (q.v.) during World War II, Truman adopted a blustering and threatening tone. Within only a few months of taking office the Truman administration terminated Lend-Lease aid to the Soviets, made difficulties over German reparations, and condemned Soviet aggression in Iran (q.v.). In March 1947 Truman responded to a crisis in the Balkans by requesting the U.S. Congress to vote an appropriation to "save" Greece and Turkey (q.v.) from communism. The president's speech was called the Truman Doctrine (q.v.) and is often regarded as marking the beginning of the Cold War. The subsequent policy of extending American economic and military aid to Western Europe became known as containment (q.v.) and took the form of the Marshall Plan and the North Atlantic Treaty Organization (NATO) (qq.v.).

While his policy was credited with success in protecting Western Europe from communist expansion, Truman fared less well in the Far East. The Truman administration was criticized for not giving sufficient aid to Chiang Kai-shek (q.v.) in China and thereby "losing China" to communism in 1949. In 1950, however, Truman responded vigorously to the North Korean invasion of South Korea and dispatched American forces to fight for the United Nations (UN) (q.v.) in what became the Korean War (q.v.). Truman's political popularity was undermined, however, by the failure to achieve military victory in Korea. The president's controversial dismissal of General MacArthur (q.v.) in 1951 demonstrated his strong character, but only generated further controversy about the effectiveness of American military strategy.

The charge also emerged that the administration was "soft on communism" because the State Department had been infiltrated by communists. Truman had responded earlier to similar charges by creating a loyalty program for federal employees in 1947. Indeed, Truman has often been criticized not for weakness but for being too abrasive and confrontational. His staunch anticommunism was evident throughout his presidency and was exemplified by his enunciation of the Truman Doctrine, support for the Marshall Plan and NATO, and his determination to repel the invasion of South Korea. Nevertheless, criticism over the "loss of China" and the military tactics adopted in the Korean War undermined Truman's reputation and influenced his decision to retire from national politics when his presidential term of office ended in 1953.

TRUMAN DOCTRINE. A seminal statement of American cold war policy made by President Harry Truman (q.v.) in 1947. The immediate cause of the Truman Doctrine was the announcement made by the British government in February 1947 that Great Britain (q.v.) must shortly withdraw its military presence from Greece. Officials in the Truman administration feared that this would lead to a communist victory in the Greek Civil War (q.v.). There was also concern that the disturbances in Greece were linked with pressure from the Soviet Union on the Turkish government to secure rights of naval access for Soviet warships to the Mediterranean. It was decided therefore that prompt action was necessary to help both Greece and Turkey (q.v.) to resist communist expansion. But doubts were expressed whether the American public and Congress would support the United States openly replacing Britain in a distant area of the world where Americans historically had little national interest or direct involvement.

Consequently, in his speech on March 12, 1947, requesting aid from Congress, President Truman deliberately magnified the extent of the communist danger and declared that it was not just limited to Greece and Turkey but threatened "free peoples" all over the world. Congress speedily assented to Truman's request for the relatively small amount of $400 million to aid Greece and Turkey. But the president's speech attracted considerable worldwide attention and was referred to as the Truman Doctrine. Its forceful language and pledge of support to "free peoples" in their fight against communism reflected the deterioration in relations between the United States and the Soviet Union and is often regarded as marking the beginning of the Cold War.

TSHOMBE, MOISE (1917–1969). Congolese political leader and prime minister. Tshombe was the leader of the Katanga secession that in 1960 contributed vitally to the crisis in the Congo (q.v.). He was associated politically with the Lunda people of the rich mining province and used European and South African mercenaries to help them break away from the Congo central government of Patrice Lumumba (q.v.). In January 1961, by arrangement with the new Congolese regime of President Joseph Kasavubu (q.v.), Lumumba was handed over to Tshombe's troops and killed. In 1964, after the Katanga secession was finally ended by United Nations (UN) (q.v.) forces, Tshombe became the Congo's prime minister and worked with Kasavubu's Western-backed forces to eliminate remaining Soviet-supported pro-Lumumba groups. Having achieved this, he was dismissed from office and in the ensuing turmoil Kasavubu's military commander Joseph Désiré Mobutu (q.v.) seized power. Tshombe died in custody in Algeria, where he was held after plotting an abortive countercoup that was exposed by Mobutu's American-trained counter-intelligence service.

TURKEY. In dominating the Black Sea straits to the Mediterranean Sea, and touching on the Transcaucasian land bridge from the Soviet Union to the Middle East, Turkey assumed geo-strategic importance throughout the Cold War. Great Britain's (q.v.) leader, Winston Churchill (q.v.), had attempted during World War II to persuade Turkey to join the Allies so that it could receive Anglo-American military aid, but this was vetoed by Joseph Stalin (q.v.), who wished to keep Turkey isolated in order to press numerous Soviet claims. They included a revision of the Montreux Convention to allow Soviet capital warships to have the right of transit through the straits and to have port facilities in the area. In addition, Stalin wanted the return of the Kars province to Soviet Armenia, after its loss to Turkey by imperial Russia during World War I.

Stalin raised the issue of transit through the straits at the Potsdam Conference (q.v.) and it was reiterated subsequently to the Council of Foreign Ministers (CFM) (q.v.), but his lack of progress led to a direct Soviet note to Turkey on August 7, 1946, pressing both demands. Soviet troop concentrations in neighboring Bulgaria (q.v.) and the Caucasus alarmed the Truman (q.v.) administration sufficiently to produce a note to Moscow on August 15 supporting Turkey's sovereign integrity, followed by American consultations with Britain on modernizing the Turkish army. By October 1946, following an earlier visit to Turkey by the battleship USS *Missouri*, a full U.S. Navy command was established in the Eastern Mediterranean. In March 1947 military aid to Turkey was promised under the Truman Doctrine (q.v.). These measures were an early example of the American strategy of containment (q.v.) and were supplemented by Turkey sending a token force to the Korean War (q.v.) before joining the North Atlantic Treaty Organization (NATO) (q.v.) in 1952 and the Baghdad Pact (q.v.) in 1954.

-U-

ULBRICHT, WALTER (1893–1973). East German communist political leader. Ulbricht was a refugee in Moscow from 1938 to 1945 and was flown into Berlin by the Soviet military authorities to begin reconstructing civil administration after the collapse of the Nazi regime. In June 1945 Joseph Stalin (q.v.) ordered the formal reconstitution of the German Communist Party with Ulbricht as executive secretary. In January 1946 Ulbricht was called to Moscow to plan his party's merger with the Social Democrats to form the Socialist Unity Party. This process was completed in April, but the new party attracted little support in the Berlin city elections, while in the Western Allied occupation zones the Social Democratic Party insisted on retaining its separate identity under Kurt Schumacher (q.v.).

In the Soviet zone, under the figurehead leadership of Otto Grotewohl (q.v.), Ulbricht continued to set up communist governmental institutions, which formed the basis for the German Democratic Republic (GDR) (q.v.) in October 1949. Ulbricht became general secretary of the Socialist Unity Party in July 1950 and dogmatically imposed Soviet-style party structures, initiated an unpopular economic Five-Year Plan, and formed a new State Security Service (Stasi) to monitor domestic political opposition. Although the Soviets recurrently tried to negotiate with the West over Germany, they were forced to back Ulbricht during the June 1953 East Berlin Workers' Uprising (q.v.) and in the 1958 and 1961 Berlin Crises (qq.v.).

Ulbricht remained an unwaveringly loyal ally of the Soviets, although after the Berlin Wall (q.v.) stabilized the GDR's demographic and economic prospects, he modified his doctrinaire insistence on following Soviet industrial and agricultural principles and adopted a partially liberalized "German model." Indeed, the GDR was to emerge as the most industrially advanced of the members of the Council for Mutual Economic Cooperation (COMECON) (q.v.). Ulbricht, nevertheless, resisted the diplomatic trend toward détente and Ostpolitik (qq.v.), seeing the GDR as a contender for exclusive social and political legitimacy against the capitalist Federal Republic of Germany (FRG) (q.v.). Ulbricht's negative attitude toward Ostpolitik irritated the Soviets and brought about his removal as leader of the Socialist Unity Party in March 1971.

UNITED KINGDOM. See GREAT BRITIAN.

UNITED NATIONS (UN). An international organization designed to promote world peace and security. The United Nations Organization was created in 1945 as a replacement for the League of Nations. The name "United Nations" had been the official title of the Grand Alliance during the war and aptly conveyed the sense of a common endeavor to work for world peace. The idealist concept was undermined, however, by the realities of power politics. The Soviet Union was suspicious of an organization too much resembling a Western parliament and likely to be dominated by the West. In order to ensure Soviet membership, various concessions were necessary. The most significant was the superior executive role accorded to the Security Council and the granting of the power of veto to its five permanent members. By using its veto, any one of the great powers could prevent the UN from taking a decision which that power considered detrimental to its national interest. Faced with a majority of pro-Western nations in both the Security Council and the General Assembly, the Soviet Union resorted to the frequent use of the veto. Soviet displeasure even extended to a boycott of the Security Council for six months in 1950 as a protest against the refusal to admit the People's Republic of China (PRC) (q.v.).

The role of the UN in responding to international crises threatening world peace was severely constrained not only by the use of the veto but also by the lack of independent military forces under its control. On occasion, the great powers agreed that the UN could serve a useful peacekeeping function, as in the Palestine Question (q.v.) or Kashmir, and member states were asked to contribute troops and military equipment for this purpose. However, as the Korean War (q.v.) and the crisis in the Congo (q.v.) demonstrated, far from prompting a spirit of compromise, the raising of cold war issues at the UN provoked only bitter and sterile debates between the superpowers. A notable change occurred during the late 1950s when the membership of the UN was almost doubled. The admission of a large number of newly independent nations from Africa and Asia shifted the balance of voting power against the West in the General Assembly.

Despite a basic lack of financial and military power, the nations of the Third World found strength in their sense of common identity and their increasing numbers. They soon discovered that their majority in the General Assembly of the UN could have an impact on international affairs. In the process, they revitalized the economic and cultural agencies of the UN. On political issues, the battle against colonialism absorbed the attention of the new members and brought them into a tactical alliance with the Communist nations. From the point of view of the United States, the UN had become an unwelcome forum for demagoguery and anti-Western propaganda. During the late 1940s, the Soviet Union had sought to detach itself from the UN. It was now the United States who pursued a strategy of disengagement beginning in the 1960s.

The founders of the UN had envisaged an instrument to preserve world peace. But the conflict of interests between the great powers ensured that the UN was effectively deprived of real power for as long as the Cold War existed. It became therefore primarily an institution to distribute economic and cultural welfare and a platform for the expression of political propaganda. UN troops continued to perform a valuable peacekeeping function especially in the Middle East and Africa. When it came to substantive discussions on cold war issues, the superpowers preferred to ignore the UN and deal directly between themselves. The virtual stalemate continued until the late 1980s when cooperation between the United States and the Soviet Union enabled the UN, under American leadership, to undertake a series of military interventions to maintain world peace most notably in the Persian Gulf War in 1991. In so doing, they affirmed the validity of the original concept that had led to the creation of the UN at the end of World War II.

USS *PUEBLO*. A diplomatic incident in 1968 illustrating the hostile relationship between the United States and North Korea (q.v.). On January 23, 1968, the USS *Pueblo,* an American intelligence-gathering vessel, and the ship's crew of 82 were captured by North Korean gunboats off the coast of North Korea. The presence of spy-ships was common in the waters of the Far East and had been tolerated by the North Koreans over a number of years. The Johnson (q.v.) administration interpreted the surprise North Korean action as a deliberate attempt to divert American attention from military events in South Vietnam (q.v.). Though no documentary evidence supports this view, it appeared to be confirmed by the outbreak of the Tet Offensive (q.v.) in South Vietnam only a few days later on January 31.

USSURI RIVER INCIDENT. Sino-Soviet border clashes in March 1969. The conflict was initiated on March 2 by troops of the People's Republic of China (PRC) (q.v.), who attacked the disputed Damansky Island/ Zhenbao in the middle of the frozen Ussuri River, which forms the border between China and the Soviet Union in Manchuria, 250 miles north of Vladivostok. Thirty-one Soviet border guards were killed, provoking a regimental strength retaliation with armor and artillery support 13 days later, with unspecified but heavy casualties on both sides. The incident may have resulted from PRC Defense Minister Lin Biao's wish for a prestigious political coup before the imminent 9th Chinese Communist Party Congress. His forces performed poorly, however, and were beaten in subsequent skirmishes along the Soviet border with the western province of Xinjiang. Moreover, the assignment to the latter area of senior commanders from the Soviet Strategic Rocket Forces (q.v.) sobered the PRC leadership, and in September 1969 in Beijing, Foreign Minister Zhou Enlai (q.v.) conferred with Soviet premier Alexei Kosygin (q.v.) on the subject of restoring relations frozen since the Sino-Soviet Split (q.v.) of the early 1960s. The border clashes also increased the PRC's sense of vulnerability and made a rapprochement with the United States desirable, a policy that was actively pursued after 1971.

USTINOV, DMITRI (1908–1984). Soviet politician and defense minister. Ustinov served with distinction as armaments minister during World War II, occupying this position until the death of Joseph Stalin (q.v.) in 1953, by which time he had also risen to membership of the Central Committee of the Soviet Communist Party. Under Nikita Khrushchev (q.v.) he was minister of defense industry, a deputy premier, and member of the Supreme Council of National Economy. His technocratic merits ensured that he survived Khrushchev's fall and in 1965 he was promoted to the Politburo and became secretary of the Central Committee, the post formerly occupied by Leonid Brezhnev (q.v.). His closest political relationship was with the director of the KGB (q.v.), Yuri Andropov (q.v.), and the foreign minister, Andrei Gromyko (q.v.), with whom he formed a ministerial inner-circle upon succeeding Andrei Grechko (q.v.) as defense minister in 1976. Ustinov supervised the continuing modernization and expansion of Soviet conventional and nuclear forces and assumed a guiding role in the formulation of the SALT II Treaty (q.v.), which American critics denounced as institutionalizing Soviet strategic superiority over the West.

Ustinov supported Andropov in the succession struggle following Brezhnev's death in 1982, but kept his position nonetheless under Konstantin Chernenko (q.v.). He died unexpectedly in office on December 20, 1984.

U-2 AFFAIR. The U-2 was a high altitude American reconnaissance aircraft, which entered service in 1955 and was used for spying on Soviet nuclear missile and test installations. Although flying missions had been temporarily suspended, President Dwight Eisenhower (q.v.) authorized a resumption in April 1960 shortly before a scheduled summit meeting in Paris with the Soviet leader, Nikita Khrushchev (q.v.), French President Charles de Gaulle (q.v.), and British Prime Minister Harold Macmillan (q.v.). On May 1, 1960, 16 days before the summit in Paris, a U-2 piloted by Francis Gary Powers was shot down over Soviet Kazakhstan. Having been assured that neither plane nor pilot could be recovered, Eisenhower issued public denials, only to suffer supreme embarrassment on May 7 when the capture of Powers was announced in Moscow, and his equipment along with U-2 wreckage exhibited in Gorky Park. Khrushchev held an inflammatory press conference, denouncing American aggression and making threats of retaliation against Norway, Pakistan, and Turkey (q.v.), where American U-2s were based. Eisenhower was unapologetic, thereby aggravating Khrushchev's rhetoric, which indeed continued into the summit. The latter therefore collapsed after only one recriminatory day. U.S.-Soviet relations were to be frozen for the remaining eight months of Eisenhower's term. Powers was jailed for espionage after a show trial in August 1960, but was released in February 1962 in exchange for a Soviet spy in American custody.

- V -

VANCE, CYRUS R. (1917–2002). American diplomat and secretary of state. Vance served in the U.S. Navy during World War II before embarking on a career in law. He joined the Kennedy (q.v.) administration in 1961 as counsel to the Department of Defense. In 1962 Vance was appointed secretary of the army and later served as deputy secretary of defense from 1964 to 1967. In 1968 President Lyndon Johnson (q.v.) recognized Vance's negotiating skills by appointing him as one of the U.S. representatives at the Paris peace talks with North Vietnam. During the presidencies of Richard Nixon and Gerald Ford (qq.v.) Vance returned to law practice.

In 1977 Vance resumed public offices as secretary of stat in the Carter (q.v.) administration. Vance emphasized "quiet" diplomacy and achieved his most notable success in assisting the agreement made at Camp David between Israel and Egypt (q.v.). He also favored détente (q.v.) and the conclusion of a strategic arms limitation treaty (SALF II) (q.v.) with the Soviet Union. However, Vance's pragmatic approach was criticized by National Security Adviser Zbigniew Brzezinski (q.v.) who argued that the United States should adopt a much more aggressive policy toward the Soviets. The clash of views was highlighted by Jimmy Carter's decision to proceed with the helicopter mission to rescue American hostages in Iran (q.v.) in April 1980. After the failure of the mission Vance resigned.

Vance exemplified the "eastern establishment" lawyer who alternated between law practice and periods in government office. Vance's undoubted skills and reputation for integrity were highlighted after the end of the Cold War when he was invited by the United Nations (q.v.) in 1993 to work with former British Foreign Minister David Owen to bring peace to Yugoslavia.

VANDENBERG, ARTHUR H. (1884–1951). American senator who was influential in the creation of the North Atlantic Treaty Organization (NATO) (q.v.). Although Vandenberg was a Republican senator from Michigan and had been an isolationist during the 1930s, after 1945 he cooperated closely with the Democratic president, Harry Truman (q.v.), in what became known as the bipartisan approach to foreign policy. Vandenberg demonstrated his support for American involvement in world affairs by his agreement to represent the United States at the 1945 San Francisco Conference (q.v.) that led to the creation of the United Nations (UN) (q.v.). Using his considerable influence as chairman of the Senate Committee on Foreign Relations from 1947 to 1949, he supported the initiatives of the Truman administration to set up the Marshall Plan (q.v.) in 1947 and NATO in 1949.

VANDENBERG RESOLUTION. Resolution passed by the U.S. Senate that led to the creation of the North Atlantic Treaty Organization (NATO) (q.v.). In March 1948 the governments of Great Britain, France (qq.v.), Belgium, Luxembourg, and the Netherlands signed the Brussels Treaty (q.v.) to provide for mutual military assistance in the event of war. The signatories hoped that the United States would join the treaty. The Truman (q.v.) administration publicly commended the efforts to defend Western Europe from communist expansion, but felt constrained from participating because of America's traditional aversion to entering into entangling alliances in peacetime. There was, however, considerable bipartisan political support in Congress for some form of American association with the Brussels Treaty. This was demonstrated in June 1948 by a vote of 64 to 4 in the Senate to pass the Vandenberg Resolution urging the government to enter into a regional security arrangement as laid down by Article 51 of the Charter of the United Nations (UN) (q.v.). The Vandenberg Resolution was important in giving the Truman administration a mandate to enter into discussions with the Brussels Treaty countries that resulted in the conclusion of the North Atlantic Treaty (q.v.) in 1949.

"VELVET REVOLUTION." *See* CZECHOSLOVAKIA, "VELVET REVOLUTION" IN, 1989.

VIENNA SUMMIT, 1961. A summit meeting of the superpower leaders, John Kennedy and Nikita Khrushchev (qq.v.), held in Vienna on June 3–4, 1961. The meeting was regarded as an opportunity for Kennedy and Khrushchev to learn more about each other rather than to engage in substantive diplomatic business. The discussions were difficult and abrasive. Khrushchev adopted an insensitive and forceful attitude and threatened to renew the crisis over Berlin (q.v.) by signing a peace treaty with the German Democratic Republic (GDR) (q.v.). Kennedy came away from the summit in a despondent mood. His advisers complained that the Soviet leader had treated the president as an inexperienced junior. The perception that Kennedy was weak may have influenced Khrushchev to put pressure on the West over Berlin and to attempt to place missiles in Cuba (q.v.). On both occasions, however, Kennedy acted firmly and effectively dispelled any perception that he had deferred to Khrushchev at Vienna. The 1961 summit illustrated that such meetings could worsen rather than improve relations between the superpowers. With the exception of the Glassboro "mini-summit" (q.v.) in 1967, more than a decade was to elapse before the next summit meeting took place at Moscow in 1972.

VIETMINH. A communist movement founded in 1941 with the formal title of the Vietnam Independence League. Guided by the charismatic Ho Chi Minh (q.v.) and the military genius of Vo Nguyen Giap (q.v.), the Vietminh emerged as a formidable political and military force in northern Vietnam. The Vietminh led resistance to the Japanese and brought about the military defeat of France in the Indochina War (qq.v.).

VIETNAM, NORTH. *See* VIETNAM WAR.

VIETNAM, SOUTH. *See* VIETNAM WAR.

VIETNAM WAR. An undeclared war taking place in Vietnam from 1964 to 1973 in which the United States directly committed its military forces to maintain the independence of South Vietnam from communist control. An earlier conflict known as the Indochina War (q.v.) had occurred in the same region from 1946 to 1954 and resulted in the division of Vietnam into two separate states. North Vietnam proclaimed itself a communist country and established close relations with the Soviet Union and the People's Republic of China (PRC) (q.v.). The United States gave its support to South Vietnam in an attempt to create a strong and stable noncommunist nation that would serve as a beacon of freedom throughout Southeast Asia.

In 1957 communist forces known as the Vietcong began a guerrilla campaign in South Vietnam with the aim of overthrowing the government and reunifying Vietnam. They were backed by North Vietnam, which infiltrated military supplies, and later troops, into the South via a series of paths and tracks through the jungle that became known as the "Ho Chi Minh Trail." In what was popularly referred to as the domino theory (q.v.), Presidents Dwight Eisenhower and John Kennedy (qq.v.) viewed events in global terms and regarded North Vietnam as the instrument of a communist plot to take over South Vietnam to be followed by the rest of Southeast Asia, Australia, New Zealand, the Pacific Islands, and ultimately the United States. Consequently, American assistance for the government of South Vietnam was steadily increased in terms of military equipment and advisers.

Although guerrilla fighting had been taking place in South Vietnam since 1957, the Vietnam War technically began in 1964 when President Lyndon Johnson (q.v.) deliberately expanded the conflict beyond South Vietnam, and using the authority given to him by the U.S. Congress in the Gulf of Tonkin Resolution, ordered a series of bombing raids on North Vietnam. In 1965 large numbers of American troops were dispatched for combat duty in South Vietnam and eventually formed an army in excess of 500,000. Johnson ruled out an invasion of North Vietnam and preferred to pursue a strategy of gradually escalating the fighting on the ground in South Vietnam and especially in the air until the enemy was forced to admit defeat. However, American faith in the efficacy of strategic bombing proved misplaced. Instead of lowering morale, the policy of escalation merely stimulated North Vietnamese determination to continue the war and increase infiltration into the South. The Soviet Union and the People's Republic of China also gave material support to North Vietnam although this stopped short of their direct military participation.

Johnson's decision to commit American troops to fighting a war on the Asian mainland proved a disastrous miscalculation. Despite suffering enormous losses and damage, North Vietnam and the Vietcong remained resolutely committed to the struggle. In contrast, American public opinion grew more and more confused and divided. The turning point came in January 1968 when the Tet Offensive (q.v.) dealt a severe psychological blow to American confidence about winning the war. President Johnson reversed the policy of escalation and publicly announced America's willingness to enter into negotiations to end the fighting. Although peace talks were started in Paris in May 1968, it was under Johnson's successor, Richard Nixon (q.v.), that a negotiated settlement was eventually secured in January 1973. Nixon favored the strategy of "Vietnamization" in which the American military presence was steadily decreased while the burden of fighting the Vietcong was transferred to the South Vietnamese army. A cease-fire was established in January 1973 that allowed American military withdrawal disguised as "peace with honor."

In reality, a humiliated United States had abandoned South Vietnam. Despite the expenditure of billions of dollars and the loss of 58,000 American lives and more than 150,000 wounded, successive presidents from Eisenhower to Nixon had failed to create a bulwark of anticommunism in the South. Without the continuing military, financial, and political support of the United States, South Vietnam could not survive as an independent country. This was demonstrated to the world on April 30, 1975, when North Vietnamese troops seized Saigon, the capital city of South Vietnam, and forcibly secured the reunification of Vietnam.

The failure to win the Vietnam War illustrated the relative decline of the global power of the United States and led to a period of détente (q.v.) between the superpowers during the 1970s. The desire to avoid "another Vietnam" also made it more difficult for American presidents to send troops to deal with overseas crises. On the other hand, the fall of South Vietnam to the communists did not lead to the establishment of similar regimes throughout Asia and the Pacific. In fact, the new Socialist Republic of Vietnam sought to include Laos and Cambodia (qq.v.) within its sphere of influence. This resulted in the dispatch of Vietnamese troops to Cambodia in 1978, an action that prompted the brief retaliatory invasion of northern Vietnam by China in 1979. In retrospect, it appeared that American policy had been mistaken in automatically regarding the North Vietnamese as communist puppets and that the attempt to maintain an independent South Vietnam had merely complicated and prolonged what was essentially a local conflict for hegemony in Indochina.

VLADIVOSTOK SUMMIT, 1974. A meeting between the American President, Gerald Ford (q.v.), and the Soviet General Secretary, Leonid Brezhnev (q.v.), held at Vladivostok in the Soviet Union on November 23–24, 1974. Ford had only recently succeeded to the American presidency on the resignation of Richard Nixon (q.v.) in August. The meeting at Vladivostok was, therefore, regarded as an opportunity for Ford to have a personal meeting with the Soviet leader, Leonid Brezhnev. The summit was also intended to affirm the desire of both superpowers to continue the policy of détente (q.v.). This was demonstrated by the conclusion of the "Vladivostok Accords," a draft agreement that was meant to form the basis of a new arms limitation treaty to be known as SALT II (q.v.). The proposed arrangement provoked so much criticism in the United States that Ford did not submit it to the Senate for ratification as a treaty.

VO NGUYEN GIAP. *See* GIAP, VO NGUYEN.

VYSHINSKY, ANDREI (1883–1954). Soviet diplomat and foreign minister. Vyshinsky rose to notoriety as public prosecutor during the purge trials of the 1930s in which Joseph Stalin (q.v.) eradicated all real and potential political resistance to his complete control of the Soviet system. Vyshinsky became deputy foreign minister in 1940 and attended the Yalta, Potsdam, and San Francisco Conferences (qq.v.). He also led the Soviet delegation to the inaugural General Assembly of the United Nations (UN) (q.v.) in London in 1946. His characteristic tirades against alleged Western infractions contributed greatly to depriving the UN of an effective role as a mediator of international disputes. Vyshinsky was promoted Soviet foreign minister in March 1949 and oversaw policies on Germany, China, and the Korean War (q.v.) that were unimaginative, doctrinaire, and invariably negative. He was demoted to deputy foreign minister after Stalin's death and then transferred to the post of Soviet permanent representative at the UN in New York, where he died from a heart attack in November 1954.

-W-

WALESA, LECH (1943–). Polish trade unionist and president. Walesa was an electrician at the Lenin Shipyard, Gdansk, where he served on the strike committee during the industrial unrest that in 1970 toppled Wladyslaw Gomulka (q.v.). He coordinated further strikes in August 1980 against austerity measures imposed by the government of Edward Gierek (q.v.), and his organization furnished the basis of what by September had become the independent Polish trade union Solidarity (q.v.). Walesa emerged as the union's main negotiator during subsequent talks on official recognition with the communist authorities. In November 1980 these resulted in the Gdansk agreements. Walesa gained international recognition when he was received in Rome by Pope John Paul II (q.v.) in January 1981 before returning to Poland (q.v.) for further negotiations to improve material conditions, extend independent unionization, and for Solidarity to take on quasi-managerial roles in Polish industry. His principal bargaining tool was to threaten paralyzing general strikes. The resulting governmental capitulations suggested a vital erosion of communist political authority.

In December 1981 the government imposed martial law. Walesa was imprisoned for 11 months and remained under close surveillance after his release. He had another papal audience in 1983 and was awarded the Nobel Prize for Peace. In May 1988 renewed industrial unrest led to Walesa's recall as a negotiator that led in turn to Solidarity's relegitimization in August. The union developed a political platform during semifree elections in June 1989 and went on to dominate Poland's subsequent coalition government. Walesa's political triumph was completed in December 1990 when he was elected president of Poland.

WALLACE, HENRY A. (1888–1965). American politician and vice president. Wallace served as vice president to Franklin D. Roosevelt (q.v.) from 1941 to 1945 and was appointed secretary of commerce in the Truman (q.v.) administration. A political liberal with populist leanings, Wallace dissented from Truman's increasingly anti-Soviet policies and believed that they increased the risk of another world war. Wallace courted public controversy on September 12, 1946, when he made a major speech at Madison Square Garden, New York, in which he denounced the emerging Cold War as a product of British imperialism, called for an American rapprochement with the Soviet Union and also for United Nations (UN) (q.v.) control of the atomic bomb (q.v.). Secretary of State James Byrnes (q.v.), attending the Council of Foreign Ministers (CFM) (q.v.) in Paris, was highly embarrassed because Truman had unwittingly approved the speech before its delivery. Nevertheless, Wallace was dismissed from the cabinet.

Wallace ran unsuccessfully as the Progressive Party's presidential candidate in 1948, during which time he attacked the European Recovery Program (ERP or Marshall Plan) (q.v.) and defended the communist seizure of power in Czechoslovakia (q.v.). After his retirement from politics, Wallace recanted his sympathetic view of the Soviet Union in his book *Why I Was Wrong*.

WARSAW PACT. Formed on May 14, 1955, by the Soviet Union, Albania, Bulgaria, Czechoslovakia, the German Democratic Republic (GDR), Hungary, Poland, and Romania (qq.v.). It was a collective military alliance that cited itself as a response to the rearmament of the Federal Republic of Germany (FRG) (q.v.) as a member of the North Atlantic Treaty Organization (NATO) (q.v.). The Warsaw Pact had a joint military command and staff under ultimate Soviet direction with accompanying bilateral agreements that legitimized the continuing Soviet military presence in each of the Eastern European member states. Its main value to the Soviet Union was in maximizing the military potential of its satellite states through standardized equipment, joint training, and command structures.

Membership of the Warsaw Pact also served as a benchmark of, and a means of maintaining, Eastern bloc political discipline and related Soviet security requirements. For example, Hungary's declaration of neutrality in 1956 was the signal for the Soviet invasion. Albania was effectively expelled in 1962 for siding with the People's Republic of China (PRC) (q.v.). Warsaw Pact command structures enabled GDR, Hungarian, and Polish forces to participate in the 1968 invasion of Czechoslovakia, thereby lending the intervention bloc legitimacy. Nicolae Ceausescu (q.v.) of Romania tempered his demonstrations of autonomy by continuing to adhere to the Warsaw Pact's political strictures. Throughout its negotiations with Solidarity (q.v.), the Polish government similarly repeated its full adherence, regardless of any domestic political changes.

An expanded Warsaw Pact secretariat after 1969 remained a mainly nominal body. It nevertheless served as a political counterpart to NATO as both blocs negotiated the Conventional Forces in Europe (CFE) Treaty (q.v.). The GDR left the Warsaw Pact on September 24, 1990, prior to its assimilation by the FRG. On July 1, 1991, the Political Consultative Committee, under acting chair Vaclav Havel (q.v.), formally dissolved the Warsaw Pact altogether, finally severing military ties between the Soviet Union and its former satellites in Eastern Europe.

WARSAW TREATY, 1970. Signed on December 7, 1970, by Poland and the Federal Republic of Germany (FRG) (qq.v.). It was the product of Willy Brandt's Ostpolitik (qq.v.) and was similar in nature to the Treaty of Moscow (q.v.) signed earlier in 1970 by the FRG and the Soviet Union. The treaty recognized the Oder-Neisse Line (q.v.) as Poland's western boundary in return for allowing the repatriation of 300,000 ethnic Germans to the FRG. It also affirmed economic accords between the two powers made in October 1970. After the formal signing, Brandt attracted worldwide attention for his silent tribute in kneeling at the monument to those killed in 1943 during the Nazi annihilation of the Warsaw ghetto.

WESTMORELAND, WILLIAM C. (1914–). American general and commander of United States forces in South Vietnam. As an army officer, "Westy" Westmoreland fought in World War II and the Korean War (q.v.) and was superintendent of West Point from 1960 to 1963. In June 1964 Westmoreland became commander of American forces in South Vietnam, a post he held until March 1968. As a combat veteran and outstanding administrator, Westmoreland symbolized the modern American military officer. He approached his command in South Vietnam with supreme confidence, but his optimistic public statements were belied by failure to win the Vietnam War (q.v.).

Critics argued that Westmoreland did not understand the complexity of guerrilla warfare and was outmaneuvered by General Vo Nguyen Giap (q.v.). Supporters of the American commander argued that President Lyndon Johnson (q.v.) denied him the military resources that were needed to defeat the Vietcong. This was exemplified in the internal debate within the Johnson administration after the Tet Offensive (q.v.) in January 1968 when Westmoreland's request for additional troops was rejected.

-X-

X-ARTICLE. An important article that brought the term containment (q.v.) to the attention of the American public. In July 1947 the influential journal *Foreign Affairs* published an anonymous article entitled "The Sources of Soviet Conduct." The pseudonym "X" was used by the author, George Kennan (q.v.), because he was currently holding an office in the State Department as chief of the Policy Planning Staff. The identity of the author, however, did not long remain a secret. The X-Article repeated many of Kennan's ideas contained in his long telegram (q.v.) and notably stressed the need for "a long-term, patient but firm and vigilant containment of Russian expansive tendencies." The term containment was soon widely adopted to describe the aim of American policy in its dealings with the Soviet Union.

-Y-

YALTA CONFERENCE, 1945. A summit meeting held at the Crimean resort of Yalta on February 4–11, 1945. The conference was attended by President Franklin Roosevelt (q.v.) of the United States, Prime Minister Winston Churchill of Great Britain (qq.v.), and Premier Joseph Stalin (q.v.) of the Soviet Union, and took place at a time when military victory over Germany was considered to be imminent. Consequently, the "Big Three" met not so much to discuss wartime military strategy but to consider postwar issues. Among these were arrangements for the surrender and partition of Germany into four military zones. The principle of German reparations to compensate for wartime destruction was agreed though detailed discussion was deferred to a later meeting. The political status of Eastern Europe was to be resolved by the "Declaration on Liberated Europe" that sought to provide for democratic elections in the territories liberated from Nazi Germany. On the particular problem of Polish territory, the Soviets were to retain possession of a large section of eastern Poland while the Polish border would be extended to the west at the expense of Germany. The conference also endorsed the creation of a new international organization to be known as the United Nations (UN) (q.v.). In a separate and secret arrangement between Roosevelt and Stalin, the latter agreed that the Soviet Union would join the war against Japan (q.v.) three months after the defeat of Germany.

The elation of imminent victory over Germany stimulated harmony and made the Yalta Conference a high point of amity and cooperation between the "Big Three." But deep divisions existed and were revealed soon after the end of World War II. The United States came into conflict with the Soviet Union over the administration of Germany, the exact amount of German reparations, and especially Poland (q.v.) where the establishment of a communist government aroused American charges that Stalin had gone back on his undertaking to allow democratic elections.

In the United States, the controversy over Yalta at the time of the meeting and later was greatly influenced by party politics. Democrats generally supported Roosevelt, while Republicans condemned the conference as a Democratic failure. Critics of Roosevelt argued that Yalta represented a sell-out to communism. They described Roosevelt as too naive and trusting in his dealings with Stalin. As a result, he had been tricked into giving away too much territory and had thereby allowed the

Soviets to take control of Eastern Europe. Supporters of Roosevelt contended that, so long as the Red Army was effectively in control of Eastern Europe, there was little that the West could do to moderate Soviet desires for territory in that region. In their opinion, the interests of achieving lasting peace and prosperity were best served by Roosevelt's strategy of avoiding confrontation in favor of seeking agreement and cooperation.

YAZOV, DMITRI (1923–). Soviet general and defense minister. Yazov rose through various Central Asian and Far Eastern commands to the rank of general in 1984. In May 1987 Mikhail Gorbachev (q.v.) promoted him over several senior candidates to the post of defense minister. Yazov operated as an ally of Gorbachev and supported the 1987 Intermediate-range Nuclear Forces (INF) Treaty, the 1990 Conventional Forces in Europe (CFE) Treaty, and the tacit abandonment of the Brezhnev Doctrine (qq.v.) that preceded the collapse of communism in Eastern Europe. In 1991 Yazov was a prominent leader of the August coup against Gorbachev. The coup's failure marked the end of his career, followed by conviction and imprisonment for antistate conspiracy.

YELTSIN, BORIS (1931–). Soviet political leader and Russian president. In 1985 Yeltsin was installed by Mikhail Gorbachev (q.v.) as secretary of the Central Committee of the Soviet Communist Party. Yeltsin had been party secretary in Sverdlovsk and was known as an outspoken critic of ineffective Soviet management techniques. However, he fell from favor when his continuing political attacks were seen to exceed the limits of glasnost (q.v.). He was demoted in November 1987 to deputy chair of the state construction committee.

In March 1989, under the reformed Soviet constitution, Yeltsin was elected from a multicandidate ballot to the Congress of People's Deputies, representing a Moscow constituency with 89 percent of the vote. In 1990 he publicly resigned from the Communist Party and continued to attack restrictions on the autonomy of the Soviet republics, even if this effectively meant their independence. When in May 1990, the Soviet Union adopted a federal structure, Yeltsin was elected president of the Russian republic, and during the following month he secured a Russian parliamentary motion for legislative precedence over the Soviet government. Yeltsin's rising political ascendancy was confirmed by his symbolic leadership of resistance to the August 1991 military coup whose collapse permitted him to press for the final dismantling of the vestigial Soviet state, which was completed in December 1991, leaving him as unchallenged president of Russia. Although in poor health, Yeltsin remained the most prominent figure in Russian politics after the end of the Cold War.

YEMEN, PEOPLE'S DEMOCRATIC REPUBLIC OF. A state created from the former British territory of Aden, on the southwest tip of the Arabian Peninsula, which gained independence in November 1967. Its ruling National Front was merged into the Yemen Socialist Party, which formally adopted Marxism-Leninism in 1978. It received $400 million in aid per year in the treaty of friendship with the Soviet Union that followed in 1979, allowing intermittent Soviet use of its ports and airfields. Despite its strategic proximity to the Horn of Africa (q.v.), the country's practical value to the Soviets during the Cold War was considerably limited by its internal political instability and hostile relations with its pro-Western neighbors, the Yemen Arab Republic and Saudi Arabia.

-Z-

ZHOU ENLAI (1898–1976). Chinese communist statesman and prime minister, also known as Chou En-lai. From a middle-class background, Zhou traveled overseas and became a communist while living in France from 1920 to 1924. Returning to China, he participated in the Long March with Mao Zedong (q.v.) and the establishment of the People's Republic of China (PRC) (q.v.) in 1949. For more than two decades afterward Zhou was China's prime minister and appeared to the world as Mao's second-in-command. He took a special interest in foreign affairs serving as foreign minister from 1949 to 1958 and representing his country at important diplomatic meetings, most notably the 1954 Geneva Conference that ended the Indochina War (q.v.). Zhou's legendary diplomatic skills were also in evidence in 1972 when he played a prominent role in organizing President Nixon's (q.v.) visit to Beijing and in securing American endorsement of the Shanghai Communiqué (q.v.).

ZHUKOV, GEORGI (1896–1974). Soviet marshal and defense minister. One of the most outstanding Soviet military figures of World War II, Zhukov was removed by Joseph Stalin (q.v.) as chief of the Soviet general staff in 1946. After Stalin's death in 1953 he was recalled to Moscow from provincial duties and became deputy defense minister and commander-in-chief of Soviet land forces. Zhukov plotted with Nikita Khrushchev (q.v.) in June 1953 for the arrest and deposition of his former nemesis, Stalin's state security chief Lavrenti Beria (q.v.). As an ally of Khrushchev, Zhukov was appointed Soviet defense minister in February 1955. He presided over the debate on the role of nuclear weapons in modern Soviet strategy and carried out a reduction of about one-third in Soviet conventional forces. Zhukov also directed plans for the suppression of the 1956 Hungarian Uprising (q.v.) and in June 1957 helped Khrushchev survive the attempted coup to remove him by his Politburo opponents. But his high profile speeches on the military's role in defending political reform unsettled Khrushchev, who secured his dismissal from office in October 1957.

Select Bibliography

GENERAL SURVEYS

Ambrose, Stephen. *The Rise to Globalism: American Foreign Policy Since 1938.* 7th rev. ed. New York: Penguin Books, 1993.

Boyle, Peter G. *American-Soviet Relations: From the Russian Revolution to the Fall of Communism.* New York: Routledge, 1993.

Crockatt, Richard. *The Fifty Years War: The United States and the Soviet Union in World Politics, 1941–1991.* New York: Routledge, 1994.

Dunbabin, John. *International Relations Since 1945: A History in Two Volumes.* New York: Longman, 1994.

Gaddis, John Lewis. *We Now Know: Rethinking Cold War History.* New York: Oxford University Press, 1997.

Harbutt, Fraser J. *The Cold War Era.* Malden MA: Blackwell, 2002.

LaFeber, Walter. *America, Russia, and the Cold War, 1945–2000.* 9th ed. Boston, MA: McGraw Hill, 2000.

McMahon, Robert J. *The Limits of Empire: The United States and Southeast Asia since World War II.* New York: Columbia University Press, 1999.

Nogee, Joseph, and Robert H. Donaldson. *Soviet Foreign Policy since World War Two.* 3rd ed. New York: Pergamon, 1988.

Paterson, Thomas G. *Meeting the Communist Threat: Truman to Reagan.* New York: Oxford University Press, 1988.

Smith, Joseph. *The Cold War, 1945–1991.* 2nd ed. Malden, MA: Blackwell, 1998.

Walker, Martin. *The Cold War: A History.* New York: Holt, 1994.

Young, John W. *Cold War Europe, 1945–89: A Political History.* London: Edward Arnold, 1991.

THE EARLY COLD WAR

Alperovitz, Gar. *Atomic Diplomacy: Hiroshima and Potsdam: The Use of the Atomic Bomb and the American Confrontation with Soviet Power.* Boulder, CO: Pluto Press, 1994.

Feis, Herbert. *From Trust To Terror: The Onset of the Cold War, 1945–1950.* New York: Norton, 1970.

Gaddis, John L. *The United States and the Origins of the Cold War, 1941–1947.* New York: Columbia University Press, 1972.

Harbutt, Fraser J. *The Iron Curtain: Churchill, America, and the Origins of the Cold War.* New York: Oxford University Press, 1986.

Kolko, Gabriel. *The Politics of War: The World and United States Foreign Policy, 1943–1945.* New York: Pantheon, 1990.

Leffler, Melvyn P. *A Preponderance of Power: The World and United States Foreign Policy, 1945–1954.* Stanford CA: Stanford University Press, 1992.

Leffler, Melvyn P. and Painter, David, eds. *Origins of the Cold War.* New York: Routledge, 1994.

Mastny, Vojtech. *The Cold War and Soviet Insecurity: The Stalin Years.* New York: Oxford University Press, 1996.

Naimark, Norman and Leonid Gibianskii, eds. *The Establishment of Communist Regimes in Eastern Europe, 1944–1949.* Boulder, CO: Westview Press, 1997.

Offner, Arnold. *Another Such Victory: President Truman and the Cold War, 1945–1953.* Stanford, CA: Stanford University Press, 2002.

Paterson, Thomas G. and Robert J. McMahon, eds. *The Origins of the Cold War.* Lexington, KY: Heath, 1991.

Raack, R.C. *Stalin's Drive to the West, 1938–1945: The Origins of the Cold War.* Stanford CA: Stanford University Press, 1995.

Taubmann, William. *Stalin's American Policy: From Entente to Detente to Cold War.* New York: Columbia University Press, 1992.

THE 1950s

Ambrose, Stephen. *Eisenhower: The President.* New York: Simon and Schuster, 1984.

Divine, Robert A. *Eisenhower and the Cold War.* New York: Oxford University Press, 1981.

Dockrill, Saki. *Eisenhower's New Look National Security Policy, 1953–61.* London: Macmillan, 1996.

Halliday, Jon, and Bruce Cumings. *Korea: The Unknown War.* London: Viking, 1988

Kaufman, Burton I. *The Korean War: Challenges in Credibility, Crisis and Command.* New York: Knopf, 1986.

Paterson, Thomas G. *Contesting Castro: The United States and the Triumph of the Cuban Revolution.* New York: Oxford University Press, 1994.

Stueck, William W. *Rethinking the Korean War*. Princeton, NJ: Princeton University Press, 2002.
Zubok, Vladislav M. *Inside the Kremlin's Cold War: From Stalin to Khrushchev*. Cambridge: Harvard University Press, 1996.

THE 1960s

Beschloss, Michael. *The Crisis Years: Kennedy and Khrushchev, 1960–1963*. New York: Edward Burlinghame, 1991.
Buzzanco, Robert. *Masters of War: Military Dissent and Politics in the Vietnam Era*. New York: Cambridge University Press, 1996.
Dallek, Robert. *Flawed Giant: Lyndon Johnson and His Times, 1961–1973*. New York: Oxford University Press, 1998.
Freedman, Lawrence. *Kennedy's Wars: Berlin, Cuba, Laos and Vietnam*. New York: Oxford University Press, 2001.
Halberstam, David. *The Best and the Brightest*. New York: Random House, 1964.
Herring, George C. *America's Longest War: The United States and Vietnam, 1950–1975*. 3rd ed. New York: McGraw Hill, 1996.
Kaiser, David. *American Tragedy: Kennedy, Johnson, and the Origins of the Vietnam War*. Cambridge, MA: Harvard University Press, 2000.
Karnow, Stanley. *Vietnam: A History*. 2nd ed. New York: Penguin Books, 1997.

THE 1970s

Ambrose, Stephen. *Nixon*. New York: Simon and Schuster, 1987.
Bundy, William P. *A Tangled Web: The Making of Foreign Policy in the Nixon Presidency*. New York: Hill and Wang, 1998.
Edmonds, Robin. *Soviet Foreign Policy: The Brezhnev Years*. New York: Oxford University Press, 1983.
Garthoff, Raymond L. *Détente and Confrontation: American-Soviet Relations From Nixon to Reagan*. Washington, DC: Brookings Institution Press, 1994.
Haslam, Jonathan. *The Soviet Union and the Politics of Nuclear Weapons in Europe, 1969–1987*. Ithaca, NY: Cornell University Press, 1990.
Hersh, Seymour. *The Price of Power: Kissinger in the White House*. New York: Summit Books, 1983.
Steele, Jonathan. *Soviet Power: The Kremlin's Foreign Policy—From Brezhnev to Andropov*. New York: Simon and Schuster, 1983.

THE 1980s AND THE END OF THE COLD WAR

Beschloss, Michael, and Strobe Talbott. *At the Highest Levels: The Inside Story of the End of the Cold War.* Boston, MA: Little, Brown, 1993.

Brown, Archie. *The Gorbachev Factor.* New York: Oxford University Press, 1997.

Garthoff, Raymond L. *The Great Transition: American-Soviet Relations and the End of the Cold War.* Washington, DC: Brookings Institution Press, 1994.

Hogan, Michael, ed. *The End of the Cold War: Its Meanings and Implications.* New York: Cambridge University Press, 1992.

Lebow, Ned, and Janice G. Stein. *We All Lost the Cold War.* Princeton, NJ: Princeton University Press, 1994.

Oberdorfer, Don. *The Turn: From the Cold War to a New Era.* New York: Poseidon, 1991.

Stokes, Gale. *The Walls Came Tumbling Down: The Collapse of Communism in Eastern Europe.* New York: Oxford University Press, 1993.

ASIA, AFRICA, SOUTH AMERICA AND THE MIDDLE EAST

Blasier, Cole. *The Giant's Rival: The USSR and Latin America.* Pittsburgh, PA: University of Pittsburgh Press, 1983.

Brands, H.W. *India and the United States: The Cold Peace.* Boston, MA: Twayne, 1990.

Buckley, Roger. *US-Japan Alliance Diplomacy, 1945–1990.* New York: Cambridge University Press, 1989.

Fraser, T.G. *The USA and the Middle East Since World War 2.* New York, St. Martin's Press, 1989.

Golan, Galia. *Soviet Policies in the Middle East from World War Two to Gorbachev.* New York: Cambridge University Press, 1990.

Li, Xiaobing, and Hongshan Li, eds. *China and the United States: A New Cold War History.* Lanham, MD: University Press of America, 1998.

Marte, Fred. *Political Cycles in International Relations: The Cold War and Africa.* Amsterdam: VU University Press, 1994.

Nelsen, Harvey. *Power and Insecurity: Beijing, Moscow, and Washington, 1949–1988.* Boulder, CO: Lynee Rienner Publishers, 1989.

Pastor, Robert A. *Whirlpool: U.S. Foreign Policy Toward Latin American and the Caribbean.* Princeton, NJ: Princeton University Press, 1992.

Schraeder, Peter J. *United States Foreign Policy Towards Africa: Incrementalism, Crisis, and Change.* New York: Cambridge University Press, 1994.

Sheng, Michael. *Battling Western Imperialism: Mao, Stalin, and the United States.* Princeton, NJ: Princeton University Press, 1997.

Smith, Gaddis. *The Last Years of the Monroe Doctrine, 1945–1993.* New York: Hill and Wang, 1994.

Tibi, Bassam. *Conflict and War in the Middle East, 1967–91: Regional Dynamic and the Superpowers.* New York: St. Martin's Press, 1993.

Index

About the Authors

Joseph Smith (B.A., Durham University; Ph.D., London University) is a reader in American diplomatic history in the department of history at Exeter University, England. An expert on American foreign relations, especially with Latin America, he has conducted archival research in Brazil, Argentina, and Chile. He is a fellow of the Royal Historical Society of Great Britain and is a member of the Council of the Historical Association of Great Britain. He has written several books, including *The Cold War, 1945–1991*, published in 1998, and *A History of Brazil*, published in 2002; he has also been the editor for several years of *History*, the journal of the Historical Association of Great Britain.

Simon Davis (M.A., Oxford University and London University; Ph.D., Exeter University) is an assistant professor of history at the Bronx Community College, City University of New York. A specialist on Anglo-American diplomatic relations in the 20th century, he is also interested in military and naval history, having taught for some years at the Britannia Royal Naval College in Dartmouth, England. His publications include articles in *Diplomacy and Statecraft* and the *Annual Bulletin of Historical Literature* and the *R.U.S.I./Brasseys' Defence Yearbook*.